DEVELOPING STAFF COMPETENCIES FOR SUPPORTING PEOPLE WITH DEVELOPMENTAL DISABILITIES

DEVELOPING STAFF COMPETENCIES FOR SUPPORTING PEOPLE WITH DEVELOPMENTAL DISABILITIES

AN ORIENTATION HANDBOOK

Second Edition

by

James F. Gardner, Ph.D., M.A.S.
Chief Executive Officer
Accreditation Council on Services
for People with Disabilities
Landover, Maryland
and

Michael S. Chapman, M.Ed.
Assistant Vice President
Kennedy Krieger Community Resources
Kennedy Krieger Institute
Baltimore, Maryland

·P A U L·H·
BROOKES
PUBLISHING CO.

Baltimore • London • Sydney

Paul H. Brookes Publishing Co.
Post Office Box 10624
Baltimore, Maryland 21285-0624
www.brookespublishing.com

Typeset by The Composing Room of Michigan, Inc., Grand Rapids, Michigan.
Manufactured in the United States of America by
IBT Global, Troy, NY·

Twelfth Printing, August 2017

Library of Congress Cataloging-in-Publication Data

Gardner, James F., 1946–
    Developing staff competencies for supporting people with
developmental disabilities : an orientation handbook / James F.
Gardner, Michael S. Chapman. — 2nd ed.
      p.   cm.
   Rev. ed. of: Staff development in mental retardation services.
© 1985
     Includes bibliographical references and index.
     ISBN-13: 978-1-55766-107-4
     ISBN-10: 1-55766-107-3
     1. Social work with the mentally handicapped—Programmed
instruction. 2. Social work administration—Programmed instruction.
I. Chapman, Michael S. II. Gardner, James F., 1946–   Staff
development in mental retardation services. III. Title.
HV3004.G35 1993
362.3′8—dc20   92-14330
                                                   CIP

British Library Cataloguing-in-Publication data are available from the British library.

To Our Families:
Diane Jean Gardner
Kathy Michelle and Tracy Lynn Gardner

Sally Kees Chapman
Lauren Reed and Katherine Logan Chapman

Contents

Introduction

The first edition of this handbook was published in 1985 as *Staff Development in Mental Retardation Services: A Practical Handbook*. At that time, family support programs were engaged in an initial growth phase. Supported employment was confined to a limited number of demonstration projects, and supported living was virtually unknown.

Since then, the provision of supports by both formal organizational structures and informal networks has increased the range of living, work, and recreational options for people with developmental disabilities. This is important because where people live, work, and spend recreational time depends on where and how services and supports are provided.

The continued decentralization of services and supports within community settings has increased social integration and community participation. In addition to agency staff who provide services and supports in traditional locations, other staff now provide supports and services in homes, work sites, schools, neighborhood parks, and social settings. Families, neighbors, friends, and volunteers can provide individualized supports.

This second edition of the handbook has been redesigned as an introductory guide for the range of people who provide services and supports. The decentralization of services and the provision of supports through informal systems will succeed only if people have the necessary values, knowledge, and skills to perform their own individualized responsibilities. *Developing Staff Competencies for Supporting People with Developmental Disabilities: An Orientation Handbook* is designed to provide basic information about the provision of services and supports to people with disabilities. The handbook is intended for students, new employees, volunteers, and other groups and individuals who will provide these supports and services. The basics provided have become useful from the moment you meet a person with a disability.

As a potential or new employee, volunteer, or friend in a service or support program, you will find this manual valuable in providing the information about the basic skills, knowledge, and values you need to function successfully during the first months of involvement with persons with disabilities. The goal of this book is not only to better your decision-making skills, but, more importantly, to prepare you to assist people with disabilities to make their own decisions. The content provided here is fundamental and is not intended to be detailed or complex. When you have finished this book, you will be ready for further reading and learning.

HOW TO USE THIS HANDBOOK

The chapters of the handbook are designed as interactive learning and orientation packages. Each chapter of this book contains several learning exercises. These exercises require, for example, that you observe a program, read an individualized program plan, or study agency policies and procedures. The exercises may ask you to review basic documents not in this book—such as the agency mission statement, values and philosophy, behavior management practices, and legal rights requirements. In this connection, instructors and agency administrators should consider packaging the documents in a loose-leaf binder that is made available to students, employees, and volunteers.

Each chapter in this handbook contains eight major sections. One of these, the Self-Appraisal (featured after the Bibliography and Additional Resources), is a quiz to help you determine how much you know about the subject matter. Before reading each chapter, you may want to take the quiz. If you answer all or most of the questions correctly (an Answer Key is provided in each chapter), you may want to simply skim the chapter, look at the tables and exercises, and move on to the Case Study. In this instance, you would have extra time to study some of the suggested readings and resources. However, if you do not know many of the answers, a careful reading of the chapter is advisable, beginning with the learning objectives. Following is a suggested approach to reading each chapter.

Learning Objectives

The learning objectives identify the major points you should learn while reading the chapter. Study them carefully; then move on to the Introduction and Summary.

Introduction and Summary

Read the Introduction. It tells you the purpose of the chapter and contains the major chapter themes. After studying the Learning Objectives and the Introduction, you should know what to look for in the chapter. Next, read the Summary at the end of the textual part of the chapter. Reread the Summary. Now recall the main points in the Learning Objectives and Introduction. Skim through the chapter and see if you can spot any of these points. Are they in the beginning, the middle, or the end of the chapter? Once you know what you will be reading, begin the chapter.

Chapter Content

Read the content. Pay special attention to the examples, tables, figures, and exercises. Make sure you complete all of the exercises. You will need to use them in later chapters. If possible, read the narrative and do the exercises with a friend. Talk about the exercises and problems with coworkers. When you finish the content narrative, go to the Summary and then back to the Learning Objectives. Have all the Learning Objectives been met?

Self-Appraisal

After completing the narrative, Summary, and Learning Objectives, turn to the Self-Appraisal. Complete the questions. Could you answer the questions after studying the chapter? If so, you have documented for yourself what you have learned. This should give you a sense of achievement. If some answers are incorrect, go back and review the material.

Case Study

The last part of each chapter is a Case Study. Read and then answer the questions at the end of the Case Study. There are no right or wrong answers to these questions. However, in the Case Study Answer Guidelines, list the important items that should be considered. Do your answers contain some of the important issues? Did you come to the same general conclusions? When you have finished thinking about the Case Study, close the handbook. Take a break before going on to the next chapter.

Bibliography and Additional Resources

The Bibliography contains the references that were used to write the chapters. You should consult these books and articles if you want to learn more about a topic. The Additional Resources lists other books, articles, and video and other instructional materials related to the chapter topic.

DEVELOPING STAFF COMPETENCIES FOR SUPPORTING PEOPLE WITH DEVELOPMENTAL DISABILITIES

section
I

FOUNDATIONS
OF
SERVICES

chapter	An Introduction to
1	Developmental Disabilities

LEARNING OBJECTIVES

Upon completing this chapter, the reader will be able to:

1. Define the categorical definition of developmental disabilities.
2. Define the functional definition of developmental disabilities.
3. Compare and contrast the categorical and functional definitions of developmental disabilities.
4. Define mental retardation.
5. Define cerebral palsy.
6. Define epilepsy.
7. Define autism.
8. Define dyslexia.
9. State the importance of using labels in the design and implementation of services for individuals with developmental disabilities.

INTRODUCTION

You have chosen a career in human services for people with developmental disabilities at an important and exciting time. The past 3 decades have produced major advances in legislation, programs, and services in this area. New opportunities for and expectations of people with developmental disabilities have occurred. Many individuals now live independently in the community and are no longer confined in isolated institutions. They are moving from activity centers to supervised employment settings and workstations in industry. They participate in community recreational activities and attend classes in community colleges.

Numerous innovative and exciting programs for persons with developmental disabilities have been developed in recent years. Successful parent training and in-home support programs enable families to raise children at home. Parent-to-parent support groups provide peer assistance. Children with severe disabilities, previously considered "beyond help," are now receiving a public education in community schools. Community colleges have developed special programs; such courses as money management, riding the bus, cooking, assertiveness training, and white-water rafting are designed with the assumption that individuals with developmental disabilities can learn. Like everyone else, they possess a range of skills and abilities.

The fact that an individual has a developmental disability does not, in itself, indicate what that person can or cannot do or what he or she likes to do. Applying the term *developmental disabilities* to an individual does not help to identify his or her strengths and needs. Because of these different capabilities, instruction, training, and counseling must be individualized for each person. Such an approach enables you to work on personal strengths and needs. It also allows you to concentrate on what each individual with developmental disabilities thinks is important.

The work of employees in the human services field should assist individuals with developmental disabilities to increase their functional independence and to make their own decisions. This does not mean that you or your agency should not provide the necessary supportive services to the individuals; in fact, they often need support. For instance, a person who fails to meet his or her own goals may need support. Whenever possible, however, the responsibility for decision making should be returned to the individual with a developmental disability. As the person gains new skills and behaviors, your role changes. At that time, you should step back and exert less influence and control.

You will encounter many labels, diagnoses, and other technical terms in your work. These are important in some situations, but the individual is more important than the diagnosis or label. His or her basic needs are the same as yours. In addition to the bare necessities of food, clothing, and shelter, each individual needs recognition, opportunity for self-expression, and friendships.

This book offers insight into working with individuals with developmental disabilities. It is important for the employee to have a clear understanding of the term *developmental disability*. In exploring the term, this chapter begins by defining it and describing the changes in its definition that have occurred during recent years. The chapter includes a discussion of the shift from the former categorical approach in defining developmental disabilities to the current functional approach.

Also provided are definitions and overviews of disabilities—mental retardation, cerebral palsy, epilepsy, autism, and dyslexia.

DEFINITIONS OF DEVELOPMENTAL DISABILITY

Categorical Approach

The definition of developmental disability has changed over time from a categorical definition to a functional one. The categorical approach to developmental disability was evident in this 1973 definition by the American Association on Mental Deficiency:

> a disability attributable to mental retardation, cerebral palsy, epilepsy, or another neurological condition of an individual which is closely related to mental retardation or to require similar treatment, and which originates in childhood, is likely to continue, and constitutes a substantial handicap to the individual. (Grossman, 1973, p. 132)

A developmental disability, as defined above, must have three critical features: 1) the condition becomes manifested before the age of 18, 2) it continues indefinitely, and 3) it represents a significant limitation for the individual.

THE CATEGORICAL DEFINITION OF DEVELOPMENTAL DISABILITY HAS THREE COMPONENTS: IT IS MANIFESTED PRIOR TO THE AGE OF 18, CONTINUES INDEFINITELY, AND IS A SIGNIFICANT LIMITATION FOR THE INDIVIDUAL.

The definition and subsequent revisions refer to mental retardation, cerebral palsy, epilepsy, autism, and dyslexia as specific categorical conditions. It is important to understand that mental retardation may be a developmental disability, but a developmental disability may not be mental retardation. Individuals with developmental disabilities do not necessarily have mental retardation. For example, a person with cerebral palsy has a developmental disability but may not have an intellectual impairment.

MENTAL RETARDATION, CEREBRAL PALSY, EPILEPSY, AUTISM, AND DYSLEXIA ARE INCLUDED IN THE CATEGORICAL DEFINITION OF DEVELOPMENTAL DISABILITIES.

The first requirement of the 1973 definition, that the disability has to originate in childhood, refers to the period from birth through 18 years. The second requirement indicates that the disability is likely to continue indefinitely, even though the individual learns skills and behaviors and has supports in achieving increased independence. The final requirement that the developmental disability must constitute a substantial disability refers to its severity and its impact on the individual's ability to function in daily life. The disability must be severe enough to interfere with daily living.

THE ORIGINATION PERIOD OF A DEVELOPMENTAL DISABILITY IS DEFINED AS BETWEEN BIRTH AND AGE 18 YEARS. IN ADDITION, THE DISABILITY MUST BE SEVERE ENOUGH THAT IT INTERFERES WITH DAILY LIVING.

Functional Approach

The categorical definition of developmental disabilities above resulted in an emphasis on the person's condition or label. The labeling process stigmatized the individual. Rather than being a person or being viewed as a person first, the individual became the disability. Terms such as "spastic quad," "the Down's baby," "slow learner," or "retardate" were common descriptive terms used by professionals in the field when describing individuals with developmental disabilities.

THE LABELING PROCESS IS STIGMATIZING FOR THE INDIVIDUAL. RATHER THAN BEING A PERSON OR BEING VIEWED AS A PERSON FIRST, THE INDIVIDUAL BECOMES THE DISABILITY.

In addition, such terms provide no information about the person. "Retardate" does not describe the person's likes, interests, and abilities. The term does not indicate what supports are needed to assist the individual to achieve his or her goals.

In order to de-emphasize the label, the definition of developmental disabilities has changed. PL 101-496, the Developmental Disabilities Assistance and Bill of Rights Act of 1990, defines developmental disability as:

> a severe, chronic disability of a person 5 years of age or older which is attributable to a mental or physical impairment or combination of mental and physical impairments; is manifested before the person attains age 22; is likely to continue indefinitely; results in substantial functional limitations in three or more major life activities; and reflects the person's need for a combination and sequence of special, interdisciplinary, or generic care, treatment, or other services which are of lifelong or extended duration and are individually planned and coordinated; except that such term, when applied to infants and young children, means individuals from birth to age 5, inclusive, who have substantial developmental delay or specific congenital or acquired conditions with a high probability of resulting in developmental disabilities if services are not provided.

The seven major life activities defined in PL 101-496 include: self-care, receptive and expressive language, learning, mobility, self-direction, capacity for independent living, and economic self-sufficiency. On this basis, Table 1 further refines the definition of developmental disabilities.

The definition above, with its categorical labels of mental retardation, cerebral palsy, epilepsy, autism, and dyslexia, was abolished in favor of a functional definition. It has become more important to understand, rather than label, the individual with a developmental disability. The assessment process and the subsequent intervention strategies now focus on the strengths and abilities of the individual.

Although the functional definition has replaced the categorical definition in federal legislation, the diagnostic terms mental retardation, cerebral palsy, epilepsy, dyslexia, and autism remain. These terms

Table 1. Definition of developmental disability

The term *developmental disability* means a severe, chronic disability of a person 5 years of age or older that:

A. Is attributable to a mental or physical impairment or combination of mental and physical impairments;

B. Is manifested before the person attains age 22;

C. Is likely to continue indefinitely;

D. Results in substantial functional limitation in three or more of the following areas of major life activity:

    1. *Self-care* (daily activities enabling a person to meet basic life needs for food, hygiene, and appearance);

    2. *Receptive and expressive language* (communication involving verbal and nonverbal behavior enabling a person both to understand others and to express ideas and information to others);

    3. *Learning* (general cognitive competence and ability to acquire new behaviors, perceptions, and information; apply experiences to new situations);

    4. *Mobility* (ability to use fine and gross motor skills; ability to move one's person from one place to another with or without mechanical aids);

    5. *Self-direction* (management and taking control over one's social and personal life; ability to make decisions affecting and protecting one's self-interest);

    6. *Capacity for independent living* (the extent to which the person exerts control and choice over his or her own life);

    7. *Economic self-sufficiency* (maintaining adequate employment and financial support).

E. Reflects the person's need for a combination and sequence of special, interdisciplinary, or generic care, treatment, or other services that are of lifelong or extended duration and are individually planned and coordinated; except that such term, when applied to infants and young children, means individuals from birth to age 5, inclusive, who have substantial developmental delay or specific congenital or acquired conditions with a high probability of resulting in developmental disabilities if services are not provided.

---

can provide information about the possible cause of the disability, some of its general characteristics, and classification systems for the disability. Knowledge of the general terms of mental retardation, cerebral palsy, epilepsy, dyslexia, and autism helps human services employees to identify differences and similarities.

The diagnostic category of the disability, however, does not provide any information about an individual's capabilities or needs. Diagnostic labels do not indicate what the individual wants to do, can do, or cannot do. In fact, differences among individuals within a single diagnosis can be as great as those among individuals in different categorical groups.

MENTAL RETARDATION

The most current and common criteria for determining who has mental retardation are included in the definition of mental retardation established by the American Association on Mental Retardation (AAMR) in 1992:

> Mental retardation refers to substantial limitations in present functioning. It is characterized by significantly subaverage intellectual functioning, existing concurrently with related limitations in two or more of the following applicable adaptive skills areas: communication, self-care, home living, social skills, community use, self-direction, health and safety, functional academics, leisure, and work. Mental retardation manifests before age 18.

According to the AAMR guidelines for the application of the definition, there are four critical assumptions that must be met, including:

1. Valid assessment considers cultural and linguistic diversity, and differences in communication and behavioral factors.
2. The existence of limitations in adaptive skills occurs within the context of community environments typical of the individual's age peers and is indexed to the person's individualized needs support.
3. Specific adaptive limitations often coexist with strengths in other adaptive skills or other personal capabilities.
4. With appropriate supports over a sustained period, the life functioning of the person with mental retardation will generally improve.

A SCORE ON AN INTELLIGENCE TEST ALONE IS NOT SUFFICIENT TO MAKE A DETERMINATION OF MENTAL RETARDATION.

More than 200 clinical or biological causes of mental retardation exist, but these specific known causes account for only 25% of the population with mental retardation. For most people, there is no clear physical or biological cause of mental retardation.

Some genetic disorders can result in mental retardation. Down syndrome, for example, is a condition that results in mental retardation because of the presence of an extra chromosome. Disorders of metabolism can also result in mental retardation.

Infections and intoxications during a woman's pregnancy can cause the child to be born with mental retardation. The occurrence of German measles during pregnancy can cause blindness, a heart defect, and/or mental retardation in the newborn. Venereal disease during pregnancy can also cause mental retardation in the child. Excess consumption of alcohol by a pregnant woman can result in the birth of a child with fetal alcohol syndrome and brain damage. Finally, smoking during pregnancy appears to be connected with low birth weight and mental retardation in young infants.

There are many other causes of mental retardation. For example, injury to the brain and central nervous system during birth can lead to mental retardation. Premature birth and low birth weight are associated with an increased incidence of mental retardation.

In approximately 75% of persons with mental retardation a definite cause cannot be identified. These unexplained causes are thought to be due to one or more factors, such as genetic and hereditary conditions that are not fully understood, poor environmental factors in early life that may deprive infants of the opportunity to learn and cause mild mental retardation, and minimal brain damage that cannot be detected but that may cause mental retardation.

Mental retardation is sometimes confused with mental illness, but the two conditions are entirely different. Mental illness can occur at any age. People can recover from mental illness because it is a disease. Mental retardation is not a disease. Various tensions, experiences, traumas, and possible genetic factors can result in mental illness. These same factors do not cause mental retardation.

Of course, some people with mental retardation can have emotional problems and may be mentally ill, just as they may become physically sick and have, for instance, high blood pressure or a bout with the flu. However, mental retardation is not commonly considered a cause of mental illness. In addition, mental illness is absolutely not a cause of mental retardation.

MENTAL RETARDATION IS NOT THE SAME AS MENTAL ILLNESS.

Estimates of the number of people with mental retardation range from 0.3% to 3.1% of the general population. About 65% of these individuals have mild mental retardation, however, and can generally master basic academic skills. In many instances people with mild mental retardation disappear from the social service, health, and educational systems when they reach adulthood.

People with severe mental retardation display a wide range of social competencies, learning rates, and personality traits. Despite the diagnosis of mental retardation, a "personality of the retarded" cannot be generalized. Each person is unique. Also, the range of capabilities among people with mental retardation is greater than that existing between those with and those without mental retardation.

THERE IS NO "PERSONALITY OF THE RETARDED."

Staff expectations influence how people with mental retardation perform tasks and accomplish goals. Employees should be aware that if they set expectations that are both reasonable and high, people with mental retardation will often meet those expectations. Low expectations generally result in small accomplishments. A major responsibility of the staff is to set reasonable but high expectations.

CEREBRAL PALSY

Batshaw and Perret (1992) define cerebral palsy as "a disorder of movement and posture due to a nonprogressive defect of the immature brain" (p. 581). Cerebral palsy is not one condition. Rather, the term is often used to describe a variety of neurological conditions that result in impaired motor functioning.

Although the exact cause of cerebral palsy in many individuals is unknown, it results from brain damage to the child that can occur prior to birth, during birth, or shortly after birth. Basically, anything that interferes with the developing brain can result in cerebral palsy. For example, a mother's poor nutritional status prior to the birth of her child, the premature birth of the baby, insufficient oxygen, infections, or brain damage as a result of an accident are all known causes of cerebral palsy.

FOR MOST INDIVIDUALS, THE CAUSE OF CEREBRAL PALSY IS UNKNOWN.

The three classifications of cerebral palsy are based on the areas of the brain that are affected: 1) the area that controls voluntary movements, 2) the area that regulates those movements, or 3) both areas. The body is affected in accordance with the areas of the brain that are involved.

When the area of the brain that controls voluntary movement is affected, spasticity results. In spasticity, or high muscle tone, the muscles in the affected area are tight or stiff. Body movements are difficult to control. In contrast, cerebral palsy can result in involuntary or purposeless movements. The individual may display abrupt movements of the arms or legs that he or she cannot control. This classification is sometimes referred to as athetoid cerebral palsy. In mixed cerebral palsy, the individual demonstrates traits of both spastic and involuntary movements.

Cerebral palsy may involve different areas of the body. Monoplegia, diplegia, hemiplegia, and quadriplegia are common terms used to describe the resulting motor involvement. Monoplegia is rare and involves one arm or leg. In other words, damage to the developing brain is evident in the motor functioning of only one arm or leg. In diplegia, damage involves both legs. The term *hemiplegia* is used to describe involvement of half the body—the arm and leg on the same side of the body. *Quadriplegia* is the term used to describe involvement of the entire body—both arms and both legs. Table 2 provides a summary of the different types of cerebral palsy and the resulting motor involvement.

An individual with cerebral palsy also may have other disabilities, such as mental retardation, epilepsy, vision problems, or hearing problems. However, a diagnosis of cerebral palsy does not automatically indicate that a person has mental retardation. Great care should be taken by staff members so as not to assume that an individual with cerebral palsy has mental retardation. In fact, they should assume that the individual has normal intelligence.

An individual with cerebral palsy does not necessarily have mental retardation as well. The staff should assume that the individual has normal intelligence.

EPILEPSY

Simply stated, epilepsy describes a condition of abnormal brain activity that results in a seizure. A seizure may last from several seconds to several minutes. The individual may or may not lose consciousness

Table 2. Types of cerebral palsy in relation to affected areas of the body

Type	Affected areas
Monoplegia	One arm or leg
Diplegia	Both legs
Hemiplegia	Arm and leg on the same side of the body
Quadriplegia	Both arms and both legs

while having a seizure. Seizures may be present at birth or may develop during childhood or adolescence. They are often controlled through the use of medications and medical monitoring.

The exact cause of epilepsy is not known for the majority of individuals with epilepsy. Head trauma, infections, hypoglycemia, drug withdrawal, and anoxia, however, have been identified as causes. Although an individual may develop epilepsy at any age, the majority of cases are diagnosed during early childhood.

FOR MOST INDIVIDUALS, THE CAUSE OF EPILEPSY IS NOT KNOWN.

Seizures are classified by categories of partial or generalized, depending on whether part or all of the brain is involved. Partial seizures may be simple or complex.

Partial Seizures

During a simple partial seizure, the individual does not lose consciousness. This type of seizure is also referred to as a focal-motor seizure because it focuses on one leg or arm. The leg or arm on one side of the body may jerk.

A complex partial seizure usually results in loss of consciousness, and it may affect the senses. The individual may experience an unusual smell, sight, or noise. The psyche may be involved: the individual may experience a sense of déjà vu, or "having done this before"; time may become distorted; or the person may experience intense feelings of fear, anger, anxiety, or other strong feelings. A complex partial seizure is also referred to as a psychomotor seizure.

SEIZURES ARE CLASSIFIED BY CATEGORIES OF PARTIAL OR GENERALIZED, DEPENDING ON WHETHER PART OR ALL OF THE BRAIN IS INVOLVED.

Generalized Seizures

Generalized seizures involve the entire brain. The most common generalized seizures are absence, myoclonic, and tonic-clonic.

Absence Seizures

The absence seizure was once referred to as petit mal. During an absence seizure, the individual does not lose consciousness but experiences momentary loss of mental functioning. He or she may appear to stare blankly into space, the eyelids may flutter, the eyes may roll slightly, or the individual may drop any object that he or she is holding.

The absence seizure begins and ends abruptly; it usually lasts between 5 and 15 seconds. An individual may experience from a few to several hundred absence seizures each day. The degree to which an individual's learning is impaired by absence seizures greatly depends on the frequency of seizure activity. Absence seizures in an individual experiencing a few each day may go unnoticed to other people, and the individual's learning may not be impaired. The learning process may be impaired, however, if several hundred absence seizures occur each day.

Myoclonic Seizures

The myoclonic seizure involves a sudden, brief jerking of one or more affected muscle groups. When one muscle group is involved, the individual experiences the sudden jerking of the arms or legs. When more than one muscle group is involved, the myoclonic seizure may cause the individual to lose total control and drop to the ground. Seizures of this nature, also called jackknife seizures, may be responsible for multiple injuries to the individual as a result of frequent falls.

Although myoclonic seizures last only a few seconds, they may occur frequently throughout the day. These seizures are difficult to control, usually worsen as the individual becomes older, and often lead to more advanced forms of epilepsy.

Tonic-Clonic Seizures

The tonic-clonic seizure, or grand mal, is the most common seizure disorder. It occurs in two phases. During the tonic phase, the body becomes quite rigid. If standing or sitting, the unconscious individual may fall to the ground during this phase and sustain injury.

The clonic phase that follows also affects the entire body. During this phase, the body jerks in a rhythmic pattern. As time passes, the jerking becomes less intense. The individual will often awaken very tired, confused, and in need of sleep.

The individual may lose bladder control and urinate during a tonic-clonic seizure. Some individuals report experiencing unusual odors, sights, or sounds prior to the occurrence of a tonic-clonic seizure. These experiences are referred to as an "aura." For other individuals, absence or partial seizures may occur prior to the tonic-clonic seizure. Tonic-clonic seizures often can be controlled and their frequency reduced with the use of medications.

Treatment of Seizures

Staff reactions to seizures are an important aspect of an individual's treatment. Historically, it was felt that individuals could swallow their tongues during tonic-clonic seizures. This is not true. They may bite their tongues, but will not swallow them. Table 3 provides general guidelines as to what should be done in the event of a seizure.

AUTISM

Autism is defined as:

a pervasive lack of responsiveness to other people, gross deficits in language and communication, bizarre responses to the environment, absence of delusions and hallucinations, with onset before 30 months of age. (Grossman, 1983, p. 160)

Autism is a difficult disability to explain because a number of different characteristics result in the diagnosis of autism. Four traits are associated with autism: socialization, communication, behavior, and learning. Although all four must be present in a diagnosis of autism, the complexity and severity of each trait vary among individuals. This variability makes an initial diagnosis and the subsequent intervention strategies difficult to define and implement.

AUTISM IS DIFFICULT TO DEFINE. FOUR TRAITS ARE ASSOCIATED WITH AUTISM: SOCIALIZATION, COMMUNICATION, BEHAVIOR, AND LEARNING. ALL FOUR TRAITS ARE REQUIRED FOR A DIAGNOSIS OF AUTISM.

Individuals with autism have difficulty in establishing social relationships with others. They may appear uninterested in people, including their parents, and may treat people as objects. These individuals

Table 3. Staff reactions to a seizure

1. Immediately note the time of onset and the type of seizure.
2. If the individual is having a tonic-clonic seizure, the greatest danger is in the immediate environment around the individual during the clonic phase. Therefore, make sure the environment is free of sharp or hard objects against which the individual may hit himself or herself.
3. Do not move the individual while the seizure is active.
4. Loosen tight clothing.
5. Turn the individual on his or her side. This will prevent the individual from choking on saliva or other body fluids.
6. Monitor the time. If the seizure lasts more than 5 minutes, seek medical assistance.
7. When the seizure ends, assist the individual in changing any wet or soiled clothing.
8. Provide a comfortable place for the individual to rest.
9. Report the occurrence to the supervisor and note occurrence in the individual's record or in other appropriate places as required by agency policy.

often prefer to be alone and generally do not display empathy for others.

Communication traits include both receptive and expressive language. In normally developing children, language links them with people around them. Children with autism appear to retreat into a world of their own, where communicating with others is of little or no interest. Individuals with autism may not demonstrate an understanding of nonverbal language, such as gestures. In addition, if they are verbal, they may be exceedingly repetitive on one topic. Frequently, they do not initiate communication with others, or they may use behaviors to communicate. For example, an individual with autism may become aggressive, throw objects, or hit himself or herself to express frustration or dissatisfaction in completing a task.

In addition to the above behavior traits, individuals with autism may exhibit stereotypic behaviors, such as rocking or finger flicking. Some individuals constantly repeat particular tasks or insist on following routines without changing them, whereas others may exhibit short attention spans. They may show little or no understanding of danger and unknowingly place themselves in dangerous situations.

Learning traits also vary among individuals with autism. They may demonstrate uneven learning and/or splinter skills. Uneven learning occurs when an individual's scores vary across the developmental domains of learning, such as fine and gross motor skills, receptive and expressive language, cognition, and social-emotional responses. Splinter skills occur when the individual's scores vary within a given domain. Additional problems in learning may include difficulty with abstract reasoning skills and the lack of ability to generalize from one skill to another or from one environment to another.

One final characteristic necessary for an individual to be diagnosed with autism is his or her age at onset, which must occur during infancy or childhood. It is generally recognized that autism must be present before 30 months of age.

Individuals with autism do not necessarily have mental retardation; in fact, some have normal IQs. It would be an incorrect assumption for staff members to assume that an individual with autism also has mental retardation.

A DIAGNOSIS OF AUTISM DOES NOT MEAN THE INDIVIDUAL IS ALSO MENTALLY RETARDED. THE STAFF SHOULD BE CAREFUL NOT TO ASSUME THAT THE INDIVIDUAL WITH AUTISM ALSO HAS MENTAL RETARDATION.

The American Psychiatric Association establishes standards by which individuals are diagnosed as having autism. Its publication, *Diagnostic and Statistical Manual of Mental Disorders* (DSM-III-R)

(1987), lists diagnostic criteria. Table 4 describes difficulties in developing a diagnosis of autism. Note the numerous variations in combinations of characteristics and the number that must be present for a diagnosis. The table also shows why it is so difficult to plan instructional programs for individuals with autism.

DYSLEXIA

Grossman (1983) defined dyslexia as a:

> term used in inconsistent ways; generally indicates serious reading difficulty; condition characterized by an inability to read more than a few words with understanding. (p. 170)

Dyslexia is a learning disability. It is used to identify those individuals who experience difficulty in learning to read. As noted in the definition above, the term dyslexia is used inconsistently. Some people use the term to describe reading difficulties that result from brain

Table 4. Diagnostic criteria for autism

At least eight of the following sixteen items are present, these to include at least two items from A, one from B, and one from C.

Note: Consider a criterion to be met *only* if the behavior is abnormal for the person's developmental level.

A. Qualitative impairment in reciprocal social interaction as manifested by the following:

(The examples within parentheses are arranged so that those first mentioned are more likely to apply to younger persons or those with more disabilities, and the later ones to older persons or those with fewer disabilities.)

1. marked lack of awareness of the existence or feelings of others (e.g., treats a person as if he or she were a piece of furniture; does not notice another person's distress; apparently has no concept of the need of others for privacy)

2. no or abnormal seeking of comfort at times of distress (e.g., does not come for comfort even when ill, hurt, or tired; seeks comfort in a stereotyped way, for example, says "cheese, cheese, cheese" whenever hurt)

3. no or impaired imitation (e.g., does not wave bye-bye; does not copy mother's domestic activities; mechanical imitation of others' actions out of context)

4. no or abnormal social play (e.g., does not actively participate in simple games; prefers solitary play activities; involves other children in play only as "mechanical aids")

5. gross impairment in ability to make peer friendships (e.g., no interest in making peer friendships; despite interest in making friends, demonstrates lack of understanding of conventions of social interaction, for example, reads phone book to uninterested peer)

(continued)

Table 4. *(continued)*

B. Qualitative impairment in verbal and nonverbal communication and in imaginative activity, as manifested by the following:

(The numbered items are arranged so that those first listed are more likely to apply to younger persons or those with more disabilities and the later ones to older persons or those with fewer disabilities.)

1. no mode of communication, such as communicative babbling, facial expression, gesture, mime, or spoken language

2. markedly abnormal nonverbal communication, as in the use of eye-to-eye gaze, facial expression, body posture, or gestures to initiate or modulate social interaction (e.g., does not anticipate being held, stiffens when held, does not look at the person or smile when making a social approach, does not greet parents or visitors, has a fixed stare in social situations)

3. absence of imaginative activity, such as playacting of adult roles, fantasy characters, or animals; lack of interest in stories about imaginary events

4. marked abnormalities in the production of speech, including volume, pitch, stress, rate, rhythm, and intonation (e.g., monotonous tone, questionlike melody, or high pitch)

5. marked abnormalities in the form or content of speech, including stereotyped and repetitive use of speech (e.g., immediate echolalia or mechanical repetition of television commercial); use of "you" when "I" is meant (e.g., using "You want cookie?" to mean "I want a cookie"); idiosyncratic use of words or phrases (e.g., "Go on riding" to mean "I want to go on the swing"); or frequent irrelevant remarks (e.g., starts talking about train schedules during a conversation about sports)

6. marked impairment in the ability to initiate or sustain a conversation with others, despite adequate speech (e.g., indulging in lengthy monologues on one subject regardless of interjections from others)

C. Markedly restricted repertoire of activities and interests, as manifested by the following:

1. stereotyped body movements (e.g., hand-flicking or -twisting, spinning, head-banging, complex whole-body movements)

2. persistent preoccupation with parts of objects (e.g., sniffing or smelling objects, repetitive feeling of texture of materials, spinning wheels of toy cars) or attachment to unusual objects (e.g., insists on carrying around a piece of string)

3. marked distress over changes in trivial aspects of environment (e.g., when a vase is moved from usual position)

4. unreasonable insistence on following routines in precise detail (e.g., insisting that exactly the same route always be followed when shopping)

5. markedly restricted range of interests and a preoccupation with one narrow interest (e.g., interested only in lining up objects, in amassing facts about meteorology, or in pretending to be a fantasy character)

D. Onset during infancy or childhood.

Specify if childhood onset (after 36 months of age).

From American Psychiatric Association. (1987). Diagnostic and statistical manual of mental disorders (3rd ed.-rev., pp. 38–39). Washington, DC: American Psychiatric Association; reprinted by permission.

damage. Others use it in describing a child who experiences difficulty in learning to read through traditional methods as taught in classroom settings.

DYSLEXIA IS A LEARNING DISABILITY THAT REFERS TO AN INDIVIDUAL WHO EXPERIENCES READING DIFFICULTIES.

A diagnosis of dyslexia provides few clues of remediation strategies needed to teach an individual how to overcome his or her reading disability. After the diagnosis, it is still important to understand the nature of the individual's reading difficulties. The reading skills that are lacking must be understood before appropriate strategies can be developed to assist the individual in learning to read. For example, the individual with dyslexia may experience directional difficulties. The individual with dyslexia must understand the nature of reading English. It requires both left-to-right and up-and-down orientations. Individuals with confused left-to-right orientation often reverse words, such as "saw" for "was"; reverse letters within words, such as "from" for "form"; and reverse single letters, such as "b" for "d." Individuals with confused up-and-down orientation may confuse "b" for "p," where "but" becomes "put"; or "m" for "w," where "make" becomes "wake"; and so on.

In addition, individuals with dyslexia often experience difficulties with mathematical and writing skills. They may see "54" as "45" and reverse letters or numbers while writing—"3" is written as "ε" or "e" as "ə".

AN INDIVIDUAL WITH DYSLEXIA WHO EXPERIENCES DIFFICULTY IN READING MAY ALSO EXPERIENCE PROBLEMS WITH MATHEMATICAL AND WRITING SKILLS.

It is important to understand that many children during the early school years experience reversals, such as those described above. This does not necessarily mean that the child is dyslexic but may be a normal part of development. In order for an individual to be diagnosed as dyslexic, the dyslexia must be likely to continue indefinitely and be considered a substantial disability for the individual, as stated in the definition of developmental disabilities.

SUMMARY

The field of developmental disabilities has changed during the past 2 decades. It will continue to change as more knowledge about individuals with developmental disabilities emerges. A significant change is the definition of developmental disabilities. For many years, advocacy organizations struggled to have their respective special interest groups included in the definition of developmental disabilities. Inclusion was a means of obtaining much needed federal money for support services for individuals with developmental disabilities. The original definition specified mental retardation, cerebral palsy, and epilepsy as developmental disabilities. Subsequent revisions in the federal legislation authorizing funds for developmental disabilities expanded the definition to include autism; later revisions included dyslexia.

Although human services workers in the field of developmental disabilities should have a working knowledge of each of these disability categories, it is more important for them to recognize that the labels of mental retardation, cerebral palsy, epilepsy, autism, or dyslexia provide little information about the individual. It is far more important to understand an individual's abilities, interests, dreams, and likes than to know what diagnostic label is used.

Current practice in the field of developmental disabilities is to focus on the functional abilities of the individual. In keeping with this practice, the definition of developmental disabilities has also changed. The definition eliminates the emphasis on disability categories and the practice of labeling individuals in favor of a functional approach to identify individuals with developmental disabilities.

As the field continues to evolve, more emphasis will be placed on the functional approach in the design and delivery of services. Group homes, work enclaves, and group recreational activities will yield to individual support services. An understanding of the individual will become a critical component of the team process and subsequent program development and implementation.

BIBLIOGRAPHY

Aicardi, J. (1986). Epilepsy in children. New York: Raven Press.

American Psychiatric Association. (1987). Diagnostic and statistical manual of mental disorders. Washington, DC: Author.

Batshaw, M.L. (1991). Your child has a disability: A complete sourcebook of daily and medical care. Boston: Little, Brown.

Batshaw, M.L., & Perret, Y.M. (1992). Children with disabilities: A medical primer (3rd ed.). Baltimore: Paul H. Brookes Publishing Co.

Cohen, D.J., Donnellan, A.M., & Paul, R. (1987). Handbook of autism and pervasive developmental disorders. New York: John Wiley & Sons.

Dawson, G. (1989). Autism: Nature, diagnosis, and treatment. New York: Guilford Press.

Donnellan, A.M. (1985). Classic readings in autism. New York: Teacher's College Press.

Duffy, F.H., & Geschwind, N. (Eds.). (1985). Dyslexia: A neuroscientific approach to clinical evaluation. Boston: Little, Brown.

Freeman, J.M., Vining, E., & Pillas, D.J. (1990). Seizures and epilepsy in childhood: A guide for parents. Baltimore: The Johns Hopkins University Press.

Geralis, E. (1991). Children with cerebral palsy: A parents' guide. Kensington, MD: Woodbine House.

Gollay, E. (1979). *The modified definition of developmental disabilities: An initial exploration.* Columbia, MD: Morgan Management Systems.

Grossman, H.J. (1973). *Manual on terminology and classification in mental retardation.* Washington, DC: American Association on Mental Deficiency.

Grossman, H.J. (1983). *Classification in mental retardation.* Washington, DC: American Association on Mental Deficiency.

Holms, G.L. (1987). *Diagnosis and management of seizures in children.* Philadelphia: W.B. Saunders.

Landau, E. (1991). *Dyslexia.* New York: Franklin Watts.

Maloney, M.P., & Ward, M.P. (1979). *Mental retardation and modern society.* New York: Oxford University Press.

McGowen, T. (1989). *Epilepsy.* New York: Franklin Watts.

Powers, M.D. (1989). *Children with autism: A parents' guide.* Kensington, MD: Woodbine House.

Reisner, H. (1988). *Children with epilepsy: A parents' guide.* Kensington, MD: Woodbine House.

Richard, A., & Reiter, J. (1990). *Epilepsy: A new approach.* New York: Prentice Hall.

Rutter, M., & Schopler, E. (1978). *Autism: A reappraisal of concepts and treatment.* New York: Plenum.

SELF-APPRAISAL

INSTRUCTIONS

The following questions will help you evaluate your knowledge about developmental disabilities. For true-false questions, check the correct answer. For multiple choice questions, circle the correct answer(s).

Note: There may be more than one correct answer for some questions.

1. Which of the following were included in the categorical definition of developmental disabilities?
   a. Mental retardation
   b. Cerebral palsy
   c. Epilepsy
   d. Autism
   e. Dyslexia
2. Which of the following were required as part of the categorical definition of developmental disabilities?
   a. Naming of the disability
   b. The origination period
   c. Substantial limitations to the individual
   d. None of the above
3. The origination period refers to the state in which the child with a disability was born.
   ____ True   ____ False
4. Mental retardation and mental illness refer to the same disability.
   ____ True   ____ False
5. Which of the following are included in the definition of mental retardation?
   a. Substantial limitations in present functioning
   b. Significantly subaverage intellectual functioning
   c. Manifest before age 18
   d. All of the above
6. An individual who meets the definition of mental retardation also meets the definition of developmental disabilities.
   ____ True   ____ False
7. Cerebral palsy classification is based on the area of the brain and body affected.
   ____ True   ____ False

8. Match the following:

   Monoplegia   Both legs

   Diplegia   Both arms and both legs

   Hemiplegia   One arm or leg

   Quadriplegia   Arm and leg on the same side of the body

9. Individuals with cerebral palsy are always mentally retarded as well.

   ___ True   ___ False

10. Which of the following describe seizure disorders?
    a. Simple partial seizures
    b. Complex partial seizures
    c. Absence
    d. Myoclonic
    e. Tonic-clonic

11. Objects should be placed in the mouth of an individual having a seizure to prevent swallowing of the tongue.

    ___ True   ___ False

12. Individuals with epilepsy always have mental retardation as well.

    ___ True   ___ False

13. Which of the following traits are associated with autism?
    a. Social
    b. Communication
    c. Behavior
    d. Learning
    e. None of the above

14. Individuals with autism always have mental retardation as well.

    ___ True   ___ False

15. Dyslexia is a learning disability that refers to an individual who experiences reading difficulties.

    ___ True   ___ False

16. The diagnosis of dyslexia provides great insights to needed intervention strategies and the remediation of reading difficulties.

    ___ True   ___ False

17. Individuals with dyslexia also have mental retardation.

    ___ True   ___ False

18. Which of the following are acceptable labels for use when describing individuals with developmental difficulties?
    a. Spastic quad
    b. Hemi
    c. Down baby
    d. Retardate
    e. All of the above
    f. None of the above

19. Appropriate labels are critical aspects of the functional definition of developmental disabilities.
    ____ True   ____ False
20. Which of the following life activities are included in the functional definition of developmental disabilities?
    a. Self-care
    b. Receptive and expressive language
    c. Learning
    d. Mobility
    e. Self-direction
    f. Capacity for independent living
    g. Economic self-sufficiency

CASE STUDY

Eric Roberts is a young adult with cerebral palsy. He has limited range of motion and his mobility is enhanced through the use of an electric wheelchair. He is able to communicate with an augmentative communication system.

Mr. Roberts graduated from the local community college 6 months ago. He earned an associate in arts degree with a major in computer-assisted design. Mr. Roberts has applied to numerous local businesses for employment. He is particularly interested in architectural firms and engineering companies.

Mr. Roberts needs a personal care attendant to assist him in getting up and preparing for work. He has arranged for transportation to a number of possible employment situations.

He has a support network of friends from school and family and participates in community life. He is generally optimistic that the Americans with Disabilities Act will increase opportunities for him in the near future.

Situation

Mr. Roberts recently applied for support services to assist him in activities of daily living and to attend to his personal needs at an employment site. The support services in the state are administered by local health departments. The county health department, in refusing Mr. Roberts's application for services, stated that he did not have mental retardation. The health department's policy and procedures for services were developed in the early 1970s and have not been updated to incorporate the functional and administrative definition of developmental disabilities.

1. How should Mr. Roberts explain the difference between the definitions of mental retardation and developmental disabilities?
2. What are the advantages and disadvantages of the term *developmental disability*?

ANSWER KEY TO
SELF-APPRAISAL AND CASE STUDY

1. a, b, c, d, e
2. a, b, c
3. False
4. False
5. a, b, c
6. False
7. True
8. Monoplegia — One arm or leg

   Diplegia — Both legs

   Hemiplegia — Arm and leg on the same side of the body

   Quadriplegia — Both arms and both legs
9. False
10. a, b, c, d, e
11. False
12. False
13. a, b, c, d
14. False
15. True
16. False
17. False
18. f
19. False
20. a, b, c, d, e, f, g

CASE STUDY ANSWER GUIDELINES

1. Mr. Roberts should explain that mental retardation and developmental disabilities are related but are different terms. An individual with mental retardation could also meet the definition of developmental disabilities. However, an individual with developmental disabilities is not necessarily mentally retarded. The term *mental retardation* addresses only a person's cognitive and adaptive abilities, whereas the term *developmental disabilities* also considers physical impairments and the individual's ability to function in seven areas of life. Mr. Roberts should review the definition of developmental disabilities with the health department worker.

2. The major advantage of the definition of developmental disabilities is that funding becomes available for individuals identified as having developmental disabilities. Disadvantages are that the term does not indicate what the person can and cannot do and does not suggest the individual's strengths, interests, and needs.

chapter 2

Historical and Contemporary Trends in Services

LEARNING OBJECTIVES

Upon completing this chapter, the reader will be able to:

1. Define the purpose of residential programs for persons with developmental disabilities during the years 1850–1860.
2. Explain why people with developmental disabilities acquired negative images in the years 1850–1900.
3. Define custodial care.
4. Identify the origins of the parents' movement.
5. Identify the importance of President John F. Kennedy's Panel on Mental Retardation.
6. Define Medicaid reform.
7. Define community integration.
8. Define the support services model.

INTRODUCTION

The availability and quality of services for people with developmental disabilities have changed over time. The types and quality of services depend on society's attitude toward people with developmental disabilities. Early services were intended to educate and train children and adolescents in special settings. The early experiments failed, however, and new reasons were advanced to justify the continuation of special settings. During the late 1800s, professionals in this field depicted people with disabilities as dangerous, deviant, and incapable of learning. The public and their elected representatives have retained these images to the present time.

After World War II, organizations of parents of people with disabilities gained greater political strength and began to advocate for reforms in services. Under President Kennedy's administration, mental retardation became part of the social reform movement and the numbers of people with disabilities living in institutions began to decline. Litigation and legislation during the 1970s resulted in an emphasis on integration and comprehensive services. The principle of normalization provided an important argument for the development of services in the community.

Certain trends are evident in the provision of services to people with developmental disabilities. Services in the community are replacing services in isolated settings, such as special schools and institutions. The choice and satisfaction of people with developmental disabilities are the features of primary concern. Services that support people in their own homes, neighborhoods, and jobs are increasing in popularity. Finally, the quality of services is being defined by the people with developmental disabilities who use the services.

SCHOOLS OF THE PRE–CIVIL WAR ERA

The first residential schools were developed for people labeled as "idiotic" and "feebleminded." These residential programs began in the era of social reform prior to the Civil War. Such reformers as Samuel Howe and Dorothea Dix opposed slavery and supported prison reform, public education, and poor law reform. They also promoted the early efforts to identify people with developmental disabilities in Massachusetts. Howe conducted a census of persons with developmental disabilities in Massachusetts during the late 1840s and, in 1850, began the first public residential program for children with developmental disabilities in Boston.

The first private school, called the Massachusetts School for Idiotic and Feeble Minded Youth, opened in Barre, Massachusetts, in 1848. During the decade before the Civil War, public residential schools opened in New York (1851), Pennsylvania (1852), Ohio (1857), Connecticut (1858), and Kentucky (1860).

The early reformers mistakenly concluded that developmental disabilities (then called mental retardation) resulted from bad habits or unlawful or immoral behavior. They believed that bad behavior on the part of parents resulted in birth defects. This belief in the cause of mental retardation led the early reformers to stress out-of-home care. Because they considered parents to be responsible for their children's disabilities, the early reformers ruled out the family as a proper source of support and development. Howe and his associates believed that the special school could train children in an artificial and uncorrupted environment.

The early schools stressed discipline of a student's physical, mental, and moral faculties. Keynotes of the schools were cleanliness, obedience, and promptness, followed by patience and industry. In the beginning, the residential schools attempted academic training; by the late 1850s, however, the focus shifted to strengthening the physique, correcting bad habits, and training for simple labor.

The early reformers were disappointed in their accomplishments (Gardner, in press). Howe noted that even the early years of the new school were disappointing. He had feared that the special school might turn into an asylum where bad habits prevailed. He felt that students should remain in the school only for education and training. Faced with a continued lack of success and increasing numbers of students during the mid-1870s, Howe warned against segregating people in asylums. Instead, he proposed that the state appoint advocates for people with developmental disabilities. The advocates would assist these individuals to live in the homes of responsible citizens.

DURING THE 1870s, SAMUEL HOWE PROPOSED A FORM OF CHILD AND ADULT FOSTER CARE AS AN ALTERNATIVE TO THE INSTITUTION.

INSTITUTIONS AND CUSTODIAL CARE

Howe's suggestion for community care was ignored. Instead, the early special schools evolved into custodial institutions that substituted work for education. By assigning people with developmental disabilities to work on farms or in industrial shops, the institutions attempted to become self-sufficient through the labor of residents. Those unable to work were assigned to custodial departments that provided little training or education. By 1880 in the United States, 15 public institutions served 4,216 individuals. That number grew to about 15,000 people residing in state institutions in 1900 (Switzky, Dudzinski, Van Acker, & Gambro, 1988, p. 27).

EARLY INSTITUTIONS ATTEMPTED TO BECOME SELF-SUFFICIENT THROUGH THE LABOR OF THE RESIDENTS.

During the years between the Civil War and World War I, only 3%–5% of all people with developmental disabilities resided in custodial institutions (Switzky et al., 1988; Tyor & Bell, 1984, p. 88). The significance of the custodial ethos lies not in the numbers but in the rationale for the custodial institution. The depiction of people with developmental disabilities as dangerous and deviant still influences social thinking today. The images that were formed at the end of the 19th century remain strong as the 21st century approaches.

THE IMAGES OF PEOPLE WITH DEVELOPMENTAL DISABILITIES
FORMED AT THE END OF THE 19TH CENTURY REMAIN STRONG
AS THE 21ST CENTURY APPROACHES.

Social reformers at the turn of the 20th century incorrectly believed that developmental disabilities were hereditary and that they were the cause of many social problems of the era. Researchers at the turn of the century examined the history of families in search of hereditary patterns of mental retardation. Studies of the Jukes and Kallikaks families indicated that mental retardation was passed from generation to generation. To prevent the spread of mental retardation, many professionals called for segregation in custodial institutions or sterilization surgery.

The concern over hereditary transmission of mental retardation was heightened by the development of the intelligence test by Alfred Binet in the early 1900s. Soon after, social welfare workers, psychologists, physicians, and others began to administer the tests to institutional populations, such as criminals, prostitutes, unwed mothers, and the poor in immigrant ghettos. The early tests were unreliable and indicated that whole populations were mentally retarded.

The connection between mental retardation and both criminality and immorality was heightened by the classification of some people as "moral imbeciles" and "defective delinquents." These individuals, though normal in intelligence, had deranged moral perceptions. Unfortunately, the label was applied to those whose social behaviors were different or excessive. Martin Barr defined the moral imbecile as "a plotter of mischief . . . with a genius for evil" (Scheerenberger, 1983, p. 140).

SPECIAL EDUCATION

The first special education programs, initiated in the large eastern cities at the turn of the century, were designed for students with mild mental retardation. There was no uniform approach to special education, with little in the way of teacher training.

By the early 1920s, 113 cities in 23 states had more than 23,000 students enrolled in a variety of special education classes. The majority of the students were male because "boys were more troublesome" (Scheerenberger, 1983, p. 169). Many of the children in the special education classes lived in urban areas of severe poverty.

A significant number of educators believed that the purpose of the special education program was to prepare children for the eventual transition to an institution. For that reason, many special education programs were intended for persons with severe disabilities.

FROM HYSTERIA TO CALM

The concern over the menace of people with mental retardation reached a high point during the period 1912–1917. This disability was considered the reason for almost all deviant behavior. Sixteen states constructed new facilities for people with mental retardation. The number of people living in such facilities increased from 20,731 in 1910 to 51,731 in 1923 (Tyor & Bell, 1984). Fifteen states had passed eugenic sterilization laws by 1917, and more than 3,000 people had been sterilized by 1921.

The hysteria about people with mental retardation declined after 1917 for several reasons. First, conclusions of a number of studies indicated that people with mental retardation could live in the community. Second, advocates of segregation realized that it was not economically possible to place all persons with mental retardation in institutions. Third, institutions began to develop parole programs, outpatient clinics, and other forms of community care. Fourth, fear of immigrants with mental retardation declined when more restrictive immigration laws were passed in 1924.

Perhaps the most important reason for the decline in hysteria, however, was criticism of the shoddy research used in previous heredity studies. In addition, the firm connection between mental retardation and criminality was broken when intelligence tests revealed that 47.3% of Caucasian draftees and 89% of African American draftees during World War I had mental ages of 12 or lower. The resulting low scores of the testing on the general population led to a reexamination of the early tests and testing procedures. These doubts about intelligence testing raised questions regarding the supposed link between mental retardation and criminality.

From 1920 to 1950, research studies indicated an absence of any direct link between mental retardation and criminality (Switzky et al., 1988, p. 29). Many professionals began to question the doctrines that had been previously developed for mental retardation. The general public and their political representatives, however, remembered the old hysteria and retained the images of deviant behavior associated with mental retardation. Despite some attempts at reform, institutions increased in number and size; living conditions became more dehumanized. The Great Depression of the 1930s and World War II diverted both resources and concern for people living in institutions.

DEINSTITUTIONALIZATION

Although the movement to improve living conditions in public institutions and to get people out of them began to escalate during the 1970s, the origins of this movement are found in earlier decades. The rise of parents' organizations, the changing nature of the population in institutions, and reforms of the Kennedy administration initiated the changes.

During the 1930s, parent groups began to organize. The Cuyahoga County (Ohio) Council for the Retarded Child began in 1933. It financed and operated a school program for severely disabled children (Scheerenberger, 1983). Eighty-eight parent groups were operating in 19 states by 1950. That year, 90 delegates representing 23 parent groups met in Minneapolis to organize a national organization. The Association for Retarded Citizens of the United States of America (ARC/USA) has since grown in membership and influence. In 1991, ARC/USA changed its name to The Arc in order to lessen the emphasis on any stigma still attached to mental retardation.

During its formative years, The Arc directed attention to the dehumanizing conditions in institutions, the lack of educational opportunities in the community, the inability of professionals to work with parents, and the mismanagement of services for people with mental retardation. As early as 1953, The Arc issued its "Education Bill of Rights for the Retarded Child," which set forth the right of every child with mental retardation to an educational program.

The parents had become alarmed by the change in the population of the institutions. Prior to World War II, teenagers with mild mental retardation accounted for the largest proportion of first admissions. With the "baby boom" that occurred after the war, however, the number of first admissions of children with severe mental retardation began to increase dramatically (Tyor & Bell, 1984). In addition, advances in medicine had extended the life span of persons with severe disabilities.

The increasing number of children with such disabilities was reflected in the growth of the institutional population. In 1940, approximately 101,164 people lived in institutions. By 1967, the number increased to 194,650 (Lakin, 1979). During the early 1980s, Scheerenberger (1983) noted that 75% of the institutions had been constructed since 1960.

THE NUMBER OF PERSONS LIVING IN INSTITUTIONS ALMOST DOUBLED BETWEEN 1940 AND 1967.

The Kennedy administration's concern for mental retardation represented the third major source of change and deinstitutionalization. The report of the President's Panel on Mental Retardation identified three major needs—research, a system of services, and social action to prevent mental retardation. The passage of the Mental Retardation Facilities and Community Mental Health Centers Construction Act of 1963 (PL 88-164) allocated federal funding for personnel training and the construction of research and clinical service facilities. More importantly, the Kennedy administration made mental retardation a social reform issue.

EXERCISE 1

Agency Origins

Through conversations with the senior staff, a review of the early minutes of the meetings of the board of directors, or a review of early scrapbooks, determine the reasons that led to the opening of your agency. Did the early goals of the organization address those reasons?

Deinstitutionalization also became a social reform issue. The exposure of deplorable conditions in institutions contributed to an increase in legal actions during the 1960s and 1970s. Wolfensberger's principle of normalization (described in Chapter 3), which questioned the institution itself, intensified social reform. The normalization principle stresses the importance of using typical and normal methods to establish valued outcomes for people. Tension arose between the advocates of the principle of normalization and those who wished to maintain the institution. The method of teaching and training individuals in institutions to live and work in the community was not considered normative.

THE NORMALIZATION PRINCIPLE QUESTIONED INSTITUTIONAL SERVICES AND SETTINGS.

LITIGATION AND LEGISLATION

Court actions were filed during the 1970s in response to the dehumanizing conditions of state institutions. The Partlow State School in Alabama and the Willowbrook State School on Staten Island, New York, were the focus of major legal proceedings. These and other court cases attracted public attention to state institutions.

Advocates also took legal action against state education agencies. In two 1971 decisions, the *Pennsylvania Association for Retarded Children v. the Commonwealth of Pennsylvania* (the PARC case) and *Mills v. the Board of Education* (District of Columbia), the courts found that children with mental retardation have a right to a free and public education.

The parents movement, pressure from advocates for social reform, and litigation resulted in major legislation during the mid-1970s (later reenacted and expanded during the 1980s and 1990s). The Rehabilitation Act of 1973 (PL 93-112) has been described as the civil rights act for individuals with disabilities. The law prohibits discrimination on the basis of disability.

The Education for All Handicapped Children Act of 1975 (PL 94-142) mandates that public school systems provide a free, appropriate public education to handicapped children, ages 3–21. The law requires that all children must have an individualized education program (IEP). Finally, the law mandates that children, whenever possible, be educated with children who do not have disabilities.

The Developmental Disabilities Services and Facilities Construction Act of 1970 (PL 91-517), the Developmental Disabilities Assistance and Bill of Rights Act of 1975 (PL 94-103), and the Rehabilitation, Comprehensive Services, and Developmental Disabilities Act of 1978 (PL 95-602) extended the original Mental Retardation Facilities and Community Mental Health Centers Construction Act of 1963 (PL 88-164). The 1970s legislation added the Developmental Disability Council formula grant program, the Protection and Advocacy System, and the functional definition of developmental disabilities.

Also in 1971, Congress amended the Social Security Act (PL 92-223) and authorized the payment of federal Medicaid funds to public institutions serving people with mental retardation. State institutions rushed to meet the new standards for an intermediate care facility for persons with mental retardation (ICF/MR) in order to receive federal funds (see Title XIX below). Some states also began to apply the ICF/MR standards to small residences (4–15 beds) to increase funding for community programs.

TITLE XIX—A FEDERAL FUNDING CONTROVERSY

Although federal funding through the ICF/MR program has undoubtedly increased the level of care provided in institutions, critics point to four failures of the program:

1. ICF/MR program standards and requirements have an outdated medical orientation.
2. Attempts by the states to obtain the maximum in federal dollars have led to greater state expenditures for institutional programs, rather than community programs.
3. Community-based programs built around the ICF/MR model are too expensive. The model is also too rigid to promote community integration and participation.
4. The ICF/MR program promoted out-of-home placement. Individuals with developmental disabilities were not eligible for service while living at home if their families did not qualify for Medicaid.

However, if the individual resided in an ICF/MR, services would be provided without regard to family income.

During an 8-year period (fiscal years 1977–1984), more than 80% of federal money paid out under the ICF/MR program went to institutions. This disproportionate use of funds between institutional and community-based services became increasingly inconsistent with current research studies indicating that community-based alternatives were more effective than institutional care in both service delivery and cost.

In an attempt to reform the Medicaid bias for institutions, Congress enacted the Home and Community-Based (Medicaid) Waiver in 1981. Under this legislation, the states could "waive" certain Medicaid requirements in order to provide services to persons with developmental disabilities in community-based settings. The next piece of Medicaid reform was introduced by Senator John Chafee in 1984 as the Community and Family Living Amendments. The original legislation was amended during the next 6 years and finally signed into law in 1990 as a new Medicaid state plan option. Known as the community living arrangements program, this option enables states to use Medicaid funding in a greater variety of community settings. However, the law limits the number of participating states and the amount of available federal money.

EXERCISE 2

Dollars and Services

Ask if any of the programs provided by your agency are linked with Medicaid. If they are, identify any special conditions attached to the use of the money.

THE SUPPORT SERVICES MODEL

The debate about Medicaid reform was strengthened when the support services model emerged. The principle of support services is that where people live or work depends on the presence of support services. Instead of developing specialized group homes or workshops, special support services can be taken to individuals in their own homes and work settings. Attendants, special equipment, and therapies can be provided in natural settings.

WHERE PEOPLE LIVE AND WORK DEPENDS ON THE AVAILABILITY OF SUPPORT SERVICES.

The support services model is important because it focuses on changing the social and physical environments, rather than just helping the individual with the developmental disability. Focusing exclusively on the individual reinforces the stigma of disability. When attention is given to social and physical supports, however, there are more opportunities for change.

Within the past decade, three distinct support services models have emerged:

1. *Family support services*—These services are designed to support people with developmental disabilities in their homes, rather than move them to special schools, nursing homes, or other facilities for needed services. In addition, many traditional services typically provided in clinics, hospitals, schools, and offices are now provided in the home. For example, instead of placing a child in a special residential school to receive behavior intervention services and physical therapy, such services can be brought to the child's home. Attendant care, Meals on Wheels, and special transportation can assist an adult with a developmental disability to live at home and work in the community.

2. *Supported employment*—On-the-job support allows people with developmental disabilities to work. Traditional vocational training stresses assessment of skills or work readiness, vocational training, and placement in employment when the necessary skills are learned. In this employment model, an individual is first trained and then placed in a job. Supported employment provides training and support while the individual is actually working. A job coach accompanies the individual to work and conducts on-the-job training. As the trainee learns the job tasks and becomes familiar with the social setting, the job coach gradually reduces the on-site training and support.

3. *Supported independent living*—Typically, residential services and supervision have been provided to individuals in a centralized setting, such as a group home. In supported independent living programs, special services and supervision are available to individuals within their own homes or apartments. Supervision is adjusted to meet the needs of each individual. Some people with developmental disabilities need only occasional drop-in monitoring; others need attendant care every morning and evening.

POSITIVE BEHAVIOR INTERVENTION

The emphasis on the positive aspects of behavior intervention programs is an indication that people with developmental disabilities have motives and reasons for their behaviors (see chap. 9, this volume). During the early and mid-1970s, behavior intervention strategies in residential, educational, and vocational settings stressed the consequence or reinforcement that followed a behavior. The staff focused attention on what happened after a particular behavior occurred. For example, the staff might ignore, redirect, or punish a person who walked away from a workstation.

It is now considered more appropriate to focus attention on the reasons for the behavior. The staff assume that the behavior serves a purpose. Most behaviors communicate messages. For example, a person may walk away from the workstation because of boredom with the task, because of frustration in not being able to do the task, or because he or she wants to take a break. The staff should search for the message that a behavior communicates.

BEHAVIOR CAN BE A FORM OF COMMUNICATION.

The focus on positive behavior intervention also emphasizes the environmental causes for the behavior. The behavior can then be altered by changing the environment. Such changes might include the introduction of new peers and/or support staff, a new setting for services or supports, different teaching techniques, and different types of work. This approach indicates that individual behavior depends on many factors in the environment. As a result, the best places for an individual to learn how to behave appropriately are those where he or she lives, works, and plays.

The change in focus of behavior intervention programs reflects the positive growth in programs for people with developmental disabilities during the past 2 decades. The institutions of the 1960s and 1970s were overcrowded and understaffed. Habilitation efforts were limited, programs were not individualized, and the staff were unable to alter the causes of behaviors. Thus, the focus was placed on the consequence of a behavior. The staff stressed the reinforcement that followed the behavior as the key to changing the behavior.

Because of the present trend toward smaller, more normalized work and living situations, the staff are now able to control many of the variables that might cause a behavior. Causes of the behavior can be identified and changed. Living space can be rearranged. Noise, light, and temperature can be altered. Staffing levels can be shifted and specific staff members assigned or reassigned. A rich array of supports is available to alter a behavior.

THE CHANGING DEFINITION OF QUALITY

The definition of quality in services for people with developmental disabilities has changed over the course of the past 15 years (Jaskowski,

1991) (see also chap. 19, this volume). The discovery of inhumane conditions in institutions and subsequent lawsuits resulted in a focus on protection from harm, freedom from abuse and neglect, and legal rights of people with developmental disabilities. The focus shifted during the early 1980s to the coordination of services and the development of individualized service plans for people with developmental disabilities. The concern over legal rights and protection from harm did not disappear, but the need for comprehensive and coordinated services was highlighted.

During the mid-1980s, a new focus on quality related to outcomes for people with developmental disabilities. The question had evolved from "What services are needed or provided?" to "What difference does the service make for the individual?" The most common measures of outcome were productivity, independence, and integration.

QUALITY IS BEST DEFINED BY THE CONSUMER, RATHER THAN THE PROVIDER, OF THE SERVICE.

The emphasis on quality has again shifted. Attention is directed toward the quality of life available for people with developmental disabilities. Individual choice and satisfaction with services and supports are important concerns. There is a growing recognition that informal networks of family, friends, and neighbors can provide important services and supports. Finally, quality in services and supports is best defined by the user of the services and supports, rather than by the provider.

EXERCISE 3

Identifying What Is Important

Talk informally with a number of people who receive supports and services through your agency. Ask them to list what is important to them. What do the people with developmental disabilities list as important to them?

SUMMARY

Images of people with developmental disabilities have changed since the Civil War era. These images and the public's attitudes about people with developmental disabilities have influenced the kinds of services received by these individuals. Many of the images and attitudes that were prevalent during the late 1800s, however, still exist.

Within the past 15 years, the institution has been replaced as the focus of service. There is a growing emphasis on providing services and supports to people with developmental disabilities in their own homes, jobs, and communities, rather than in special schools, group homes, and sheltered workshops Increased attention is placed on making changes to an individual's social and physical environment. The individual with a developmental disability is no longer required to make all of the changes so that he or she can "fit in." Finally, there is recognition that the informal service and support systems of family, neighborhood, and community can assist individuals to live and work in natural settings.

The definition of quality in services is also changing. The current emphasis is on individual choice, satisfaction, and quality of life for the individual.

BIBLIOGRAPHY

Bradley, V.J., & Knoll, J. (1990). Shifting paradigms in services to people with developmental disabilities. Unpublished paper.

Gardner, J.F. (in press). The era of optimism, 1850–1870: A preliminary reappraisal. Mental Retardation.

Jaskowski, T. (1991). The changing definition of quality. Unpublished paper, Columbia, MD.

Lakin, K.C. (1979). Demographic studies of residential facilities for the mentally retarded: An historical overview of methodologies and findings. Minneapolis: University of Minnesota, Development of Psychoeducational Studies.

Scheerenberger, R.C. (1983). A history of mental retardation. Baltimore: Paul H. Brookes Publishing Co.

Scheerenberger, R.C. (1987). A history of mental retardation: A quarter century of promise. Baltimore: Paul H. Brookes Publishing Co.

Switzky, H.N., Dudzinski, M., Van Acker, R., & Gambro, J. (1988). Historical foundations of out-of-home residential alternatives for mentally retarded persons. In L.W. Heal, J.I. Haney, & A.R. Novak Amado (Eds.), Integration of developmentally disabled individuals into the community (2nd ed., pp. 19–35). Baltimore: Paul H. Brookes Publishing Co.

Tyor, P.L., & Bell, L. V. (1984). Caring for the retarded in America: A history. Westport, CT: Greenwood Press.

ADDITIONAL RESOURCES

D. Braddock and G. Fujiura (1991), in Politics, public policy, and the development of community mental retardation services in the United States, American Journal of Mental Retardation, 95(4), 368–387, discuss the strength of consumer advocacy organizations and the history of state policies promoting racial equality as the significant predictors of variance in state spending for community programs.

E. Dwyer (1987), in Homes for the mad: Life inside two nineteenth century asylums (New Brunswick, NJ: Rutgers University Press); Gerald Grob (1975), in Mental institutions in America: Social policy to 1875 (New York: Free Press, 1975); and Nancy Tomes (1984), in A generous confidence: Thomas Story Kirkbride and the art of asylum-keeping, 1840–1883 (New York: Cambridge University Press), provide a history of psychiatry and the social history of mental illness.

D. Fullwood (1990), in *Chances and choices: Making integration work* (Baltimore: Paul H. Brookes Publishing Co.), provides a practical approach for staff, parents, educators, and the general public who want to promote integration within their own communities.

The discussion and debate over the science and technology of "aversive" interventions and "nonaversive" behavioral supports are found in (1990), *Journal of The Association for Persons with Severe Handicaps*, 15(3), 125–159. The same general topic is covered in a series of articles, (1990), *American Journal on Mental Retardation*, 95(2), 137–181.

T. Kastner, P. DeLotto, B. Scagnelli, and W. Testa (1990) have written Proposed guidelines for agencies serving persons with developmental disabilities and HIV infection, *Mental Retardation*, 28(3), 139–146.

D.J. Rothman has written two volumes on the history and meaning of institutions in the United States. See Rothman (1971), *The discovery of the asylum: Social order and disorder in the new republic* (Boston: Little, Brown) and Rothman (1980), *Conscience and convenience: The asylum and its alternatives in progressive America* (Boston: Little Brown).

Symposium on aging and mental retardation (1988), *Mental Retardation, 26*(4), 177–222, notes the increasing attention given to older Americans with mental retardation.

Symposium, Developmental Disabilities and HIV Infection (1989), *Mental Retardation, 27*(4), 197–262, covers the topic of human immunodeficiency virus infection.

SELF-APPRAISAL

INSTRUCTIONS

The following questions will help you evaluate your knowledge about the history and current trends in services to people with developmental disabilities. For true-false questions, check the correct answer. For multiple choice questions, circle the correct answer(s).

Note: There may be more than one correct answer for some questions.

1. The early reformers were disappointed in the successes of the early residential schools for individuals with mental retardation.
   ___ True   ___ False
2. The images of people with disabilities that resulted in custodial institutions remain today.
   ___ True   ___ False
3. In the late 1800s and early 1900s, people mistakenly believed that mental retardation was hereditary. As a result, they proposed to prevent conception and birth of people with mental retardation in the future by:
   a. Surgical sterilization
   b. Segregation of men and women in custodial institutions
   c. Prevention of travel by people with disabilities outside their own towns or cities
   d. Incentives for childless marriages
4. A significant reason for early special education programs was to prepare children for the eventual transition to the custodial institution.
   ___ True   ___ False
5. The hysteria about people with mental retardation declined after 1917 for the following reasons:
   a. Studies concluded that people with mental retardation could live in the community.
   b. Professionals and political leaders recognized that it was not economically possible to place all people with mental retardation in institutions.
   c. Institutions began to develop community-based parole programs and other outpatient services.
   d. New immigration laws decreased the fear of the growing number of immigrants with disabilities.
   e. New evidence indicated that mental retardation was not hereditary.

6. During its formative years, the parents' movement focused attention on:
   a. Dehumanizing conditions in institutions
   b. Lack of educational opportunities in the community
   c. Inability of professionals to work with parents
   d. Mismanagement of services for people with disabilities

7. The major forces behind deinstitutionalization were:
   a. The parents' movement
   b. The change in the population in institutions
   c. The reforms of the Kennedy administration
   d. New federal funding for community programs

8. The concerns about Medicaid funding for the Intermediate Care Facility for Persons with Mental Retardation (ICF/MR) program focused on:
   a. Increased federal funding for an outdated program
   b. Expense of community-based ICF/MR programs
   c. Promotion of out-of-home placement to receive services
   d. Difficulty of providing adequate clinical services in ICFs/MR

9. The support services model is important because:
   a. People live and work in the natural community with the necessary supports.
   b. Avenues for change are not limited to the individual with the disability. The physical and social environments can be altered to increase the functional abilities of individuals.
   c. Reimbursements for supports are higher than for traditional services.
   d. Supports can be found in both formal systems and informal networks.

10. The current focus on quality emphasizes:
    a. Quality in institutional services
    b. Quality assurance through utilization review
    c. Quality of life
    d. Quality from the consumer's point of view

CASE STUDY

Billy Hughes is a 20-year-old man with a moderate degree of cognitive impairment; he is graduating from the Oak Hills Special Education School next year. Billy currently lives at home and enjoys going to fast-food restaurants, watching sporting events, and helping with chores around the house.

Oaks Hills school personnel, Billy, and his family have been discussing the range of residential, vocational, and leisure options available during the next 3–4 years. Billy has indicated that he would like to continue to live at home. He has also expressed a desire to work in the produce department at the local Lucas Supermarket. There is general agreement that Billy is capable of supported employment and may even be able to secure independent employment.

Situation

During the discussions of Billy's future work options, the parents began to voice some concerns about the perceived lack of structure and supervision in a supported independent living program that the school personnel suggested as a possible future residential option. They indicated that neighbors would have negative images of Billy, and that he would be unable to fit into the neighborhood. In addition, they worried that the drop-in coverage was insufficient to meet Billy's needs.

1. How would you respond to the parents' concern that the neighbors might have negative perceptions of people with developmental disabilities?
2. How would you explain the advantages of the support services model in residential services?

ANSWER KEY TO
SELF-APPRAISAL AND CASE STUDY

SELF-APPRAISAL

1. True
2. True
3. a, b
4. True
5. a, b, c, d, e
6. a, b, c, d
7. a, b, c
8. a, b, c
9. a, b, d
10. c, d

CASE STUDY ANSWER GUIDELINES

1. Don't deny that the general public can have some misguided beliefs about people with disabilities. These beliefs were formed over a century ago and have become embedded in our social thinking. However, most neighbors are reasonable and will make final decisions based on their own experience and observations. Billy's participation in the supported living program will be evidence that people with disabilities are not dangerous or deviant.
2. In the support services model, the support services, such as drop-in supervision, can be increased or decreased depending on the needs of the individual with the disability. Services can be adjusted without Billy having to move to a different program with different levels of service. Support services models actually promote stability because the supports change, rather than the residential placement. Billy has the advantage of living in the same setting without having to move every time services need to be adjusted.

chapter 3

The Principle
of
Normalization

LEARNING OBJECTIVES

Upon completing this chapter, the reader will be able to:

1. Define the normalization principle.
2. State the difference between being different and being different and devalued.
3. Identify three targets for effecting change.
4. Identify the five major components of the normalization principle.
5. Identify three arguments that state the normalization principle is not realistic.

INTRODUCTION

In October 1974, more than 500 people with developmental disabilities gathered at a conference in Otter Crest, Oregon. The theme of the conference, which they planned and conducted, was "We have something to offer." The next year, more than 700 people attended a second conference in Bend, Oregon. In the following years, People First conventions have been held across North America.

Several important messages have emerged from these self-advocacy efforts. Participants at the meetings have been able to speak out, and they have listened to each other. The most common message has been that participants hate the term "retarded."

It is not surprising that People First members dislike the term *mental retardation*. The term has many negative implications. The primary assumption is that a person with "mental retardation" cannot perform certain tasks or accomplish personal goals. Yet many people with developmental disabilities live independently in the community. They are moving from activity centers to supervised employment settings, participating in community recreational activities, and attending classes in community colleges.

The normalization principle has helped to focus attention on what people with developmental disabilities can achieve. Various writers in the United States and Europe have provided definitions of the normalization principle. Perhaps the most common and useful definition of the term is provided by Wolf Wolfensberger (1972), in *The Principle of Normalization in Human Services*. "Normalization," says Wolfensberger, "is . . . the utilization of means which are as culturally normative as possible, in order to establish and/or maintain personal behaviors and characteristics which are as culturally normative as possible" (p. 28).

Sensitivity to the normalization principle is important because it can prevent devaluation of people. It can also decrease discrimination against people that occurs simply because they have developmental disabilities. Wolfensberger (1983) has recently suggested changing the term *normalization* to *social role valorization*. Services and practices for people with developmental disabilities would then be judged by the extent to which they enhance the social role of the individual.

The normalization principle is also important because it can help you to make decisions. It can assist you in deciding what services to provide and how they should be provided. Finally, the normalization principle can help people with developmental disabilities to make decisions about their own lives.

"NORMALIZATION IS . . . THE UTILIZATION OF MEANS WHICH ARE AS CULTURALLY NORMATIVE AS POSSIBLE, IN ORDER TO ESTABLISH AND/OR MAINTAIN PERSONAL BEHAVIORS AND CHARACTERISTICS WHICH ARE AS CULTURALLY NORMATIVE AS POSSIBLE."

STIGMA OF DEVELOPMENTAL DISABILITIES

People with developmental disabilities have not been fully accepted by society. They have been perceived as significantly different. In addition, this difference is negatively valued. The combination of being both different and devalued results in people being stigmatized.

The distinction between the terms *different* and *devalued* is important. Many individuals are different but not devalued. The late Howard Hughes or Hugh Heffner, for example, may have acted or act quite differently from most people, but their actions have not caused them to be devalued by most people. Like the absentminded professor or the million-dollar athlete, some people can act differently because they are valued. If you are valued and accepted by your friends, you can deviate from the norm in certain ways and your friends will still tolerate you. However, people who have developmental disabilities and are devalued are not allowed to act differently.

Society is not as willing to tolerate differences in people with developmental disabilities. For instance, you might not be admonished for playing your stereo too loudly on a Friday night, but the same behavior by a person with developmental disabilities may not be so easily tolerated. To be socially accepted, people who are negatively valued because they are different must act in a conservative manner.

The normalization theory suggests that you, as an employee of a human services agency, should minimize the perceived differentness of people with developmental disabilities. Human services agencies should attempt to reduce the stigma and deviancy associated with disability. The normalization principle does this by encouraging people with developmental disabilities to establish behaviors and experiences that are similar to those of other people. It also promotes the use of valued means to achieve goals. Both the means to the end and the end behavior or experience should be valued as typical of the norm.

The normalization principle focuses on two aspects of programs and services to people with developmental disabilities. First, the principle concentrates on such program outcomes as the following:

1. Skills, abilities, and behaviors of people with developmental disabilities
2. Quality of life experienced by people with developmental disabilities in residential, vocational, and leisure-time activities
3. Public perception of persons with developmental disabilities

Second, the normalization principle is concerned with how the program achieves its outcomes. The process, or the manner in which the outcomes are achieved, includes attention to such factors as the following:

1. Methods used in teaching skills, abilities, and behaviors
2. Grouping of people
3. Physical location of the program
4. Vocabulary and language that describe people with developmental disabilities

---

THE NORMALIZATION PRINCIPLE STRESSES WHAT A HUMAN SERVICES PROGRAM DOES AND HOW IT IS DONE.

PROGRAM MESSAGES

The normalization principle also stresses the difference between what a program accomplishes and the impression it makes on the public.

The success of a program, for example, that increases the skills and abilities of people with developmental disabilities will be negated if the program depicts them as devalued or dependent. The message that your program sends to the public is as important as what the program accomplishes.

The language that describes programs and people is a part of the message sent to the public. Unfortunately, people are sometimes described as a disability type. This happens when the staff refer to a person as a "quad," a "CP," or a "non-amb." As a result, individuals are reduced to members of a devalued disability status group. If an employee refers to individuals with physical disabilities as "vegetables and pretzels," what value and status are conveyed to the public? Similarly, characterizing people with dated terms, such as "retardate," "mongoloid," or "trainable," only reinforces negative messages from the past.

Another example of a negative message is treating people with developmental disabilities as if they were perpetual children. Programs and publications frequently refer to adults with developmental disabilities as "children who never grew up." Employees sometimes use childhood activities in adult programs. Common examples are scheduling visits by Santa Claus during the holidays, the use of crayons and coloring books to teach fine motor skills, and the use of child-oriented decorations in programs for adults.

The use of age-equivalent developmental levels and intelligence test scores sometimes leads to age-inappropriate practices. Test scores and assessments frequently report, for instance, that a person has a mental age of 2 years, or a developmental level of 3 years. This does not mean that the person is 2 or 3 years old because he or she has a developmental disability. And it certainly does not mean that the individual should be treated as a child.

Your challenge as an agency staff member is to provide a variety of age-appropriate programs, settings, and activities for people with developmental disabilities. This is the intent of the normalization principle. You should also encourage and reinforce the choice of age-appropriate activities and personal possessions.

You should be aware that some people with developmental disabilities have been deprived of age-appropriate opportunities and expectations. They may thus have a distinct preference for age-inappropriate activities and possessions. In this instance, the staff are presented with a conflict between encouraging decision making and allowing the possibly devaluing choice of an age-inappropriate possession or activity. Your response should not be, "Get rid of the Donald Duck hat." Instead, you should provide a variety of age-appropriate alternatives and also give the necessary guidance and reinforcement for the age-appropriate choices.

In summary, the messages relayed by your program are important. The public's perception and reception of people with developmental disabilities are shaped by the messages you send. Advocates frequently blame the state agency or the legislature for lack of funds or poor services for people with developmental disabilities; however, your messages influence the attitudes of state agency representatives, legislators, and the voting public.

THE MESSAGE THAT YOUR PROGRAM SENDS TO THE PUBLIC IS AS IMPORTANT AS WHAT THE PROGRAM ACCOMPLISHES.

VALUED SOCIAL ROLES

A role is an expected behavior that is usually determined by the status, occupation, and/or wealth of an individual in a community. Roles can include formal job-related requirements; for example, we expect different behaviors from bankers than we do from airline jet mechanics. Football players generally behave differently than college professors. Other roles can include less formal social roles—the expected behavior of individuals in group situations, for instance.

Most people play many different formal and informal roles. People play multiple roles within the same day. You may be a parent and prepare breakfast for your children. As a commuter, you drive to work where you assume the role of a worker. At work, you assume a specific role, such as boss, technical coordinator, or residential associate. After work, you may play the roles of softball player and tavern patron. Later, when you return home for dinner, you may again play a role of parent, spouse, or both.

Some roles are more highly valued than others. People generally prefer the role of boss or manager rather than that of the newest employee. Most people would rather be a theater patron than an usher. But even the usher recognizes that the role is temporary and that he or she can return to another role as a student, parent, or aspiring actor. Although many people recognize that they will occupy nonvalued social roles for some time, they do so with the belief that they will move on to more valued roles.

People with developmental disabilities, however, often have the opportunity to play only one role—that pertaining to the type of disability—for two reasons. First, the opportunity to play other valued social roles is not provided. People with disabilities may not have the opportunities to be a theater patron or an usher, to become a university student or a worker, to play softball, or to frequent a tavern. This reason involves the concept of self-fulfilling prophecies (see below).

Second, people with developmental disabilities are restricted from playing multiple and valued social roles. Even when they do perform social roles, they are not seen in those roles but continue to be perceived as people with developmental disabilities. For example, a person filling the roles of aspiring actor, tavern patron, and softball player is still assigned the role of a person with a specific type of disability by the larger community. He or she is unable to change, grow, and succeed in other roles.

EXERCISE 1

Opportunities To Fill Valued Social Roles

Think of the people with developmental disabilities with whom you interact at work. Do they have the opportunity to play different and valued social roles? How often do they get to fill the role of:

Student _____   Citizen _____
Good friend _____   Winner, leader _____
Sports team   Husband, wife,
  member _____   lover _____
Sporting event, theater, or movie   Employee _____
  patron _____   Diner patron _____
Church/synagogue
  member _____

PLANNING FOR CHANGE

The normalization principle is also useful in planning for change. As an employee in a human services agency, you can focus on three targets for change:

1. The person with a developmental disability
2. Professionals and human services agencies
3. The general public

THE NORMALIZATION PRINCIPLE PROVIDES GUIDELINES FOR PLANNING AND DELIVERING SERVICES.

The normalization principle recognizes that the focus for change cannot rest on the people with developmental disabilities alone. Significant changes can occur at the human services agency and the general public levels. Many problems in how services are planned and provided can be solved only at the service system level. To focus on the individual is to ignore many other possibilities for change.

SELF-FULFILLING PROPHECIES

The messages from human services programs either alter or continue self-fulfilling prophecies about people with developmental disabilities. Self-fulfilling prophecies are formed according to the following sequence:

1. *Prejudiced beliefs* about the capabilities of people with developmental disabilities lead to—
2. *Low expectations* of what they can accomplish, which lead to—
3. *Withholding of opportunities* for learning and decision making, which leads to—
4. *Limited growth and development,* which—
5. *Confirms the prejudiced belief*

One example of a self-fulfilling prophecy is provided by the diagnosis of Down syndrome during the 1970s. At that time, most authorities believed that children with Down syndrome lacked the capacity to learn preacademic skills (to count, differentiate colors, recognize basic words). Because no educational system would waste resources on a child who could not learn, no preacademic skill training was provided. It is not surprising that the prediction for children with Down syndrome came true in many instances; those children who were not educated could not count or recognize basic words.

A second illustration of a self-fulfilling prophecy is found when parents or agency personnel do not believe that people with developmental disabilities can make decisions. As a result, they are not taught *how* to make decisions. They do not learn how to cope with failure, nor are they allowed to learn by making small mistakes over time. It is not surprising that these individuals cannot make decisions as adults without additional help and supervision.

The normalization principle is particularly helpful in thwarting the first and second steps in the self-fulfilling prophecy. The portrayal of people with developmental disabilities as unique individuals who have strengths and capabilities decreases prejudiced beliefs. Expectations are changed. For example, an agency may provide an excellent work training program that leads to supervised employment. The goal of placing people in work situations is compromised, however, if any of the following situations occur:

The trainees arrive at the program and depart on a yellow special education bus.
The trainees carry Super Heroes lunch boxes.
The trainees are underpaid.

If you were a potential employer visiting the work training program, what would you conclude from these three examples? Would you view the trainees as potential employees? Would the program send you a message of low expectations? What conclusions would you make about expanding employment opportunities for people with developmental disabilities?

EXERCISE 2

Values Influencing Quality of Life

Following is the result of a study (Dalkey, Rourke, Lewis, & Snyder, 1972) that asked students at the University of California at Los Angeles to identify the values that contributed to the quality of life. The values are listed in order of importance, as rated by respondents.

1. Love
2. Self-respect
3. Peace of mind
4. Sex
5. Challenge
6. Social acceptance
7. Accomplishment
8. Individuality
9. Involvement
10. Well-being (economic, health)
11. Change
12. Power (control)
13. Privacy

The next set of values represents the consensus of a group study of the American Academy of Arts and Sciences. These are the values expected to be most important in the year 2000. They are listed in order of importance, as rated by respondents.

1. Privacy
2. Equality
3. Personal integrity
4. Freedom
5. Law and order
6. Pleasantness of environment
7. Social adjustment
8. Efficiency and effectiveness of organizations
9. Rationality
10. Education
11. Ability and talent

The two value surveys listed above were cited in Rubinstein (1975). Now conduct your own value survey as follows:

(continued)

EXERCISE 2

(continued)

Consider the agency in which you work. List below the policies, procedures, and practices that increase the qualities listed on the left in the lives of people with mental retardation.

Value	Policy, procedure, practice
1. Love	_____
2. Self-respect	_____
3. Peace of mind	_____
4. Sex	_____
5. Challenge	_____
6. Social acceptance	_____
7. Accomplishment	_____
8. Individuality	_____
9. Involvement	_____
10. Well-being	_____
11. Change	_____
12. Power and control	_____
13. Privacy	_____
14. Equality	_____
15. Personal integrity	_____
16. Freedom	_____
17. Law and order	_____
18. Pleasantness of environment	_____
19. Social adjustment	_____
20. Efficiency and effectiveness of organizations	_____
21. Rationality	_____
22. Education	_____
23. Ability and talent	_____

Were the policies, procedures, and practices supporting the values easy to identify? Does the agency consider the values important?

THE FIVE DIMENSIONS OF THE PRINCIPLE OF NORMALIZATION

The extent to which an agency incorporates the principle of normalization is assessed by a Program Analysis of Service Systems (PASS) evaluation. This evaluation measures service quality in terms of the agency's adherence to the principle of normalization. A newer evaluation, Program Analysis of Service Systems' Implementation of Normalization Goals (PASSING), measures service quality in terms of the agency's implementation of normalization. Both evaluations contain numerous items and groupings. Most of the major items can be included under five groupings:

1. Community presence
2. Community participation
3. Skill enhancement
4. Image enhancement
5. Autonomy and empowerment

Community Presence

The first dimension of the normalization principle is community presence. This means that both the programs and the people themselves must be situated in the community. Community presence can be considered as physical integration.

Services and activities should be provided in local neighborhoods and communities. Isolation should be avoided. Programs and services for people with developmental disabilities can be located in rural, suburban, and urban settings. Proximity is one measure of community presence. This measures how close the program is to a major population center. Two aspects of proximity are involved: 1) cost and time required to participate in community life (potential for participation is increased by closeness to the community), and 2) distance from a service or activity (this affects the perception of who is entitled to the service).

Residence in a neighborhood or community provides a sense of belonging or ownership. People residing in a group home outside the neighborhood cannot make the same claim on services or activities as people on your block. Access to services and activities also influences community presence; speed of transit and convenience influence access. Public transportation, parking, traffic congestion, and physical safety determine ease of access. A supervised apartment program in a high-crime area does not promote community presence. Similarly, a work training program distant from public transportation prevents some people from making full use of the training opportunity.

LIVING IN THE COMMUNITY GIVES PEOPLE A CLAIM TO LOCAL SERVICES.

The availability of socially integrative resources also influences community presence. Opportunities for social integration require the presence of shopping options, public services, opportunities for religious expression, recreational and leisure-time activities, and educational programs. Most people choose a residence because of the environmental setting, proximity to work, and availability of other resources in the neighborhood or community. Residential options for people with developmental disabilities should also consider the distance and access to the same resources commonly used by persons without disabilities.

Community presence is further affected by the number of people in a program and the ability to integrate those people into neighborhood settings. This ability is influenced by three factors. The first is the size or capacity of the neighborhood. An industrial park with ancillary services for 125 businesses nearby could absorb a work training program for 50 people. If the same program were located in a village center with 5 businesses, the trainees could not be as easily integrated. The second factor is the size of the program. A supervised apartment program serving 3 people with developmental disabilities can be absorbed with greater ease than a 15-person group home. The third factor is the number of other devalued people who might want to engage in community life. The local recreation council, for example, might meet the needs of 3 people from an apartment program. Integrating those 3 people with 12 people from the mental health program and 53 people from the work-release program would be a more difficult task.

Community Participation

Community participation, the second dimension of the normalization principle, is a measure of the extent to which people are socially integrated into the community. This includes both impersonal and personal interactions. The impersonal interactions take place, for example, while purchasing an item at the neighborhood variety store, while ordering a meal in a restaurant, and during work or work training. Impersonal interactions require mutual respect and esteem. Public attitudes and the behavior and appearance of people with developmental disabilities should be positive. When public attitudes are not positive, they should become targets for change. Public awareness meetings; newspaper, television, and radio advertisements; and educational seminars may help to change public attitudes.

Community participation also involves personal interactions, including the opportunity for meaningful relationships with friends and family. For children, such interactions involve parents, siblings, relatives, and school and neighborhood friends. For adults, these interactions extend to friends, relatives, spouses, and perhaps their own children.

Both personal and impersonal interactions are influenced by how services are provided by an agency. Services for people with developmental disabilities in any community should be comprehensive. All needed services should be available in the community, but no single agency or organization should provide all of the services. The residential program should be separated from the recreational program. Vocational and work training programs should take place apart from the residential program. Agencies that provide a wide range of services often become all-encompassing, so that people with developmental disabilities never have to go outside the agency for services or supports. This limits community participation.

SERVICE SYSTEMS SHOULD BE COMPREHENSIVE, BUT A SINGLE AGENCY SHOULD NOT PROVIDE ALL THE SERVICES AN INDIVIDUAL NEEDS.

Community participation is increased by using generic rather than specialized services for people with developmental disabilities. A generic service is one that is available to all persons in the community. For example, the public library and the waterfront park are generic resources. The neighborhood recreation council is also a generic service. People with developmental disabilities should be able to participate in the programs and activities sponsored by the recreation council.

In some instances, however, the generic service excludes people with developmental disabilities. When society excludes these people, specialized services are developed. In the past, special schools for children with developmental disabilities, blindness, or deafness were founded because the public schools refused to admit them. Specialized medical clinics and recreational programs were also established. Such services may be necessary in very limited cases, but community participation is not achieved through specialized and segregated services. The alternative is to assist the generic service to meet the needs of people with developmental disabilities. It is up to the generic service agency itself, however, to ensure that their needs are addressed. A child with mental retardation who attends school but receives no individually designed instruction is present but is not participating in the community. A recreation council that sponsors a bowling league for people with disabilities is offering a specialized and segregated service. Instead, the council should provide a bowling league that is open to all people. To do this, the council may need assistance from a consumer or provider agency.

Impersonal and personal community participation can take place in residential programs and in developmental programs, such as education, work, or work training. Community participation also occurs in recreational programs and other leisure-time activities.

Residence in a large institution, nursing home, or regional center provides few opportunities for community participation. Group homes and supervised apartment programs offer more possibilities for informal and formal personal interactions. Foster care, independent living, and shared living opportunities provide even more possibilities for community participation.

The extent of community participation in developmental programs can range from low to high. Totally segregated special education schools and vocational programs offer few opportunities for social integration. Generic early education programs, workstations in industry, and other on-the-job training programs can result in greater community participation. For community participation to be meaningful, however, the early education and employment training programs must meet the needs of people with developmental disabilities. Otherwise, they are merely integrated physically into the community. Physical integration *only* is almost the same as being dumped into the community.

Skill Enhancement

The third dimension of the normalization principle implies that people should perform according to the expectations of the culture for a particular age range. In some limited and exceptional instances where an individual may fail to grow and to adapt, the culture's value system supports the idea of individual growth and adaptation throughout the life cycle. A developmental growth orientation should be present in residential, vocational, and recreational programs. Realistic, yet firm, expectations should be set for people with developmental disabilities.

Human services agencies should be committed to helping each person achieve greater independence. This can be accomplished through intensive and relevant services. The intensity of a program can be judged by the extent to which the time span of the program compares with that of similar services to people who are not developmentally disabled. For example, an afternoon special education program conducted 3 days a week is not similar to other educational programs. A sheltered employment program that operates from 10 A.M. to 2 P.M. because it utilizes public school transportation is also inappropriate. The length of the program should approximate the normal work day.

Intensity is influenced by the number and skills of the staff, as well as the use of modern adaptive equipment, new technologies, and recent clinical innovations. Regularly scheduled in-service training and workshops for the staff are other indications of intensity.

EXERCISE 3

Determining Intensity of Programming

Check those items that indicate intensity of programming in your agency:

1. Hours of operation _____
2. Number of skilled staff _____
3. Staff training opportunities _____
4. Modern adaptive equipment _____
5. Staff training requirements _____

The relevance of services is determined by the extent to which the services meet the individualized needs of people with developmental disabilities. These needs should be outlined in each person's individualized service plan (ISP). The plan will detail goals, objectives, and strategies to accomplish objectives, as well as initiation, target, and completion dates and staff members who are responsible for teaching the skills and behaviors.

Services should be developed for each person according to the ISP. As an illustration, if the ISP indicates that the person chose a work training program in landscape maintenance rather than a packaging task, services should be developed to improve the skills needed in landscape work. Availability alone is not a sufficient reason for providing a service. Staff convenience is also not a legitimate reason for including a person in one program rather than another.

Individualization means, in addition, that the staff differentiate persons with developmental disabilities from each other. Respect for the uniqueness and autonomy of each person should result in toleration for individual differences. Regimentation, group management techniques, and lack of privacy should be avoided as much as possible.

Finally, individualization can be related to the increase in the person's functional independence, decision-making ability, and control over the environment. These are highly individualized outcomes. Programs that are not relevant will fail to meet these goals.

One common obstacle to growth and development is physical and social overprotection. This occurs when programs unnecessarily lower the person's exposure to normative dangers, risks, and growth and learning challenges. All people learn through making a series of mistakes. The series moves in the direction of increasing complexity and danger. If people do not learn from minor failures, they are ill prepared to make more important decisions and may face potentially dangerous consequences. Overprotection prevents people from learning.

Physical overprotection occurs when too much risk has been removed from the environment. Common practices include regulated water temperature, "indestructible" furniture, shatterproof glass, lack of eating utensils to spear or cut food, and stairs with handrails on both sides. Of course, regular safety measures considered typical for all people, such as covers on electrical outlets in locations with young children and smoke detectors, would be appropriate.

Social overprotection takes place through rules, commands, role expectations, and peer pressure. Unnecessary restrictions on the use of community resources, prohibitions on certain recreational or leisure-time activities, and dress codes are examples of social overprotection.

OVERPROTECTION PREVENTS PEOPLE FROM LEARNING.

Programs that serve many people with developmental disabilities are frequently forced to set up extra rules and procedures in order to control large numbers of people. Unfortunately, this approach results in group management practices that ignore individual needs. In addition, the rules and procedures are usually designed for those persons with the most needs. As a result, those with fewer needs and supports must accommodate themselves to the overprotected environment. Instead of designing programs around the person with the greatest needs, human services agencies should allow each person with a developmental disability the dignity of risk and the opportunity to learn from mistakes.

Image Enhancement

The fourth dimension of the normalization principle is the consideration that the public perception of human services programs is as important as what the programs accomplish. As such, human services programs should assist people with developmental disabilities to project positive images. There are two reasons why a positive image is vital. First, it is human nature to treat people as they are perceived; thus a person who projects a negative image is treated in a negative manner. Second, a person who is treated in a negative fashion starts to act accordingly. The self-fulfilling prophecy occurs as the person with a developmental disability begins to act out the negative expectations.

Agency staff members have a particular responsibility to act as role models for people with developmental disabilities. For some people, you may be one of several role models or even their only one. You have a very powerful influence on the self-image of those people. You also have a major responsibility for how they are perceived. By acting in a conscientious and prudent manner, you encourage similar behavior in others.

Enhancing the image of people with developmental disabilities exerts a direct and positive influence on the public's perception. Improvement of their self-image and personal appearance and the development of skills and behaviors in these individuals contribute to a more positive public perception. The public's expectations are increased, and the self-fulfilling prophecy yields positive results.

The public perception is frequently confused because of the age-inappropriateness of programs for people with developmental disabilities. Developmental services for adults are frequently offered in old school buildings. Transportation is provided by the yellow special education bus, and the interior decorations of facilities are associated with childhood. Similarly, adults sometimes dress in a childlike fashion. This is particularly evident in grooming, dress, hairstyle, and mannerisms. The issue of age-appropriate possessions is similar to that of dress and fashion. The staff can have a direct influence in these instances. Although you may have little control over transportation to the vocational center, you can encourage a person to have and value those appearances appropriate for his or her age. Age-appropriate labels and forms of address should be used. You can refer to children by their first names, but adults should be introduced as Mr., Ms., or Mrs.

The names of human services programs, facilities, and locations also influence the public perception of people with developmental disabilities. The principle of normalization does not deny that people have developmental disabilities. However, it does caution you to avoid adding to the negative image that already exists. For example, Rochester Diversified Industries is a more positive name for a sheltered employment program than Rochester Workshops for the Retarded. The value of the program is not enhanced by publicizing to the larger community that all who attend the program have the negative label of developmental disabilities. Instead, the normal and valued aspects should be noted. Similarly, residential facilities can be referred to by the address, for example, 55 Brookwood Road, rather than the Home for Hyperactive Children.

Labels that suggest pity, charity, and dependence also should be avoided. Facility names, such as Angel's Haven, Friendship Center, Sunrise Acres, and New Hope Workshop, do not enhance the valued status of people participating in a program but broadcast a message to the public that the people in the program are different and negatively valued.

The public perception of people with developmental disabilities is often severely damaged by charity events that raise money for programs. In an effort to obtain funds, persons with developmental disabilities are depicted as incapable and dependent. The public is asked to contribute money because of pity. Instead of minimizing the differences that are negatively valued, charity events highlight these differences.

EXERCISE 4

Recent Images

Think of the most recent fund-raising event or advertisement you have witnessed for people with developmental disabilities. This could be a telethon, ride-a-bike, skate-a-thon, white elephant sale, or other promotion. What image did it portray of people with developmental disabilities?

Finally, public perceptions become confused when facilities do not look like the services they provide. For example, a special education program in a church basement does not convey the message of high-quality education. Similarly, a work training program in the gymnasium of an old school sends out the message that the sponsoring agency is only half serious about work training. A different perception would be fostered if the program were located in an industrial park.

Autonomy and Empowerment

The final and most important component of normalization is autonomy and empowerment. In one sense, these issues are related to legal rights. People of all ages have basic rights. Due process, equal protection of the law, freedom from abuse, and the right to medical treatment are rights accorded all people regardless of age. Other rights are acquired gradually with age. The law often sets forth specific ages at which adolescents gain specific rights. The legal age of maturity generally corresponds to the time period when people attain greater autonomy.

Autonomy and empowerment, however, have important meanings quite apart from the legal sense. Autonomy and empowerment mean transferring power and control to people with developmental disabilities. Responsibility for making decisions rests with each individual, regardless of developmental disability.

During the past 20 years, the number of human services agencies has increased dramatically. Many of these agencies have contracted with state agencies to provide a wide range of services to people with developmental disabilities. In this process, the person often becomes dependent on the service provider, and, in some instances, the provider makes decisions for the person. Advocacy efforts and consumer-driven service coordination programs are designed to focus the decision-making responsibility on the person with a developmental disability.

Human services agencies should periodically review policies and procedures concerning rules or restrictions placed on people with developmental disabilities. Limitations with regard to smoking, drinking, choice of residence or roommates, and leisure-time activities should be clearly justified.

EXERCISE 5

Choice and Autonomy

Review your agency's policies, procedures, and practices concerning choice and autonomy.

Are adults treated like adults?
Are adults allowed to make choices?
Are the choices meaningful?
List the choices:

1.
2.
3.

Then, ask a friend who does not work in human services if the choices are meaningful.

People with developmental disabilities often need assistance in making decisions. They can better learn to make choices when the physical setting provides opportunities for choices. The living environment, for example, should allow for control over water and room temperature. People with developmental disabilities should be allowed to turn on lights, radios, stereos, and televisions at their discretion. They should have access to a variety of recreational and leisure-time activities. Each individual should be assisted in choosing among different activities and also be free to choose no activity. In addition, staff members in residential programs should support these choices, even if their preferences rest elsewhere.

STAFF SHOULD TEACH AND ASSIST PEOPLE WITH MENTAL RETARDATION TO MAKE AND EXECUTE RESPONSIBLE DECISIONS.

The autonomy of people with developmental disabilities can best be ensured by making them the key to developing the individualized service plan. They should be present at their individualized service plan meetings and reviews, even if the staff question their ability to understand or contribute.

Participation of people with developmental disabilities in their individualized service plan meetings can be enhanced by the following methods:

1. Simulated team meetings can teach people their roles and responsibilities.
2. An advocate or service coordinator can assist the person with a developmental disability with his or her role and responsibility.
3. All questions concerning likes, strengths, and needs should be first directed toward the person with a developmental disability. The staff should contribute to the meeting only after that person has spoken or if he or she cannot respond to the question.

Finally, the person with a developmental disability should determine what services are provided and the manner in which they are provided. The question of what is best for that person should resume a secondary position to the more important question of "What does the person choose to do?" The responsibility of the staff is to teach and assist people with developmental disabilities to make responsible decisions.

BUT—BE REALISTIC

People frequently conclude that the normalization principle is not realistic. It is considered to be too ideal and therefore unattainable. Such arguments include:

1. "The world doesn't work that way. . . ." Of course it doesn't. The normalization principle suggests how services *should* be provided. It does not state how services *are* provided. The principle indicates where changes need to be made. It is used in planning how to provide services.

2. "There are no alternatives. . . ." There may be no appropriate alternatives. If this is true, you need to become an advocate and demand change. As an illustration, assume that no work training program for people with developmental disabilities exists in your community. The only program is an activity center that provides day care. There may be no other alternative but to enroll people in the program; however, you need to change the program.

3. "Be realistic. Everybody knows. . . ." All self-fulfilling prophecies begin with an assumption about what a person can accomplish. Double-check and question your assumptions.

4. "I can't do it all the time. . . ." The normalization principle suggests how services should be provided. Since you live in an imperfect world, you have to make compromises. The normalization principle helps you to understand and evaluate the concessions and trade-offs in the compromises you make.

5. "You can't make all people normal." This is true. But normalization is not something done to a person. Rather, it provides guidelines for planning and delivering services for the person.

SUMMARY

People with developmental disabilities are considered different. In addition, this differentness is negatively valued by others. Their perception of people with developmental disabilities has shaped the pattern of services. The normalization principle provides a vehicle for reversing this pattern of discrimination. The principle prescribes the utilization of means that are as culturally normative as possible in order to establish and maintain personal behaviors and characteristics that are also as culturally normative as possible.

The normalization principle suggests that you should minimize the perceived differentness of people with developmental disabilities. Human services agencies can decrease differentness by improving the skills and behaviors of people with developmental disabilities. Agencies should also consider the messages that their programs send to the public. These messages shape public opinion. In the long term, public opinion determines the quantity and quality of services provided to people with developmental disabilities.

The normalization principle also challenges the false assumptions that support self-fulfilling prophecies. Changing the assumptions about what people can do with proper support and training can alter society's expectations for them.

The five major components of the normalization principle are: 1) community presence, which is similar to physical integration; 2) community participation, which means social integration; 3) development of skills and behaviors; 4) influence on public perception, which refers to the messages sent by human services programs; and 5) autonomy and empowerment, which means returning the responsibility of decision making to the consumer.

BIBLIOGRAPHY

Dalkey, N., Rourke, D., Lewis, R., & Snyder, D. (1972). *Studies in the quality of life: Delphi and decision making*. Lexington, MA: D.C. Heath.

Flynn, R.J., & Nitsch, K. (1980). *Normalization, social integration, and community services*. Baltimore: University Park Press.

Gardner, J., & O'Brien, J. (1990). The principle of normalization. In J. Gardner & M. Chapman (Eds.), *Program issues in developmental disabilities: A guide to effective habilitation and active treatment* (2nd ed., pp. 39–57). Baltimore: Paul H. Brookes Publishing Co.

Rubinstein, M.F. (1975). *Patterns of problem solving*. Englewood Cliffs, NJ: Prentice-Hall.

Wolfensberger, W. (1972). *The principle of normalization in human services*. Toronto: National Institute on Mental Retardation.

Wolfensberger, W. (1983). Social role valorization: A proposed new term for the principle of normalization. *Mental Retardation, 21*, 234–239.

Wolfensberger, W., & Glenn, L. (1975). *Program analysis of service systems: Field manual*. Toronto: National Institute on Mental Retardation.

ADDITIONAL RESOURCES

B. Blatt and F. Kaplan (1966), in *Christmas in purgatory* (Boston: Allyn & Bacon), and Blatt (1970), in *Exodus from pandemonium: Human abuse and the reformation of public policy* (Boston: Allyn & Bacon), provide a number of photographic essays on dehumanization.

E. Goffman (1963), *Stigma: Notes on the management of spoiled identity* (Englewood Cliffs, NJ: Prentice-Hall), was published in several editions in the late 1950s and early 1960s. It is an invaluable resource for understanding deviancy. James R. Dugley (1983), *Living with stigma* (Springfield, IL: Charles C Thomas), specifically covers the stigma of developmental disabilities.

SELF-APPRAISAL

INSTRUCTIONS

The following questions will help you evaluate your knowledge about the principle of normalization. For true-false questions, check the correct answer. For multiple choice questions, circle the correct answer(s).

Note: There may be more than one correct answer for some questions.

1. The normalization principle is concerned with *how* programs accomplish objectives. The process includes:
   a. Methods for teaching skills, abilities, and behaviors
   b. Groupings of people
   c. Vocabulary and language that describe people
   d. Skills, abilities, and behaviors
2. The following are devaluing labels:
   a. Quad
   b. CP
   c. Retardate
   d. Non-amb
3. An adult with a developmental level of 7 years should be treated as a 7-year-old.
   ___ True   ___ False
4. The following are major dimensions of the normalization principle:
   a. Community participation
   b. 24-hour supervision
   c. Legal rights and empowerment
   d. Access to specialized services for special populations
5. The following services are usually generic in scope:
   a. Public library
   b. Parks and playgrounds
   c. Crippled children's clinics
   d. Food stamp program
6. The greatest potential for social integration is provided by the:
   a. Institution or regional center
   b. Group home or supervised apartment
   c. Foster care or independent living
   d. Nursing home
7. One measure of program intensity is the extent to which the time span of the program approximates that of similar services to people who do not have developmental disabilities.
   ___ True   ___ False

8. Indicators of physical overprotection are:
   a. Mixer valves that control water temperature
   b. Indestructible furniture
   c. Smoke detectors
   d. Stairs with handrails on both sides

9. Which of the following would confuse the public perception of people with developmental disabilities?
   a. A work training program in a gymnasium of an old school
   b. A special education program in the basement of a church
   c. A workshop in an industrial park
   d. A counseling program in a converted tavern

10. The normalization principle does not make people normal. Instead, it provides guidelines for planning and delivering services for people.
    ____ True   ____ False

CASE STUDY

Robert Daniels is a 53-year-old male with a diagnosis of a severe developmental disability and a seizure disorder. Mr. Daniels has lived in a large state-operated intermediate care facility for the mentally retarded (ICF/MR) since he was 18 years old. The county service coordination program has been working with Mr. Daniels, the ICF/MR, and a local residential provider to begin Mr. Daniels's transition into a four-person group home.

The institution staff have expressed concern about Mr. Daniels's ability to change his place of residence at age 53, as well as about the possibility of injury resulting from seizures. The community residential staff are concerned about these issues but feel Mr. Daniels should move to the group home.

The service coordinator has identified a day program for Mr. Daniels. Many of Mr. Daniels's friends from the institution attend the program, which stresses socialization and leisure-time skills. The day program supplements the leisure-time program by transporting all 38 participants on community field trips to the local playground, swimming pool, restaurant, and other places. The group home staff plan to develop more age- and culturally appropriate leisure-time activities for Mr. Daniels. They also plan to collect data over a 2-month period to document the frequency and type of his seizure activity. This information will be used in determining whether or not Mr. Daniels should continue to wear a protective helmet. Mr. Daniels has indicated to the service coordinator that he does not want to wear a helmet.

Situation

The group home staff are attempting to design a more age-appropriate leisure-time program for Mr. Daniels. They feel that the day program should stress vocational skills and work rather than socialization skills and leisure-time activity. The day program staff, however, argue that people at age 53 are too old to begin vocational training.

1. What age- and culturally appropriate leisure-time activities would you recommend to the group home staff?
2. How could the day program further incorporate the principle of normalization in developing leisure-time skills?
3. Should a day program be concentrating on skill development with a 53-year-old man? Is this an example of providing excessive programming? Does it make any difference if these are vocational or leisure-time skills?

ANSWER KEY TO
SELF-APPRAISAL AND CASE STUDY

SELF-APPRAISAL

1. a, b, c
2. a, b, c, d
3. False
4. a, c
5. a, b, d
6. c
7. True
8. a, b, d
9. a, b, d
10. True

CASE STUDY ANSWER GUIDELINES

1. Age- and culturally appropriate activities might include attending major sporting events, participating in neighborhood and community functions, and joining church, civic, and/or recreational organizations. Leisure-time activities, such as walking, jogging, and swimming, can promote good health. The choice of specific activities would depend on Mr. Daniels's preferences.

2. The day program should include only small groups on the field trips. It would be exceedingly difficult for any community resource to accommodate all 38 people at one time. However, small groups of two or three people could use those same resources and blend in with other people without disruption. Also, field trips to the community playground are not appropriate for middle-age people.

3. The key issue in this situation is the preference of Mr. Daniels. Like many other men in their early 50s, he may wish to work until age 65. However, he could choose early retirement. Either choice could enhance his social role status.

Providing services to Mr. Daniels is not excessive programming. However, providing structured programs from 7:30 A.M. to 9:00 P.M. would be excessive programming.

Mr. Daniels's choice should be the deciding factor in stressing either vocational or leisure-time skills. In addition, Mr. Daniels may need to work to earn money to purchase leisure-time activities.

<table>
<tr><td>chapter
4</td><td># Legal Rights of Persons with Developmental Disabilities</td></tr>
</table>

LEARNING OBJECTIVES

Upon completing this chapter, the reader will be able to:

1. Define how the rights of due process and equal protection apply to persons with developmental disabilities.
2. Define how to implement the rights of least restrictive alternative.
3. Identify the two major requirements for informed consent.
4. Identify how the advocacy system can be helpful to staff in human services agencies.
5. Identify and explain 10 rights guaranteed by the U.S. Constitution.
6. List eight strategies for safeguarding rights in community programs.

INTRODUCTION

On December 15, 1791, the Bill of Rights became part of the U.S. Constitution. Article Five of the Constitution declared that "no person shall be . . . deprived of life, liberty, or property without due process of law."

After the Civil War, Article Fourteen was added to the Constitution. That amendment stated that "no state shall make or enforce any law which shall abridge the privileges or immunities of citizens." The amendment repeated the guarantee of due process for all citizens. It also added that no state could "deny to any person within its jurisdiction the equal protection of the laws."

These articles of the Constitution mean that people cannot be treated differently solely because of developmental disabilities. The government is not allowed to discriminate against any group of people. It makes no difference whether the group consists of people of a specific race, sex, or nationality or of people with developmental disabilities.

The government cannot deny benefits to one group that it routinely provides to other groups.

Unfortunately, the Constitution does not always guide social behavior. Historically, people with developmental disabilities have been discriminated against. They have been denied access to public education, involuntarily sterilized, prohibited from voting, incarcerated in public institutions, and excluded from life in the community. Recently, however, the pattern of discrimination has started to lessen. As the civil rights movement of the 1960s and 1970s has resulted in gains for minorities and women, the courts have given increased recognition to the legal rights of persons with developmental disabilities.

GENERAL LEGAL CONCEPTS

The Constitution and various federal and state laws clearly state that all citizens are due fair and equal treatment. This does not mean that all people have equal ability. It does mean, however, that all citizens are due the same opportunity to use their ability, knowledge, and property.

Equal Protection and Due Process

Equal protection means that people with developmental disabilities must have equal access to all the services and opportunities available to other persons. They cannot be treated differently simply because of their disabilities.

In some instances, however, it is necessary to restrict a person's rights. For example, a person may not be competent to live independently, to maintain a bank account, to raise children, or to distribute an estate. In this event, the government must follow due process. It must inform the person that his or her rights may be restricted. The government must also allow the person to present his or her case. Due process also requires the government to curtail only the minimum freedom necessary to ensure the interest of the state. If the state restricts a right for the purpose of providing a treatment or service, then the state is obligated to provide this treatment or service.

IF THE STATE RESTRICTS A RIGHT FOR THE PURPOSE OF PROVIDING A TREATMENT OR SERVICE, THEN THE STATE IS OBLIGATED TO PROVIDE THIS TREATMENT OR SERVICE.

When the rights of people with developmental disabilities are restricted, the human services agency staff should pay particular attention to four questions of safeguards:

1. What type of right is being restricted? The more important the right is, the higher the level of review that is required. Some rights are

safeguarded by the Constitution. They can be abridged only in a court of law. Sterilization, for example, requires court review. Other rights might be limited upon review by a human rights committee. Limitations on use of the telephone or television, spending of personal funds, or participation in a behavior management program might require approval by a human rights committee.

2. How long will the restriction last? Rights should not be restricted for any longer than necessary. Rights should never be abridged indefinitely.

3. Is the restriction the least intrusive measure possible? For example, assume that a young man spends all the money he has. An intrusive step would be to remove his personal funds in the future. A less restrictive alternative would be to provide instruction and reinforce him for saving some money.

4. What training or rehabilitation is provided to the person to make the restriction unnecessary? For example, assume that a woman is restricted from making long-distance telephone calls for which she cannot pay. What training is provided to teach the woman the consequences of the long-distance calls for which she cannot pay?

Least Restrictive Alternative

The concept of least restrictive alternative means that services, programs, and life situations should be provided in the most typical setting possible while still meeting the person's needs. Least restrictive setting does not mean a program without supports and special services. A setting without supports could be very restrictive for some people. For example, a person who uses a wheelchair requires a residential setting with special adaptations. A less supportive setting without wide doors, grab bars in the bathroom, and lowered kitchen appliances would be very dysfunctional and restrictive.

In addition, you should not provide a more supportive alternative than is necessary. A teenager with a developmental disability may require a special education class in a regular school. A separate school would be considered too restrictive. Similarly, a middle-age man may require an apartment living program. Placement in a group home would be too restrictive.

LEAST RESTRICTIVE ALTERNATIVE DOES NOT MEAN A PROGRAM WITHOUT SUPPORTS AND SPECIALIZED SERVICES.

Least restrictive alternative, then, has two meanings. It requires an agency to provide the most typical setting or service. The service or setting must also meet the particular needs of the person by providing the necessary support services.

Informed Consent

Staff members in human services agencies have no authority to do anything to or for a person with developmental disabilities without that person's consent. In the case of minors or those who have been declared incompetent, consent of the parent or guardian is required.

If a person chooses not to give consent to a procedure, he or she has the right to be left alone. This situation can cause problems for the staff. You sometimes work with people who cannot make some decisions or perform complicated tasks. Often, these people have not been declared legally incompetent. They have the right to make decisions even though they may lack the capacity.

The staff have two alternatives in this situation. The first alternative requires that the staff teach the person to make the necessary decisions after providing sufficient information about the choice. Informed consent requires both that the person have the capacity to make decisions and that information be provided that is relevant to the decision. Under the second alternative, a guardianship proceeding should be started for the person who cannot give informed consent in important decisions. Table 1 outlines conditions for informed consent.

Guardianship

The decision that a person is legally incompetent usually results in the appointment of a guardian. This means that the decision-making authority is taken from the person and given to the state or another individual. The guardian then makes decisions for the incompetent person or ward.

In the past, guardianship was an all-or-nothing situation. Being declared legally incompetent meant a total loss of all decision-making authority. In reality, however, a person can be competent in some matters but not in others. For example, a person could be competent to live independently but not to manage a large and complicated estate.

Table 1.   Conditions for informed consent in human services agencies

1. Written consent must be placed in the person's record.
2. For research or medical purposes, the person obtaining the consent must be different from the person performing the research or medical procedure.
3. Coercion is not allowed.
4. The following must be explained to the person:
   a. Nature and outcome of the procedure or program
   b. Side effects and risks of the treatment procedure or program
   c. Risks of not proceeding with the procedure or program
   d. Less intrusive or dangerous alternative procedures or programs
   e. Withdrawal of consent at any time without penalty

In order to avoid this all-or-nothing choice, some states have developed a limited guardianship approach. The state can then appoint a guardian for limited and well-defined decision areas. This enables the person with developmental disabilities to make all other choices and decisions.

Guardianship is not an all-or-nothing choice. Limited guardianship is an alternative.

You will often face difficult choices about guardianship and decision making. You will want to assist people to make responsible decisions and also prevent them from harming themselves or others or wasting personal resources. However, you should recognize that you can only identify people who appear unable to make important decisions. Only the court can make a determination of legal incompetence and appoint a guardian. Sometimes, in emergency situations, the staff may have to make decisions for people with developmental disabilities, but the agency should then notify the court or an advocacy agency and request a guardianship hearing.

EXERCISE 1

Reviewing Legal Competence

Determine if any person served by your agency has been declared incompetent. If so, who is the legal guardian? What are the legal guardian's rights? Summarize these rights on a separate sheet of paper.

Confidentiality

The legal basis for the concept of confidentiality is derived from communications between an individual and his or her physician, lawyer, or pastor. When the concept of confidentiality is extended to human services agencies, it means that information about a person with developmental disabilities cannot be released to others without the consent of the person.

This privilege belongs to the person served by the agency. The staff need permission to release information. However, the person with a developmental disability does not require staff or agency permission to release any confidential information about him- or herself.

Finally, people with developmental disabilities should have access to their records. In order to guarantee privacy and ensure accuracy, they (or a parent, guardian, or advocate) may need to examine the records.

Punishment

Increasing attention has been paid to the constitutional rights of protection against harm and psychological autonomy. In the past, human services agencies have caused harm to people even when the intention was to help.

In addition to the constitutional limitations on the use of punishment, recent research has pointed to the limited success of punishment in making long-term changes in behavior. Also, positive behavior intervention techniques can be more effective than punishment.

Various federal laws and professional standards prohibit physical and chemical restraint; corporal punishment and verbal abuse; and seclusion when used as punishment, for convenience of the staff, or as a substitute for habilitation programs.

EXERCISE 2

Review of Policy and Procedure

Review the agency policy and procedure concerning punishment, restraint, seclusion, and other aversive behavior management methods. Summarize the policy and procedure.

A general guideline is to not use aversive behavior management methods. However, if you do use an aversive procedure, it must be done only as a part of a defined, approved, and documented behavior management program. Consent must be obtained from the individual, or from the parents if the individual is a minor, or from a guardian if one has been appointed by the court. Also, you must be able to demonstrate that the aversive procedure is the least intrusive alternative and that the risks of using the procedure are not greater than the risks involved in not using the procedure. You must also document that other less restrictive alternatives have not been successful. Finally, the aversive behavior management program must be designed, implemented, and monitored by highly trained, experienced staff members. The number of persons qualified to perform aversive procedures is very limited.

Protection of Rights

Advocacy

Federal legislation has created advocacy systems for persons with developmental disabilities. Whether working with a formal advocacy program or as a friend, an advocate should protect the rights and interests of persons with developmental disabilities. Table 2 lists the commonly

Table 2. Commonly recognized rights of persons in community-based residential programs

---

Right to services in the least restrictive environment
Right to normalized living conditions
Right to dignity and respect
Right to freedom from discomfort and deprivation
Right to appropriate clinical, medical, and therapeutic services
Right to vote
Right to religious worship
Right to private communication
Right to free association
Right to physical exercise
Right to seasonal, clean, neat clothing
Right to manage personal funds
Right to bed, dresser, and storage area
Right to privacy
Right to access to public media
Right to adequate nutrition
Freedom from unnecessary medication and mechanical, chemical, or physical restraints
Freedom from involuntary servitude
Right to equal protection and due process

---

recognized rights of persons in community-based residential programs. The advocate's job is to work only for the person with developmental disabilities. The presence of an advocate should not imply that you or your agency are negligent.

In correctly carrying out their jobs, advocates make sure that the human services network respects the rights of people. Sometimes an advocate will point out rights of persons with developmental disabilities that the staff may have overlooked or not even been aware of. If the concern of the advocate is valid, address the issue. Do not become defensive.

In addition, do not view advocates as potential problem finders. Rather, use the advocacy system as a problem solver. Agency staffs frequently encounter instances where, for example, a guardian will not consent to a person moving to a new residential program. Another example may involve a person who appears incompetent by spending large sums of money. You can ask the advocacy system for aid in solving such problems. Advocates can often help you to avoid making mistakes.

THE ADVOCACY SYSTEM CAN HELP YOU SOLVE PROBLEMS.

Human Rights Committee

Agencies can also protect the rights of people by forming a human rights committee. This committee reviews the ongoing work of the agency and monitors all policies, procedures, and services to protect the rights of persons with developmental disabilities. Human rights committees should include members from outside the agency, such as civic leaders, advocates, lawyers, persons with developmental disabilities, and parents. The committee can discuss issues and concerns voiced by parents, staff, administrators, advocates, or persons with developmental disabilities. Finally, the human rights committee can serve an important function by referring particularly difficult problems to outside independent advocacy programs.

EXERCISE 3

Human Rights Committee

Determine if your agency has a human rights committee. If so, who are the members of the committee? When does the committee meet? How are issues placed on the agenda? How are issues resolved? Summarize these issues.

Refusal of Services

One basic choice that people with developmental disabilities can make is to refuse to participate in services provided by the agency, even if such services are in accordance with the person's individualized service plan (ISP). Assume that the person participated in developing the plan and that the services rendered are relevant and provided in the least intrusive manner. Does the person have the right to refuse the services? Does he or she have the right to continue in the program without participating in his or her habilitation program? In general, the answer is no. This is especially true in instances where public funds support the program.

The person with a developmental disability has a responsibility to try to achieve the goals and objectives of the ISP. If the person does not accept the responsibility and if the agency has counseled the person and attempted other less drastic alternatives, the person could be asked to leave the program.

This same situation would apply to a person who refused to comply with basic policies and procedures. The agency should counsel the person and explain the possible consequences of the action. If other alternatives do not succeed, the agency could ask the person to leave.

Table 3. Suggestions for safeguarding rights in community programs

1. Know the relevant laws. Keep up to date on local ordinances and regulations.
2. Maintain a policy and procedure manual that describes in detail how employees are to respond to various situations.
3. Provide services that are based on the goals and objectives in the individualized service plan.
4. Hire only the best staff after a rigid interview process and reference check.
5. Provide an intense pre- and in-service training program.
6. Provide feedback to staff through regular professional consultation.
7. Implement a solid but practical program of informed consent, ISP development, data collection and review, and confidentiality.
8. Provide periodic staff evaluation by the people within the program.

SOURCES AND IMPLEMENTATION OF RIGHTS

Certain specific rights are guaranteed to all citizens by the U.S. Constitution. These rights are fundamental and can be removed only through a due process procedure. The president, the Congress, and the states are all unable to alter these constitutional rights.

Statutory rights result from laws passed by local, state, and federal governments. Rights guaranteed through this legislative process may change as the laws are changed. Regulations developed to implement legislation are also a part of statutory law. Finally, many agencies develop policies and procedures to ensure conformity with laws and regulations (see suggestions for safeguarding rights in Table 3).

As staff members, you should be aware that citizens with developmental disabilities have the same rights as other citizens. People are entitled to these constitutional and statutory rights unless, through a due process proceeding in court, the rights are restricted.

PEOPLE WITH DEVELOPMENTAL DISABILITIES HAVE THE SAME CONSTITUTIONAL AND STATUTORY RIGHTS AS OTHER CITIZENS.

Constitutional Rights

Certain rights are guaranteed by the U.S. Constitution to each citizen, regardless of disability:

1. Access to the courts and legal representation
2. Free association
3. Right to contract, own, and dispose of property
4. Equal educational opportunity
5. Equal employment opportunity

6. Equal protection and due process
7. Fair and equal treatment by public agencies
8. Freedom from cruel and unusual punishment
9. Freedom of religion
10. Freedom of speech and expression
11. Right to marry, procreate, and raise children
12. Privacy
13. Services in the least restrictive environment
14. Right to vote.

Access to the Courts and Legal Representation

Persons with developmental disabilities, like all citizens, have the right to use, and benefit from, the legal system. They can retain lawyers to represent them. The expense of legal representation is not an excuse for denying a person access to legal representation. State protection and advocacy programs can assist the indigent. Legal aid programs, state public defender programs, and other services sponsored by public and private organizations are available for persons with limited resources. Human services agencies that provide services to persons with developmental disabilities should take positive steps to promote access to the courts and legal representation. These agencies should inform people of their rights and assist them in contacting advocates and representatives of the legal profession.

EXERCISE 4

Requesting Legal Assistance

Is there a policy and procedure for responding to requests for legal assistance? Identify the duties and responsibilities.

Free Association

People with developmental disabilities can choose to associate with and form friendships with neighbors, roommates, or even strangers. This is a basic right in a democratic society. A person should be able to choose friends, to share his or her home with a friend, and to attend gatherings in the community. People should be encouraged to communicate with others in person or by telephone, audiotape, or letter. This not only promotes their legal rights but also encourages social integration. In addition, it provides a way for people with developmental disabilities to inform others if something is wrong.

The freedom of association is not absolute. It carries responsibilities. The right to free association, for example, does not mean that a person can disturb others who are working or otherwise occupied. It does not mean that a person living in a group situation can invite four friends to a party at 1 A.M. without consulting the other roommates. The right to communicate and interact with others means that the right must be exercised at a responsible time and in a responsible manner.

THE RIGHT TO FREEDOM OF ASSOCIATION REQUIRES RESPONSIBLE CONDUCT.

Right To Contract, Own, and Dispose of Property

Americans continually exercise the right to own and dispose of property. They buy and sell items ranging from stereo equipment to clothing to magazines. Sometimes, lacking cash, a person charges a purchase to a credit card. This is a contract in which the buyer agrees to pay interest and the seller agrees to a delay in payment.

People with developmental disabilities are frequently prevented from exercising the right to contract and to buy and sell property, because society believes they are unable to make decisions. In addition, because of bias, they are often unemployed, have little money, and cannot purchase items or obtain credit.

The right to contract and buy and sell property is not an all-or-nothing situation. Many people, including those with developmental disabilities, might not have the ability to buy and sell stocks and bonds. Most people, however, can make normal day-to-day purchases. Likewise, some people with developmental disabilities might not be legally competent to finance the purchase of an automobile, but they could purchase a radio, television, or telephone.

People also have the right to spend money on whatever they wish. Agency staff must recognize that taste and preference vary from person to person, and that what might be considered a waste of money by one person would not by another.

Society's commitment to letting people with developmental disabilities make responsible decisions is reflected in the extent of training they receive. What training is given them in the use of money, in shopping, and in banking? Do they have access to their own money?

Equal Educational Opportunity

Each of the 50 states provides a public education to children. The age requirement, the quality of the education, and the cost of the education vary within and among states. However, the same educational opportunity must be provided all children without regard for disability. No child can be denied a free and appropriate education because of a disability. Congress confirmed this constitutional right when it passed the Education for All Handicapped Children Act of 1975 (PL 94-142), discussed later in this chapter.

Equal Employment Opportunity

The United States does not guarantee a job for every citizen, but employers cannot discriminate against a person solely because that person has a developmental disability. Unfortunately, because of long-held stereotypes and social devaluation, many employers do discriminate against people with developmental disabilities.

Although there is no constitutional right to employment or even to job training, day habilitation programs should be designed to train people for real jobs in the local community. Many workshops fail to provide training for work in the competitive market.

Equal Protection and Due Process

These concepts are discussed in a previous section of this chapter. They are most often implemented by ensuring that people receive fair and equal treatment from public agencies and officials. This requirement also extends to human services agencies that are licensed and/or funded by the public sector.

EQUAL PROTECTION AND DUE PROCESS MEAN THAT PEOPLE CANNOT BE DISCRIMINATED AGAINST OR TREATED DIFFERENTLY SIMPLY BECAUSE THEY HAVE DEVELOPMENTAL DISABILITIES.

Freedom from Cruel and Unusual Punishment

People cannot be punished for the "offense" of having a developmental disability. In the past, it was not uncommon for individuals with developmental disabilities to be subjected to corporal punishment, electric shock, isolation, seclusion, and restraint for nonconforming behavior. The use of punishment and various forms of aversive behavioral procedures can become complicated and confusing. Therefore, you should ask four basic questions before using any such procedure:

1. What less intrusive behavior management program was previously attempted?
2. Was it correctly implemented over a sufficient time period?
3. What specific behavior is desired as a result of the behavior management program?
4. Who consented to the procedure?

Unless there are clear and concise answers to these questions, you should not continue the procedure.

You must consider three important issues when working with people who have developmental disabilities. First, corporal punishment and mental and emotional abuse are simply not allowed. Second, you should not institute an aversive behavioral program before you have demonstrated that other less intrusive programs have not produced the desired result. For example, very few behaviors require aversive techniques, such as restraint or water spray. These techniques should be used only when other nonaversive techniques, such as social reinforcement, extinction, or withdrawal of privileges, do not change the behavior, and when the procedure has been approved by a human rights committee. Third, the person (or parent/guardian in the case of a minor or ward) must consent to the procedure.

CORPORAL PUNISHMENT AND MENTAL AND EMOTIONAL ABUSE ARE NEVER PERMITTED UNDER ANY CIRCUMSTANCES.

Freedom of Religion

The U.S. Constitution guarantees citizens the right to practice any religion they choose. This right extends from believing in any particular creed to attending any church or religious service. It also means that people are free to choose not to practice a religion or attend church or religious services.

Like other rights, the exercise of freedom of religion cannot impinge on the rights of others. For example, the right to read aloud or recite the Bible or the Koran may not extend to the living room of an apartment if the other people living there want to watch television.

The staffs of human services programs, particularly in residential facilities, should assist people to exercise their religious freedom (if indeed they choose a religion and want to attend services). Religious services should be made accessible; transportation may be needed. Churches and synagogues should be barrier free. Moreover, people should be able to attend religious services of different denominations according to their preferences. Too often, people from a single residential program all attend the same church. This may not provide room for individual preference.

Right To Marry, Procreate, and Raise Children

The fundamental right to marry, procreate, and raise children is protected by the Constitution. Because of the confusion and anxiety over both human sexuality and developmental disabilities, however, these constitutional guarantees often have been overlooked. People have been involuntarily sterilized, have been prevented from marrying, and have had their children removed from their custody solely because they had developmental disabilities.

In addition, developmental disability has been considered a reason for the presumed inability of a person to function as a parent. This argument is used to deny the options of marriage and children, but no similar "test" of parenting skill is applied to other people. The Constitution prevents the administration of an "ability to parent test" as a precondition for marriage for any special group. One can only imagine what would happen if such a test were applied to the general population, where so many marriages end in divorce.

More so perhaps than any other right, the right to have children carries with it a major responsibility. People with developmental disabilities should examine that responsibility carefully when making decisions.

Privacy

The Constitution grants all citizens the right to conduct the private aspects of their lives in whatever manner they choose. Thus, people with developmental disabilities should be accorded privacy, especially in the bedroom and bathroom. They also need the time and privacy to be alone when they choose. In addition, all written and verbal communications should be considered confidential.

An agency's relative concern (particularly in residential programs) for privacy can be easily evaluated. For instance: Who is given the keys for doors and storage lockers, the staff or the person with a developmental disability? Are staff members allowed to enter a person's room without permission on a routine basis? Are the bathrooms provided with doors and shower curtains? Where can a person go to be alone?

Services in the Least Restrictive Environment

People with developmental disabilities must be provided services in the least restrictive environment. Courts have ruled that states must create new services if existing programs do not provide the least restrictive program for any individual. Agencies are also responsible for determining on a regular basis whether people have gained new skills and capabilities and whether they could move to less restrictive environments. In fact, the choice of a program should not be made until the staff can document why a less restrictive program cannot be recommended. Table 4 lists questions that an agency staff can ask in evaluating whether a person's rights are being met.

Right To Vote

The Constitution guarantees the right to vote. Many states, however, have passed laws preventing felons and people with "mental disabilities" from voting. Because the term *mental disability* is generally not defined, it is often extended to include persons with developmental disabilities. State advocacy systems can represent people with developmental disabilities who have not been allowed to vote. The right to vote also means that agency staff should assist people to understand the issues and responsibilities of voting.

Table 4. Questions to ask in evaluating agency concern for the rights of a person with a developmental disability

1. Does the person belong in your program? Are the person's characteristics, strengths, and needs consistent with agency mission statements and admission policy?
2. Has the person (parent/guardian for a minor or ward) given informed consent? Does the person realize consent can be withdrawn at any time?
3. Does the person have an individualized service plan, and are services provided in accordance with that plan?
4. Is there a periodic review of progress toward meeting goals and objectives?
5. Is the program provided in the most normal and least restrictive environment possible?
6. Are the staff members trained to perform their job functions?
7. Does the agency have a policy and procedure manual that provides staff direction in making decisions?
8. Does the agency maintain accurate written records?
9. How would you investigate allegations of abuse? Does the policy and procedure manual provide information?
10. Are you ever required to seek approval of a human rights committee for certain training or behavior management programs? How many times has the human rights committee reviewed proposals during the past year?

Statutory Laws and Regulations

In addition to rights guaranteed by the Constitution, federal and state laws also define and protect the rights of people. Four major federal laws, with their respective public law (PL) numbers (by which they are often referred) are:

1. The Rehabilitation Act of 1973 (PL 93-112)
2. The Education for All Handicapped Children Act of 1975 (PL 94-142) (retitled in 1990 as the Individuals with Disabilities Education Act, IDEA)
3. The Developmental Disabilities Assistance and Bill of Rights Act of 1975 (PL 94-103)
4. The Americans with Disabilities Act of 1990 (PL 101-336)

The Rehabilitation Act of 1973

Often referred to as the first civil rights act for persons with disabilities, this law prohibits discrimination on the basis of disabilities and requires employers and educational programs to make reasonable accommodations to meet the needs of persons with disabilities. Section 504 of the law, as amended in 1978, specifically prohibits discrimination against people because of disabilities.

The 1978 amendments authorize grants to assist the states in providing services for independently living individuals whose disabilities are so severe that they do not have the potential for employment. Independent living centers are intended for those individuals to live and function independently. The amendments also establish state independent living councils and require that a majority of each council consist of individuals with disabilities or guardians of such individuals.

In 1991, debate arose over the traditional time-limited services through vocational rehabilitation programs. Many advocates suggested major changes in the law and a greater emphasis on continuity of services. Congress reenacted The Rehabilitation Act (PL 102-52) for only 1 year to allow time for a study of the major issues.

The Education for All Handicapped Children Act of 1975

This law requires that all children with disabilities be provided a free and appropriate public education and that they should be educated in the least restrictive environment. In addition, the law provides many due process provisions. It places a heavy reliance on parental consent to the individualized education program (IEP) that must be developed for each child. Although no law can guarantee the provision of quality services, this Act clearly defines the responsibility of local education agencies to provide education to children with disabilities.

The Education for All Handicapped Children Act was amended in 1983 to include children from birth to age 3 (at each state's discretion). In 1986, the law was again amended and expanded (PL 99-457) to provide grants to states for the development of coordinated interagency systems to provide early intervention programs. In 1990 under another amendment (PL 101-476), the law was reauthorized and further expanded. The name of the law was changed to the Individuals with Disabilities Education Act (IDEA). PL 101-476 has also been subsequently amended, namely by PL 102-119, which further strengthened the early intervention services authorized by PL 99-457. Opportunities for infants and toddlers with disabilities were expanded, and the definition of early intervention services was also expanded to include transportation, assistive devices, and technology services.

IDEA requires that each eligible student be given transition services as part of his or her IEP. These services are intended to promote the individual's movement from school to post-school programs, which include postsecondary education, vocational training, supported employment, continuing education, employment, and community living.

The Developmental Disabilities Assistance and Bill of Rights Act of 1990

This law authorizes federal financial support for planning, coordinating, and delivering specialized services to people with developmental disabilities (as defined in PL 94-142) and has continued to be extended through amendments in 1984, 1987, and 1990.

The Developmental Disabilities Assistance and Bill of Rights Act of 1990 (PL 101-496) redefines services required in state plans. The Act continues federal support for state planning councils on developmental disabilities, state protection and advocacy (P & A) systems, and university-affiliated programs (UAPs).

The Americans with Disabilities Act of 1990

This law (PL 101-336) is referred to as the second civil rights act for persons with disabilities. It protects people with disabilities from discrimination in employment, transportation, public accommodations, telecommunications, and activities of state and local governments. The law offers the same protections that are extended to other groups on the basis of race, sex, national origin, age, and religion. People with disabilities have recourse to the same remedies as other minorities under Title VII of the Civil Rights Act of 1964.

The Americans with Disabilities Act establishes time-lines and requirements for accessibility to bus and rail transportation. It also reinforces the intent of The Rehabilitation Act of 1973 by stating that an employer cannot refuse to hire a person with a disability when the person is capable of performing the job. This and other employment provisions of the Act became law in 1992.

SUMMARY

As an employee of a human services agency, you are not expected to know all the federal laws and regulations regarding the rights of people with developmental disabilities. You probably are not expected to know the state laws, but you may need to be familiar with state regulations that implement these laws and outline how programs and services should be provided. Finally, you must know your agency's policies and procedures.

The human services agency is responsible for issuing and implementing policies and procedures that protect both staff and people with developmental disabilities. The policies and procedures should specify routines that any reasonable, prudent, and careful person would follow in similar circumstances. By being familiar with them, you can ensure the rights of people with developmental disabilities and markedly decrease the probability that you would act in an unreasonable, imprudent, or careless manner.

BIBLIOGRAPHY

Brakel, S., Parry, J., & Weiner, B. (1985). *The mentally disabled and the law* (3rd ed.). Washington, DC: American Bar Foundation.

Castellani, P.J. (1987). *The political economy of developmental disabilities.* Baltimore: Paul H. Brookes Publishing Co.

Goldberg, L.J. (1990). Legal rights of persons with developmental disabilities. In J.F. Gardner & M.S. Chapman (Eds.), *Program issues in developmental disabilities: A guide to effective habilitation and active treatment* (pp. 19–38). Baltimore: Paul H. Brookes Publishing Co.

World Institute on Disability. (1991). *A brief summary of disability legislation in the United States of America.* Oakland, CA: Research and Training Center on Public Policy in Independent Living.

ADDITIONAL RESOURCES

D.R. Kemp (1983), Assessing human rights committees: A mechanism for protecting the rights of institutionalized mentally retarded persons, *Mental Retardation, 21*(1), 13–16, provides a review of human rights committees in state institutions.

F.J. Laski (1985), Right to habilitation and right to education: The legal foundation, and Valerie Bradley (1985), Implementation of court and consent decrees: Some current lessons, both in R.H. Bruininks and K.C. Lakin (Eds.), *Living and learning in the least restrictive environment* (Baltimore: Paul H. Brookes Publishing Co.).

M.S. Moon, W. Kiernan, and W. Halloran (1990), School-based vocational programs and labor laws: A 1990 update, *Journal of The Association for Persons with Severe Handicaps, 15*(3), 177–185, cover the application of the Fair Labor Standards Act to School-Based Vocational Programs.

S. Spreat and F. Lanzi (1989), Role of human rights committees in the review of restrictive/aversive behavior modification procedures: A national survey, *Mental Retardation, 27*(6), 375–382, discuss the role of human rights committees in the review of aversive behavior intervention programs.

SELF-APPRAISAL

INSTRUCTIONS

The following questions will help you evaluate your knowledge about the legal rights of people with developmental disabilities. For true-false questions, check the correct answer. For multiple choice questions, circle the correct answer(s).

Note: There may be more than one correct answer for some questions.

1. The Constitution states that all people:
   a. Have equal potential
   b. Should have the same opportunity to use their abilities
   c. Have equal rights
   d. Can do the same tasks
2. People cannot be treated differently solely because of a developmental disability.
   ____ True   ____ False
3. A person can be determined to be mentally incompetent only by:
   a. A physician
   b. A physician and psychologist
   c. A qualified developmental disabilities professional
   d. A court proceeding
4. Which of the following questions should be raised when rights are restricted?
   a. The type of right being restricted
   b. The length of time the restriction will be in effect
   c. Whether the restriction is the least intrusive measure possible
   d. Whether training is provided to make the restriction unnecessary
5. The concept of least restrictive alternative means that services should be provided in the most typical setting and still meet individualized needs.
   ____ True   ____ False
6. Informed consent requires that the following must be explained:
   a. Nature and outcome of the procedure
   b. Side effects and risks of the procedure
   c. Withdrawal of consent without penalty
   d. Cosignature of the program supervisor on the consent form
7. Commonly recognized rights of persons in community-based residential programs include:
   a. The right to services in the least restrictive environment
   b. The right to dignity and respect

    c. The right to appropriate clinical, medical, and therapeutic services

    d. The right to private communications

8. The human rights committee in community services agencies:

    a. Links the agency to outside independent advocacy programs

    b. Protects the rights of persons with developmental disabilities

    c. Monitors policies and procedures of the agency

    d. Files legal briefs in state court proceedings

9. Legal rights require responsible behavior in the exercise of these rights.

    ____ True   ____ False

10. Major laws providing legal guarantees for people with disabilities are:

    a. The Individuals with Disabilities Education Act Amendments of 1991 (PL 102-119)

    b. The Developmental Disabilities Assistance and Bill of Rights Act of 1990 (PL 101-496)

    c. The Rehabilitation Act of 1973 (PL 93-112)

    d. The Crippled Person Reform Act of 1979 (PL 109-78)

CASE STUDY

Brian Dawson is a 14-year-old male diagnosed as having a moderate developmental disability, cerebral palsy, and severe acting-out behaviors. Brian lives at home with his mother (47 years old), three brothers (ages 17–25 years), and three sisters (ages 16–21 years). The family income is low but is above the cutoff for public assistance.

Brian attends Midland Special Education Center 5 days a week. Until recently, the local education agency provided bus transportation between the home and school.

During the past 6 months, Brian's teacher, Linda Johnson, has reported that the incidence of his aggressive behavior in the classroom has steadily increased. She reports that Brian hits other students, has tantrums, moves furniture, and screams.

Ms. Johnson requested a behavior management consultation from the local mental health clinic. The consulting psychologist has indicated that the aggressive behaviors are symptoms of a neurological condition. Therefore, he feels unable to help.

Feeling frustrated, Ms. Johnson recommends a comprehensive reassessment of Brian, and a team meeting to revise his individualized education program (IEP).

Situation

The Midland Special Education Center no longer provides transportation to Brian's school because of his aggressive behaviors. Without prior discussion, the principal informed Brian's mother that the team has developed a new IEP for Brian. The new IEP provides for a more restrictive placement in a new school and makes no provision for transportation. Ms. Dawson was told that because Brian is disruptive, the school is not obliged to provide the same transportation services to Brian that it routinely provides to other students.

1. What legal rights are violated in this situation?
2. What appropriate process should the school have followed to involve the parents in the decision process?

ANSWER KEY TO
SELF-APPRAISAL AND CASE STUDY

SELF-APPRAISAL

1. b, c
2. True
3. d
4. a, b, c, d
5. True
6. a, b, c
7. a, b, c, d
8. a, b, c
9. True
10. a, b, c

CASE STUDY ANSWER GUIDELINES

1. The Individuals with Disabilities Education Act of 1990 (PL 101-476) requires that the parents or guardian of a school-age child must give informed consent to any changes in the individualized education plan. Also, the school has the obligation to involve the parents in the team process. The school also violated the right of due process and equal protection by denying Brian the same transportation services routinely provided to other students. Finally, the team placed Brian in a more restrictive setting than was justified by any assessment data or by the disruptive behaviors alone.

2. Federal law defines the parent as a member of the team that makes decisions. The parents must also consent to the individualized education plan. The school should have scheduled a meeting at a time convenient for the parents. During the meeting, the parents and school personnel should develop the individualized education program.

section II

PROGRAM DEVELOPMENT FOR PERSONS WITH DEVELOPMENTAL DISABILITIES

The Process
of
Assessment

LEARNING OBJECTIVES

Upon completing this chapter, the reader will be able to:

1. Describe the different types and purposes of assessments.
2. Define norm-referenced, criterion-referenced, and informal instructor-designed assessments.
3. Interpret the assessment data for determining program goals and objectives.
4. Describe the difference between the form and function of a behavior.
5. Describe an assessment process using the functional approach to assessing a behavior.

INTRODUCTION

The process of obtaining assessment information about an individual with developmental disabilities requires two steps. The assessment strategy is the first step. It is designed to identify the service needs of the individual in order to determine which community agencies can provide the various services. No one agency can meet all the needs of the individual. For example, based on the assessment of the individual's strengths and interest, agency A may provide residential support services, agency B supported employment, and agency C functional academic skills training. Agencies that provide the needed services also change over time as the individual gains new skills and experiences.

The second step of the assessment process takes place at the agency level. After appropriate agencies are chosen for the needed services, each agency must further assess the individual in order to develop plans for effective intervention and support. This chapter discusses this assessment process as it occurs within an agency.

PLANNING

The staff, with the assistance of the individual, must plan the assessment and the services to be provided. The four phases of planning are:

1. Completing assessments
2. Determining program objectives
3. Selecting the teaching strategy that will accomplish the program objectives
4. Conducting the teaching process

Before beginning the planning process, however, it is important for staff members to understand clearly the agency's mission or purpose. The mission statement provides the staff with critical information and guidelines for each phase of the planning process. For example, consider two agencies with different mission statements. The first agency's mission statement reads that its purpose is to assist individuals with developmental disabilities to achieve their maximum potentials. The second agency's mission statement reads that its purpose is to integrate individuals with developmental disabilities into community life. The assessment process used to determine an individual's abilities would be different for each agency. In the first statement, the staff may not know exactly what to assess. Every individual has the potential to achieve within a variety of areas. The mission statement thus implies that all areas are to be assessed, but that would be almost impossible to achieve. In contrast, the second mission statement provides the staff with a better understanding of the areas to assess. It provides a clearer direction for the staff to follow in implementing the planning process. The assessment here would focus on the community and the skills needed by the individual for successful community integration.

The planning process is a building process: Assessments provide information for determining program objectives; program objectives aid in selecting appropriate teaching strategies; and teaching strategies help determine how to design the teaching process. Each step is dependent on each other. Because the process is interdependent, the quality of one step in the process affects the outcomes in the remaining steps. In other words, a poor assessment will result in poor objectives, poor strategies, and poor instructional consequences. Therefore, the staff should clearly understand the planning process, beginning with the agency's mission statement and its implications for the assessment.

Assessment refers to the process of collecting and studying information about a person that is used to plan, provide, and evaluate the goals and objectives of the person's individualized service plan (ISP). Assessment information can be obtained by various agency personnel and allows them to look at the individual's development in different areas. For example, an instructor may be concerned with the way a person uses a pencil for writing. An assessment for fine motor skills allows the instructor to evaluate that specific area of development. This chapter discusses the different types of assessment and how to determine which type to use for the desired information. It also focuses on the use of assessment information in making decisions about ISPs.

The assessment process is continuous. Once you complete the four steps, you begin the process over again. You continually assess the individual to determine what changes have occurred as a result of the teaching process. For example, a physical therapist assesses a person's ability to get from home to the store. The therapist then determines the training needed to improve the person's mobility. This training will enable the person to go shopping independently or to live independently in the community. Gaining these new skills, however, changes the person's ability to interact with the environment. As a result of this change, the physical therapist reassesses the person to determine additional areas of training needed for further independence.

THE ASSESSMENT PROCESS IS CONTINUOUS.

EXERCISE 1

Assessment Identification

Ask your supervisor what assessments are used in the agency's program. Determine why the assessment instruments were picked for use and review each assessment. List the assessments on a separate sheet of paper.

PURPOSE OF ASSESSMENTS

A primary purpose for gathering assessment information is to learn what a person *can* do. This information permits you to develop an ISP based on the individual's strengths. A second purpose is to determine what a person *likes* to do. Individuals perform better when they like what they are doing. Finally, assessment information assists you in deciding what skills a person *should* learn. This determination is made by the interdisciplinary team.

The first step in the assessment process is to determine what information is needed. This dictates the type of assessments to be administered and assists in choosing a specific assessment.

ASSESSMENT INFORMATION CAN ASSIST YOU TO DETERMINE:
WHAT A PERSON CAN DO
WHAT A PERSON LIKES TO DO
WHAT SKILLS OR BEHAVIORS A PERSON SHOULD LEARN

The process of determining whether a person has developmental disabilities is vastly different from that of determining whether a person is accomplishing program objectives. Not only are the assessments different, but the information you need is different.

METHODS OF ASSESSMENT

Assessment information is collected by two methods: 1) interview, and 2) direct observation. An interview is directed to the individual or to someone who knows the individual well. In this method, the examiner asks the individual a list of questions. The questions may be standardized or may be a list developed by the examiner to assess a specific area. The examiner must ask the questions carefully to make sure that the person understands them.

The second method, observation, requires that the observer pay close attention to the person and to the specific task being completed. Observation may take place over several days, which allows an evaluation of the person in various settings. While observing an individual during an assessment, note how the person responds and performs when presented with:

Written materials, such as books or instructions
Visual or auditory cues
Correction procedures, modeling, physical assistance, gesturing, or altered environment
Positive reinforcement techniques.

During the observation, also determine:

The effects that any possible medications may have on performance
The presence of a physical disability as a barrier to completing a task
How performance is enhanced with the use of adaptive technology

TYPES OF ASSESSMENTS

The three primary types of assessments are 1) norm-referenced, 2) criterion-referenced, and 3) instructor-designed.

Norm-Referenced Assessments

Norm-referenced assessments are typically used to evaluate an individual's performance against that of others who were given the same assessment. They are often referred to as standardized tests because of the way they are developed. Designers give the test to hundreds or thousands of people and determine the average or "normal" score. One individual score can be compared with the group assessment score. The most common norm-referenced tests are standardized intelligence tests.

A NORM-REFERENCED TEST COMPARES THE SCORE OF ONE PERSON WITH THE GROUP SCORE OF HUNDREDS OR THOUSANDS OF PEOPLE ON WHOM THE TEST WAS STANDARDIZED.

Highly trained individuals, such as psychologists, give norm-referenced tests. A test is always uniformly administered. As a result, the psychologist can ensure that the responses are not influenced by the way in which the questions are asked, by facial expressions, or by other "hints" given during the test.

The purpose of norm-referenced tests is to compare a person's relative performance with the group performance on the test. The results are generally given in the form of an intelligence quotient (IQ) or social quotient (SQ). The scores obtained on norm-referenced assessments provide diagnostic information about the person. Agencies frequently require this information prior to enrollment in a program. The information also may be needed to establish eligibility for federal and state programs and may be used to document the need for a specific type of service.

Although a norm-referenced assessment provides assistance in establishing eligibility or securing placement in a program, it does not provide specific information for developing an ISP. Norm-referenced assessments are frequently misused when scores are interpreted in a way that limits individual potential. This may result in decreased opportunities for learning because low expectations can sometimes affect the individual's achievement. For example, a teacher reviews the records of a student having difficulty reading. The teacher notes that the student performed poorly on a standardized reading test. Rather than providing remedial work, the teacher changes her expectation of the student's reading. She expects him or her to do poorly as a result of the test score. The opportunity to improve is therefore not provided, and the student continues to lag behind his or her peers.

Another major misuse of norm-referenced assessments is the grouping of individuals in programs based on IQ scores. Many people equate IQ scores with ability. Measures of IQ, however, do not take into account an individual's strengths or any information about his or her abilities. An IQ of 75, 100, or 125 does not provide specific information about this individual.

Criterion-Referenced Assessments

Criterion-referenced assessments, designed to determine the program needs of individuals, compare individuals with themselves. That is, an assessment indicates the skills of a person and the specific tasks that he or she can do.

Criterion-referenced tests compare individuals with themselves.

These assessments are particularly useful in program development because assessment results provide the information needed to design ISPs. Three general purposes of criterion-referenced assessments are: 1) to obtain a direct assessment of a behavior in real or simulated settings, 2) to obtain a measure of a person's performance in a specific area of development, and 3) to determine how a person learns a new concept.

Some criterion-referenced assessments focus on performance in different developmental areas, such as fine motor, gross motor, cognitive, receptive language, expressive language, and social/emotional development of the person. Others look at a person's ability to handle money, do laundry, or perform kitchen skills. An agency's mission statement determines the assessment to use. If its mission is to provide instruction in academics, a criterion-referenced assessment designed to measure academic abilities should be used. If the purpose of a program is to provide on-the-job training, it would be helpful to use a criterion-referenced assessment to measure components of vocational training programs. The assessment should reflect the mission of the agency that uses the assessment results.

Most criterion-referenced assessments are designed in a developmental sequence—in order to do task D, a person must first be able to do tasks A, B, and C. For example, one section of a developmental assessment for gross motor skills may include the following test items:

Can the person sit unsupported?
Can the person pull to standing?
Can the person cruise holding onto furniture?
Can the person stand unsupported?
Can the person take independent steps?

This assessment lists the motor skills in the order they occur in the person's normal development. He or she cannot go directly from "sits unsupported" to "walks independently." To learn to walk independently, the person must first sit unsupported, then pull to stand, then cruise, and then stand unsupported.

MOST CRITERION-REFERENCED ASSESSMENTS ARE DESIGNED IN A DEVELOPMENTAL SEQUENCE.

Criterion-referenced assessments divide the measured behavior into simple steps. This is called *task analysis*. The examiner determines what tasks or steps the person can do. Often, staff members believe that items a person passes on criterion-referenced tests should be listed as strengths and failed items are needs. The focus of the intervention program then becomes remediation of the person's deficits. To use test results in this manner is a misuse of the assessment. In order to appropriately identify an individual's needs, the staff must clearly understand why he or she has failed a test item. Furthermore, contemporary practice suggests that ISPs and subsequent program objectives provide better results when they are based on the individual's strengths. The needs of the individual are viewed as an extension of his or her strengths and interests. The focus of instructional programs is not on remediation but on building the natural abilities and strengths of individuals with developmental disabilities. Criterion-referenced assessments can be designed also for a specific job or program area and the results are for appropriate ISPs.

Skill development in the different areas overlap. For instance, development of fine motor skills is related to the development of language skills. The two occur simultaneously and are interrelated. The criterion-referenced assessment is divided into these developmental areas only to aid the examiner in the organization of each assessment. Information obtained from one assessment area should not be examined in isolation but reviewed in relation to other areas. In designing the ISP, the team must approach the individual as a whole person.

EXERCISE 2

Agency Use of Assessments

Examine the assessments used by your program. Do the assessments look at the person by developmental areas or by the specific task the agency wants the person to perform?

Criterion-referenced assessments have limitations. The assessment may contain only a few items in each assessment category. For example, a gross motor development assessment may list three items to determine the person's ability at one level and four items at another level. In reality, many gross motor skills are developing at any one level or in a particular time period. The designers of this assessment simply chose to shorten the list to include only samples of the types of gross motor skills developing at that time.

In addition, many items on a criterion-referenced assessment are the curriculum activities that describe only the behavior assessed, rather than the skills needed to perform the behavior. The performed behavior, however, is not what the test designer is attempting to measure. Consider, for example, an assessment item that measures whether a person can stack three blocks. Stacking blocks is not the critical issue. Instead, the abilities to reach, grasp, and release an object in a coordinated manner are the vital skills being measured. Many people confuse such tasks as block stacking with what the task measures. As a result, when a person with developmental disabilities fails the task, stacking blocks is mistakenly included as a teaching objective. Many useless tasks find their way into ISPs in this manner. The ISP should stress basic skills, such as coordinated reaching or grasping and coordinated eye-hand movements. In addition, no analysis is made of the reason why the person failed the task. When stacking blocks, for example, was the person unable to reach for the object, to grasp the object, or to pick up the object?

Instructor-Designed Assessments

Instructor-designed assessments focus on a specific program need. They can be as complex or as simple as needed. The four steps in designing an assessment tool are:

1. Identifying the skill to be learned
2. Listing the simple behaviors in sequence
3. Listing other factors to be measured, such as completion of task with assistance, without assistance, with reinforcers, or without reinforcers
4. Administering the assessment and determining the results

Table 1 presents an example of an instructor-designed assessment that measures an individual's ability to use a telephone. The assessment results will indicate where you should begin your teaching strategy. For example, after giving the assessment in Table 1, you may discover that the person needs assistance in identifying the numbers 3 and 6, in dialing the number 0, and in initiating phone conversation.

FUNCTIONAL ASSESSMENT PROCESS

A new approach to the assessment process for individuals with severe disabilities is the functional assessment. This is an alternative to the traditional developmental assessment, which may not provide the necessary information for developing programs for these individuals. A

Table 1. Instructor-designed assessment in independent use of the telephone

Task: To telephone community residence—532-6410	With assistance	Without assistance
The individual:		
1. Picks up telephone		
2. Puts telephone to ear		
3. Listens for dial tone		
4. Identifies the number 5		
5. Dials the number 5		
6. Identifies the number 3		
7. Dials the number 3		
8. Identifies the number 2		
9. Dials the number 2		
10. Identifies the number 6		
11. Dials the number 6		
12. Identifies the number 4		
13. Dials the number 4		
14. Identifies the number 1		
15. Dials the number 1		
16. Identifies the number 0		
17. Dials the number 0		
18. Says "hello"		
19. Carries on conversation		
20. Says "good-bye" to end conversation		

developmental assessment focuses exclusively on the individual with the disability and does not measure whether the individual can do some form of a behavior. For example, developmental assessments primarily list various forms of behaviors, such as crawling, walking, and running.

In contrast, the functional assessment emphasizes the environment and functions of behavior. It identifies external resources and adaptations that can assist the person to accomplish the behavioral function. For some people with severe disabilities, the function of the behavior may be more important than the form the behavior takes. For instance, getting from the dining room to the den is more important than how it is done. A person who cannot walk could use a wheelchair, a walker, or staff assistance (all different forms of movement) to accomplish the task desired.

THE FUNCTIONAL ASSESSMENT MODEL FOCUSES ATTENTION ON THE ENVIRONMENT AND FUNCTIONS OF THE BEHAVIOR.

The goal of any person's ISP is increased skill development and greater independence. For example, the function, or purpose, of eating is to obtain nourishment for the body. There are many different ways or forms of accomplishing this behavior. The developmental approach focuses on the form of eating, and the staff designs programs to increase fine motor ability, eye-hand coordination, or lip closure. In cases of severe physical disability, the staff can focus on accomplishing the function of eating by adapting a spoon with a special handle that allows the person to perform the skill. The person could also eat by using special food-dispensing devices, or another individual could provide assistance during the meal.

In the past, too much concern has been placed on what a person with severe disabilities cannot do. Not enough time has been spent in exploring resources that can enable the person to perform a function. In evaluating the form a behavior takes (e.g., does the person drink from a cup, a bottle, or use a straw?), the function of the behavior, obtaining liquids, is ignored.

As another example, assume that you are assessing an individual's ability to wash his or her face, but his or her physical limitations prevent this. In a traditional assessment the person would fail the test item. Face washing would then become a goal on the ISP, without considering that the person may never be able to independently wash his or her own face. However, this function can be accomplished in other ways. Could a roommate or caregiver assist him or her in washing? Is it possible to pay someone to perform this function? These are only two solutions to the problem. The team should explore all possible options and select the most functional one. Table 2 provides additional examples of various forms that a behavior may take in order to accomplish a required function.

The functional approach to assessment is not designed to replace developmental assessments. Rather, it is aimed at supporting and enhancing the assessment process in those instances where a person's disability prevents him or her from accomplishing the next task in a developmental sequence. The functional approach is most applicable to people with severe disabilities. The majority of individuals with less severe developmental disabilities and those who are young may benefit from a criterion-referenced test.

ENVIRONMENTAL CONSIDERATIONS

In addition to norm- and criterion-referenced tests, instructor-designed assessments, and functional assessments, the staff should consider the potential effects the immediate environment may have on an individual. Everyone responds to environmental factors, and the staff must un-

Table 2. Examples of alternative behavioral forms to accomplish required functions

Behavioral function	Behavioral forms
The individual must:	The individual may:
1. Obtain adequate nutrition	a. Independently eat with appropriate utensils
	b. Independently eat with utensil
	c. Independently eat with adapted utensil
	d. Eat with utensil when assisted by another person
	e. Eat when fed by another person
	f. Eat when fed by another person and when more finely textured foods are used
	g. Independently eat by activating special feeding machine
	h. Eat through nasal gastrostomy tube
	i. Eat through gastrostomy tube
2. Demonstrate good oral hygiene	a. Independently use toothbrush to brush teeth
	b. Independently use water pic to clean teeth
	c. Independently use adapted toothbrush
	d. Be assisted by staff member in brushing teeth
	e. Have teeth brushed twice a day by a staff member/family member/friend
3. Demonstrate effective written communications	a. Independently use pencil
	b. Independently use adapted pencil
	c. Independently use typewriter
	d. Independently use computer
	e. Use typewriter/computer with assistance
	f. Dictate message while staff person/family member/friend writes
4. Drive a nail	a. Independently drive nail with hammer
	b. Independently drive nail with hammer with adapted handle
	c. Independently drive nail with hammer secured in hand with Velcro fasteners
	d. Drive nail with assistive device holding nail
	e. Drive nail by activating machinery

derstand how they affect the individual with developmental disabilities who is learning, working, or playing.

In assessing the environment to identify variables that may influence the individual's abilities, the staff should consider at least seven areas:

1. Lighting—bright or low lights, direct or indirect lighting
2. Noise—loud, soft, or no noise; background music or no music
3. Work space—large or small room, large or small work space; bright-colored or soft-colored walls; work cubicle or worktable
4. Room temperature—summer/winter temperatures, room ventilation, air circulation
5. Group size—1, 2, 3, 8, or 10 individuals in a group
6. Time of day—A.M. or P.M. for maximum attention to task
7. Recent changes in the person's life—increase/decrease in medication dosage, changes in medication, increase/decrease in visitations from family members or advocate, new work supervisor, new direct care worker assigned to living environment, new roommate

Understanding these factors and how they affect the performance of individuals with developmental disabilities increases the effective development of program plans.

USE OF ASSESSMENT DATA

Assessment data provide an understanding of a person's abilities. Multiple assessments offer a broader picture of capacities and strengths from which to develop program objectives. The use of several assessments can also prevent the development of goals and objectives based only on a failed test item of a single assessment. Using several assessment tools thus increases the list of the individual's strengths. The focus on strengths rather than on what is wrong with a person results in a program plan that stresses the growth of the individual, whereas a plan built around weaknesses often frustrates the individual and the staff. The latter type of plan often results in little or no progress and may lead to disruptive behaviors as the individual attempts to avoid the instruction. This process can become a vicious cycle when a program, based on weaknesses, causes noncompliant behaviors that, in turn, lead to a behavior intervention program in which the behaviors become identified weaknesses.

For most individuals, the human services agency staff should use information obtained from all types of assessments in order to determine an appropriate program. Programs should be recommended for an individual only after a variety of tests yield comprehensive information and the staff understand the person's skill development in the different developmental areas. Administering the various assessments ensures that individuals receive services that are best designed to meet their needs.

SUMMARY

Assessment is the first step in designing an individualized service plan. It is also the most critical aspect of the instructional process. The assessment provides the information needed to set goals and objectives. The staff should use the agency's mission statement as a guide in the selection of assessment tools.

Norm-referenced assessments are standardized in design and are usually administered by a psychologist or other highly trained individuals. The information obtained from a norm-referenced test is typically given in the form of an IQ score or a statement that describes the overall traits of the individual. This information is not particularly useful in the design of an ISP.

Because criterion-referenced assessments are designed to measure what people can do, they are helpful in developing ISPs. These assessments can be purchased or designed by the staff. They can be administered by most staff members with minimal training. Criterion-referenced assessments are generally developmental in design. Because you use the assessment results, you are in a position to modify assessment items so that the person can successfully complete the task. Changing assessment items is acceptable and even advisable if it can increase your understanding of the person with a developmental disability. However, you should note the assessment items changed and try to understand the reason for needing the changes.

The purpose of assessments is to measure a person's abilities. Assessment data can also identify the best approach for working with the individual. Assessment results should not only indicate the person's score on the assessment but also how the person learns, the type and degree of assistance required, and the need for reinforcement.

The functional model of assessment is an assessment approach. It is particularly helpful in assessing individuals with severe disabilities because it focuses attention on factors other than the individual's ability to perform behaviors in a developmental sequence. Effective assessment emphasizes the function of the behavior, as well as the form the behavior takes. Stressing the form of a behavior enables the development of an ISP that emphasizes progress toward increased independence.

Finally, the staff must consider environmental factors that can influence learning, working, and playing. These include lighting, noise, work space, room temperature, group size, time of day, and recent changes in the person's life. An understanding of the environment's effects on people with developmental disabilities can increase the team's success in planning appropriate ISPs.

BIBLIOGRAPHY

Browder, D.M. (1991). *Assessment of individuals with severe disabilities: An applied behavior approach of life skills assessment* (2nd ed.). Baltimore: Paul H. Brookes Publishing Co.

Lakin, K.C., & Bruininks, R.H. (Eds.). (1985). *Strategies for achieving community integration of developmentally disabled citizens.* Baltimore: Paul H. Brookes Publishing Co.

Meyer, L.H., Peck, C.A., & Brown, L. (Eds.). (1991). *Critical issues in the lives of people with severe disabilities.* Baltimore: Paul H. Brookes Publishing Co.

ADDITIONAL RESOURCES

B. Bolton (1987), in *Handbook of measurement and evaluation in rehabilitation* (2nd ed.) (Baltimore: Paul H. Brookes Publishing Co.), provides an in-depth discussion of various elements of assessment, including validity, reliability, and norm-referenced and criterion-referenced tests. An excellent resource book.

M.S. Chapman (1990), Assessments, in J.F. Gardner and M.S. Chapman, *Program issues in developmental disabilities: A guide to effective habilitation and active treatment* (2nd ed.) (pp. 129–143) (Baltimore: Paul H. Brookes Publishing Co.), provides an overview of the assessment process. Although written for an intermediate care facility for the mentally retarded (ICF/MR), the chapter contains interesting points on the assessment process relevant to all settings.

A.P. Kaiser and C.M. McWhorter (1990), in *Preparing personnel to work with persons with severe disabilities.* (Baltimore: Paul H. Brookes Publishing Co.), provide the reader with additional information on assessment and the needs of individuals with developmental disabilities.

SELF-APPRAISAL

INSTRUCTIONS

The following questions will help you evaluate your knowledge about the process of assessment. For true-false questions, check the correct answer. For multiple choice questions, circle the correct answer(s).

Note: There may be more than one correct answer for some questions.

1. The two primary methods of assessment are the interview and direct observation.
   ____ True   ____ False
2. Which of the following should be noted during the assessment process?
   a. Behavior when presented with correction procedures
   b. Presence of medications
   c. Response to reinforcement
   d. Physical inability to complete a task
3. The purpose of assessment is to determine what:
   a. The person is capable of doing
   b. The person likes to do
   c. Skills and behaviors the person wants to acquire
   d. Previous learning experiences occurred
4. An assessment to assist in the diagnosis of a person is:
   a. Norm-referenced
   b. Criterion-referenced
   c. Developmentally tested
   d. Instructor-designed
5. Norm-referenced assessments help:
   a. Document the need for certain services
   b. Determine eligibility for services
   c. Provide specific information for developing the ISP
   d. Identify skills for working in programs
6. A norm-referenced test does not identify an individual's specific capabilities.
   ____ True   ____ False
7. The three purposes of criterion-referenced tests are to:
   a. Obtain direct assessment of a behavior
   b. Obtain a measure of the person's knowledge
   c. Evaluate how a person learns new concepts
   d. Compare one person against the group standard

8. Common misuses of assessment results are:
    a. Making placement decisions from only one test
    b. Administering assessments that are not related to the mission of the program
    c. Interpreting assessment results as limitations rather than capabilities
    d. Formulating failed assessment items as goals or objectives without further assessment
9. If the function of a behavior is to obtain liquids, which of the following is a form of the behavior?
    a. Drink from a cup
    b. Drink through a straw
    c. Drink with one's hands
    d. Drink from a bottle
10. The form of a behavior is an important consideration for persons in their developmental years and for persons with less severe disabilities.
    ____ True   ____ False

CASE STUDY

Brian Dawson is a 14-year-old male diagnosed as having moderate mental retardation, cerebral palsy, and severe acting-out behaviors. Brian lives at home with his mother (47 years old), three brothers (ages 17–25 years), and three sisters (ages 16–21 years). The family income is low but is above the cutoff for public assistance.

Brian attends Midland Special Education Center 5 days a week. Until recently, the local education agency provided bus transportation between the home and school.

During the past 6 months Brian's teacher, Linda Johnson, has reported that the incidence of his aggressive behavior in the classroom has steadily increased. She reports that Brian hits other students, has tantrums, moves furniture, and screams.

Ms. Johnson requested a behavior management consultation from the local mental health clinic. The consulting psychologist indicated that the aggressive behaviors are symptoms of a neurological condition. Therefore, he feels unable to help. Feeling frustrated, Ms. Johnson recommends comprehensive reassessment of Brian, and a team meeting to revise his individualized education program (IEP).

Situation

Completed assessment data revealed that there was no neurological problem. The team also concluded that Brian needed a classroom setting with greater structure and more support services. Finally, the team concluded that Brian's cerebral palsy interfered with his ability to write with a pen or pencil.

1. How would you respond if norm-referenced tests were used to identify program goals and objectives for the classroom?
2. Brian has difficulty writing with a pen. This is one form of communication. What other form would accomplish the function of communication?
3. How would you respond if you attended the IEP meeting and the staff used assessment data to identify what Brian could not do?

ANSWER KEY TO
SELF-APPRAISAL AND CASE STUDY

SELF-APPRAISAL

1. True
2. a, b, c, d
3. a, b, c, d
4. a
5. a, b
6. True
7. a, b, c
8. a, b, c, d
9. a, b, c, d
10. True

CASE STUDY ANSWER GUIDELINES

1. Norm-referenced assessments are typically used to assist in the development of a diagnosis. Norm-referenced assessments do not provide specific information for developing program goals and objectives. Rather, they provide diagnostic information about the person. They are also used to establish eligibility or to secure placement in a program.

2. Communication can assume many different forms. A few of these forms may include:
   Writing with an adapted pencil
   Using a typewriter
   Using a computer
   Using a tape recorder
   Dictating to a friend, family member, or staff person
   Using video equipment

3. The primary purpose for gathering assessment information is to determine what Brian can do. IEPs are based on the strengths of the person. Identifying what Brian cannot do may result in decreased opportunities for learning, owing to low expectations of his behaviors. Finally, the focus on Brian's strengths results in a program plan that stresses Brian's growth and development.

chapter 6

The
Interdisciplinary
Team Process

LEARNING OBJECTIVES

Upon completing this chapter, the reader will be able to:

1. Define the purpose of the interdisciplinary team.
2. Define the contributions of the following individuals to the team process:

   Person with developmental disability
   Speech-language pathologist
   Occupational therapist
   Physical therapist
   Psychologist
   Parents and/or residential personnel
   Physician
   Day program staff

3. Define two general approaches to the interdisciplinary team process.
4. State the advantages of the contemporary approach to interdisciplinary team planning.
5. State three barriers to effective team interactions.
6. Define the difference between a goal and an objective.
7. State the three components of a behavioral objective.

INTRODUCTION

In programs for persons with developmental disabilities, many types of professionals participate in the assessment process (discussed in Chapter 5). These individuals meet and share information in a gathering that is usually referred to as an interdisciplinary team meeting. This chapter covers interdisciplinary team composition and professional responsibilities.

PURPOSE OF THE INTERDISCIPLINARY TEAM PROCESS

The interdisciplinary team process exists to help individuals with developmental disabilities to make decisions. The team meeting, by providing the opportunity for members to discuss data and information, results in decisions. Team members assist people with developmental disabilities or their advocates to arrive at decisions about life goals. The team meeting should identify the programs and services needed to achieve those goals.

THE INTERDISCIPLINARY TEAM ASSISTS INDIVIDUALS WITH DEVELOPMENTAL DISABILITIES IN MAKING DECISIONS.

COMPOSITION OF THE INTERDISCIPLINARY TEAM

The composition of the team depends on the needs of the person with a developmental disability. In other words, what other professionals and agency staff have information that the person needs in order to make decisions? These individuals should be members of the team. The person with a developmental disability, however, is the most important team member.

EXERCISE 1

Interdisciplinary Teams

At the next interdisciplinary team meeting you attend, list the members of the team and their roles.

To the extent possible, the person with a developmental disability should assume a major role on the team. Some persons can actively join in the team process. Some need assistance in attending the meeting and making contributions, and others may not have the ability to make contributions. In such cases, an advocate, service coordinator, or staff member serves as the person's representative. The team also includes other people who have information and opinions about the person with a developmental disability. Some of these people can provide specialized information.

Speech-Language Pathologist

A speech-language pathologist is interested in how people communicate. The assessment data tell how the person with a developmental disability can best communicate and share information. The speech-language pathologist can determine if the person would benefit from an alternative communication system, such as signing, a communication board, or an electronic device. The speech-language pathologist may also recommend speech therapy. In addition, the pathologist can generally screen the individual to determine if he or she has a hearing loss and if additional hearing tests are recommended.

A speech-language assessment is conducted when a discrepancy between the person's cognitive abilities and the level of communication exists. For example, consider a 15-year-old adolescent who is communicating at about the 5-year-old level. The psychological report indicates that the person demonstrates a mental ability at the 8-year-old level. Because of the difference between the person's cognitive abilities and communication skills, he or she should be referred for speech-language evaluation.

Occupational Therapist

In general, the occupational therapist focuses on three skill areas: fine motor development, activities for daily living, and oral motor skills. The occupational therapist considers both the mastery and the quality of skills.

In the area of fine motor development, the occupational therapist studies a person's use of his or her hands to perform a task. The task may range from opening mail to cutting with scissors to using tools in a shop. The occupational therapist also assesses skills needed in activities for daily living, including bathing, dressing, grooming, toileting, eating, housekeeping, and cooking.

In evaluating oral motor skill development, the occupational therapist assesses the muscles used for eating, drinking, and/or speaking. The evaluation focuses on such skills as chewing food, swallowing, speech sounds, and lip closure while drinking.

The occupational therapist works with the physical therapist in evaluating a person's wheelchair. The person's positioning in the wheelchair and his or her ability to move the wheelchair are observed. The occupational therapist also evaluates the positioning of materials on a table or tray in front of the person in the wheelchair. The occupational therapist determines how the person can best use his or her arms and hands to complete tasks.

Physical Therapist

The physical therapist is concerned with the person's gross motor development. The physical therapist evaluates the manner in which a person moves from one point to another and checks coordination, balance, muscle strength, endurance, and the range of motion in the joints necessary for gross motor activity. The therapist can provide specialized assistance for people in wheelchairs or for those who demonstrate some difficulty in walking. A physical therapy assessment also considers how well a person walks up and down stairs and over curbs and uneven ground.

Psychologist

The clinical psychologist provides information to the team regarding the person's intelligence. This includes rate of learning and preferred learning methods. The psychologist typically reports an intelligence quotient (IQ) score or age equivalent. For example, the psychologist might report that the person has an IQ of 50 and is functioning at around the 15-year-old level. By itself, an IQ score is not particularly relevant. It is significant, however, when combined with the information of other team members.

Parents

When the person with a developmental disability is a child, the parents can offer additional information to the team. Most parents do not come to a team meeting with a formal assessment but they do have a special perspective of the child. Parents generally are not experts in academic or clinical fields. They are, however, the experts who may spend the most time with the child and who may best know the child. Often, parents are able to offer unique observations.

Because the home environment is probably not as structured as the classroom, workshop, or employment setting, a person with a developmental disability may behave differently in the home. Parents can provide insights on this behavior. They are also concerned about the total life of the individual, not just one program. Parents can support and enhance in the home setting the goals and objectives set by the team.

Physician or Other Medical Personnel

The physician provides medical information about the person. This may include a medical diagnosis, medical history, and special health concerns. The physician can also describe the potential side effects of any medications taken by the person.

Residential or Day Program Staff

In general, the residential or day program staff have the responsibility for implementing the goals and objectives of an individualized service plan (ISP). The staff also provide the team with assessment information about the individual's performance in a specific program. Staff observations are critical in forming appropriate goals and objectives for the person with a developmental disability.

Other Team Members

The professionals mentioned above do not represent the full range of possible team members. Other individuals, such as behavioral psychologists, social workers, nutritionists, educators, music therapists, art therapists, and vocational rehabilitation counselors, may be part of the team. In some programs, the assessment is done by consultants or community practitioners, rather than by full- or part-time staff members. In such cases, the consultant may not be able to attend interdisciplinary team meetings. All team members should have access to the assessment, however, and one staff member should review the assessment before the meeting.

EXERCISE 2

Information Identification

For each team member listed earlier, identify the information that person provides to other team members.

APPROACHES TO INTERDISCIPLINARY TEAM PLANNING

The traditional approach to team planning focuses on the individual who is involved in a day or residential program. The interdisciplinary team develops goals and objectives that are based, in large part, on the services provided by the day or residential program, and the team consists of employees of the program. The goals and objectives reflect the services available within the program. This type of interdisciplinary team process takes a narrow approach to planning for the person with a developmental disability and is considered inappropriate by today's standards.

In a second, more contemporary planning approach, the agency responsible for service coordination arranges for the completion of comprehensive evaluations. These evaluations are performed by the staff of the residential or day program or by professionals outside the program. The results of the assessments are shared by the team members. The focus of the team meeting is to determine what services in the community can help the person to reach his or her goals. Decisions as to the long-range goals are based on the person's needs without regard to availability of services. If the needed services are not available in the particular day or residential program, they often can be obtained elsewhere in the community.

In a third approach, called *personal futures planning*, team membership is expanded to include friends, relatives, neighbors, and even local business representatives. The purpose of personal futures planning is to provide an opportunity for the individual with a developmental disability to express personal interests and desires. Professionals, family members, friends, and community representatives all commit to assist the individual in achieving his or her stated goals. Unlike the first two approaches, goals and objectives stated during personal futures planning include issues related to community participation. The individual states the goals that he or she wishes to achieve in the community and actively solicits the help of the team in pursuing them. Should the goals not be reached, the individual and team members critically review their roles in not fulfilling their obligations.

BARRIERS TO THE TEAM PROCESS

The interdisciplinary team meeting provides an opportunity for mutual communication and planning, but several barriers can prevent the process from working. Professional jargon, for instance, is sometimes used in team discussions and written reports. It can inhibit the team process if some people do not understand the discussion. Assessments and discussions should be free of jargon because it interferes with, and may even prevent, necessary dialogue.

"Turf tending," a second barrier, occurs when staff members become possessive of persons or of services provided to individuals with developmental disabilities. They feel that only certain professionals or programs can make decisions or provide services. This attitude is often carried over into the team meeting and prevents the members from acting as a team. Rather, they act as individuals with individual interests.

Another barrier, the lack of clear role definition, occurs when team members do not clearly understand either the team process or purpose or their roles as team members. Lack of role definition is evident when one team member attempts to control the meeting. In some cases, team members play out personal agendas during the meeting. At other times, team members may not share information with other members for fear of ridicule.

Having a team leader may also result in a barrier and affect the team process. When an agency establishes one leader or chairperson for the interdisciplinary team, the dialogue is usually between the team leader and the person presenting an assessment or other pertinent information. Rarely does dialogue take place among all team members. A chairperson needs special skills to create and maintain a team culture where all members feel comfortable and speak openly about issues.

The reading of assessment reports during the interdisciplinary team meeting presents another barrier to the team process. Written reports, as part of the agency's records for individuals receiving services, are documents of work that has been completed. At team meetings, they should be used only as guides to ensure that all relevant new information is shared with all team members. The team process is designed to be a discussion about the individual. Reading discourages discussion.

A final barrier to an effective team may be the attitude of team members toward the individual with a developmental disability. The purpose of the team meeting is to have an open dialogue with that individual. The team that meets with the individual once a year with the intention of creating a dialogue among the group puts the individual with a developmental disability at a disadvantage in understanding the process. There should be numerous meetings with the individual throughout the year to ensure ongoing dialogue among all team members.

PROFESSIONAL JARGON, TURF TENDING, LACK OF CLEAR ROLE DEFINITION, USE OF TEAM LEADERS, READING OF ASSESSMENT REPORTS, AND LACK OF OPPORTUNITIES FOR DIALOGUE INTERFERE WITH THE INTERDISCIPLINARY TEAM PROCESS.

EFFECTIVE TEAM PROCESS

In the first part of the team meeting, each team member shares with the other members assessment data and other pertinent information related to the individual with a developmental disability. Each member develops a comprehensive view of the individual from this information, which includes listings of the individual's strengths, likes, and dislikes, as well as program needs. It is important that each team member not only evaluate the individual from his or her area of expertise but also carefully consider information from the other team members. The team is then able to develop an ISP based on the strengths and interests of the individual with a developmental disability, and the team members agree on the focus or direction of the program.

Characteristics of effective team meetings include group leadership, participation by all members, and summarization. As stated above, a single team leader may inhibit a good group process. The leadership of effective teams shifts among its members. As the meeting progresses, team members gather information from each other and begin to focus on the potential service needs of the individual with a developmental disability. Various members of the team assume leadership roles as insights and direction are revealed. This natural process of team leadership should be encouraged and supported.

An effective team invites and reinforces the active participation of all team members. Recognition is given to the significant contributions each member makes to the team process and the resulting ISP. In addition, differences among team members are viewed as a natural part of the process and are worked out by the team.

Summarization is a critical component of a successful meeting. A large volume of data about the individual with a developmental disability is presented by team members. Constantly summarizing this information helps the members to draw conclusions and make recommendations for the ISP, as well as for future directions of the agency in assisting the individual to achieve his or her stated goals and objectives.

A written plan is then developed by the team that emphasizes the individual's capabilities and preferences. The plan also specifies the team members who will assume responsibilities for each identified program area. A major portion of this program plan is the statement of its goals and objectives that are written by the team during the interdisciplinary team meeting.

GOAL STATEMENT

The goal statement is a written expression of direction that identifies priorities for the person with a developmental disability. It also assists agency staff and other personnel in focusing on a shared outcome.

A GOAL DEFINES THE DIRECTION OF A PERSON'S PROGRAM.

Agencies use different approaches in writing goal statements. In some agencies, the goal statement indicates what the person will accomplish within 1 year. Such a statement is considered a long-range goal. For other programs, the time frame of the goal statement extends to only 6 months. Short-range goals are generally accomplished in 3 months. Each human services agency adopts its own definition of the content and time frame of long- and short-term goals and objectives. Consistent use of the terms by each agency's staff is more important than differences between agencies. The long-term goals should be established without regard to the availability of services. All goals should be based on the person's needs.

LONG-TERM GOALS SHOULD BE WRITTEN WITHOUT CONSIDERING WHAT SERVICES ARE AVAILABLE FOR THE PERSON.

EXERCISE 3

Go to your program supervisor. Determine how the agency defines goals.

Goal statements can be regarded as expectations. Consider the following goal statements and note how they are written:

John will dress himself.
Sarah will complete a job application.
Doug will tune a car engine.
Jerry will demonstrate the ability to stack objects.

All of these goals state what is expected. They reflect the belief that these individuals will live in the community, find meaningful employment, and participate in leisure and recreational activities. Finally, the goals are stated in a positive manner. They indicate what the individuals will do.

A WRITTEN GOAL IS A STATEMENT OF THE STAFF'S EXPECTATIONS OF THE PERSON WITH A DEVELOPMENTAL DISABILITY.

The number of goals established on the ISP varies from agency to agency and depends on several factors. One factor is the agency's policy for the development of ISPs. The second factor relates to the desires of the person with a developmental disability. These desires also affect the number of established goals. The person's energy level and interest in programs are additional factors that influence the development of goal statements. This is especially true for adults with developmental disabilities who advocate on their own behalf.

BEHAVIORAL OBJECTIVES

Behavioral objectives, like goal statements, are written statements that define the progress a person is expected to make in a program. An objective differs from a goal in that it is a specific statement of one step that is necessary to complete a goal. The objective is also accomplished in a shorter time period, usually 3–6 months. A goal may consist of several behavioral objectives that specify the steps the person must complete to meet the goal. The team often identifies the objectives during the interdisciplinary team meeting.

A BEHAVIORAL OBJECTIVE IS A MORE SPECIFIC STATEMENT THAN A GOAL AND IS ACCOMPLISHED IN A SHORTER TIME PERIOD.

Three critical elements of a behavioral objective are the behavior to be learned, the conditions under which the behavior is to occur, and how well or to what criterion the behavior must be performed. Without these three elements, the statement is not a behavioral objective.

THE THREE CRITICAL ELEMENTS OF A BEHAVIORAL OBJECTIVE ARE:

1. THE BEHAVIOR TO BE LEARNED
2. THE CONDITIONS UNDER WHICH THE BEHAVIOR IS TO OCCUR
3. HOW WELL OR TO WHAT STANDARD THE BEHAVIOR MUST BE PERFORMED

Written Statement of Behavior

The first element of the behavioral objective is a statement of the behavior to be learned. A behavior is anything a person does that is observable and measurable. Therefore, behavioral objectives identify skills or activities that are observable and measurable. For example, assume that an ISP goal states that John will dress himself. The behavioral objectives for this goal define the steps necessary to accomplish the goal of dressing. They may include:

John will recognize the front of each clothing item.
John will put on his shirt.
John will put on his pants.
John will put on his shoes.
John will tie his shoe laces.

Note that in each case the desired outcome or behavior is positively stated. In addition, each objective is a behavior.

Written Statement of Conditions

The second component of the behavioral objective is a statement of the conditions under which the behavior will occur. The condition statement defines where (e.g., a classroom or bedroom) the behavior will occur, who (if anyone) will assist in the performance of the behavior, when the behavior will occur, or what assistance is needed. Note how the condition statement affects the desired outcome of the same behavior in the following examples:

Given the verbal command to button his shirt and the use of a buttoning hook, John will button his shirt.
Given the verbal command to button his shirt, John will button his shirt.
Given the command to button his shirt, John will button his shirt with physical assistance.

In each example, the behavior is the same: John will button his shirt. However, the conditions under which the behavior will occur are different.

Written Statement of Criterion

The final requirement of a behavioral objective is the statement of how well or to what criterion the behavior must be performed. This element is critical because it defines when the person has accomplished the objective. Different methods can be used to determine this. The most common approach involves statements about the accuracy, speed, duration, or quantity of the behavior.

Accuracy statements are the most commonly used. They describe how correctly a person performs the desired behavior. Accuracy statements are written in the form of a percentage of completed tasks. For example, you may see the statement: "Doug will correctly identify the number 7 with 80% accuracy." This means that when given 10 opportunities to perform the behavior, Doug will do it correctly on 8 trials.

Accuracy statements also can be written in terms of correct responses on a specific number of trials. For example, using this same behavior, the criterion statement could have read: "Doug will identify the number 7 on 8 out of 10 times when asked."

A third option would be to state: "Doug will correctly identify the number 7 when asked." In this case, the word *correctly* is an accuracy statement that means the behavior will be performed the right way each time it is attempted.

The *speed* at which a behavior is learned is another standard. For example, the person in the work center who takes 5 minutes to stuff one envelope is not performing at a functional level. An objective would be needed for the person to decrease the amount of time it takes to complete the task, such as: "When given the needed materials, Susan will put the material in an envelope within 30 seconds." Consider another example in the area of mealtime behavior. Doug is able to feed himself, but it takes 45 minutes to complete the meal. An objective might read, "Doug will eat his meal within 20 minutes." This will help to make his mealtime behavior more functional.

A third criterion is *duration*. In some instances, time spent on a behavior should be increased. An example of a duration statement would be: "Given a worksheet, Doug will remain in his seat for 5 minutes." Similarly, in the work setting, a person may need to hold a lever down for 15 seconds or a clamp closed for 30 seconds. Stating the duration of the task is necessary to determine if the task is accomplished.

Quantity is also a criterion. Examples of quantity include counting the number of streets between work and home, identifying the number of program supervisors, or counting 25 nails in a box.

In writing some behavioral objectives, a combination of statements concerning accuracy, speed, duration, and/or quantity may be needed. It may not be enough, for instance, to state that a person will correctly identify the color red three out of five times when asked. The objective may need to be expanded to read; "When asked, the person will identify the color red three out of five times requested on 3 consecutive days." By addition of "on 3 consecutive days" to the objective, the person must perform the behavior in a consistent manner over time before the behavior is considered to have been learned.

EXERCISE 4

Objectives

Look at a recently developed ISP. Do the established objectives contain the required statements of the behavior to be learned, the conditions under which the behavior is performed, and the standards?

SUMMARY

This chapter stresses the importance of the interdisciplinary team planning process and the use of goals and objectives in writing the individualized service plan. The concept of the interdisciplinary team planning process allows and encourages the sharing of information. The goal of the meeting is to assist the person with a developmental disability and/or his or her advocate in making decisions.

Decisions about long-term goals for the person should be made regardless of the services available. This allows the person with a developmental disability or the advocate to choose from a variety of program options. It also provides the agency staff with suggestions for future program development.

The agency staff must develop an ISP for the program that is chosen. The team meeting initiates the development of an ISP and determines the statements of behavioral goals and objectives.

Personal futures planning is an expanded model for team planning. Team members include professionals, agency staff, family members, friends, and community representatives. All are committed to assist the individual with a developmental disability in achieving his or her stated goals.

The goal is a statement defining the direction of the person's program plan. The terms used are general in nature. The goal statement usually covers a period of 1 year. The number of goal statements established by the team varies among agencies.

An objective is a statement of one step that is necessary to complete or reach the goal. An objective is usually written for a period of 3–6 months. It has three component parts: a statement of the behavior to be learned; a statement of the conditions under which the behavior is performed; and a statement of criterion, or when the behavior is considered learned.

BIBLIOGRAPHY

Golin, A.K., & Ducanis, A.J. (1981). *The interdisciplinary team: A handbook for the education of exceptional children.* Rockville, MD: Aspen Systems.

Meyer Children's Rehabilitation Institute. (1980a). *Setting goals.* Omaha: Author.

Meyer Children's Rehabilitation Institute. (1980b). *Writing behavioral objectives and measuring behavior.* Omaha: Author.

ADDITIONAL RESOURCES

G.M. Parker (1990), in *Team players and teamwork: The new competitive business strategy* (San Francisco: Jossey-Bass), looks at what makes effective and ineffective teams, with a focus on developing a team and achieving tasks through teamwork within organizations.

S.L. Philip and R.L. Elledge (1989), in *The team-building source book* (San Diego: University Associates), provide readers with information about teams, purposes of teams, and strategies for team building. This is an excellent "how to" book.

W.B. Reddy and K. Jamison (1988), in *Team building: Blueprints for productivity and satisfaction* (San Diego: University Associates), offer the reader more strategies on building effective teams.

SELF-APPRAISAL

INSTRUCTIONS

The following questions will help you evaluate your knowledge about the interdisciplinary team process. For true-false questions, check the correct answer. For multiple choice questions, circle the correct answer(s).

Note: There may be more than one correct answer for some questions.

1. The purpose of the interdisciplinary team process is to assist individuals with developmental disabilities to make decisions.
   ___ True   ___ False

2. The most important person(s) on the interdisciplinary team is (are):
   a. The professional staff
   b. Parents
   c. The person with a developmental disability
   d. The program administrators

3. A person is usually referred for speech-language therapy if there is a discrepancy between the person's cognitive abilities and the level of functioning in the area of language development.
   ___ True   ___ False

4. The occupational therapist is concerned with which of the following:
   a. Fine motor development
   b. Activities for daily living
   c. Oral motor skills
   d. All of the above

5. The professionals responsible for a positioning evaluation of a person in a wheelchair are:
   a. Occupational therapist and speech-language therapist
   b. Speech-language therapist and physical therapist
   c. Occupational therapist and physical therapist
   d. Psychiatrist and orthopedist

6. The interdisciplinary team members set goals with a person with developmental disabilities by:
   a. Considering agency resources
   b. Considering all available resources
   c. Considering available funds
   d. Not considering available resources

7. Common problems that impede the interdisciplinary team process include:

    a. Use of jargon
    b. Turf tending
    c. Lack of role definition
    d. Feedback questions

8. A goal statement should be:
    a. Measurable
    b. Stated positively
    c. Accomplished within 2 weeks
    d. Based on assessment data

9. The three critical elements of a behavioral objective are:
    a. A statement of the behavior, the conditions under which the behavior occurs, and the criteria
    b. A goal statement, conditions of the behavior, and length of training required
    c. The behavior to be learned, materials needed for instruction, and reinforcers
    d. Who is providing instruction, who will evaluate the instruction, and what will be used to test the behavior

10. Measurement criteria in behavioral objectives include statements of:
    a. Accuracy
    b. Speed
    c. Length of time
    d. Quantity

CASE STUDY

Brian Dawson is a 14-year-old male diagnosed as having moderate mental retardation, cerebral palsy, and severe acting-out behaviors. Brian lives at home with his mother (47 years old), three brothers (ages 17–25 years), and three sisters (ages 16–21 years). The family income is low but is above the cutoff for public assistance.

Brian attends Midland Special Education Center 5 days a week. Until recently, the local education agency provided bus transportation between the home and school.

During the past 6 months, Brian's teacher, Linda Johnson, has reported that the incidence of his aggressive behavior in the classroom has steadily increased. She reports that Brian hits other students, has tantrums, moves furniture, and screams.

Ms. Johnson requested a behavior management consultation from the local mental health clinic. The consulting psychologist indicated that the aggressive behaviors are symptoms of a neurological condition. Therefore, he feels unable to help. Feeling frustrated, Ms. Johnson recommends a comprehensive reassessment of Brian and a team meeting to revise his individualized education program (IEP).

Situation

Following Ms. Johnson's request, a team completed a series of assessments on Brian. They met to revise the IEP. The meeting was scheduled at a time convenient to the parents. During the meeting, the team reviewed the assessment data. The parents indicated they had difficulty understanding the reported information. The team was able to list goals for the IEP.

1. Identify the people who should attend the meeting.
2. What are the effects of using professional jargon in the team meeting?
3. One objective established by the team stated, "Brian will become more cooperative with staff." What are the limitations of this objective?
4. Some team members expressed concerns about cerebral palsy. They asked if the occupational therapist could design a program to improve Brian's ability to walk up and down stairs. Discuss the appropriateness of this request.

ANSWER KEY TO
SELF-APPRAISAL AND CASE STUDY

SELF-APPRAISAL

1. True
2. c
3. True
4. d
5. c
6. d
7. a, b, c
8. a, b, d
9. a
10. a, b, c, d

CASE STUDY ANSWER GUIDELINES

1. Any person who completed assessment data should attend—in this case, the school psychologist, teacher, neurologist, and behavioral psychologist. A school administrator, the parents, and any other people who would be involved in Brian's program should also be present.
2. Jargon tends to alienate parents and other team members. In addition, it contributes to turf tending.
3. The statement is not behavioral. It is a label; as such, there is no way to measure "cooperation." In addition, condition and criterion statements are not included.
4. The question to the team is appropriate. However, the occupational therapist is generally not responsible for mobility issues. The team members should refer the question to the physical therapist.

Developing Instructional Strategies

LEARNING OBJECTIVES

Upon completing this chapter, the reader will be able to:

1. Define instruction.
2. Define and complete a task analysis.
3. Define error-free learning.
4. Define four error-free teaching techniques.
5. Define fading.
6. Complete an instructional objective sheet.
7. State the importance of data collection.
8. State the importance of providing practice and generalization on a regular basis.

INTRODUCTION

After goals and objectives have been identified, the next step is to develop instructional strategies that will assist the individual with a developmental disability to acquire new skills. Instructional strategies enable the staff to define the support services required by each individual. They also allow the staff to pinpoint the natural environments within which learning will take place. The staff should employ the strategies only in the environments where the new skills will be used. To teach skills in artificial environments is not a good instructional strategy.

This chapter tells you how to develop effective instructional strategies and organize the learning environments. Three critical steps in organizing a learning environment are: 1) planning the instruction, 2) implementing the instruction, and 3) providing opportunities for the practice and generalization of the skill.

PLANNING THE INSTRUCTION

Providing instruction is a planned and systematic process. Learning, for the most part, does not happen accidentally. Successful planning enhances the learner's ability to accomplish the goals and objectives in the individualized service plan (ISP). Table 1 details the planning steps in establishing an instructional strategy.

Determine Whether Behavior Is Simple or Complex

The first step in planning for instruction is to distinguish simple behaviors from complex behaviors. Simple behaviors are those that cannot be broken down any further. They stand alone and do not involve other behaviors. For example, sitting is a simple behavior. You would be unable to list behaviors that make up the behavior of sitting. Looking, standing, or holding are other examples of simple behaviors.

In contrast, complex behaviors are combinations of several other behaviors. Driving a car is a complex behavior composed of hundreds of simple behaviors. The study of behaviors and the listing of the simple behaviors that make up a complex behavior constitute a process called a *task analysis*.

TASK ANALYSIS IS THE PROCESS OF STUDYING A BEHAVIOR BY BREAKING THE BEHAVIOR INTO SMALLER, LOGICAL, AND SEQUENTIAL STEPS.

Task analysis simplifies the teaching of new skills by breaking a new behavior into logical steps within a sequence. To complete a task analysis, list the simple behaviors in the order they occur. You can do this from memory or by actually completing the behavior and listing

---

Table 1. Planning instructional strategies

Steps in planning an instructional strategy include:

1. Determine if the behavior is simple or complex. If the behavior is complex, determine if a task analysis is needed.
2. Select the instructional methods and a strategy for eliminating any assistance.
3. Determine your reaction to a correct or incorrect response.
4. Decide when to move to the next step in your instructional strategy.
5. Select instructional materials and the appropriate setting for instruction.
6. Identify opportunities for practice and generalization of the new behavior.

---

the steps you performed. For example, consider the skill of washing your hands. What is the sequence of steps in this behavior? A list might include the following eight steps:

1. Turn on water
2. Pick up soap
3. Rub soap on hands
4. Put soap down
5. Rub hands together
6. Rinse hands
7. Turn off water
8. Dry hands

The steps in the task analysis are listed in the order in which the behavior will be learned. In addition, each of the steps can be broken down into additional steps. For example, "turn on water" can be broken down into grasping the faucet, turning the faucet, adjusting the temperature, and controlling the water force.

Most tasks can be broken down into simpler steps. These simpler tasks, in turn, probably can be broken down into even simpler tasks. Some people with developmental disabilities may require additional simple tasks. The strengths and needs of the person determine the number of steps in your task analysis.

In a second example, an individual is learning to spread mustard on a hot dog. The task analysis may include the following eight steps:

1. Open jar of mustard
2. Pick up teaspoon
3. Put teaspoon in jar of mustard
4. Stir contents of jar until smooth
5. Remove spoon from jar
6. Turn spoon on its side and lay it on one end of hot dog
7. Pull spoon across hot dog from one end to the other
8. Return spoon to jar

As in the previous example, each of these steps can be broken down further, depending on the needs and abilities of the individual.

Select Instructional Methods and Strategy for Eliminating Assistance

The second step in developing a teaching strategy is to select the instructional methods. Five methods are frequently used in providing instruction: verbal cueing, modeling, arranging the environment, gesturing, and providing physical assistance. These are all "error-free" teaching approaches. Error-free methods ensure that the person learning a new skill makes a correct response and that learning takes place in a positive manner.

ERROR-FREE TEACHING REFERS TO THOSE TECHNIQUES DE-
SIGNED TO ASSIST THE PERSON TO BE SUCCESSFUL IN
LEARNING A NEW SKILL.

The goal of error-free teaching is to assist people to progress from dependence to independence in performing a skill or behavior. Error-free techniques are gradually withdrawn as the skill is learned. Procedures to reduce or eliminate the assistance are called *fading techniques*. By systematically reducing the amount of assistance provided, these techniques contribute to independent performance of the behavior.

FADING INVOLVES THE GRADUAL WITHDRAWAL OF AS-
SISTANCE UNTIL IT IS NO LONGER NEEDED.

Verbal Cues

Verbal cues help the person to be successful in learning new behaviors by providing the desired response to the person. This method can provide all or part of the necessary feedback. For example, to teach a person how to verbally identify an object, your verbal cue might be, "What is this? Say 'pants.'" Success is guaranteed by providing the answer. The appropriate use of verbal cues in an instructional strategy depends on the person. Verbal cues are generally appropriate for the person who understands one- or two-step commands and some abstract words, but they do not help the person who does not understand verbal messages.

VERBAL CUES PROVIDE SPOKEN INFORMATION TO ENSURE A
CORRECT RESPONSE.

Fading Procedures

Fading procedures are used to eliminate assistance. For instance, to add a fading procedure to the example above, you provide less and less of the cue until the cue is no longer needed. Table 2 demonstrates the fading of verbal cues into such an instructional program. Notice how the sequence goes from dependence to independence in logical steps.

FADING PROCEDURES ARE LISTED IN SEQUENTIAL, LOGICAL
ORDER FROM DEPENDENCE TO INDEPENDENCE.

Modeling Procedures

Modeling involves demonstrating the behavior to be learned. The amount of the behavior you model when you begin the instruction

Table 2. Fading of verbal cues

1. The counselor asks "What is this?" and then says, "pants."
2. The counselor asks "What is this?" and then says, "pan--."
3. The counselor asks "What is this?" and then says, "p---."
4. The counselor asks "What is this?"

depends on the needs of the individual. For example, in teaching a person to hammer a nail, you might say, "Hammer the nail." Then you would pick up the hammer and hit the nail.

MODELING INVOLVES DEMONSTRATING THE BEHAVIOR TO BE LEARNED.

Modeling procedures are generally appropriate for individuals who have the visual, cognitive, and motor abilities to imitate your movements. Modeling is not appropriate for persons who cannot imitate simple motor tasks. After modeling the appropriate behavior for a time, you include fading procedures. Table 3 represents the combination of modeling and fading procedures. Again, the instructional sequence goes from dependence to independence in a logical order.

Arranging the Environment

Arranging the environment is another error-free teaching technique. This method makes it easier for a person to perform a behavior by changing aspects of the person's immediate environment. The focus of the instructional strategy is on the environment, not on the individual. For example, oversized bags can be helpful in teaching a person how to package products in bags. Fading can be combined with arranging the environment. Over time, the size of the bag can be decreased until a regular bag is used.

Table 3. Fading of modeling procedures

1. The job coach says,"Hammer the nail" and then picks up the hammer, raises the hammer overhead, lowers hammer, strikes nail, and puts the hammer down.
2. The job coach says,"Hammer the nail" and then picks up the hammer, raises the hammer overhead, lowers the hammer, and strikes the nail.
3. The job coach says,"Hammer the nail" and then picks up the hammer, raises the hammer overhead, and lowers the hammer.
4. The job coach says, "Hammer the nail" and then picks up the hammer and raises the hammer overhead.
5. The job coach says,"Hammer the nail" and then picks up the hammer.
6. The job coach says, "Hammer the nail."

> MAKING CHANGES IN THE ENVIRONMENT ASSISTS THE PERSON TO COMPLETE A TASK.

Table 4 illustrates the use of physical changes in the environment, along with a fading technique, to teach a person to put letters in an envelope. Arranging the environment is useful in most instructional situations. It can be especially helpful for the person learning or performing motor behaviors.

Gesturing

Gesturing is another type of error-free teaching technique. Gestures are movements or expressions that bring about the desired behavior. Most people use gestures in communicating with others. For example, you may point to the desk when asking for a piece of paper, shake your head to express disapproval of a person's behavior, or develop a gesture code to indicate to a friend when you wish to leave a party.

> GESTURES CONSIST OF MOVEMENTS OR EXPRESSIONS THAT ELICIT THE DESIRED BEHAVIOR.

Gestures are effective teaching techniques for the person who needs only a little assistance in completing a desired behavior. A program to instruct a person to recognize his or her house key by using gestures is illustrated in Table 5. The program also includes fading techniques.

Physical Assistance

In this error-free teaching technique, you physically assist the person through a desired behavior. This procedure is commonly used for people with severe disabilities. It is also often used as an instructional approach in learning activities of daily living, such as dressing and eating. Finally, it is useful for teaching sequential motor tasks. Table 6 illustrates a program that combines physical assistance and fading to teach a person to take off his or her socks.

Table 4. Fading of arranging the environment

1. The job coach says,"Put the letter in the envelope" and hands the employee a 13" × 18" envelope.
2. The job coach says,"Put the letter in the envelope" and hands the employee a 10" × 15" envelope.
3. The job coach says,"Put the letter in the envelope" and hands the employee a 7" × 12" envelope.
4. The job coach says,"Put the letter in the envelope" and hands the employee a letter-size envelope.

Table 5. Fading of gestures

---

1. Roommate says, "Show me your house key" and then holds a finger on the key.
2. Roommate says, "Show me your house key" and then holds a finger 2 inches from the key.
3. Roommate says, "Show me your house key" and then holds a finger 4 inches from the key.
4. Roommate says, "Show me your house key."

PHYSICAL ASSISTANCE INVOLVES PHYSICALLY ASSISTING THE PERSON THROUGH A BEHAVIOR.

Determine Your Reaction to a Correct or Incorrect Response

Error-free learning techniques provide the person with opportunities for repetition of the desired behavior. Positive reinforcement is provided for completing the behavior even though assistance is given. You must carefully consider the person and his or her abilities and preferred learning styles. The method of instruction must follow logical steps that lead from dependence to independence.

Successful use of error-free learning techniques requires that you decide ahead of time how you will respond to behaviors. If these responses are not planned, they may be inconsistent or random and delay learning. What do you plan to do when the person accomplishes a task? Will you use verbal praise? What exactly will you say? You must also decide what to do if the person gives an incorrect response. Will you say, "No," ignore the response, or turn your head for 3–5 seconds? Again, you must plan your response in advance. Your behavior must be predictable.

DURING THE INSTRUCTION, YOUR BEHAVIOR MUST BE PREDICTABLE TO THE PERSON WITH WHOM YOU ARE WORKING.

Table 6. Fading of physical assistance

---

1. The counselor says, "Take off your socks" and then grasps the person's hand and removes the sock.
2. The counselor says, "Take off your socks" and then guides the person's hand from the wrist.
3. The counselor says, "Take off your socks" and then taps the person's hand. The person completes the behavior.
4. The counselor says, "Take off your socks."

Decide When To Move to the Next Step

You must decide when to move the person from dependence to increased independence. For example, assume you are using physical assistance to teach a person to take off his or her socks. You will have to change from physically completing the behavior to guiding the person with your fingertips. The time spent on each step in the fading sequence is extremely important. If you spend too much time on a step, the person may become dependent on your help. If you move too quickly, however, the person may become confused. He or she may not have completely mastered the previous step, and moving to the next step will only decrease the chance for success. The decision to move to the next step depends on successful performance of the previous step. A general rule is to move to the next step in the fading sequence after the person demonstrates three consecutive correct responses.

Select Instructional Materials and Appropriate Setting

Planning the teaching strategy also requires selection of the materials and location for the instruction. Decide on the materials in advance. Do you need, for example, paper, pencils, a sink, a hammer, or drill? In terms of location, the instructional environment affects the person's performance. You must determine, for example, whether the person works best alone or in a group situation. Whenever possible, teaching should occur in the place where the skill or behavior will be most frequently performed. For instance, dressing skills should be taught in the bedroom or bathroom, not in a classroom. It is best to teach a new skill step-by-step in a real-life setting.

THE PREFERRED METHOD FOR TEACHING A NEW SKILL IS TO TEACH IT STEP-BY-STEP IN A REAL-LIFE SETTING.

Identify Opportunities for Practice and Generalization

Finally, you should identify opportunities for the individual to practice and generalize the new behavior or skill. Practice and generalization mean that the individual can try out the skill under different circumstances. Having time to practice and generalize a new skill in natural settings is as important as having the opportunity to learn the skill. Finally, if the individual has few opportunities to learn and practice the skill in natural settings, you should question why you are teaching it.

IF THERE ARE FEW OPPORTUNITIES TO LEARN AND PRACTICE THE SKILL IN NATURAL SETTINGS, QUESTION WHY YOU ARE TEACHING IT.

IMPLEMENTING THE INSTRUCTIONAL PLAN

The best instructional plans are written documents. Figure 1 depicts a form for organizing your instructional strategies, all the elements of which have been discussed here. Figure 2 is an example of a completed form. Note how the information is placed on the form. After completing this form, you are prepared to teach the behavior. In addition, should you be unable to continue working with an individual, another staff member may pick up the form and know exactly what you are working on, what materials and settings to use, and even what to say during your absence.

Teaching Procedures

Teaching requires a systematic procedure that allows the individual to learn a skill in a step-by-step sequence. Two such procedures are *forward chaining* and *backward chaining*.

Forward chaining involves teaching the skill beginning with the first step in the task analysis coupled with the first step in the selected sequence of fading. The trials are presented until the criterion for movement between program steps is achieved. The instructor proceeds to the second step in the sequence of fading while remaining on the first task in the task analysis. Instruction continues until the person performs the first task of the task analysis independently. The training session then focuses on the second step of the task analysis. Figure 3 visually describes this process.

Backward chaining involves teaching the skill beginning with the last step in the task analysis coupled with the first step in the sequence of fading. In backward chaining, the instructor applies the full support of the selected error-free strategy for all tasks in the task analysis but is concerned with applying the sequence of fading with the last step. Trials are presented until the criterion for movement between program steps is achieved. Providing total support for all tasks except the last, the instructor then proceeds to the second step in the sequence of fading. Once the task is performed independently, the next to the last step becomes the focus of fading procedures. Figure 4 visually represents this process.

Individuals with developmental disabilities learn skills faster with the use of backward chaining, but the training technique generally has no effect on retention of the skills once they have been learned.

FORWARD CHAINING INVOLVES WORKING FROM BEGINNING TO END UNTIL THE BEHAVIOR IS LEARNED.

BACKWARD CHAINING INVOLVES WORKING FROM END TO BEGINNING UNTIL THE BEHAVIOR IS LEARNED.

138

Person's name: _____   Date started: _____
Program implementor: _____   Date completed: _____
Program area: _____
Behavioral objective: _____

Instructional statement: _____
Task analysis: _____   Sequence for fading cues: _____
_____   _____
_____   _____
_____   _____
_____
_____
_____

Consequences: A.   Correct response — _____
                B.   Incorrect response — _____

Criterion level of acceptable behavior for movement between program steps: _____

Materials: _____
Setting: _____
Opportunities for practice/generalization: _____

Figure 1.   Form for organizing an instructional strategy.

Person's name: _John Smith_   Date started: _1-4-93_

Program implementor: _Tom Winner_   Date completed: _____

Program area: _Activities of Daily Living_

Behavioral objective: _Given a command, John will wash his hands correctly 4 out of 5_
times requested on 3 consecutive days.

Instructional statement: _"John, wash your hands."_

Task analysis:

1. Turn on water.   6. Rinse hands.

2. Pick up soap.   7. Turn off water.

3. Rub soap on hands.   8. Dry hands.

4. Put soap down.

5. Rub hands together.

Sequence for fading cues:

     A. Grasp John's hands; complete the behavior.

     B. Guide John's hands with finger tips.

     C. Guide John's hands from wrist.

     D. Tap John's hands; John completes the
         behavior.

Consequences: A. Correct response — _"Good hand washing."_

            B. Incorrect response — _State firmly, "No, John," plus ignore response by_
                                   turning head 3-5 seconds.

Criterion level of acceptable behavior for movement between program steps: _3 consecutive correct_
responses

Materials: _soap, towel, data sheet, pencil_

Setting: _bathroom, kitchen_

Opportunities for practice/generalization: _In the morning, prior to meals._

Figure 2. Example of a completed instructional strategy form.

139

Task analysis

1. Turn on water
2. Pick up soap
3. Rub soap on hands
4. Put soap down
5. Rub hands together
6. Rinse hands
7. Turn off water
8. Dry hands

Sequence of fading

1. Grasp hands and complete the behavior
2. Guide hands with fingertips
3. Tap hand to initiate behavior
4. Instructional command only

Figure 3. Forward chaining method of teaching. (From Gardner, J.F., & Chapman, M.S. [1990]. *Program issues in developmental disabilities: A guide to effective habilitation and active treatment* [2nd ed.] [p. 176]. Baltimore: Paul H. Brookes Publishing Co.; reprinted by permission.)

Regardless of the chaining sequence used, instruction should focus on the individual's ability to learn each step and to combine the step with other steps in the sequence to complete the desired behavior. Instruction moves from one step to the next when the individual demonstrates the ability to complete the step without assistance. During the teaching process, assistance is provided to help the individual learn the steps in the program. This assistance must be systematically reduced to allow the individual to perform the step as independently as possible. Fading procedures reduce the assistance needed by the individual with a developmental disability during each step. After he or she has correctly completed a step with the least assistance, you begin teaching the next step in the sequence.

Data Collection

The success of your instruction is increased by effective data collection methods. Data collection and analysis are as important as the written

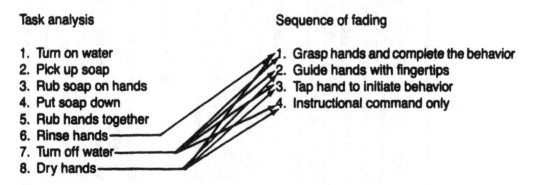

Task analysis

1. Turn on water
2. Pick up soap
3. Rub soap on hands
4. Put soap down
5. Rub hands together
6. Rinse hands
7. Turn off water
8. Dry hands

Sequence of fading

1. Grasp hands and complete the behavior
2. Guide hands with fingertips
3. Tap hand to initiate behavior
4. Instructional command only

Figure 4. Backward chaining method of teaching. (From Gardner, J.F., & Chapman, M.S. [1990]. *Program issues in developmental disabilities: A guide to effective habilitation and active treatment* [2nd ed.] [p. 177]. Baltimore: Paul H. Brookes Publishing Co.; reprinted by permission.)

program. Like windows to your program, they show whether your planned teaching procedure is successful and may help you determine why your teaching is not more effective. Compiling results also provides a way to communicate to others what your program is accomplishing.

EXERCISE 1

Data Collection

Determine what type of data is collected on programs for two people. Are the data similar? If not, why are they different?

There are many different ways to collect data. Figure 5 shows one method used to document the progress made on a program. This data sheet is designed to use with the instructional strategy form (see Figure 1). It has spaces for restating information about your program; you do not have to refer back frequently to the written program. Space is also provided for responses to 10 separate trials. Figures 6 and 7 illustrate two examples of completed data sheets for a hand-washing program. A trial is provided each time the instructional statement, "John, wash your hands," is given. A "+" in the box indicates a correct response. A "−" in the box indicates an incorrect response. Studying your data at the end of each day helps you to evaluate the teaching strategy.

The data in Figure 6 suggest the following:

1. In 15 minutes of teaching, the person accomplished two steps in the program, A and B, and is currently working on step C: Drying hands while the instructor guides hands from wrist.
2. The task analysis and fading procedures appear correct.
3. The choice of reinforcers appears appropriate.
4. The correction procedures appear effective.

The data in Figure 7 suggest the following:

1. The person moved from step A to step B in the fading procedures: dry hands while instructor guides hands with fingertips.
2. The person appears to be stuck on step B.

If the person continues to show little success you should reevaluate the following (in the order listed):

1. The reinforcer used
2. The task analysis
3. The sequence of fading
4. The assessment data

DATA SHEET

Person's name: _____

Behavioral objective: _____

Task analysis:

1. _____
2. _____
3. _____
4. _____
5. _____

Sequence of fading:

A. _____
B. _____
C. _____
D. _____
E. _____

Date	Reinforcer used	Task analysis	Sequence of fading	Trials										Comments
				1	2	3	4	5	6	7	8	9	10	

Figure 5. Data sheet for documenting program progress.

DATA SHEET

Person's name: _John Smith_

Behavioral objective: _Given a command, John will wash his hands correctly 4 out of 5 times requested on 3 consecutive days._

Task analysis:
1. Turn on water.
2. Pick up soap.
3. Rub soap on hands.
4. Put soap down.
5. Rub hands together.
6. Rinse hands.
7. Turn off water.
8. Dry hands.

Sequence of fading:
A. Grasp hands and complete the behavior.
B. Guide hands with fingertips.
C. Guide hands from wrist.
D. Tap hands.
E. _____

Date	Reinforcer used	Task analysis	Sequence of fading	Trials										Comments
				1	2	3	4	5	6	7	8	9	10	
1-4-93	Tokens	(1-7)8	A	+	+	+								
1-4-93	Tokens	(1-7)8	B	+	+	+								
1-4-93	Tokens	(1-7)8	C	+	-	+	-	+	+	-	+			

Figure 6. Example No. 1 of a completed data sheet for documenting program progress.

DATA SHEET

Person's name: ___John Smith___

Behavioral objective: ___Given a command, John will wash his hands correctly 4 out of 5 times requested on 3 consecutive days.___

Task analysis:
1. Turn on water.
2. Pick up soap.
3. Rub soap on hands.
4. Put soap down.
5. Rub hands together.
6. Rinse hands.
7. Turn off water.
8. Dry hands.

Sequence of fading:
A. Grasp hands and complete the behavior.
B. Guide hands with fingertips.
C. Guide hands from wrist.
D. Tap hands.
E.

Date	Reinforcer used	Task analysis	Sequence of fading	1	2	3	4	5	6	7	8	9	10	Comments
1-4-93	Potato chips	(1-7) 8	A	+	+	+								
1-4-93	Potato chips	(1-7) 8	B	-	-	+	-	-	-	-	+	-	-	

Trials

Figure 7.   Example No. 2 of a completed data sheet for documenting program progress.

Begin with a review of the reinforcers. Noneffective reinforcers will not motivate people to work. Use another reinforcer from the reinforcement menu. Immediate changes in performance signal a solution to the problem.

If there is no change in performance after introducing the new reinforcer, review the task analysis. Are the steps in the task analysis too large? Is a particular step in the program too difficult? The step in the task analysis may need to be further broken down. For example, the step "dry hands" could be broken down into the following seven steps:

1. Pick up towel in left hand
2. Rub back of right hand with towel
3. Rub palm side of hand with towel
4. Transfer towel from left hand to right hand
5. Rub back of left hand with towel
6. Rub palm of left hand with towel
7. Put towel on counter

If the task analysis is sufficient, review the selected fading technique. Should you have chosen a different technique? Do you need to add additional steps to the fading procedure?

Finally, if the adjustments do not increase learning or performance, review the assessment data. The objective may be inappropriate for the person. The interdisciplinary team may have to set new program objectives.

PROVIDING OPPORTUNITIES FOR PRACTICE AND GENERALIZATION

In addition to teaching the skill in natural settings, it is also important to provide multiple opportunities for the individual to practice the skill as it is being learned. Generalization refers to the use of a skill in various settings and situations. An important aspect of planning an instructional strategy is to make sure that the person with a developmental disability has opportunities to practice and generalize the skill being taught. If you cannot readily identify multiple opportunities for the individual to use the skill you are teaching, the skill may not be that important to the individual. You should then consider substituting a skill that is more useful.

SUMMARY

Instruction is a planned, structured activity. Certain techniques are helpful in developing instructional strategies. The six steps of planning are:

1. Determine if the behavior is simple or complex. If the behavior is complex, determine if a task analysis is needed.
2. Select the instructional methods and a strategy for eliminating assistance.
3. Determine your reaction to a correct or incorrect response.
4. Decide when to move to the next step in the instructional strategy.
5. Select instructional materials and identify the appropriate setting for the instruction.
6. Identify opportunities for practice and generalization of the new behavior.

The instructional objective sheet is needed for development of a written intervention plan. The form provides areas for delineating the task analysis, fading procedures, and correct and incorrect responses. The sheet also lists the opportunities for practice and generalization of the skill being learned. Practice and generalization refer to the performance of the behavior in a natural setting. Teaching should, when possible, take place in natural settings.

The instructional strategy form is a working document of the instruction provided to the person with a developmental disability. Because this form is a working document, it will change. In fact, it is rare that a program is written and implemented without being changed in some way.

Data collection is a critical aspect of your instruction. Data provide information regarding the effectiveness of the program and document the need for changes within the program. This information offers a means of communication with other team members and can be used to plan and record successes in accomplishing program goals and objectives.

BIBLIOGRAPHY

Chapman, M.S. (1990). Implementation strategies. In J.F. Gardner & M.S. Chapman, *Program issues in developmental disabilities: A guide to effective habilitation and active treatment* (pp. 161–185). Baltimore: Paul H. Brookes Publishing Co.

Lakin, K.C., & Bruininks, R.H. (Eds.). (1985). *Strategies for achieving community integration of developmentally disabled citizens.* Baltimore: Paul H. Brookes Publishing Co.

ADDITIONAL RESOURCES

M.A. Falvey (1989), in *Community-based curriculum: Instructional strategies for students with severe handicaps* (2nd ed.) (Baltimore: Paul H. Brookes Publishing Co.), provides additional information on instructional strategies.

R. Gaylord-Ross and J. Holvoet (1985), in *Strategies for educating students with severe handicaps* (Boston: Little, Brown), focus on intervention strategies for school-age individuals.

SELF-APPRAISAL

INSTRUCTIONS

The following questions will help you evaluate your knowledge about developing instructional strategies. For true-false questions, check the correct answer. For multiple choice questions, circle the correct answer(s).

Note: There may be more than one correct answer for some questions.

1. Providing instruction to another person is a planned, systematic process.
    ___ True   ___ False
2. Simple behaviors stand alone; they cannot be broken down.
    ___ True   ___ False
3. Complex behaviors include:
    a. Sitting
    b. Starting a car
    c. Holding an object
    d. Washing your hands
4. Task analysis is:
    a. A list of behaviors in the order in which they occur
    b. Based on medical diagnosis
    c. Completed with gestures and verbal cues only
    d. Not an instructional strategy
5. Error-free teaching techniques ensure that the person learning a new skill will make a correct response.
    ___ True   ___ False
6. Error-free teaching techniques include which of the following:
    a. Verbal cues
    b. Modeling
    c. Gestures
    d. Physical assistance
7. Fading procedures involve the gradual withdrawal of assistance until it is no longer needed.
    ___ True   ___ False
8. Gesturing refers to which of the following:
    a. Showing or demonstrating the behavior
    b. Changing the environment to expedite the performance of a behavior
    c. Using movement or expressions to indicate the desired behavior
    d. Physically putting the person through the behavior

9. The best instructional plan is written.
   ___ True   ___ False

10. Data collection on the instructional strategy will tell you which of the following:
   a. If the reinforcer is effective
   b. If correction procedures are appropriate
   c. If the task analysis is appropriate for the person with a developmental disability
   d. If the fading procedures are effective

CASE STUDY

Robert Daniels is a 53-year-old male with a diagnosis of severe mental retardation and a seizure disorder. Mr. Daniels has lived in a large state-operated intermediate care facility for the mentally retarded (ICF/MR) since he was 18 years old. The county service coordination program has been working with Mr. Daniels, the ICF/MR, and a local residential provider to begin Mr. Daniels's transition into a four-person group home.

The institution staff have expressed concern about Mr. Daniels's ability to change his place of residence at age 53, as well as about the possibility of injury resulting from seizures. The community residential staff are concerned about these issues, but feel Mr. Daniels should move to the group home.

The service coordinator has identified a day program for Mr. Daniels. Many of Mr. Daniels's friends from the institution attend the program, which stresses socialization skills and leisure-time skills. The day program supplements the leisure-time program by transporting all 38 participants on community field trips to the local playground, swimming pool, restaurant, and other places.

The group home staff plan to develop more age- and culturally appropriate leisure-time activities for Mr. Daniels. They also plan to collect data over a 2-month period to document the frequency and type of his seizure activity. This information will be used in determining whether Mr. Daniels should continue to wear a protective helmet. Mr. Daniels has indicated to the service coordinator that he does not want to wear a helmet.

Situation

During a recent meeting, the group home staff reviewed their instructional strategies developed to assist Mr. Daniels in learning a new task. One staff member felt that Mr. Daniels was not making progress as rapidly as he is capable of doing; however, he had no data on the progress made. Mr. Daniels has indicated a desire to prepare hot meals.

1. Discuss the relationship between data collection and instructional strategies.
2. Identify and discuss key questions that the staff should ask in the development of an instructional strategy to teach Mr. Daniels how to prepare hot meals.
3. Develop a task analysis for preparing a can of hot soup.

ANSWER KEY TO
SELF-APPRAISAL AND CASE STUDY

SELF-APPRAISAL

1. True
2. True
3. b, d
4. a
5. True
6. a, b, c, d
7. True
8. c
9. True
10. a, b, c, d

CASE STUDY ANSWER GUIDELINES

1. Data collection is a critical part of the instructional strategy. It provides information regarding the effectiveness of the established program and documents the need for changes within the program. It also provides the means for communicating information about Mr. Daniels to other people. It documents the success of your instructional strategies.

2. For any instructional strategy, the success of your program depends on the planning involved. The following should be determined for each instructional program:

    Determine if the behavior is simple or complex. If the behavior is complex, determine if a task analysis is needed.

    Select the instructional method and a strategy for eliminating any assistance provided.

    Determine your reaction to a correct or incorrect response.

    Decide when to move to the next step in the instructional strategy.

    Select instructional materials and the appropriate settings for the instruction.

    Identify opportunities for the practice and generalization of the new behavior.

3. The number of steps in the task analysis depends on Mr. Daniels's abilities. The steps in the task analysis appear in the sequence in which they occur. New steps can be added or existing steps omitted after instruction begins. The task analysis for preparing a can of hot soup includes:

Open can
Pour contents into a saucepan
Add water to saucepan
Put saucepan on burner
Turn on burner to low heat
Bring soup to boil
Turn off burner

| chapter 8 | Identifying and Measuring Behaviors |

LEARNING OBJECTIVES

Upon completing this chapter, the reader will be able to:

1. Define the word *behavior* and list five behaviors.
2. Identify the difference between a "behavior" and an "attitude."
3. State two reasons why it is important to speak in behavioral terms.
4. State two ways of measuring behaviors.
5. Graph a behavior by using percentages.
6. Graph a behavior by using tally data.

INTRODUCTION

This chapter explores behaviors. It defines what behaviors are and what they are not. It also discusses the importance of defining another person's behavior. Methods of observing and recording the behavior are reviewed. The importance of using behavioral terms in the design of behavior management programs is presented. The chapter concludes with a discussion on how to use a graph to present a visual picture of the information about a behavior.

DEFINING BEHAVIORS

A behavior is anything a person does that is observable and measurable. A behavior can be seen and counted. Some words are used to describe attitudes or feelings that you cannot see or measure. These words are not behaviors. Consider the word *happy*. Happy is an attitude or feeling. You cannot see happy. What you can see are behaviors, such as smiling or laughing, which only make you think that a person is happy.

Someone else could look at that same person and think that he or she is not happy, even though what you both see are smiles and laughter. This is the difference between a behavior and an attitude. Such words as *lazy*, *sad*, *fearful*, and *nervous* are other examples of attitudes or feelings. They are labels, not behaviors.

EXERCISE 1

Identifying Behavior

Observe a person for 3–5 minutes. List the behaviors you see during this time. Check to make sure you have listed behaviors and not attitudes by asking yourself these three questions about each item on your list:

1. Can you observe it (see and/or hear)?
2. Can you count it?
3. If someone else observed the same person, would his or her list of observed behaviors be the same as yours?

If the answers to these three questions are yes, then you have identified behaviors.

When describing a person's behavior use specific words to indicate what the individual is doing. Using concise words that characterize behavior and not attitudes or feelings improves your communication with other people. Other staff members have a clearer understanding of the person with whom you are working when you use behavioral terms. Table 1 illustrates the difference between behaviors and attitudes.

To many people, the word *behavior* implies bad things. When asked to describe a person's behavior, many agency staff members use negative words in their descriptions. Examples are: "He screams constantly," "Her behavior is awful," or "She hits her sister." It is important to remember that the definition of a behavior requires that it be observed and counted. Not only can you observe a person scream, but you can also see that person sit quietly.

BEHAVIORS ARE OBSERVABLE AND MEASURABLE.

"Good" behaviors are as important to recognize as "bad" behaviors. Behaviors also include skill performance. It is necessary to observe and measure new skills that people learn.

Consider the statement, "Mary cries all day long." "Cries" is a behavior. Analyze the rest of the statement, "all day long." What do you think of when you hear someone say that Mary cries all day long? You probably envision Mary waking in the morning and crying *all day long*

Table 1. Examples of behaviors versus attitudes

Common behaviors	Attitudes or labels
Ties shoes	Lazy
Stacks blocks	Sad
Writes name	Disobedient
Shaves	Fearful
Screams	Sluggish
Adds 1 + 1	Joyful
Drives car	Depressed
Types letter	Lucky
Washes hands	Cheerful
Kicks ball	Courageous
Puts on shirt	Unhappy
Cuts food with knife	Melancholy
Sits in chair	Dismal
Uses napkin	Passive
Slams door	Loyal
Walks	Friendly
Folds clothes	Nice
Makes tea	Bored
Follows directions	Aggressive
Swims	Angry

until she goes to bed at night. Now that is a big behavior problem! Do you think the staff member meant all day long, or did it only seem like all day long? With further questioning, you might discover that Mary did not, in fact, cry all day long. Rather she cried three times a day for about 15 minutes each time. Without clarifying the terms used, Mary's behavior would have been interpreted incorrectly and poor recommendations made on how to handle the situation.

Here is another example: "Tony has several seizures a day." How many seizures are several: 10, 7, 2, 18, 20? What kind of seizures did Tony have? How serious is the problem? The word *several* is too vague. The statement, "Tony had three tonic-clonic seizures today," provides a more exact statement of the situation.

These examples emphasize the need for being specific and for using behavioral terms when discussing skills and behaviors. By stating information in exact behavioral terms you:

1. Have a better understanding of what the situation is.
2. Provide clear communication to other staff members.
3. Give precise information about the person with whom you are working.
4. Identify actions that must be taken.

EXERCISE 2

Using Exact Behavioral Descriptions

Compare the following two reports written by different schoolteachers. Which report gives you more information about the student?

Report One

Michael has shown a great deal of progress during the past quarter. This is especially true in math, which he greatly enjoys learning. He has also shown progress in reading.

He could still improve his lazy attitude toward his other assignments. He doesn't like art, is a poor communicator, and becomes easily frustrated in social situations.

Please work on these skills at home. Thank you.

Report Two

Jane has shown a great deal of progress during the past quarter. This is especially true in math. She has learned to add fractions and to divide two digits by 2 and 3. In reading, Jane has completed the third-year reader.

She could use some help in her art classes. She compares her artwork with that of other children and often feels that hers is not as good. We have been encouraging her to work independently and to judge her own art projects without making comparisons to others. We have been helping Jane to state what she wants to do during free time. In social situations, Jane is learning to introduce one friend to another by saying, for example, "Mr. Jones, I want you to meet my friend, John. John, this is Mr. Jones."

Which report would be most helpful to you if you wanted to work on these skills at home? By comparing these two reports, you can see the importance of speaking or writing in behavioral terms.

DATA COLLECTION AND GRAPHING

In order to analyze a person's behavior in detail, it may be necessary to collect written information, or data, about the behavior. The data give a precise report about the skill or behavior. You can use the information to design a behavior management program. Sometimes, staff members use words such as "all the time," "most of the time," "frequently," or "many" to describe a behavior. If the staff members then collect and graph data, they may find that the behavior is occurring more or less frequently than they had thought. For this reason, data are collected before a behavior management program is started.

GRAPHING DATA PRODUCES A PRECISE REPORT ABOUT A SKILL
OR BEHAVIOR.

Baseline Data

Quantitative information collected before the beginning of a program is called baseline data. This information (expressed in terms of quantity) describes a person's behavior before you begin an intervention program. Later, these data can be compared with data collected during the program. By analyzing this information, you will know whether your program is effective in changing the behavior. You can determine:

1. If your procedure is working
2. If your procedure caused an unintended effect on the behavior

BASELINE DATA ARE COLLECTED BEFORE THE INTERVENTION
PROGRAM.

Collection Methods

Two methods used in collecting data are: 1) the tally, or frequency, method and 2) the interval method.

Tally Method

This method is generally used when the behavior occurs infrequently or lasts only for a short time. For example, assume you are an instructor in a day program. You are concerned with the number of times a person inappropriately places objects in his mouth. Pick a time of the day that you are free to collect data. Also select a duration of time for observation. Once you have chosen an amount of time, collect the data at the same time every day for the same amount of time.

THE TALLY METHOD FOR COLLECTING DATA IS MOST HELPFUL
WHEN THE BEHAVIOR:

OCCURS INFREQUENTLY
LASTS FOR A SHORT PERIOD OF TIME

On a piece of paper provide columns for recording the date, the time of day, and the behavior you are observing. Insert a mark on the paper each time the person puts inappropriate objects in his mouth. At the end of the observation period, simply total the number of times the behavior has occurred. Continue this process until you can identify a frequency in the behavior. The baseline data indicate the average number of times the behavior occurs.

Once the baseline data are collected, you can begin the intervention program. Continue collecting data every day. Data collected during the intervention phase can then be compared with the baseline data. This comparison tells you if a change has occurred in the specific skill or behavior. A form for utilizing the tally method is illustrated in Figure 1.

Interval Method

This method is used for measuring behaviors that occur frequently, perhaps almost constantly, or for long periods of time. Examples of these behaviors are constant movement, rocking, and talking. It would be difficult to use the tally method for collecting continuous and accurate data on these types of behaviors. In addition, the tally method is not appropriate with behaviors of long or continuous duration. For example, if you collected data on talking between 9:00 A.M. and 9:10 A.M. and the person talked the entire 10 minutes, do you conclude that he or she talked only once?

When using the interval method, pick a time of day to collect the information and decide how long to collect it. Write this on a piece of paper. Then divide the paper into intervals of time—perhaps 10-second intervals—for the entire 10 minutes. Using a stopwatch or the

Behavior observed: _____

Date	Time	Number of times behavior occurred	Total

Figure 1. Form for utilizing the tally method of collecting data.

second hand on your watch, place an X in the interval box if the behavior occurs at all during the interval of time. Continue to record data in this manner until the entire 10 minutes have passed. The data can be described in terms of the percentage of 10-second intervals during which the behavior occurred. The 10-minute, 10-second interval method sheet is shown in Figure 2.

To calculate the percentage of 10-second intervals the behavior occurred, use the following formula: Divide the number of boxes containing an X by the total number of boxes and multiply the result by 100.

TO CALCULATE THE PERCENTAGE OF 10-SECOND INTERVALS
THE BEHAVIOR OCCURRED:

$$\frac{\text{BOXES WITH X}}{\text{NUMBER OF BOXES} \times 100} = \text{PERCENTAGE}$$

As with the tally method, continue to collect the baseline data until you can detect a pattern in the behavior. Continue to collect data after you begin your intervention program. Compare the data collected during the intervention program with the baseline data to determine if there is a change in the skill or behavior.

THE INTERVAL METHOD FOR COLLECTING DATA IS MOST USE-
FUL WHEN THE BEHAVIOR:

OCCURS FREQUENTLY
OCCURS FOR LONG PERIODS OF TIME

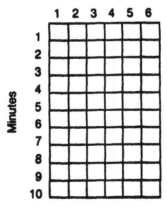

Figure 2. Form for utilizing the 10-minute, 10-second interval method of collecting data.

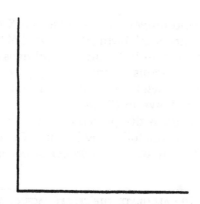

Figure 3. Step 1 in building a graph: Make two lines, one vertical and one horizontal.

Graphing

The data collected for your behavior management program can be shown as a picture in the form of a graph. A graph visually shows what is happening to the behavior you are attempting to change. To build a graph, begin by making two lines, one vertical and one horizontal, as shown in Figure 3.

Then add hash marks that are at an equal distance from each other, as shown in Figure 4. Uniform distance ensures that any changes in behavior are graphed in a uniform manner.

Number the vertical line to show either tally marks or percentages, as represented in Figure 5.

The sessions, days, or dates are inserted on the horizontal line as depicted in Figure 6.

You are now ready to graph the data you have collected. For example, assume that for 5 days you collected baseline data for the person

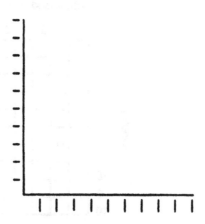

Figure 4. Step 2 in building a graph: Add hash marks at an equal distance from each other.

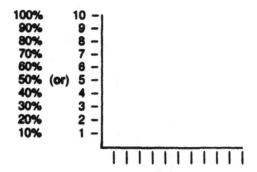

Figure 5. Step 3 in building a graph: Number the vertical line to show either tally marks or percentages.

who put inappropriate objects in his mouth. The following information was collected for the number of times the person placed objects in his mouth between 9:00 A.M. and 9:15 A.M.:

Day 1—10 times
Day 2— 8 times
Day 3— 7 times
Day 4—11 times
Day 5— 9 times

To obtain a visual picture of the baseline data, place a dot on the graph where the number of each day and the number of behaviors for that day intersect, as shown in Figure 7.

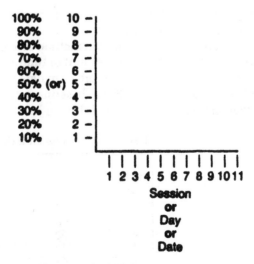

Figure 6. Step 4 in building a graph: Add sessions, days, or dates to the horizontal line.

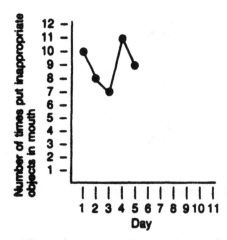

Figure 7. Graph showing baseline data for the number of times a behavior occurred.

Next, draw another vertical line on the graph corresponding to the day that the intervention program began. Assume that the following information was collected on the number of times the person placed inappropriate objects in his mouth between 9:00 A.M. and 9:15 A.M. for each of 5 days after the program begins:

Day 6—10 times
Day 7— 6 times
Day 8— 7 times
Day 9— 4 times
Day 10— 4 times

By graphing this information, you can demonstrate the change in the behavior, as shown in Figure 8.

Data collected by the interval method also can be graphed. Assume that you want to increase the amount of time a person spends on a task. Your baseline and intervention program data were taken from 9:30 A.M. to 9:40 A.M. each day. The 5-day baseline data and the 5-day intervention program data indicate the following:

Day % of the time on task

Day	% of the time on task
1	10
2	0
3	15
4	10
5	10
6	20
7	30
8	25
9	40
10	30

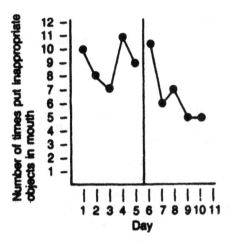

Figure 8. Completed graph for comparison of baseline data with intervention program data.

When using the interval method of data collection, put percentages on the vertical line and sessions on the horizontal line. Your completed graph, as shown in Figure 9, identifies changes in the behavior. The graph clearly shows that the percentage of time the person spent working on a task increased after the intervention program began. Graphing the data is a useful method for showing the impact of your program.

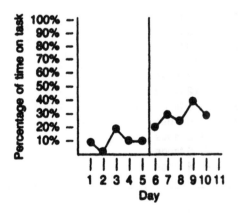

Figure 9. Graph showing data collected by the interval method.

EXERCISE 3

Graphing Your Data

Situation

Assume that you want to teach a person in your program to do light assembly work for longer periods of time. Your baseline data tell you the following about his work behavior:

Day 1—35% of the time working
Day 2—20% of the time working
Day 3—20% of the time working
Day 4—40% of the time working
Day 5—30% of the time working

On day 5, you decide to begin a program to increase the amount of time he works. The data over the next several days are:

Day 6—30% of the time working
Day 7—25% of the time working
Day 8—40% of the time working
Day 9—30% of the time working
Day 10—20% of the time working
Day 11—40% of the time working
Day 12—35% of the time working

Graph this data and indicate if the treatment program is working.

Situation

Using the tally method of data collection, you obtain data on a person who throws objects. The baseline was taken for 4 days and the treatment program for 7 days. Graph the following information and indicate if the treatment program is working:

Day 1—12 times
Day 2— 9 times
Day 3—10 times
Day 4—10 times
Day 5—13 times
Day 6—12 times
Day 7— 8 times
Day 8— 9 times
Day 9— 6 times
Day 10— 6 times
Day 11— 4 times

SUMMARY

This chapter stresses the importance of identifying and measuring behaviors. A behavior is anything a person does that is observable and measurable. Speaking in behavioral terms helps people to communicate and present clear information about behavior programs.

Data collection is a process whereby information is obtained and analyzed for a precise report about a skill or behavior. It also provides information about the seriousness of a problem and demonstrates the effectiveness of an intervention program.

A graph is a visual representation of the data collected. A graph shows patterns of behavior that result from your intervention. It tells you how effective the program is for the individual based on increases or decreases in the behavior.

BIBLIOGRAPHY

Baldwin, J.D., & Baldwin, J.I. (1986). *Behavior principles in everyday life.* Englewood Cliffs, NJ: Prentice Hall.

Walker, J.E., & Shea, T.M. (1988). *Behavior management: A practical approach for educators.* Columbus, OH: Charles E. Merrill.

ADDITIONAL RESOURCES

P.A. Alberto and A.C. Troutman (1990), in *Applied behavior analysis for teachers* (Columbus, OH: Charles E. Merrill), present information on identifying behaviors and collecting and graphing data on behaviors.

G. Bernstein, J. Ziarnik, E. Rudrud, and L. Czajkowski (1982), in *Behavioral habilitation through proactive programming* (Baltimore: Paul H. Brookes Publishing Co.), provide an overview of writing objectives and the use of behavior management in programs.

SELF-APPRAISAL

INSTRUCTIONS

The following questions will help you evaluate your knowledge about identifying and measuring behaviors. For true-false questions, check the correct answer. For multiple choice questions, circle the correct answer(s).

Note: There may be more than one correct answer for some questions.

1. Behaviors are learned. They can be unlearned.
   ___ True   ___ False
2. Which of the following describe a behavior?
   a. Observable and measurable
   b. Describable and measurable
   c. Observable and describable
   d. Observable only
3. Which of the following are behaviors?
   a. Runs
   b. Cries
   c. Sad
   d. Chews
4. Given the following information, complete a graph. Data were collected on the number of times a person puts objects in his mouth. The baseline behaviors took place over 5 days and the treatment program over the next 5. The data collected were:

   Day 1—10 times
   Day 2— 8 times
   Day 3— 7 times
   Day 4—11 times
   Day 5— 9 times
   Day 6—10 times
   Day 7— 6 times
   Day 8— 7 times
   Day 9— 4 times
   Day 10— 4 times

5. Using exact behavioral terms will:
   a. Clarify communications between staff
   b. Provide a clearer understanding of a situation
   c. Help determine the necessary actions to be taken in any situation
   d. All of the above

166

6. Collecting data will not help in designing a behavior management program.

    ___ True   ___ False

7. Which of the following provide(s) a good description of the frequency of a behavior?
   a. All of the time
   b. Most of the time
   c. Frequently
   d. 7 out of 10 times

8. Baseline data are collected at the end of every behavior management program.

    ___ True   ___ False

9. Data collection will tell you:
   a. If the behavior management procedure is working
   b. If the procedure is not working
   c. If the procedure has an unplanned effect on the behavior
   d. All of the above

10. The data you collect on your behavior management program can be shown as a picture in the form of a graph.

    ___ True   ___ False

CASE STUDY

Susan Williams is a 34-year-old woman who lives with her parents in Washington County, Maryland. She has Down syndrome and severe mental retardation. She is 43 pounds overweight. Her hearing and eyesight are normal.

At age 28, she entered a job training program at the county vocational center, operated by Tri-County Employment, Inc. She remained in that program for 6 years. For the past 6 months, she has worked in a job station at the nearby Holloway Inn.

Situation

Following her recent annual medical checkup, Ms. Williams received a follow-up note from her physician regarding her weight reduction program. In the report, the physician indicated the following:

a. You need to lose 43 pounds (reduce your weight from 153 pounds to 110 pounds).
b. You need to change personal and dietary habits to obtain this goal.
c. You need to become more energetic and less lethargic.
d. Your diet program will require that you be highly motivated and consistent in your approach.
e. You should consume no more than 1,200 calories per day.
f. For exercise, you should walk at least ½ mile per day.

Ms. Williams's parents are concerned about her ability to successfully follow the doctor's recommendations. Their major concern is that she snacks for ½ hour before each meal. They constantly remind her to refrain from snacking each day.

On the diet, Ms. Williams lost 2 pounds per week for the first 5 weeks, gained 1 pound during the 6th week, and didn't lose any weight during the next 3 weeks.

1. Review the physician's report. Underline those words that are labels and circle those words that are behaviors.
2. Design a data collection system to monitor Ms. Williams's snacking behavior.
3. Graph Ms. Williams's weight loss.

ANSWER KEY TO
SELF-APPRAISAL AND CASE STUDY

SELF-APPRAISAL

1. True
2. a
3. a, b, d
4.

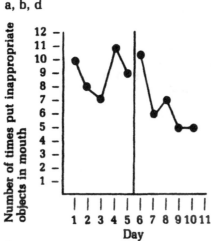

5. d
6. False
7. d
8. False
9. d
10. True

CASE STUDY ANSWER GUIDELINES

1. a. You need to (lose 43 pounds) (reduce your weight from 153 pounds to 110 pounds).
   b. You need to change personal and dietary <u>habits</u> to obtain this goal.
   c. You need to become more <u>energetic</u> and less <u>lethargic</u>.
   d. Your diet program will require that you be <u>highly motivated</u> and <u>consistent</u> in your approach.
   e. You should (consume) no more than 1,200 calories per day.
   f. For exercise, you should (walk) at least ½ mile per day.
2. In designing your collection system, use the tally method. You will need to consider the time when you will collect the data. Ms. Williams's mother reports that Susan snacks for ½ hour before

breakfast, lunch, and dinner. You need to clearly define the target behavior of snacking in writing prior to data collection.

3.

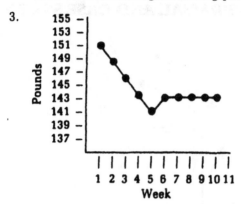

chapter	Principles of Behavior
9	Intervention

LEARNING OBJECTIVES

Upon completing this chapter, the reader will be able to:

1. Define behavior intervention strategies that focus on the antecedent of behaviors.
2. Define functional analysis.
3. Define strategies for selecting behaviors for change.
4. Define positive reinforcement.
5. Give four examples of secondary reinforcers.
6. State at least four rules for selecting reinforcers.
7. Define and give an example of the Premack principle.
8. State the differences between aversive and nonaversive behavior change strategies.

INTRODUCTION

This chapter is about behavior change. The process of behavior change requires an understanding of the purpose or function that the behavior serves for the person with a developmental disability. The chapter begins with a discussion of contemporary approaches to strategies for behavior change. You may find yourself in situations that require knowledge of reinforcement strategies. Therefore, this chapter defines reinforcement and discusses the types and schedules of reinforcement.

CONTEMPORARY APPROACHES TO BEHAVIOR CHANGE

Approaches to behavior change have evolved with the shift from institutional programs for individuals with developmental disabilities to

171

community-based programs. In an institutional setting, the staff had little control over the environment. Most features of instructional programs were beyond the staff's direct control. The size of groups; assigned work areas; available choices, activities, and environments; and the lack of individualized programming could seldom be changed. In the institutional environment, behavior management programs were often developed in reaction to disruptive behaviors.

Behavior management interventions were centered on the control of individuals. For the most part, the behavior management programs were reactive in nature and focused on the consequences of behavior— the events that followed the occurrence of a behavior. The staff often manipulated reinforcement procedures as a means of controlling behaviors. Insufficient attention was given to the events that had occurred prior to the antecedents of the behavior. The realities of life in institutions prevented the staff from manipulating prior events as a means of preventing disruptive behaviors.

As more and more individuals with developmental disabilities have moved into community-based settings, interventions have become more proactive in nature. This means that the staff emphasize prevention of dysfunctional behaviors by looking at antecedents or events leading to the occurrence of the behavior. Staff members and individuals with developmental disabilities both have direct influence on the immediate environment and control many of its features. Community-based settings are typically smaller, and interdisciplinary teams focus on community integration and the ability of individuals to make choices. Multiple opportunities for decision making enable individuals with developmental disabilities to exercise more control over their lives.

In community-based settings, the staff can analyze the environment, the events immediately preceding the occurrence of a behavior, and the natural consequences of the behavior. This process enables staff members to gain insight into the nature of disruptive behaviors and to develop strategies that prevent them. Prevention is often the result of focusing on and changing the environment and events that elicit the behaviors.

CONTEMPORARY BEHAVIOR MANAGEMENT INTERVENTION STRATEGIES FOCUS ON THE ANTECEDENTS OF A BEHAVIOR AND THE EVENTS THAT ELICIT IT.

Recent research has demonstrated that maladaptive behaviors are actually a means of communicating and often result from meaningless programming, boredom, lack of control over decisions and choices, and other factors. Contemporary practice suggests that successful programs, by contrast, are meaningful, functional, and appropriate and are based on the expressed interest of the individual and his or her strengths.

Horner, Dunlap, and Koegel (1988) have offered guidelines for program development that help to create a proactive approach to behavior change. The work of individuals with developmental disabilities should:

Have immediate utility. It should produce something useful for the individual or be part of a broader skill that does so.

Have desirability. It should produce something the individual would likely choose if an appropriate choice situation were arranged.

Be acquired in a social context. The acquisition should result from interactions with more than a single caregiver.

Be acquired in the actual, physical contexts in which it will be ultimately used.

Have practicality for the individual. It should be needed and practiced with some regularity.

Be age appropriate. The behavior should facilitate social integration.

Be adaptable. The skill should be generalized to a number of settings and situations. (pp. 68–69)

These elements are critical components of effective behavior intervention programs. Staff focus on antecedents, rather than consequences, can prevent the need for many formal behavior management programs.

FUNCTIONAL ANALYSIS OF BEHAVIORS

Successful behavior intervention programs require the staff to complete a functional analysis of a behavior. A functional analysis, sometimes referred to as an ABC chart of behavior management (Figure 1), can help in the study of behaviors and their antecedents and consequences. The ABC chart can also assist in making decisions that are based on information obtained on antecedents and consequences. Construction of the ABC chart, however, requires keen observation:

A stands for antecedents—the events that have led up to the behavior's occurrence. They are important because each behavior has a cause. For many individuals with developmental disabilities, the behavior communicates a message. Without this written information, the crucial events that cause the behaviors could go unnoticed.

B stands for behavior—the specific behavior you are trying to increase or decrease.

C stands for consequences—what happens after the behavior occurs. The consequences influence the behavior and determine whether it will be repeated.

Date	Time Incident Began and Ended	A: Antecedent Stimuli	B: Description of Behavior	C: Consequences	Individual's Response	Staff initials

Antecedent Stimuli: Should include events or activities that preceded the behavior. Antecedents to consider include: what staff and other individuals were doing, environmental changes, etc.

Description of Behavior: Describe the exact behaviors exhibited.

Consequences: All the events or activities that followed the behaviors. Include response of staff and other individuals.

Individual's Response: Describe what the individual who performed the behavior did in response to the consequences.

Figure 1. ABC chart of behavior management. (From Weiss, N.R. [1990]. Positive behavioral programming: An individualized approach. In J.F. Gardner & M.S. Chapman [Eds.], *Program issues in developmental disabilities: A guide to effective habilitation and active treatment* [2nd ed.] [p. 67]. Baltimore: Paul H. Brookes Publishing Co. Reprinted by permission.)

The information on the ABC chart is carefully analyzed after it is collected over a reasonable period of time. Several observation periods may be needed before you have sufficient information for an analysis.

Equal time should be spent looking at both the A and C columns. The key to effective behavior change strategies lies in understanding what message the individual with a developmental disability may be trying to communicate through the behavior. Studying the antecedents and consequences provides important information about the individual's behavior and what the person may be attempting to communicate.

ANTECEDENTS AND CONSEQUENCES PROVIDE INFORMATION ABOUT WHAT THE INDIVIDUAL MAY BE ATTEMPTING TO COMMUNICATE.

For example, the behavior may be communicating the individual's:

Need for attention or social contact
Boredom with a task
Desire to escape from completing a task
Pleasure of engaging in an activity
Need for help or assistance completing a task
Frustration
Desire to move on to another task

This is not a complete list. For some individuals with developmental disabilities, the purpose of disruptive behaviors is not readily apparent. The staff may need to explore a variety of changes in the individual's environment before discovering the message.

Following the analysis, the staff are better able to design strategies that help the individual to communicate needs and/or desires in appropriate ways. In addition, strategies can be defined to give the individual control over his or her environment. This process of behavior change aids in preventing future occurrences of disruptive behaviors.

Assume, for example, that you are a support staff member in a two-person alternative living unit for young adults. As you prepare dinner, you are instructing one of these individuals. The second person is setting the table in the dining room. You hear a noise behind you, go into the dining room, and observe the individual throwing the silverware on the floor. The first person starts to laugh. You tell the second person, "Pick up the silverware and get back to work." After observing these behaviors, you complete an ABC chart. Under the A column you should list:

6:00 P.M.
I was instructing Joe in cooking dinner.
Sam was setting the table in the dining room.
Joe and I heard a noise and went into the dining room.

Under the B column:

Sam threw silverware on the floor, piece by piece.
Sam looked at us while dropping each piece.

Under the C column:

Joe laughed.
I told Sam to "pick up the silverware and get back to work."
Joe continued laughing.

After the chart is complete, determine if the behavior needs to be changed. Look at both the A column and C column in making a decision about intervention strategies. Column A usually describes those behaviors that triggered the disruptive behavior. In this example, it is known that Sam likes social contacts with other adults. It is possible that Sam was seeking social contacts through the use of this behavior. Column C may provide clues as to what may be causing the behavior to become stronger or weaker, depending on the responses of the individual. Again, knowing that Sam seeks social contacts, the responses listed under column C may have served to strengthen the behavior.

The next step in designing an intervention program is to identify solutions. For purposes of analysis, assume that a list of solutions includes four possibilities:

1. Talk to Sam about his behavior.
2. Ignore the behavior
3. Tell Sam, "If you set the table correctly, then I will watch a movie with you after dinner."
4. Tell Sam, "I don't like it when you throw the silverware. You may not watch TV after dinner."

Which responses to the behavior would you choose?

Option 1 may be a social contact for Sam and serve to strengthen the behavior you are trying to decrease.

With option 2, you ignore the behavior. Sam throws down the silverware and receives no reaction. The behavior got no response. Assuming that Sam likes social contact, ignoring his behavior may be an effective means to decrease the behavior.

As an example of the Premack principle (explained in the next section on reinforcement), option 3 offers Sam an opportunity for social contact after completing a task. This option may also be an effective means to decrease the behavior.

Option 4, telling Sam that he may not watch TV after dinner, may work, but it does not show respect for Sam. In fact, it is treating him as a person much younger than his age. This option is unacceptable and should not be considered.

Options 2 and 3 may be the best methods for dealing with the behavior. Option 3 offers Sam a choice and helps him to assume responsibility for his behavior. In addition, it offers an opportunity for Sam to receive social contacts in an appropriate manner. You decide to try option 3. Data collected on the occurrence of the behavior will indicate if your choice was correct. If the behavior does not improve, try a different option.

Consider another example. You are ready to check out in a grocery store, and you notice two women in line in front of you. One woman looks at the magazine rack at the checkout counter and asks the second woman for a magazine. When she is told "No," the first woman begins to shout. As the shouting gets louder and louder, the second woman, who is apparently an agency staff member, becomes increasingly nervous. She picks up a magazine and gives it to the first woman, who immediately becomes quiet. She smiles and begins looking through the magazine. What advice would you give this staff member regarding the first woman's behavior? How should the staff member handle this problem in the future? You begin again by studying the behavior and putting the available information on the ABC chart.

Under A, you list what you observed preceding the behavior while you stood at the checkout line: One woman tells the other woman that she may not have a magazine. Under B, note that the woman shouts for the magazine. Under C, list as the consequence: The staff member gives the woman the magazine. You begin a behavior management program by studying the behavior. What was causing the behavior to occur? Look at what you listed under A. Do you see anything that may have triggered the behavior? What reinforced the behavior? The magazine is a reward that reinforces the shouting and increases the behavior.

Four possible methods of decreasing the behavior might be the following:

1. Give the woman a magazine before getting to the checkout line.
2. Shout back at the woman.
3. Ignore the behavior.
4. Tell the woman, "If you are quiet, I'll give you a magazine when we get home."

Option 1, giving the woman a magazine before reaching the checkout line, is not behavior management, but bribery. Bribery is getting something for nothing. It does not influence behavior over time. Behavior management programs provide reinforcement for a desired behavior. Bribery is not a reinforcer.

Option 2, shouting back, may cause pain. A person in pain will escape from, avoid, or fight back at the person doing the shouting, so this is not a desirable option. Also, an aversive procedure, such as shouting, should be considered only in rare circumstances after all other possible techniques have been tried.

Option 3 requires that the staff member ignore the behavior. What effect will no response to the woman's shouting have? If she is not given a magazine, she will receive no reward for crying. The chances are good that the behavior will decrease. Although it may be difficult to ignore shouting in a public place, it is always more effective than giving the desired item and rewarding an undesirable behavior.

Option 4 would teach the person to be quiet by promising her a reward. At first glance, this may appear to be an option until you consider that the woman is already shouting. By giving her the magazine, she learns that she may shout and then be given a reward later.

In this situation, the best solution would be to ignore the behavior. The staff member may be embarrassed for a while, but over time the woman will learn that shouting in the checkout line does not pay off and she will stop the behavior.

REINFORCEMENT

The technique of providing a pleasant consequence following a behavior, with the aim of increasing or strengthening the behavior, is called positive reinforcement. Reinforcement means to make stronger. It is the best tool you have for strengthening a behavior or teaching new skills.

POSITIVE REINFORCEMENT IS ANYTHING A PERSON LIKES THAT IS GIVEN AFTER A BEHAVIOR TO INCREASE THE BEHAVIOR.

Positive reinforcement is classified as primary, or unlearned, and secondary, or learned. Reinforcers necessary for survival include food, water, shelter, sleep, and companionship. You did not need to learn the importance they have in your lives. They are referred to as primary, or unlearned, positive reinforcers.

Secondary, or learned, positive reinforcers are the items and events you have learned to value in your life. People generally work to obtain these items or activities. Everyone's list of learned positive reinforcers is different. They include such things as a 25-foot Catalina sailboat; a new Buick Skylark; a vacation in Charleston, South Carolina; a 19-inch color television; a new CD by Earl Kluch; dancing at the Hyatt Regency Hotel; or walking on the beach.

The key to using positive reinforcement is knowing what is important to the person with whom you are working. Although the idea may be easily understood, it is often difficult to do this. Not all people are motivated by the same reinforcers. Some people prefer dancing to sailing. Others like strawberries more than pastry. Never assume that other people are willing to work for your reinforcers. Secondary reinforcers provide strong motivation for performing a behavior. These learned positive reinforcers should be listed in each person's individualized program plan.

EVERYONE'S LIST OF LEARNED POSITIVE REINFORCERS IS DIFFERENT.

Categories of Secondary Reinforcers

Secondary reinforcers can be divided into four categories—social, material, activity, and token. Social reinforcers come from other people and are very strong motivators. They include hugs, kisses, smiles, eye-winks, nods of approval, pats on the back, or verbal comments. Children learn certain behaviors because of the attention these behaviors bring from their parents and often children carry them over into their adult lives. Many adults behave the way they do because of the attention they receive from other people. Attention is a powerful motivator.

Material reinforcers are those objects that a person may enjoy. Books, radios, boats, CDs, board games, cards, and paints and paintbrushes are examples of material reinforcers. For some people, the ownership of materials is important.

Activity reinforcers are material reinforcers that have been put to use. Owning a book is a material reinforcer; reading the book is considered an activity reinforcer. Listening to a radio or CD, sailing, swimming, and playing board games are other examples of activity reinforcers.

Tokens, the final type of secondary reinforcers, are similar to money because they can be exchanged for goods or services. Poker chips, buttons, or metal washers are examples of tokens. Like a dollar bill, these things by themselves have no value. When traded for a purchase, however, they become important.

Selection of Reinforcers

In selecting appropriate reinforcers, you must first determine what is on each person's list of secondary reinforcers. Once a list is complete, you will have a reinforcement menu. From this, you can choose the reinforcers you need to teach a new skill, to increase and maintain a desirable behavior, or to decrease undesirable behaviors. Five basic rules can guide your selection of reinforcers for the menu:

1. The reinforcer should be easy and convenient to deliver. Assume that you are trying to teach a person to wash his hands. Assume also that the person enjoys listening to music. How easy would it be to use that reinforcer for this behavior? This skill would probably be taught in the bathroom and it would be difficult to instruct the

person in hand washing and then run to another room to play his favorite music as a reinforcer. In this situation, listening to music as a reinforcer would be neither easy nor convenient.

REINFORCERS SHOULD BE EASY AND CONVENIENT TO DELIVER.

---

2. The reinforcer should not interfere with other planned activities or events. Assume that you are a staff member in a home with two women residents. You tell one woman that when she finishes doing her work, she can go for a walk with you. Hours pass. Just as dinner is ready, she announces that her work is finished and she wants to go for a walk. Going for a walk simply is not convenient for anyone at that time.

REINFORCERS SHOULD NOT DISRUPT ROUTINES.

---

3. To ensure the effectiveness of reinforcers, their use must be monitored. The chances of other people unintentionally using your program reinforcers can be minimized by effective communication. Staff members must know if coworkers are using the same reinforcers. Consider the following example: As a job coach, you are responsible for teaching a person an assembly task. You decide to use a social praise as reinforcer for each correct response. After a few days of work, you notice that you are not making much progress. You mention this at a team conference, where you discover that the recreation therapist, as well as the parents, is using social praise. Your reinforcer is no longer working because it is being overused.

To prevent this situation, it is important to inform other people who are involved with the person about your program and the reinforcers you are using. If they are not available from others, they will tend to be more effective in your program.

TO ENSURE THE EFFECTIVENESS OF A REINFORCER, MONITOR ITS USE.

---

4. In some cases, it is important to change your reinforcer on a regular basis. If that is not possible, use smaller amounts of the same reinforcer. Using the example above, how many days do you think the person will work if social praise is the only reinforcer he receives? He will probably stop doing well on his program by the end of the third or fourth day. You should establish a reinforcement menu so that you can change the reinforcer used in your program on a regular basis.

> If possible, vary the reinforcer on a regular basis. Otherwise, use smaller amounts of the same reinforcer.

5. Choose only those reinforcers that are age appropriate and that improve the image of the person. Assume that you are a staff member in a residential program responsible for teaching a 38-year-old man appropriate shaving techniques. M&Ms are on his list of favorite reinforcers. How will the person be viewed by his peers or other people of similar age if you pop M&Ms into his mouth as a reinforcer? He probably will not be viewed too favorably.

> Reinforcers should be consistent with the normalization principle.

Use of Reinforcers

Effective use of reinforcement offers better control of the environment in bringing about a change in a person's behavior. The rules for accomplishing this are important, yet simple. The following five rules apply to most learning situations, whether you are teaching a new behavior, trying to increase a desirable behavior, or trying to decrease an undesirable behavior:

1. Be consistent. The success of a program depends on how consistent the staff are in following a program plan. The success of a program depends on the predictability of *your* behavior. Over time, the person will learn that when he does X, you do Y. When he does T, you will do B. *Every* time he does X, you do Y. Your behavior is predictable.

> Be consistent. When using reinforcers, your behavior must be predictable.

2. Reinforce the behavior every time it occurs until it is learned. The speed at which a person learns a skill or behavior depends on how frequently it is reinforced. You cannot reinforce a behavior some of the time and expect the person to learn the skill or behavior.

> Reinforce the behavior consistently every time the behavior occurs until it is learned.

3. Reinforce the behavior immediately. This greatly increases the likelihood of the behavior occurring again. In addition, you can avoid accidental training. If you wait longer than a few seconds to rein-

force the desired response, you might reinforce another behavior that has occurred between the person's response and your delivery of the reinforcer. Consider this example: You are a mobility instructor teaching a 28-year-old person sign recognition. You ask a question and the person responds correctly. Hearing the correct response, you turn to reach for a reinforcer. By the time you turn back, the person is looking around the room and tapping his foot. You tell him he does good work and give him the reinforcer. What did you reinforce? Did you actually reinforce his answer? Owing to the amount of time between his response and your delivery of the reinforcer, did you actually reinforce his looking around the room while tapping his foot?

REINFORCERS SHOULD BE GIVEN IMMEDIATELY AFTER THE CORRECT RESPONSE TO AVOID ACCIDENTAL LEARNING.

---

4. Name the reinforced behavior for the person who is learning it. Unfortunately, many people who teach behaviors confuse social reinforcement with providing specific information, so that they tend to use such phrases as "That was good," "Good," or "Do that again." These statements may be secondary positive reinforcers, but they do not provide exact information. It is often difficult to be specific in verbal reinforcement. People are generally not in the habit of noticing the specifics of others' good behaviors. They are not very free with reinforcing comments, such as "Thank you for arriving on time for our meeting," or "You did a great job teaching hand washing to John." People are more apt to comment on the negative things that others do, rather than on the positive things.

WHEN USING VERBAL REINFORCEMENT, BE SPECIFIC. LET THE PERSON KNOW EXACTLY WHAT BEHAVIORS ARE PERFORMED WELL.

---

5. Be sincere. Imagine that your boss told you, "The goals you wrote were good," while at the same time he had a frown on his face? Would you question his or her sincerity? Most people have the ability to recognize when others do not really mean what they say. People with developmental disabilities are no different. If you do not mean what you say, then you are better off not saying anything at all.

REINFORCE IN A POSITIVE WAY AND MEAN WHAT YOU SAY.

The Premack Principle

The Premack principle states that when an activity a person likes to do takes place after an activity he or she does not like, the rate at which the person completes the activity he or she does not like will increase. In other words, first you work, then you play. For example, consider an instructor in a classroom telling a student, "If you work quietly at your desk for 5 minutes, you may then put a puzzle together." This example illustrates how you can effectively reinforce the student for working quietly at his or her desk with an activity—putting a puzzle together—that the student wants to do.

Notice that the Premack principle is always stated in positive terms. How do you think the student would feel if you said, "If you don't sit quietly in your seat, you can't play with the puzzle."? The student would probably feel threatened. However, when stated in a positive manner, the student can assume responsibility for making a decision. Other examples of the Premack principle are:

"If you finish your homework, then I will go for a walk with you."
"If you complete the job, you will get a paycheck."
"If you finish dinner, then you may have some cake for dessert."
"When you pick up your toys, we'll go shopping."

There are many opportunities for using the Premack principle. In order to make it work effectively, the staff must know each person's menu of learned secondary reinforcers. These reinforcers can be paired with desired behaviors to increase the frequency of these behaviors.

PUNISHMENT

To punish means to make weaker. A punisher is anything a person dislikes that is given after a behavior in order to decrease or weaken the behavior.

To punish means to make weaker.

Aversive Measures

Punishment involves the use of aversive measures. Simply stated, aversives involve the use of painful stimuli to decrease a behavior. Punishment can cause physical or mental pain. Many professionals have become increasingly alarmed at the potential side effects of punishment techniques. Consider the following example of side effects. You are at home when the doorbell rings. You look through the peephole and see that it is your friend from down the street. When you open the door, he hits you for no apparent reason and then leaves. The next day you see him again walking up to your door. What do you think you will do when he rings the doorbell? Are you going to answer it or not? Assume that you do not answer it. You are probably *avoiding* him. Suppose that he has a key and lets himself in the door. What are you going to do then? You would probably try to run or *escape* through the back door. But he catches you. Now what are you going to do? More than likely, you would try to *fight back*.

This example illustrates the general point that people try to avoid, escape from, or fight back at anyone or anything that causes pain in their lives. It can be very difficult for people to trust you, to come to you, or to learn to respect you if you are using punishers. Their response will be to avoid you, to try to escape from you, or to fight back at you.

The other major limitation of punishment is that it does not teach a new positive behavior or skill. Punishment does not teach a person what he or she should do. It is not constructive. Punishment provides no alternatives or choices to replace the undesirable behavior.

Punishment includes anything that is painful, such as spankings, slaps across the face, shouting, loud noises, certain odors, or bright lights. Because punishment can hurt people, the staff should be very cautious about ever using it. In fact, federal and state laws may not allow punishment. Agency policy and procedures should prohibit the use of punishment techniques. If the agency does allow the use of aversive measures, they must be approved by a human rights committee as part of a behavior management program.

The debate over the use of aversive procedures continues among professionals in the field of human services and has become more intense in recent years. Although many professionals have no concerns about the use of aversive procedures, many others believe that aversive techniques should be prohibited by law. As more data regarding the use of nonaversive (reinforcement) strategies are accumulated and published, the need for aversive strategies becomes less apparent.

Finally, most programs can effectively utilize positive reinforcement techniques to change behaviors. Aversive punishment techniques are usually unnecessary.

EXERCISE 1

Agency Policy and Procedures

Review the agency policies and procedures on the use of aversive measures. Are they allowed? Do they require review by a committee?

Removing Positive Reinforcement

Removing a positive reinforcer can decrease or weaken a behavior. There are three ways to decrease a behavior by taking something away. These procedures are called time-out, extinction, and response-cost.

Time-out procedures involve moving a person from one situation to another in which he or she has no opportunity to receive reinforcers. For example, a person may become disruptive during mealtime. Sending him to his room or making him sit in the corner is a time-out procedure. By doing this, the opportunities for the behavior to be reinforced are taken away.

Extinction refers to cutting off reinforcement for a particular behavior. In using this procedure, you ignore the behavior. A person may have a temper tantrum when told "No." By ignoring the behavior, you provide no reinforcement for it.

Response-cost procedures remove or take away privileges. If you are rewarding good behavior with tokens, fining the person for an undesirable behavior by taking away a certain number of tokens is an example of a response-cost procedure.

SCHEDULES OF REINFORCEMENT

When teaching a new skill or behavior, reinforcement is provided every time the behavior occurs until it is learned. Once a new skill or behavior has been learned, the schedule of reinforcement is no longer continuous. It is necessary to select a new schedule for giving reinforcement in order to maintain the desired behavior. You can select one of five different schedules of reinforcement: continuous, fixed ratio, variable ratio, fixed interval, and variable interval.

Continuous

A continuous schedule of reinforcement means that reinforcement is given every time the behavior occurs. Once the behavior has been learned, you choose a schedule of reinforcement designed to decrease the amount of reinforcement that is needed to maintain the behavior.

Fixed Ratio

With a fixed ratio method of reinforcement, the reinforcer is given after a certain number of correct responses have occurred. You may start to decrease the reinforcement from a continuous schedule by giving it after every other or after every third correct response. If the desired behavior continues on this reinforcement schedule, you continue to gradually withdraw the reinforcer on the fixed schedule (i.e., after every fourth correct response, after every fifth) until the person completes the behavior with no reinforcement. The reinforcer has become internalized, and the person no longer needs it to perform the behavior.

Variable Ratio

Sometimes a person you are working with figures out what you are doing and does not perform well until just before he or she is reinforced. If this happens, it may be necessary to use a variable ratio schedule of reinforcement. With this schedule, you provide reinforcement to the person according to an average number of correct responses. For example, you present reinforcement after the first correct response, then not again until after four more correct responses, then two more, then three more, and, finally, five more. You add these numbers together and divide by the number of times reinforcement is given $(1 + 4 + 2 + 3 + 5 = 15 \div 5 = 3)$. You are reinforcing, on the average, every third correct response.

Fixed Interval

In some instances, your objective is to increase or decrease the amount of time a person spends in an activity. In a fixed interval schedule of reinforcement, you reinforce the first correct response that is made after a certain amount of time has passed. You may decide to reinforce the first correct response that is made after 1 minute, or after 2 minutes, or maybe after 10 minutes have passed. When using the fixed interval method of reinforcement, the time interval must be decided in advance and be realistic for the person with whom you are working. As the behavior or skill is learned, the interval is gradually increased so that the person receives less reinforcement for the completed behaviors.

Variable Interval

Because some people may anticipate the reinforcement schedule, it may be necessary to reinforce the first correct response after an averaged period of time has passed. This method is called the variable interval schedule of reinforcement. For example, the reinforcer is given for the first correct response after the first minute passes. The reinforcer is then given after the next 4 minutes pass, then after the next 2 minutes, after the next 3 minutes, and after the next 5 minutes. The sum of these intervals divided by the number of times reinforcement is given yields a variable interval reinforcement schedule of 3 minutes. This method requires a prior decision of what the variable intervals will be. As the new skills and behaviors are learned, gradually decrease the reinforcement needed by increasing the intervals.

SUMMARY

Strategies for behavior intervention have changed during recent years. Traditional approaches to behavior change have focused on the consequences of the behavior and on control of the individual. The consequences were manipulated in order to produce a desired change in the individual's behavior.

Contemporary approaches to behavior change stress the importance of first understanding the environment within which a behavior occurs. They also require the agency staff to understand what the individual with developmental disabilities is attempting to communicate by exhibiting the behavior. Rather than controlling the individual, behavior intervention strategies focus on changes in the environment that teach the individual appropriate strategies to communicate needs.

A functional analysis, also called an ABC chart of behavior management, is an effective tool in studying a behavior. Functional analysis is useful for looking at the antecedents and consequences of behaviors. Data obtained over several observation periods help to determine behavior change strategies. The preferred strategy is proactive and consists of making changes in the individual's environment. This strategy prevents the need for a formal intervention program altogether.

A key to successful behavior change, as well as a tool for teaching new skills, is a reinforcement menu established and maintained for each person with whom you are working. This list may include primary (unlearned) and secondary (learned) reinforcers. The list differs for each individual. Effective use of reinforcers enables you to influence the individual's environment. Changes in the environment can lead to changes in the person's behavior.

In order to use reinforcement effectively, you must be aware of the need for consistency, the importance of being immediate and sincere, and the need to be specific in verbal reinforcement. These guidelines will contribute to the success of your behavior program.

BIBLIOGRAPHY

Alberto, P.A., & Troutman, A.C. (1990). *Applied behavior analysis for teachers.* Columbus, OH: Charles E. Merrill.

Baldwin, J.D., & Baldwin, J.I. (1986). *Behavior principles in everyday life.* Englewood Cliffs, NJ: Prentice Hall.

Horner, R.H., Dunlap, G., & Koegel, R.L. (Eds.). (1988). *Generalization and maintenance: Life-style changes in applied settings.* Baltimore: Paul H. Brookes Publishing Co.

Walker, J.E., & Shea, T.M. (1988). *Behavior management: A practical approach for educators.* Columbus, OH: Charles E. Merrill.

ADDITIONAL RESOURCES

A. Donnellan and G. LaVigna (1986), in *Alternatives to punishment: Solving behavior problems with non-aversive strategies* (New York: Irvington), present readers with detailed information regarding functional analysis and nonaversive behavior change strategies.

L.H. Meyer and I.M. Evans (1989), in *Nonaversive intervention for behavior problems: A manual for home and community* (Baltimore: Paul H. Brookes Publishing Co.), provide an excellent overview of nonaversive strategies of behavior change.

N.R. Weiss (1990), Positive behavioral programming: An individualized, functional approach, in J.F. Gardner and M.S. Chapman (Eds.), *Program issues in developmental disabilities: A guide to effective habilitation and active treatment* (2nd ed.) (pp. 59–77) (Baltimore: Paul H. Brookes Publishing Co.), is an excellent chapter on the individualized approach to positive behavioral change.

SELF-APPRAISAL

INSTRUCTIONS

The following questions will help you evaluate your knowledge about behavior management principles. For true-false questions, check the correct answer. For multiple choice questions, circle the correct answer(s).

Note: There may be more than one correct answer for some questions.

1. The best method of understanding the need for a behavior change strategy is to focus on the consequences of the behavior.
   ___ True   ___ False
2. Bribery is a form of behavior management.
   ___ True   ___ False
3. Which of the following describe a reinforcer?
   a. Reinforcers make behavior weaker.
   b. Reinforcers make behavior stronger.
   c. Reinforcers interpret behaviors.
   d. Reinforcers are caused by behaviors.
4. Which of the following describe a punisher?
   a. Punishers are used to increase behaviors.
   b. Punishers result in good behaviors.
   c. Punishers weaken behaviors.
   d. All of the above.
5. Punishment can be used as a behavior-shaping technique with the approval of the program supervisor.
   ___ True   ___ False
6. Given the following information, construct an ABC chart. You are a staff person in a group home for adolescents. It is 10:00 at night. It is time for the residents to go to bed. When told to go to bed, one adolescent whines and stomps his feet. When he does these behaviors, your coworker says, "You were told to go to bed; now hurry up and get going."
7. Secondary reinforcers are determined by:
   a. The professional
   b. The parent
   c. The individual
   d. The interdisciplinary team
8. Which of the following are potential side effects of punishment?
   a. Avoidance behaviors
   b. Escape behaviors

      c.   Aggressive behaviors

      d.   All of the above

9. An example of the Premack principle is:

      a.   "If you don't take out the trash, I'll spank you."

      b.   "If you take out the trash, I'll read you a story."

      c.   Both of the above.

      d.   None of the above.

10. Time-out, extinction, and response-cost are behavior management principles that decrease a behavior by removing a positive reinforcer.

      ____ True   ____ False

CASE STUDY

Susan Williams is a 34-year-old woman who lives with her parents in Washington County, Maryland. She has Down syndrome and severe mental retardation. She is 43 pounds overweight. Her hearing and eyesight are normal.

At age 28, she entered a job training program at the county vocational center, operated by Tri-County Employment, Inc. She remained in that program for 6 years. For the past 6 months, she has worked in a job station at the nearby Holloway Inn.

Situation

Ms. Williams's cleaning task at the Holloway Inn includes the following steps:

Strip all laundry from the room
Make beds
Dust furniture
Vacuum floors
Clean tub
Clean sink
Clean toilet
Mop bathroom floor

Ms. Williams's work supervisor has become concerned about her work performance. She has observed Ms. Williams during the past 3 weeks and noted that she completes only four tasks in the time allowed. When encouraged to increase her speed in completing the tasks, Ms. Williams whines and stops working. In addition, she engages in inappropriate talking with the supervisor and other workers, saying such things as "What do I do now?" or "Am I a good worker?"

1. What concerns would you have about Ms. Williams's behavior?
2. With which behavior would you begin your behavior management program?
3. What are the important points to consider before beginning a behavior management program?
4. Identify the important reinforcers for a person 34 years old.

ANSWER KEY TO
SELF-APPRAISAL AND CASE STUDY

SELF-APPRAISAL

1. False
2. False
3. b
4. c
5. False
6.

Staff	Date	Time incident began/ended	A: Antecedent stimuli	B: Description of behavior	C: Consequences	Individual response
	2-6	10:00 P.M. 10:05 P.M.	Adolescent told to go to bed	Adolescent whines and stomps feet	Coworker says, "You were told to go to bed; now hurry up and get going."	Whines louder, stomps feet harder, slams door

7. c
8. d
9. b
10. True

CASE STUDY ANSWER GUIDELINES

1. There are several areas of concern in the situation. They include:

   The time it takes Ms. Williams to complete the required task
   Ms. Williams's whining and refusal to work when confronted
   Ms. Williams's inappropriate talking

2. This is a difficult question. However, considering that Ms. Williams is in an employment situation, she may lose her job if her performance does not improve. Therefore, any behavior management program should be designed to increase her speed in completing the required task.

3. The primary concern here is with the supervisor's observations. *Observed* is the key word. Does it mean that actual data were collected? Is the behavior management program based on data col-

lected on the problem in a variety of situations, or is the supervisor making an inaccurate judgment about Ms. Williams?

4. The reinforcers appropriate for a 34-year-old person with a developmental disability are the same as those for other 34-year-old individuals. For most people in a work situation, the primary reinforcers received during the work day are scheduled breaks and social contacts. In addition, at the end of a given period of time, a paycheck is forthcoming.

section
III

NEW TRENDS
AND
INDIVIDUAL
DIFFERENCES

chapter
10

Human
Sexuality

LEARNING OBJECTIVES

Upon completing this chapter, the reader will be able to:

1. List five reasons for providing assistance to persons with developmental disabilities in understanding human sexuality.
2. List three sources of confusing attitudes about the sexuality of persons with developmental disabilities.
3. Define sex education.
4. Define counseling in human sexuality.
5. Identify four staff responsibilities for assisting people with developmental disabilities in exercising their sexuality in a responsible manner.

INTRODUCTION

Human sexuality is an important part of every individual's personality and self-esteem. Most people have a self-concept that is linked to their being male or female. An awareness of sexual identity is present in young children, and it remains a strong influence throughout men's and women's lives. Sexuality, then, is not something an individual does; sexuality is being a woman or a man. This chapter assists the reader to acquire a positive perception of the individual sexuality of persons with developmental disabilities.

CONFUSION ABOUT HUMAN SEXUALITY

Human sexuality is important and natural, yet it seems so difficult to talk about. This is not surprising. American society does not encourage open discussion of human sexuality. For example, consider the following five areas of anxiety about sexuality:

1. Many people have grown up with fears and incorrect facts about sexuality. Until fairly recently, sex education programs were not available.
2. Advertising in the media promotes products through sexual imagery. Yet, the same media seldom contain factual information about sexuality because it is too controversial.
3. Society tolerates adults who tell stories or jokes about sex more than it tolerates those who openly discuss it.
4. The language of sexuality is confused. There is a "proper" language drawn from medical books. There is also a "popular" language developed in the streets and in the workplace. An ear is generally an ear; a nose is sometimes a snout; but a penis has at least 30 different names.
5. The difference between "do as I do" and "do as I say" applies in the area of sexual conduct.

In general, there is a confused attitude about the sexuality of people with developmental disabilities. They are sometimes viewed as nonsexual people. Society does not allow them the same forms of sexual expression that it does the general population. This approach is also apparent in the attitudes and behaviors of people with developmental disabilities themselves. They have been taught and told not to talk about or engage in sexual activity. As a result, they often find it difficult to discuss human sexuality.

Persons with developmental disabilities have sexual identities.

Some parents, professionals, teachers, and agency staff working with people with developmental disabilities have reinforced this nonsexual approach. Parents sometimes view their sons or daughters with developmental disabilities as "perpetual children." They think their children will be forever innocent and ignorant of their own sexuality. Although many parents are able to help their children through puberty and into adulthood, others are not prepared to provide advice and counseling about sexuality.

Professionals and agencies serving people with developmental disabilities have often taken the position that sexuality is not an important issue. Implicit in this position is the attitude that helping people with their sexuality carries possible complications and risks. It can lead to discussions about feelings and emotions. Counseling can also result in decisions about expressing and sharing friendships, affection, and sex-

ual relationships. Agencies sometimes try to avoid these issues by ignoring sexuality. At other times, professionals and agencies try to prevent people from making mistakes by pretending they are not sexual.
Many agencies do not have clearly stated policies about sexuality.
Sometimes an agency staff may think there is a policy of not dealing
with sexuality, even when there is no such policy. At other times, the
staff ignore the issues when there is a policy.

Although families and program staff sometimes deny the sexuality
of persons with developmental disabilities, the general public often
holds the opposite view and believes that people with developmental
disabilities are oversexed and may molest others. This myth is cited as
an argument against social inclusion and community participation.

To sort through the myth about sexuality in American society,
Dailey (1979) (as cited in Gardner, 1986, p. 48) indicated that human
sexuality consists of five interrelated factors:

1. *Sensuality:* The awareness of body, sexual memory and fantasy, and
   orgasm.
2. *Identity:* A sense of being male or female, an acknowledgment of
   the different sexual roles, a preference for heterosexual or homosexual relationships, and a molding of different male and female
   role characteristics.
3. *Intimacy:* Mental feelings of closeness and caring that accompany
   sex.
4. *Reproduction:* Creation of new life.
5. *Sexualization:* The use of sex to control or manipulate others.

EXERCISE 1

Policy and Procedure

What are your agency policies and procedures concerning human sexuality? List them on a separate sheet of paper.

NEED FOR ASSISTANCE IN UNDERSTANDING SEXUALITY

The five major reasons for assisting persons with developmental disabilities to understand human sexuality are: difficulties in learning,
physical and social overprotection, segregated living situations, recognition of legal rights, and public health concerns. Helping people to
understand sexual roles and norms, family relations, and sexual feelings about themselves and others is an important staff responsibility.

Difficulties in Learning

Because some people with developmental disabilities have difficulty learning, they may need more help in developing positive feelings about their sexuality. They may not have access to or be able to benefit from additional information sources, such as books, magazines, films, and special classes. Because of difficulty in learning and limited exposure to the community, people with developmental disabilities often do not know when or whom to ask for assistance. Finally, they need assistance in understanding human sexuality because they may be more vulnerable to sexual exploitation and abuse than other people.

ASSISTING PEOPLE TO UNDERSTAND THEIR OWN SEXUALITY IS AN IMPORTANT STAFF RESPONSIBILITY.

Overprotection

Families and professionals have overprotected people with developmental disabilities from making mistakes regarding their sexuality. As a result, they are sometimes not allowed to learn about their own sexuality. From an early age, they are denied the small experiments and low-risk mistakes through which people learn. People who grow up without learning from one small risk to another have limited opportunity to develop good judgment about their sexuality. Instead, unfortunately, some people with developmental disabilities have to make major decisions and accept large risks without the benefit of previous learning. As Johnson (1973, p. 78) stated, "It is unrealistic of society to demand responsible sexual behavior from people who have never been taught what constitutes responsibility and irresponsibility in sexual matters."

"IT IS UNREALISTIC OF SOCIETY TO DEMAND RESPONSIBLE SEXUAL BEHAVIOR FROM PEOPLE WHO HAVE NEVER BEEN TAUGHT WHAT CONSTITUTES RESPONSIBILITY AND IRRESPONSIBILITY IN SEXUAL MATTERS."

Segregated Living Situations

Many people with developmental disabilities grow up in typical home situations, go to school, and then enter into work situations. They have the opportunity to learn in normal circumstances. Others, however, are exposed to very different learning situations. For them, many sexual behaviors and attitudes are shaped and reinforced in programs that are removed from the mainstream of society. This is particularly true in institutions, segregated schools, and other isolated programs.

The lack of community living may have prevented some people with developmental disabilities from developing appropriate social skills, behaviors, and sexual roles. What is acceptable in the isolated setting is not acceptable in most communities. For example, public nudity and gang showering may be tolerated in an institution, but they are not acceptable in apartment living. Many times, people with developmental disabilities do not understand that different places require different sexual attitudes and behaviors.

EXERCISE 2

Lack of Privacy

In many cases attention to individual sexuality is made very difficult by the limitations in segregated living situations. Imagine that you live in a group living situation and share a bedroom with three other people.

Would the lack of privacy and individuality affect your self-esteem?
How would your sense of self and sexuality be affected if you could never be alone by yourself or with another person?

As a staff person, list the difficulties of teaching people positive attitudes about sexuality and relationships when they have not lived in a typically integrated world in many years.

Legal Rights

Individuals with developmental disabilities have the full right to express their sexuality in a socially appropriate manner. Individuals with minimal cognitive impairment should have little difficulty in learning appropriate behavior. People with more severe disabilities may require more supports and training to figure out what is socially appropriate.

People with developmental disabilities have a full legal right to marry, to procreate, and to raise children. The U.S. Supreme Court has declared these to be fundamental rights protected by the Constitution. Unless, through due process, a person is declared incompetent in a court of law, these rights cannot be denied.

This right of due process has not always been recognized in the past. Many parents, agency staff, and professionals have taken the attitude that people forfeit these rights because they lack judgment or are slow learners. This is not true. It bears reemphasizing that *unless persons have been declared incompetent*, they are legally responsible for making their own decisions regarding sexuality. As a staff member, you have the responsibility to assist a person to make the most informed and responsible decision possible. Table 1 lists sexual rights that are implicit in the Constitution and opportunities that should be accorded persons with developmental disabilities.

Table 1. Sexual rights and opportunities of people with developmental disabilities

---

1. The opportunity to receive training in human sexuality that will promote social integration and community living
2. The right to be given all facts and information so that informed consent can be given
3. The opportunity to share and feel companionship
4. The right to marry, to procreate, and to raise children unless determined incompetent in a judicial proceeding
5. The opportunity to express sexuality within the framework of acceptable behavior
6. The right to birth control methods and services that are designed to meet individual needs
7. The opportunity to obtain support services that enable people to exercise these rights. This includes the supportive services that enable two people to live together and share affection and sexual relationships (if they desire) in community settings

---

Public Health Concerns

Current public health issues (Monat-Haller, 1992), such as unplanned pregnancy, abortion, substance abuse, and acquired immunodeficiency syndrome (AIDS) make education in sexuality particularly important in this decade. AIDS has made education in sexuality a matter of life and death. Monat-Haller has commented on the difficulty of convincing people with limited cognitive capability of the danger of AIDS. She identifies the difficulty as communicating the abstract concept that an individual who looks healthy can, during a pleasurable act, transfer a virus that kills. Individuals with developmental disabilities also need information about the range of other sexually transmitted diseases, as well as instruction in the use of condoms and the advantages of abstinence and monogamous, lifelong relationships.

Staff members need a basic understanding of the human immunodeficiency virus (HIV) and AIDS. HIV can infect various parts of the body. It can be passed to another person through sexual or parenteral blood contact or from an infected mother to her fetus or infant. The most severe form of HIV infection is AIDS.

More than 160,000 cases of AIDS were reported in the United States from 1981 through 1990. Over 40,000 were reported in 1990 alone. The total cost of medical care for treating people with AIDS is expected to reach $7 billion per year by 1993 (Crocker, Cohen, & Kastner, 1992).

AIDS has been a particular problem for homosexual men and intravenous drug users, but no individual or group is beyond the threat of AIDS. People who engage in heterosexual activity can also acquire

AIDS. Both the staff and people with developmental disabilities should take the threat of AIDS seriously. They need to understand seven basic facts about how HIV is passed from one person to another:

1. Although HIV has been found in other bodily fluids, only blood, semen, vaginal secretions, and, in unique circumstances, breast milk have been found to transmit HIV from one person to another (Rennert, Parry, & Horowitz, 1989, p. 9).
2. The four methods of HIV transmission are:
   a. Unprotected sexual contact
   b. Transfusion of HIV-infected blood
   c. Sharing of intravenous needles
   d. Congenital transmission from a mother to her fetus or newborn
3. HIV can be transmitted by blood *only* when infected blood comes into contact with an open wound. Unbroken skin is a barrier to transmission.
4. Transmission of HIV-infected blood through accidental needle-stick injuries in health care settings can occur, but it is rare. The risk of acquiring HIV in this type of accident is estimated at 1 per 250–350. Through 1989, only 25 cases of such transmission had been published (Crocker et al., 1992, p. 9).
5. Dentists, dental hygienists, and staff involved in dental care and toothbrushing should exercise caution because of possible exposure to bleeding gums (Rubin & Crocker, 1989, p. 473). Special gloves should be worn for dental work.
6. When handling body fluids, such as urine, stool, sweat, oral or nasal secretions, or vomitus, no special precautions other than handwashing are required if no blood is visible (Crocker et al., 1992, p. 9).
7. Studies of homes of people with AIDS indicate that the following activities (in the absence of blood) do not transmit HIV (Rennert et al., 1989, p. 9):
   a. Sharing eating utensils
   b. Sharing drinking glasses
   c. Sharing towels
   d. Sharing beds
   e. Sharing toilets
   f. Washing clothes
   g. Hugging
   h. Kissing
   i. Assisting someone to bathe, toilet, or eat.

Although accidents with infected blood do occur, the vast majority of HIV infections take place through sexual contact. HIV infection can be prevented by refraining from sexual activity. Sexual activity can be made "safer" through the use of condoms.

EDUCATION IN HUMAN SEXUALITY

In order to make responsible decisions, people with developmental disabilities must have the necessary information. The task for the agency staff is to present the correct information to each individual in the most suitable manner. In addition, the staff must convey proper feelings, attitudes, and reactions about sexuality. This is why staff behaviors, attitudes, and examples are so important.

People with developmental disabilities learn about sexuality from the way staff members act. They also learn from one another. They learn about individual dignity and human sexuality from the world around them—for example, from the public institution, shopping mall, or church. This information can be correct or it can be wrong or confusing. Similarly, they can learn to be comfortable with their sexuality or they can learn to feel ashamed and guilty about expressing their feelings of sexuality.

The term *sex education* generally refers to the provision of information about human sexuality. It also refers to the ongoing process of learning about being male or female. As stated earlier, every person's identity is tied to his or her sex. Self-concept is linked to growth and development as a male or female. The information offered in sex education covers such topics as anatomy and physiology, birth control, safe sex, sexually transmitted diseases, marriage, parenthood, and appropriate and inappropriate sexual expression and behavior.

Education in human sexuality can be provided through formal classroom instruction. It can also be rather informal, like learning to play a new sport or discovering a new neighborhood. The goal of the educational process is to develop and foster a positive attitude toward individual sexuality. The attitude people have about their own sexuality is a more important outcome of sex education than their ability to name body parts.

The basic content of a human sexuality program might include the following 10 topics (Monat-Haller, 1992, p. 42):

1. Anatomy and physiology
2. Maturation and body change
3. Birth control
4. Sexually transmitted diseases and their prevention
5. Masturbation
6. Responsibility for sexual behavior
7. Inappropriate sexual behavior and sex offenses
8. Same-sex and opposite-sex activities
9. Psychosocial-sexual aspects of behavior and psychosexual development
10. Marriage and parenthood

There is no uniform format for the presentation of the material. It can be presented to an individual or a group. However, the presentation should match the learning styles, communication methods, and cognitive capability of the individual or group.

Staff members who present information about sexuality to persons with developmental disabilities should exhibit three important characteristics: 1) they must possess the correct information; 2) they must have a positive attitude about human sexuality; and 3) they must be able to talk about sexuality in an open and honest manner, alone or in a group. Only a limited number of staff members in any agency will meet these requirements and be qualified to provide formal courses in sexuality. However, almost all of the staff should develop the attitude and ability to provide impromptu instruction in sex education.

Impromptu teaching can occur at unexpected times. Staff members must develop two skills in such situations. The first skill is to refrain from panic or overreaction in response to questions or behaviors. A panic reaction indicates that whatever the person said or did was wrong. This can only reinforce feelings of guilt or lowered self-esteem. The second skill is to provide the proper response to the person's question or a concise description of the appropriate behavior. Simplicity is the key.

Table 2 offers staff guidelines for providing education in sexuality. Whether formal or informal, the information should be given on an

Table 2. Staff guidelines for education in human sexuality

1. Be guided by the policies and procedures of your agency.
2. Teach and provide counseling that is consistent with the individualized service plan (ISP).
3. Find out what the person with a developmental disability already knows and feels about his or her sexuality. Know and understand before acting.
4. Determine the reason and goal for the teaching and/or counseling (this should be stated in the ISP).
5. Start with the person's language and communication style. When necessary, teach the use of more acceptable words.
6. Be straightforward, simple, and direct.
7. Do not interpret silence as knowledge. The person may be too shy or not know what questions to ask.
8. Always keep a sense of humor. It is often the best way out of moments of high anxiety or embarrassment.
9. Honesty and sincerity are also good responses to feelings of embarrassment and anxiety.
10. Do not lecture or moralize.
11. Emphasize that individual sexual behavior carries with it individual responsibilities.

individual basis. Each person should be provided information that is in keeping with his or her individualized service plan (ISP). The ISP should state what the person needs to know, the level of detail, and the best method of instruction. The ISP cannot anticipate all possible questions or situations, and it may not list all the answers. However, it can and should serve as a guide for the staff. If a person's ISP makes no reference to human sexuality, it may be necessary to hold an interdisciplinary team meeting to update the plan.

Greater sexual awareness and information will not necessarily result in increased sexual experimentation and activity. Instead, information helps people to think, rather than to act without thinking. In addition, correct information can lead to improved social behavior. It can also result in increased self-respect and fewer feelings of guilt and anxiety. Withholding of information, on the other hand, can result in confusion, unnecessary fear, and poorly planned actions.

The goal of education in human sexuality is to give people a positive attitude toward their own sexuality and an enhanced self-image. The purpose should not be prevention—whether of pregnancy, masturbation, or homosexuality. If prevention is the keynote and people are taught that stopping sexual activity is the goal, they develop negative attitudes toward their feelings of sexuality. As a general rule, stopping one type of sexual expression only results in a different form of sexual expression.

A PERSON'S ATTITUDE TOWARD HIS OR HER SEXUALITY IS MORE IMPORTANT THAN THE ABILITY TO NAME BODY PARTS.

In providing sex education, the staff should be aware that slow learners have difficulty grasping verbal abstractions. Instead, pictures, models of body parts, role playing, and acting are good instructional methods. Instruction should begin with simple and specific facts and become only as complicated as the person's understanding permits. It is important to find out what the person already knows. Are the facts right or wrong? Determine in the beginning how the person feels about his or her own sexuality. How can the person best communicate those feelings?

INFORMATION DOES NOT NECESSARILY LEAD TO INCREASED SEXUAL ACTIVITY.

COUNSELING IN HUMAN SEXUALITY

Counseling in human sexuality is more involved than giving information and shaping attitudes. Counseling consists of an interaction that addresses feelings and emotions about sexuality. It integrates those feelings with the self-concept of the individual. Monet-Haller (1992) notes that sexuality counseling differs from education in sexuality in that counseling attempts to match thoughts and feelings with appropriate behavior.

One aspect of sexuality counseling focuses on the remediation of problem or inappropriate behaviors. Because of a lack of previous education or counseling in sexuality, some people with developmental disabilities may have developed inappropriate forms of sexual expression. These "poor choices" (Monat-Haller, 1992) that can be addressed through counseling include:

Evasion of responsibility
Poor self control
Sexual expression based on incorrect information
Unavailability of more acceptable alternative forms of sexual expression
Physical or intellectual inability to find other means to satisfy physical desires

The person providing sexuality counseling should have a background in such counseling. Counseling is provided in a verbal mode. There may be times, however, when alternative communication systems, such as sign language, language boards, or prosthetic speech devices, may be used with people who are nonverbal. A counselor may use role-playing techniques, but "hands-on" teaching or counseling is not permitted. This type of activity is both unethical and illegal.

Dilemmas encountered in sexuality counseling are listed in Table 3. Other factors to be considered are given in Table 4.

EXERCISE 3

Counseling in Sexuality

Identify the questions that one or two people have recently asked you in the area of sexuality. Write down any sexual behaviors that indicate a need for counseling. Then review the ISPs of these persons and the agency policy and procedure manual. Do these documents provide you with direction and advice on how to respond to the person's needs?

STAFF RESPONSIBILITIES

The staff of an organization can assume various responsibilities for education in sexuality. Some staff members accept a more formal role

Table 3. Dilemmas in providing counseling

1. Counseling and education may not have been provided in the past.
2. Persons who are slow learners may have difficulty with abstract verbal learning. They generally need realistic learning situations. Teaching should be realistic and concrete, not abstract. However, this approach has obvious limitations in the area of sexuality.
3. Counseling in human sexuality can involve decisions about controversial issues, such as birth control, sterilization, marriage, and sexual preference.
4. Because many persons lack factual information, counseling generally begins as sex education.
5. Helping people make decisions about their sexuality is an important responsibility. Professional organizations, including the American Psychological Association and the American Association of Sex Educators, Counselors, and Therapists, have developed ethical guidelines for providing counseling and therapy.
6. Agency staff frequently provide counseling because there are no experts available. Staff members may have developed a trusting relationship with the person. They are there when the question is asked or the behavior takes place, but they may lack training in human sexuality counseling.

in developing an educational program, selecting instructional materials, and providing individual and group instruction. This formal approach is designed to address knowledge and skills that are identified as part of the ongoing assessment and ISP process. As such, the educational objectives and process are individualized and provide the information that each person needs to develop appropriate sexual behavior.

Other staff members may find opportunities to provide education during normal daily routines. Individuals with developmental disabilities ask questions that merit answers at that time. Community living associates, job coaches, and teachers can use natural teaching moments to convey information on sexuality. Most individuals with developmental disabilities talk with the people with whom they feel most comfortable, and these staff members should be prepared to provide basic information.

In addition, each staff member should be knowledgeable about the individual's ISP and its assessment and plan in the area of sexuality.

Table 4. Questions to be considered in counseling on human sexuality

1. Is the person who will be counseled fully informed of the counselor's qualifications, orientation, values, and limitations?
2. How will confidentiality be assured?
3. Will the counselor inform the person of all the advantages and disadvantages of his or her sexual actions?
4. Does the person fully understand his or her rights? This includes the right to stop the counseling.
5. Have referral routes to more specialized counselors been established?

The staff must act in a consistent manner, and the ISP ensures a coordinated approach to the individual's form of sexual expression. No matter how the staff feels about any sexual behavior, they must follow the ISP. Finally, the staff must also provide education in sexuality within the context of agency policy and procedure.

In order to respond consistently, staff members need to analyze their own attitudes toward sexual behaviors. They have the responsibility to understand their own biases. It is important for them to realize, for example, that they may be more tolerant of masturbation than of homosexuality or that their primary concern is pornography. Nevertheless, the staff should keep personal feelings separate. The staff should work to develop a healthy and supportive attitude toward the informed sexual choices of the person with a developmental disability. This should be the goal even if individual staff members would make different choices for themselves.

In addition to understanding their own attitudes, staff members are responsible for acquiring a basic understanding of human sexuality. This should include knowledge of human anatomy, reproduction, birth control, and the range of typical sexual behavior. Such information is available in the public library. It can also be obtained through the sources listed in the Bibliography and Additional Resources sections at the end of this chapter.

Staff members also must be responsible for their own behaviors. You should realize that your direct and indirect actions teach people, and that people with developmental disabilities will model your behavior. The manner in which you act out your own self-concept of being male or female will influence people with developmental disabilities. Also, the manner in which you carry out the agency's policies and procedures concerning sexuality can influence what people learn. For example, if you were to discourage a man from expressing affection toward a woman without also dealing with his advances toward other men, you might be indirectly teaching that homosexual relationships are more acceptable than heterosexual associations.

The staff must come to terms with the language of sex. The first step is to feel comfortable with formal terminology, including *penis* and *vagina*. However, some people, including those with developmental disabilities, simply do not talk that way. They use such words as *fuck* and *cock*. These words are not generally accepted in normal conversation, but they are part of the native language describing sexual activity. Staff members need to develop a tolerance to such language so that they do not react emotionally when they hear it.

YOUR BEHAVIORS AND ACTIONS AS A MAN OR WOMAN WILL INFLUENCE WHAT PEOPLE WITH DEVELOPMENTAL DISABILITIES LEARN AND HOW THEY BEHAVE.

Staff responsibilities in the area of counseling are more limited. In general, counseling in human sexuality is the responsibility of individuals with training in both group and individual sexuality counseling. In some instances, it is unclear whether an individual is requesting, or needs, information and education to make a decision or whether the individual needs counseling to resolve conflict and uncertainty about feelings and behaviors. As a general rule, the staff should respond to inquiries with simple and straightforward responses. These may lead to requests for more information that enables the individual to make a decision. Information and conversations that produce greater uncertainty, doubt, guilt, or inappropriate activity may indicate a need for counseling.

A final staff responsibility is ensuring that no person ever sexually exploits another person. No one should be pressured or forced into any type of sexual activity. No person should be allowed to use children sexually. Also, people should not sexually dominate one another because of greater strength, ability, or knowledge.

NO PERSON SHOULD EVER SEXUALLY EXPLOIT ANOTHER PERSON.

SUMMARY

Providing information about human sexuality may seem difficult. It may sometimes be embarrassing or confusing. You may not be able to find similar experiences from the past to guide you. You will probably make a few mistakes, but most people learn from their mistakes and do a better job the next time. So will you.

When events begin to get confusing or difficult, remember how important human sexuality is to people. For some people with severe developmental disabilities, human sexuality can be best appreciated as the warmth of another's caress or voice. For others, sexuality may have meaning in terms of masturbation or a relationship with another person.

Finally, never forget the important role you play. Your attitude and actions teach people what to think about their sexuality. You and your coworkers make the unwritten policy about sexuality. This is true whether or not your agency has formal policies and procedures. As a result, you need to be sensitive to the human sexuality and rights of people with developmental disabilities.

BIBLIOGRAPHY

Crocker, A.C., Cohen, H.J., & Kastner, T.A. (Eds.). (1992). *HIV infection and developmental disabilities: A resource for service providers.* Baltimore: Paul H. Brookes Publishing Co.

Croft, A., & Croft, M. (1983). *Sex education and counseling for mentally handicapped people*. Baltimore: University Park Press.

Gardner, N.E.S. (1986). Sexuality. In J.A. Summers (Ed.), *The right to grow up: An introduction to adults with developmental disabilities* (pp. 45–66). Baltimore: Paul H. Brookes Publishing Co.

Johnson, W. (1973). Sex education of the mentally retarded. In Felix F. De La Cruz (Ed.), *Human sexuality and the mentally retarded*. New York: Brunner/Mazel.

Kempton, W., Bass, M.S., & Gordon, S. (1980). *Love, sex, and birth control for the mentally retarded—a guide for parents* (3rd ed., rev.). Philadelphia: Planned Parenthood Association of Southeastern Pennsylvania.

Monat-Haller, R.K. (1992). *Understanding and expressing sexuality: Responsible choices for individuals with developmental disabilities*. Baltimore: Paul H. Brookes Publishing Co.

Palmer, F.B., Ziring, P.R., & Shapiro, B.K. (1989). Serious viral infection. In I.L. Rubin & A.C. Crocker (Eds.), *Developmental disabilities: Delivery of medical care for children and adults*. Philadelphia: Lea & Febiger.

Rennert, S., Parry, J., & Horowitz, R. (1989). *AIDS and persons with developmental disabilities: The legal perspective*. Washington, DC: American Bar Association.

Rubin, I.L., & Crocker, A.C. (1989). *Developmental disabilities: Delivery of medical care for children and adults*. Philadelphia: Lea & Febiger.

Simonds, R.J., & Rogerts, M.F. (1992). Epidemiology of HIV infection in children and other populations. In A.C. Crocker, H.J. Cohen, & T.A. Kastner (Eds.), *HIV infection and developmental disabilities: A resource for service providers* (pp. 3–13). Baltimore: Paul H. Brookes Publishing Co.

ADDITIONAL RESOURCES

M.O. Hyde and E.H. Forsyth (1989), in *AIDS: What does it mean to you?* (3rd rev. ed.) (New York: Walker & Co.); John Langone (1991), in *AIDS: The facts* (rev. ed.) (Boston: Little, Brown); and W. Colman (1987), in *Understanding and preventing AIDS* (Chicago: Childrens Press), address the issue of AIDS in a practical manner at a basic reading level.

E.W. Johnston (1988), in *Love and sex in plain language* (4th rev. ed.) (New York: Bantam Books), and (1990), in *Love and sex and growing up* (New York: Bantam Books), writes about love, sex, and growing up in a simple, straightforward manner at a basic reading level.

D. Sobsey, S. Grey, D. Wells, D. Pyper, and B. Reimer-Heck (1991), in *Disability, sexuality, and abuse: An annotated bibliography* (Baltimore: Paul H. Brookes Publishing Co.), provide an excellent annotated bibliography.

The James Stanfield Publishing Company, P.O. Box 41058, Santa Barbara, CA 93140 (1-800-421-6534), offers a wide variety of materials on sexuality, social relationships, sexuality education, intimacy and relationships, sexual abuse, safe sex, social skills, citizenship, and work. Materials include slide-tape programs, videos, filmstrips, and teaching graphs.

SELF-APPRAISAL

INSTRUCTIONS

The following questions will help you evaluate your knowledge about human sexuality. For true-false questions, check the correct answer. For multiple choice questions, circle the correct answer(s).

Note: There may be more than one correct answer for some questions.

1. In general, there is a conservative attitude about the sexuality of people with developmental disabilities. They are sometimes viewed as nonsexual people.
    ____ True   ____ False

2. Sexuality is not something an individual does. Sexuality is learning about being a woman or a man.
    ____ True   ____ False

3. Unless persons of legal age have been declared incompetent by a legal proceeding, they are responsible for making decisions about their own sexuality.
    ____ True   ____ False

4. The staff have a responsibility to:
    a. Provide the necessary and correct information about sexuality
    b. Support the informed decisions of people with developmental disabilities
    c. Inform the family of all decisions concerning a person's sexuality
    d. React in a consistent manner (as specified in the ISP) to the person's sexual behaviors

5. People with developmental disabilities learn about sexuality from:
    a. The way staff members act
    b. One another
    c. Their physicians
    d. The people they live with

6. Which of the following statements about teaching or counseling in the field of human sexuality is correct?
    a. Simplicity is the key.
    b. Provide only the information requested.
    c. Begin with the basic and simple facts the person already knows.
    d. Avoid verbal abstractions.

7. A goal of education and counseling in human sexuality is to:
   a. Assist people in developing a positive attitude toward their own sexuality
   b. Prevent inappropriate behaviors
   c. Enhance self-image
   d. Increase sexual activity
8. Which of the following is not a guideline for teaching and counseling?
   a. Find out what the person already knows and feels about his or her sexuality. Know and understand before acting.
   b. Do not interpret silence as knowing. People may be too shy or may not know what questions to ask.
   c. Do not lecture or moralize.
   d. Use the proper language of human sexuality, not the learner's language.
9. Which of the following should always be used as decision aids by the staff?
   a. The ISP
   b. Agency policy and procedures
   c. The staff member's value system
   d. The individual's choice
10. Important considerations in providing counseling in human sexuality are:
    a. People with developmental disabilities should be fully informed of the counselor's qualifications, orientation, values, and limitations.
    b. Confidentiality will be preserved.
    c. People with developmental disabilities should know their rights, including the right to stop the counseling.
    d. Parents and other important family members are always included in the counseling.

CASE STUDY

Susan Williams is a 34-year-old woman who lives with her parents in Washington County, Maryland. She has Down syndrome and severe mental retardation. She is 43 pounds overweight. Her hearing and eyesight are normal.

At age 28, she entered a job training program at the county vocational center, operated by Tri-County Employment, Inc. She remained in that program for 6 years. For the past 6 months, she has worked in a job station at the nearby Holloway Inn.

Situation

Ms. Williams attends a Friday night social program sponsored by the church. A 43-year-old man with a moderate developmental disability has begun to interact with Susan. Until recently, they had held hands, kissed each other on the head and face, and engaged in age-inappropriate laughing and verbalizations. Ms. Williams's family and friends were aware of the behavior, but no one provided any guidance or instruction to her. More recently, however, her brother and sister have observed Susan and her friend caressing one another in public. They suspect that Ms. Williams is currently engaged, or soon will be, in more intimate sexual activity. They are reluctant to discuss their concerns with either Ms. Williams or their parents.

1. What concerns would you have about Ms. Williams's behavior? List these concerns.
2. How would you determine what information she knows and what she needs to know?
3. What would you advise Ms. Williams's brother and sister to do about their concerns?
4. If necessary, how would you explain to Ms. Williams the possible consequences of her actions?

ANSWER KEY TO
SELF-APPRAISAL AND CASE STUDY

SELF-APPRAISAL

1. True
2. True
3. True
4. a, b, d
5. a, b, d
6. a, b, c, d
7. a, c
8. d
9. a, b, d
10. a, b, c

CASE STUDY ANSWER GUIDELINES

1. First, you need to determine what responsibility you, as a staff member, have for Ms. Williams's behaviors outside the job training program. Who should be responsible for providing assistance to her? Once the responsibility has been assigned, several behaviors need to be addressed. The first is the hand-holding, kissing, and age-inappropriate laughing and verbalizations. These have been observed. Ms. Williams's brother and sister have also seen her and her friend caressing in public. The more intimate sexual activity is an inferred behavior. You should be concerned about the age-inappropriate social interaction and the public exchange of affection. The inferred behavior is a more difficult issue. You need more information.
2. That determination could be made by talking with Ms. Williams in an honest and direct manner. An equally important question is who should talk with her.
3. This is a complex issue. They need to determine the parents' capabilities and willingness to talk with their sister. The parents should be given the opportunity. The brother and sister could decide to talk directly to Ms. Williams if the parents declined. The real question, however, is why should anyone talk with her? Why should anyone have an interest in her behavior? What is a legitimate interest in her behavior? This leads to the next question.

4. The agency staff and Ms. Williams's family do have an interest in her behavior. Their interest should focus on her being able to make an informed and conscious decision about her behavior. Either the family (the first choice) or a counselor, or both, at the agency should talk with Ms. Williams. They should determine what she knows and what she needs to know.

chapter 11

Leisure and Recreation

LEARNING OBJECTIVES

Upon completing this chapter, the reader will be able to:

1. Identify four reasons for the importance of leisure activities.
2. State the four characteristics of an appropriate leisure activity.
3. Identify common barriers to integrated leisure activities.
4. Identify specific examples of the five types of leisure activities.
5. Describe assessment methods for determining appropriate leisure activities.
6. Define four methods of promoting leisure-time activity through adaptation.

INTRODUCTION

Programs for people with developmental disabilities generally focus on residential and vocational services. A place to live and a job are necessary for survival. The staff design residential and vocational programs to enable people with developmental disabilities to live and work in more independent and integrated surroundings, but these programs do not include leisure time. A healthy and harmonious life should consist of lifelong learning, working, and leisure. For adults, work is important, but it should not exclude continued learning or significant leisure activities. In a similar manner, retirement may include a mix of leisure, learning, and work.

Leisure is an activity that individuals choose to engage in during free time. You can identify leisure time by defining the following terms (Bolles, 1981):

Nonwork time is time that is not spent in preparing for, going to, participating in, returning from, or thinking about work.

Personal care time includes dressing, eating, and hygiene activities.

Sleep includes both day (naps) and night sleep.

House and family care consists of such activities as caring for family members, shopping, cleaning, making repairs, and paying bills.

Leisure time is the time that is left over when personal care time, sleep, and house and family care time are subtracted from nonwork time.

Leisure time can now be defined by the following equation:

Leisure time equals nonwork time:

      minus personal care time

      minus sleep

      minus home and family care

THE IMPORTANCE OF LEISURE

Leisure is important because it balances the worlds of work and learning. People make important choices about their own preferences in leisure activities. These choices are individualistic and personal. The same activity may not appeal to different people. Leisure activities are important because they are personal choices about how people want to use their free time.

Leisure activities indicate how people want to use their free time.

Using Free Time

Many people with developmental disabilities have a great deal of free time because employment and learning opportunities are limited. Even those who are employed or engaged in adult education may still have significant time for leisure during the week.

For people with developmental disabilities, however, free time often becomes "waiting" time because they lack experience and training in leisure activities. In former large residential programs, people with developmental disabilities were trained to wait while the staff prepared activities, programs, and meals. They did not expect to use their free time in individualized and rewarding activities. This same routine of waiting for the staff can take place in community-based programs. The abundance of free time makes leisure activities important.

Free time makes leisure activities important.

Reducing Inappropriate Social Behaviors

A lack of individualized activities may cause people with developmental disabilities to engage in inappropriate social behaviors. Social withdrawal, self-stimulation, body rocking, and aggression can result from empty free time. People who are participating in individualized leisure activities usually find it difficult to engage in dysfunctional behaviors at the same time. The staff can replace inappropriate social behaviors with leisure-time behaviors and activities.

Teaching Social and Communication Skills

Leisure activities also present opportunities to learn and demonstrate social, communication, and work adjustment skills. Cooperative leisure behavior and good social skills are essential for community living, work, and play. Social and communication skills are vital to good relationships with coworkers and important in maintaining good job performance. They are necessary skills when living with another person.

Promoting Physical Health

Leisure activities contribute to health and wellness and can significantly reduce stress and anxiety. Active recreational activities are particularly important in promoting physical and mental health. Leisure makes a significant contribution to the quality of life.

MAJOR ISSUES IN LEISURE ACTIVITIES

The selection of leisure activities may present concerns for service agencies, family, and advocates. Because the selection reflects an individual's preference, the staff may face the issues of risk and protection. These can influence decisions about integrated and segregated leisure programs.

Autonomy and Choice

Leisure involves choices about free time. Many people discover leisure interests by experiencing a variety of activities and selecting those they most enjoy. Parents expose children to many activities as they grow up. Eventually, children and adolescents begin to choose their own leisure activities. Adults generally rely on past experiences and current preferences in making choices.

The agency staff should allow people with developmental disabilities to experience a variety of leisure activities and assist each individual to participate in those of his or her choice. The process begins with the staff providing a range of experiences and ends with the individual choosing the preferred activities.

Risk and Protection

Choice in leisure activities may involve some risks. Learning to swim creates the possibility of drowning. Going to the ballpark involves the possibility of getting lost. Leisure activities in the community expose people with developmental disabilities to many risks.

Former institutional practices sheltered people from risk, but this overprotection was too extreme. It prevented people from exploring various life options and experiences. The issues of overprotection in leisure activities are similar to those presented in the discussion on sexuality (Chapter 10). People deserve the opportunity to make choices in a graduated fashion. They should first make small choices with limited risks. Then, they can move on and begin to make bigger choices with more significant risks. Individuals with developmental disabilities can develop meaningful leisure pursuits without undue risk if they are given staff assistance and training.

Special or Generic Leisure Activities

There is disagreement about whether leisure activities should be designed specifically for people with developmental disabilities. Some advocates promote their participation in regular (generic) leisure activities with other citizens of the community. Other advocates argue that special programs provide opportunities that might not otherwise exist. The Special Olympics and parks designated for people with disabilities are examples of specialized services.

Special programs, however, do not promote community participation for people with developmental disabilities. They are often designed to protect people from failure, ridicule, and abuse. In addition, special programs continue to depict people with developmental disabilities as different and devalued and are often inferior to generic programs available to all citizens.

The debate over special or generic leisure activities can lead to heated discussions. The staff should decide the issue on an individual basis. The personal preference of each individual with a developmental disability should be the primary factor. Staff members can begin the decision process by assisting each individual in participating in integrated community leisure activities. They should provide training, counseling, and support so that the individual is as successful as possible in these activities. The choice of specialized or regular leisure rests with the individual, however, and the staff must respect that choice.

CHARACTERISTICS OF APPROPRIATE LEISURE PROGRAMS

All people have different leisure-time skills, interests, and opportunities. Individuals also differ in physical ability, mental capability, and sensory acuity. For these reasons, leisure activities require an individualized approach. Each leisure program, however, should demonstrate four characteristics:

1. Leisure services should be consistent with the principle of normalization. In particular, leisure activities should be appropriate for the individual's age and culture. Most leisure activities should be provided through integrated community programs, for example, the local 4-H Club, the neighborhood association, and the city or county parks and recreation program. Recent advances in adaptive equipment, communication systems, and environmental modification have decreased the need for special programs for people with developmental disabilities. Therapeutic recreation is being transformed into activities that are available to all citizens, including people with developmental disabilities.

LEISURE ACTIVITIES SHOULD BE PROVIDED THROUGH INTEGRATED COMMUNITY PROGRAMS.

---

2. Training in leisure skills and habilitation programs for children, adolescents, and adults that focus on leisure should take place in the community.
3. Leisure-time activities should be based on personal preferences. Individuals should be able to make choices from available options and have the necessary experience and skills to make meaningful choices. A daily schedule that provides for a crafts class between 7 P.M. and 8 P.M. for the three people living in a supervised apartment does not place the crafts class in the category of leisure activities. Individualization, choice, and a range of options are needed for leisure programs.
4. Promotion of integrated leisure activities requires a partnership among various organizations and individuals. Human services organizations, local educational agencies, the municipal parks and recreation department, families, advocates, volunteers, and individuals with developmental disabilities should all work together in planning, developing, and monitoring accessible leisure-time activities.

COMMUNITY RECREATION AND LEISURE ACTIVITIES

Leisure and recreation generally consist of physical, cultural, social, outdoor educational, and mental recreational activities (Wehman, Renzaglia, & Bates, 1985).

Physical Activities

An excellent form of exercise, physical activity can lead to improved mental and physical health. Physical activities can be individual or group events; for example, people can walk and jog alone or with others. People with developmental disabilities can participate in various physical activities for fun or in competition. Many municipalities have specialized teams and clubs, such as soccer, softball, and swimming.

Cultural Activities

Individuals with developmental disabilities can engage in cultural activities as either participants or observers. Cultural activities range from arts and crafts; to dramatic activities, such as plays, fairs, and festivals; to dance and music. They provide opportunities to discover new leisure interests and to develop social networks in the community.

Social Activities

Most leisure and recreational events are social in nature; however, the attraction of some activities is based on interaction with people. Dances, parties, picnics, and holiday celebrations bring people together. They are times for people to share and enjoy experiences with others.

Outdoor Educational Activities

Outdoor sporting events and nature study groups offer many leisure opportunities. Clubs and organizations provide many of these activities. Some, such as the Wilderness Society, Audubon Society, and Sierra Club, are national organizations with branches in most states and many local communities. Local organizations that provide similar services may include church groups, local parks and recreation clubs, and community colleges.

Mental Activities

Many individuals with developmental disabilities enjoy leisure activities that offer mental, rather than physical, satisfaction. Adult education classes, games, hobbies, and library activities can provide mental challenge and satisfaction.

EXERCISE 1

Integrated Options for Leisure and Recreation

Explore your neighborhood and surrounding community. Start with an area 3 miles from where people with developmental disabilities live. Within that area, what generic options are available for people with disabilities? List them in column A.

(continued)

EXERCISE 1
(continued)
In column B, list the leisure and recreational resources that need some changes to accommodate people with developmental disabilities. These could be architectural, attitudinal, or organizational.

Column A	Column B
_____	_____
_____	_____
_____	_____
_____	_____

LEISURE ACTIVITIES AND HABILITATION PLANNING

Assessment for leisure activities is similar to other functional assessments described in Chapter 5. In addition, the selection, training, and participation in leisure activities is part of the habilitation planning team process. The team does not need to be present when people choose leisure activities, but it should ensure that the choices are integrated with other aspects of individual habilitation programs.

Interdisciplinary Team Planning Process

Decisions about leisure are part of habilitation planning. Leisure activities should reflect the choices and preferences of the individual with a developmental disability. Functional assessment in leisure begins with an individual's self-assessment of what he or she wants to do during free time.

The self-assessment of leisure activities will be most meaningful if the individual has experienced some range of leisure activities from which to choose. This is especially important for persons with cognitive impairments who have difficulty generalizing experiences from one context to another and who find abstractions particularly difficult.

INDIVIDUALS SHOULD HAVE SOME RANGE OF PREVIOUS LEISURE EXPERIENCE FROM WHICH TO MAKE CHOICES.

Team members can help the individuals with developmental disabilities to make realistic choices of leisure activities. The team can assist them in deciding if they are able to participate independently in the chosen activities, or the team might identify training that would increase individual skills and promote independence. The team also can suggest supports and modifications in leisure programs that would help people to participate.

Finally, the team must remember that leisure activities take place during an individual's free time, that they are selected by the individual, and that the individual receives enjoyment and other reinforcement from the activities. The team should not intrude in the individual's leisure activity. The team should clearly distinguish between training in leisure skills and an individual's participation in leisure activities during free time.

Leisure Assessment

Leisure skills can be assessed by using structured leisure assessment tools, behavioral checklists, or a functional analysis of an individual's actual performance in a selected leisure activity. Table 1 identifies a number of leisure assessment tools. It also indicates the individuals for whom the assessment applies and illustrates the reliability, validity, ease of administration, and response mode of each assessment. Leisure skills also can be assessed through the use of general competency checklists.

Finally, leisure skills can be assessed by observing an individual engaged in a leisure activity. Actual observation, as well as discussion with the individual and others, may identify ways to adapt the activity, if necessary, so that the individual can participate.

ADAPTATIONS TO LEISURE ACTIVITIES

Depending on the type and degree of disability, some individuals with developmental disabilities may lack necessary motor, social, communication, or cognitive skills to participate successfully in leisure and recreational programs of their choice. However, through appropriate modifications and supports, the programs can be adapted for these individuals.

MODIFICATIONS TO LEISURE PROGRAMS AND INDIVIDUALIZED SUPPORTS ALLOW PEOPLE WITH DEVELOPMENTAL DISABILITIES TO PARTICIPATE IN LEISURE AND RECREATIONAL PROGRAMS.

Three principles should be considered in adapting leisure and recreational programs:

1. Use adaptations only when necessary to increase participation, success, and enjoyment.
2. Consider adaptations as temporary, if possible. In some instances, the adaptation may be permanent. In many instances, reasonable skill development and training enable individuals eventually to participate without adaptations.
3. Base adaptations on the functional assessment in order to meet the individual's needs.

Table 1. Leisure assessment tools

Instruments	Target population	Reliability	Validity[a]	Ease of administration[b]	Response mode
Avocational Activities Inventory (Overs, O'Connor, & Demarco, 1974)	EMR[c]	good	good	quickly	staff
I Can (Wessel, 1976)	TMR-children	good	good	quickly	direct
Joswiak's Leisure Counseling Assessment Instruments (Joswiak, 1975)	DD	N/A	good	time-consuming	examinee: direct
Linear Model for Individual Treatment in Recreation (LMIT) (Compton & Price, 1975)	DD	N/A	N/A	time-consuming	examinee: direct
Leisure Skills Curriculum Assessment Inventory (LSCDD) (Wehman & Schleien, 1979)	DD	N/A	N/A	time-consuming	direct: staff
Minimum Objective System (MOS) (Williams & Fox, 1977)	severely handicapped	N/A	good	quickly	direct: staff
Recreation Therapy Assessment (Cousins & Brown, 1979)	nonambulatory adult	N/A	N/A	time-consuming	direct

(continued)

Table 1. (continued)

Instruments	Target population	Criteria			
		Reliability	Validity[a]	Ease of administration[b]	Response mode
Sonoma County Organization for the Retarded Assessment System (SCOR) (Westaway & Apolloni, 1977)	DD	N/A	good	time-consuming	examinee: staff
State of Ohio Curriculum Guide for Moderately Mentally Retarded Learners (Ohio Department of Mental Health, 1977)	TMR	N/A	N/A	time-consuming	direct: staff
Toward Competency: A Guide for Individualized Instruction (Oregon State Department of Education, 1974)	all special populations	N/A	good	time-consuming	examinee: staff

From Hawkins, B.A. (1988). Leisure and recreational programming. In M.P. Janicki, M.W. Krauss, & M.M. Seltzer (Eds.), *Community residences for persons with developmental disabilities: Here to stay* (p. 220). Baltimore: Paul H. Brookes Publishing Co; reprinted by permission.

Adapted with permission from Wehman and Schleien (1980), pp. 14–15.

[a] The original table by Wehman and Schleien (1980) reported validity for some instruments; however, it did not provide companion reliability information. N/A = not available.

[b] "Quickly" implies 30 minutes or less, and "time-consuming" means longer than 30 minutes.

[c] EMR, educable mentally retarded (mild mental retardation); TMR, trainable mentally retarded (moderate mental retardation); DD, developmentally disabled.

Four types of adaptation pertain to community leisure and recreational activities (Wehman & Schleien, 1981): material, procedural, skill sequence, and facility adaptations.

1. *Material adaptations.* The materials and equipment used in most leisure and recreational activities are not designed for people with developmental disabilities, but many modifications are possible. Examples of these adaptations are:

   Handle-grip bowling balls
   Braille reading materials
   Lowered basketball rims
   Tee-ball, rather than pitched baseball
   Special handles on rackets

2. *Modifications in rules and procedures.* The rules and procedures for most games can be altered. Examples of such modifications to help people with developmental disabilities are:

   Reducing standard distances in horseshoes, for foul shots in basketball, or for services from the baseline in tennis
   Simplifying rules for card games, billiards, and square dancing
   Reducing the number of players in team sports

3. *Skill sequence adaptations.* Some recreational and leisure activities require that steps be performed in a certain sequence. This may be difficult or impossible for some people with developmental disabilities. Examples of adaptations in the sequence of steps for safety and better performance are:

   Dressing in exercise clothing at home rather than the gym
   Taking position earlier than other participants
   Positioning food for cooking before turning the oven on
   Starting with a prethreaded needle in sewing

4. *Facility adaptations.* In the past, cultural, leisure-time, and recreational facilities, including libraries, churches, restaurants, theaters, stadiums, and schools, were often inaccessible to many individuals with developmental disabilities. Section 503 of The Rehabilitation Act of 1973 and The American with Disabilities Act of 1990, however, have greatly reduced this inaccessibility. Examples of facility adaptations are:

   Accessible toilets, sinks, and water fountains
   Curb cuts and ramps
   Mobility buses
   Enlarged doorknobs and door handles

EXERCISE 2

Application of Adaptations

Column B in Exercise 1 contains a list of community leisure and recreational activities that require adaptations. Identify which of the four types—material, skill sequence, rules and procedures, and facility—would be required in each instance.

BARRIERS TO INTEGRATED LEISURE

Despite the passage of recent federal legislation and the increasing adaptation of materials, procedures, skills sequence, and facilities, many people with developmental disabilities are unable to participate in leisure and recreational programs.

Leisure Services Designed by and for Nondisabled People

Nondisabled people are able to use services that are not individualized because they have a greater capacity for adjustment. As a result, leisure services for nondisabled people may not meet some quality standards, but they can still be utilized.

In addition, if the able-bodied person objects to substandard programs, he or she can shop for other equivalent services and select from a variety of options. Multiple options, however, are seldom available to people with developmental disabilities.

Finally, because most leisure and recreational programs are designed for and used by nondisabled people, no design allowances are made for special supports needed by people with developmental disabilities.

MOST LEISURE AND RECREATIONAL PROGRAMS CONTAIN NO DESIGN ALLOWANCES FOR SPECIAL SUPPORTS NEEDED BY PEOPLE WITH DEVELOPMENTAL DISABILITIES.

Lack of Accessible Facilities

Nonaccessible buildings, open spaces, and transportation have historically prevented people with disabilities from participating in integrated leisure and recreational activities. The Rehabilitation Act of 1973 prohibits discrimination on the basis of disability and requires the removal of architectural barriers in some buildings. The Americans with Disabilities Act of 1990 (PL 101-336) goes well beyond the 1973 law in banning discrimination in public accommodations. It requires removal of existing physical barriers when "readily achievable." In all new construction, the law requires that public accommodations be accessible to people with disabilities. The term *public accommodation*, as used in the Act, refers to such facilities as restaurants, hotels, theaters, museums, libraries, parks, and centers for hobbies, crafts, and socialization.

EXERCISE 3

The Americans with Disabilities Act of 1990

Read and discuss the provisions of The Americans with Disabilities Act of 1990 that pertain to accessibility and transportation.

Lack of Transportation

Lack of transportation remains a major barrier to community-based leisure and recreation. The American with Disabilities Act of 1990 has set standards for accessible public transportation, but often there is no public transportation to be made accessible. Private taxi services may not be accessible and also may be too costly.

The barriers caused by lack of transportation can be addressed by advocacy efforts aimed at local transportation authorities. Some corporations, churches, and schools may donate transportation services during off-peak hours. Parents, volunteers, and service agencies can form car pools. Where public transportation is available, the best strategies are to plan services carefully so that they are accessible to public transportation and to provide mobility training for those individuals capable of using public transportation.

Lack of Qualified Staff

The staffs of many generic leisure and recreational programs may not have the necessary training and experience to work with people with developmental disabilities. In the past, therapeutic recreation specialists worked in special programs for individuals with disabilities. There was little expectation that people with developmental disabilities would or could use generic services, and many of these programs still lack the staff necessary for this purpose. In addition, the training and experience of some professionals reinforces their beliefs that people with developmental disabilities are best served in specialized programs. They are reluctant to develop resources and expertise to serve these individuals.

Employees of leisure and recreational programs often lack knowledge and experience in listening to and communicating with people with developmental disabilities, many of whom have difficulty with communication. Unfortunately, many professionals have little experience with alternative communication systems—signing, communication boards, and artificial speech.

Financial Considerations

The use of some leisure and recreational services costs money, but the majority of people with developmental disabilities have limited financial resources. Also, leisure and recreational agencies often face financial burdens when they attempt to remove architectural barriers, modify existing programs and activities for people with developmental disabilities, and hire staffs who can individualize programs for them.

Sliding-scale fees based on ability to pay are helpful for individuals with developmental disabilities. Many publicly supported recreational and leisure programs have adopted sliding fee scales.

Leisure and recreational organizations can often resolve the problem of specialized staff by collaborating with similar agencies and sharing staffs. These agencies can also organize a group of volunteers to help people with developmental disabilities move into community-based leisure and recreational programs.

SUMMARY

Leisure is as important as education and work. Because leisure activities take place during free time, they can provide special enjoyment and reinforcement. For people with developmental disabilities, leisure activities can help to reduce inappropriate social behavior and long waiting periods in service programs. Leisure programs are also used to teach social and communication skills. In addition, leisure activities and recreation promote physical and mental health.

Leisure and recreational services were traditionally provided to people with developmental disabilities through specialized services. Recreation and leisure activities were identified with special camps, bowling leagues for people with developmental disabilities, and swimming classes for people who are blind. The more contemporary approach is to attempt first to provide services through generic recreational and leisure programs. People with developmental disabilities can participate in leisure and recreation with nondisabled peers. Some families and individuals with developmental disabilities, however, prefer to participate with other persons with developmental disabilities in self-contained leisure and recreational programs. In these instances, individual choice should prevail.

Barriers to integrated leisure linger. Lack of design features for people with developmental disabilities, lack of alternatives and options, architectural barriers, lack of accessible transportation, financial constraints, and lack of professional staff may reduce the number of integrated leisure and recreational possibilities for people with developmental disabilities.

Finally, the support service model has been extended to leisure and recreation through adaptations in material, procedures, skill sequence, and facilities.

BIBLIOGRAPHY

Bates, P., & Renzaglia, A. (1979). Community-based recreation programs. In P. Wehman (Ed.), *Recreation programming for developmentally disabled persons.* Austin, TX: PRO-ED.

Bolles, R.N. (1981). *The three boxes of life and how to get out of them.* Berkeley, CA: Ten Speed Press.

Compton, D., & Price, D. (1975). Individualizing your treatment program. A case study using LMIT. *Therapeutic Recreational Journal, 9,* 127.

Cousins, B., & Brown, E. (1979). *Recreation therapy assessment.* Jacksonville, FL: Amelia Island ICF/MR.

Hawkins, B.A. (1988). Leisure and recreational programming. In M.P. Janicki, M.W. Krauss, & M.M. Seltzer (Eds.), *Community residences for persons with developmental disabilities: Here to stay* (pp. 217–227). Baltimore: Paul H. Brookes Publishing Co.

Joswiak, K.F. (1975). *Leisure counseling program materials for the developmentally disabled.* Washington, DC: Hawkins & Associates.

Ohio Department of Mental Health/Mental Retardation. (1977). *State of Ohio curriculum guide for moderately mentally retarded learners.* Columbus, OH: Author.

Oregon State Department of Education. (1974). *Toward competency: A guide for individualized instruction.* Salem, OR: Special Education Section.

Overs, R., O'Connor, E., & Demarco, B. (1974). *Avocational activities for the handicapped.* Springfield, IL: Charles C Thomas.

Putnam, J.W., Werder, J.K., & Schleien, S.J. (1985). Leisure and recreational services for handicapped persons. In K.C. Lakin & R.H. Bruininks (Eds.), *Strategies for achieving community integration of developmentally disabled citizens* (pp. 253–274). Baltimore: Paul H. Brookes Publishing Co.

Schleien, S.J., & Ray, M.T. (1988). *Community recreation and persons with disabilities: Strategies for integration.* Baltimore: Paul H. Brookes Publishing Co.

Turnbull, H.R., Turnbull, A.P., Bronicki, G.J., Summers, J.A., & Roeder-Gordon, C. (1989). *Disability and the family: A guide to decisions for adulthood.* Baltimore: Paul H. Brookes Publishing Co.

Wehman, P., Renzaglia, A., & Bates, P. (1985). *Functional living skills for moderately and severely handicapped individuals.* Austin, TX: PRO-ED.

Wehman, P., & Schleien, S. (1979). *Leisure skills curriculum for developmentally disabled persons.* Richmond: School of Education, Virginia Commonwealth University.

Wehman, P., & Schleien, S. (1981). *Leisure programs for handicapped persons: Adaptations, techniques, and curriculum.* Baltimore: University Park Press.

Wessel, J. (1976). *I can physical education program,* Northbrook, IL: Hubbard Scientific Co.

Westaway, A., & Apolloni, T. (1977). *SCOR curriculum: Volume 1. Independent living skills assessment system.* Sonoma, CA: Sonoma County Organization for the Retarded and Department of Education, Sonoma State College.

Williams, W., & Fox, T. (1977). *Minimum objective system.* Burlington, VT: University of Vermont, Center on Developmental Disabilities.

ADDITIONAL RESOURCES

The Arc (1991), *Together successfully* (Arlington, TX: The Arc Publications Department, P.O. Box 1047), a 120-page manual that provides detailed guidelines for implementing youth oriented recreation and leisure programs.

J.D. Kelley and L. Frieden (1989), in *Go for it: A book on sport and recreation for persons with disabilities* (Orlando, FL: Harcourt Brace Jovanovich), describe creative and innovative methods for involving people with disabilities in sports and recreation.

SELF-APPRAISAL

INSTRUCTIONS

The following questions will help you evaluate your knowledge about leisure activities. For true-false questions, check the correct answer. For multiple choice questions, circle the correct answer(s).

Note: There may be more than one correct answer for some questions.

1. Leisure is important for people with developmental disabilities because it can:
   a. Reduce periods of waiting
   b. Reduce inappropriate social behaviors
   c. Teach social and communication skills
   d. Promote physical and mental health
2. Major issues concerning leisure-time activities include:
   a. Autonomy and choice
   b. Risk and protection
   c. Integration
   d. Balance in team sports
3. Leisure time activities should be age and culturally appropriate.
   ___ True   ___ False
4. An individual who makes an informed choice to participate in a segregated leisure or recreational activity should be redirected into an integrated program setting.
   ___ True   ___ False
5. Barriers to integrated leisure activities include:
   a. Architectural
   b. Transportation
   c. Professional training
   d. Leisure and recreational services designed by and for non-disabled people
6. Leisure and recreational activities can be classified as:
   a. Physical
   b. Cultural
   c. Social
   d. Outdoor education
   e. Mental
7. Assessment of leisure skills should take place in the actual setting where the activity will take place.
   ___ True   ___ False
8. The following can be adapted to increase participation in leisure activities:
   a. Materials

    b. Procedures

    c. Skill sequences

    d. Response time

9. Assessment of leisure skills should always be based on formal assessment instruments.

    ____ True   ____ False

10. Federal laws that have resulted in new requirements for accessibility are:

    a. The Rehabilitation Act of 1973

    b. The Architectural Barriers Act of 1988

    c. The Americans with Disabilities Act of 1990

    d. The Community Habilitation Act of 1987

CASE STUDY

Robert Daniels is a 53-year-old male with a diagnosis of severe developmental disability and a seizure disorder. Mr. Daniels has lived in a large state-operated intermediate care facility for the mentally retarded (ICF/MR) since he was 18 years old. The county service coordination program has been working with Mr. Daniels, the ICF/MR, and a local residential provider to begin Mr. Daniels's transition into a four-person group home.

The institution staff has expressed concern about Mr. Daniels's ability to change his place of residence at age 53, as well as about the possibility of injury resulting from seizures. The community residential staff is concerned about these issues but feels Mr. Daniels should move to the group home.

The service coordinator has identified a day program for Mr. Daniels. Many of Mr. Daniels's friends from the institution attend the program, which stresses socialization skills and leisure-time skills. The day program supplements the leisure-time program by transporting all 38 participants on community field trips to the local playground, swimming pool, restaurant, and other places.

The group home staff plan to develop more age- and culturally appropriate leisure-time activities for Mr. Daniels. They also plan to collect data over a 2-month period to document the frequency and type of his seizure activity. This information will be used in determining whether or not Mr. Daniels should continue to wear a protective helmet. Mr. Daniels has indicated to the service coordinator that he does not want to wear a helmet.

Situation

The group home staff are attempting to design a more age-appropriate leisure-time program for Mr. Daniels. They feel that the day program should stress vocational skills, rather than socialization skills and leisure-time activity. The day program, however, argues that people at age 53 are too old to begin vocational training.

1. What advice would you offer to the day and residential staffs concerning vocational training and leisure-time activities?
2. What age- and culturally appropriate leisure-time activities would you recommend to the group home staff?

ANSWER KEY TO
SELF-APPRAISAL AND CASE STUDY

SELF-APPRAISAL

1. a, b, c, d
2. a, b, c
3. True
4. False
5. a, b, c, d
6. a, b, c, d, e
7. True
8. a, b, c, d
9. False
10. a, b, c

CASE STUDY ANSWER GUIDELINES

1. Mr. Daniels's informed choice should be the deciding factor in stressing either vocational or leisure-time skills and activity. The interdisciplinary team should consider the vocational and leisure activities that Mr. Daniels has experienced and that are his preferences and desires. The team should provide Mr. Daniels with a reasonable number of vocational and leisure options from which to choose. Mr. Daniels might benefit from a balance of vocational and leisure programs. With proper planning, the team might assist Mr. Daniels to participate in leisure activities with peers from work. The team might also identify leisure skills that would complement and increase attainment of vocational goals and objectives.

2. Age- and culturally appropriate activities might include attending major sporting events, participating in neighborhood and community functions, and joining church, civic, and/or recreational organizations. Leisure-time activities, such as walking, jogging, and swimming, can promote good health. The choice of specific activities would depend on Mr. Daniels's preferences.

chapter 12

Adaptive Technology

LEARNING OBJECTIVES

Upon completing this chapter, the reader will be able to:

1. Define adaptive technology.
2. Name four input devices appropriate for use by individuals with developmental disabilities.
3. Name three output devices appropriate for use by individuals with developmental disabilities.
4. Identify strategies for selecting hardware and software programs.
5. Identify strategies for evaluating the effectiveness of adaptive technology.
6. State at least one ethical consideration for using adaptive technology for individuals with developmental disabilities.

INTRODUCTION

Adaptive technology is a relatively new field. As used in this chapter, the term *adaptive technology* relates to computer hardware and software and how they can be modified to assist individuals with developmental disabilities achieve desired goals. Hardware consists of both input and output devices. In designing and implementing programs for individuals with developmental disabilities, it is important to consider the input and output devices that will aid these individuals to achieve their stated goals and objectives. This requires an in-depth understanding of each individual's strengths and abilities in order to match appropriate hardware with the person.

Software tells the computer what to do. Understanding the desired outcomes helps one to choose the proper software programs. A recognized problem with software today is the limited selection of age-appropriate programs.

This chapter explores the use of computers and adaptive technology in programs for individuals with developmental disabilities. Various input and output devices and software are discussed. The chapter also presents strategies for selecting appropriate hardware and software programs for individuals with developmental disabilities.

EXERCISE 1

Agency Computer Survey

Conduct a survey of your agency. Does it use computers? Are computers available to individuals with developmental disabilities? Have any of the computers been modified to accommodate the individual?

BACKGROUND

With the end of the industrial revolution, the information revolution and electronic revolution ushered in a new era of work. Rather than being hired for their bodies and the ability to do physical labor, employees are now hired for their brains and thinking processes. This has changed the way in which business is conducted. The mindless tasks of assembly work in factories have been replaced with mindful creative processes that can be achieved virtually anywhere. In accomplishing these processes, employers increasingly rely on computers for storing, sorting, and retrieving information. Computers are the tools used in creative processes.

EMPLOYEES ARE BEING HIRED FOR THEIR THINKING PROCESSES, RATHER THAN FOR THEIR PHYSICAL LABOR.

The field of information technology, a relatively young area of study, is approximately 40 years old. The introduction of the computer has resulted in an explosion of hardware and software applications in society. Ranging from business to recreational applications, computers are appearing in almost every aspect of civilization. As early as 1980, it was reported that the supply of microcomputers and available software applications was doubling every 6 months (Evans, 1981).

More recently, the use of computers in the field of developmental disabilities has received increased attention. Agency staff members are exploring creative options for the use of computers to assist individuals with developmental disabilities in achieving greater levels of independence. These options range from teaching new concepts in mathematics, science, history, and geography to controlling lights, television, security, and other electronic systems in an individual's home.

There are an estimated 43 million individuals with disabilities in the United States. Computers can be used to improve almost any aspect of human activity that is limited by a disability (Vanderheiden, 1981).

COMPUTERS ARE ASSISTING INDIVIDUALS WITH DEVELOPMENTAL DISABILITIES TO ACHIEVE NEW SKILLS AND ABILITIES.

The Johns Hopkins University sponsors a competition of new technologies for individuals with disabilities. Referred to as the Johns Hopkins University Search for Computing Applications to Assist Persons with Disabilities, its goal is to identify ways in which computer applications help people with disabilities in the areas of communication, movement, education, or employment. During the most recent competition, more than 700 innovations were submitted for review.

The increased use of technology in the field of developmental disabilities has been initiated by several pieces of federal legislation. The right to a free and appropriate education for all individuals with disabilities, regardless of the severity of the disabilities, is guaranteed by federal law. One provision of the Education of the Handicapped Act Amendment of 1983 (PL 98-199) is "an emphasis of federal research on the improvement of teaching methodology and curriculum, and the application of new technologies toward improved instruction."

In October 1986, Congress also reauthorized the Rehabilitation Act of 1973, as amended by PL 99-506 Rehabilitation Act Amendments of 1986. Section 603, Electronic Equipment Accessibility, of the revised law mandates that guidelines be established by each state to ensure equal access to electronic office equipment. This includes computers used in the workplace by nondisabled and disabled workers (Lander, 1989).

The Technology-Related Assistance for Individuals with Disabilities Act of 1988 (PL 100-407) authorizes grant money to help each state to develop a comprehensive adaptive technology program. The program is for individuals of all ages and all degrees of disability. The legislation also establishes a technical assistance program to help each state develop the adaptive technology program.

These public laws have ushered in a new era of recognition for individuals with developmental disabilities. Regardless of the severity of their disabilities, they can benefit from the use of technology. Adaptive technology is becoming an integral part of these individuals' daily activities throughout their lifetimes and across all areas of their lives.

> Federal legislation establishes that all individuals, regardless of the severity of their disabilities, can benefit from the use of technology.

APPLICATIONS OF ADAPTIVE TECHNOLOGY

Adaptive technology, simply defined, refers to the application of sophisticated electronic principles and/or devices to the solution of problems faced by individuals with disabilities in day-to-day living. Often, the terms *adaptive technology* and *assistive technology* are used interchangeably. The goal of adaptive technology is to improve the quality of life for individuals with disabilities. Adaptive technology may consist of software programs to aid an individual in the completion of tasks, or hardware that has been modified or adapted to fit the individual in order to perform a specified task for the individual.

> Adaptive technology refers to the application of sophisticated electronic principles and/or devices to the solution of problems faced by individuals with disabilities in day-to-day living.

> The terms *adaptive technology* and *assistive technology* are used interchangeably.

In reviewing possible adaptive technology for individuals with disabilities, Cawley and Murdock (1987) recommended the use of two broad categories in classifying modifications—hardware and software. The individual's disability often impairs, limits, or prevents the completion of an activity. Through the use of technology, many individuals have overcome such barriers and are able to engage in a variety of new activities.

Hardware

Hardware modifications are designed to provide an individual who has sensory and/or motor disabilities with systems of communication, interaction, and achievement.

Hardware modifications have proliferated in recent years and vary greatly. Adaptive hardware usually utilizes one of two devices: adaptive input or adaptive output.

Input Devices

The traditional keyboard is the most widely used input device for the general population. However, many individuals with disabilities may not be able to use the traditional keyboard as an input device. Many alternative input devices have been or are in the process of being developed. For example, an individual can use modified keyboards with smaller or larger buttons, blink an eye to move the cursor, or even blow into a tube. Depending on the assessment outcomes, other common input devices that are available and appropriate for individuals with disabilities are a light pen, mouth stick, touch-sensitive screen, touch tablet, joy stick, and mouse.

The ultimate goal is for the computer to process, understand, and act upon the human voice (Cawley & Murdock, 1987; Mahaffey, 1985). Although identified as a possible option, the technology to make its use widespread has not been fully developed. Variations in human speech create tremendous challenges for computer engineers. The human voice as an input device, however, offers many possibilities for the future.

ALTERNATIVE INPUT DEVICES THAT SHOULD BE CONSIDERED INCLUDE A LIGHT PEN, MOUTH STICK, TOUCH-SENSITIVE SCREEN, TOUCH TABLET, JOY STICK, MOUSE, AND THE HUMAN VOICE.

All of the input devices described below are designed to assist individuals with disabilities to gain access and to control the computer, whether in wheelchairs or flat on their backs in bed. These devices offer individuals increased independence and control of their environments. For example, an individual confined to bed can design jet airplanes and discuss his or her designs with other people around the world. This is accomplished through the use of computers, the appropriate software, and telephone lines.

Light Pen A light pen, or a light pointer, is shaped much like an ink pen. It uses a beam of light to activate the computer. The light shines on the desired computer instruction, and the computer activates the command. The light pen is a useful input device because it requires very little pressure. It also can be held in the mouth or attached to the end of a pointer.

Mouth Stick A mouth stick enables an individual to access the computer through a stick held between the teeth. By using the stick to strike the desired keys on the keyboard, the individual activates the software, and the computer performs the desired task. A head stick is similar to a mouth stick; rather than being held in the mouth, the stick is affixed to a strap worn around the head.

Touch-Sensitive Screen A touch-sensitive screen fits over the front of a computer monitor. The screen is divided into quadrants that the computer reads when an area of the screen is touched. Touching the screen at a desired location activates the software program, and the computer performs the desired task.

Touch Tablet Much like the touch-sensitive screen, a touch tablet activates the computer by touching a specific quadrant. The difference is that the touch-sensitive screen is attached to the monitor, whereas the touch tablet lies flat on a table. The individual can move it around and position it much like a tablet of paper.

Joy Stick A joy stick works like an arcade game. The cursor (the blinking line on the screen that tells you where you are) is moved around the screen by using a control stick attached to a base. The individual grasps the stick and moves it from side to side or from top to bottom. The cursor moves in a corresponding manner. Typically, the individual moves the cursor to a desired instruction and activates the instruction by working the joy stick.

Mouse The mouse gets its name from its shape, a small rectangular box with a tail that connects to the computer. The mouse is moved across a mat located next to the computer. This, in turn, moves a pointer on the screen. The movement of the pointer corresponds to the movement of the mouse on the pad. If the individual moves the mouse to the right, the pointer moves to the right; if the mouse is moved in a circle, the pointer moves in a circle; and so on. The mouse has a control button that is pushed once the pointer is positioned at a desired instructio This action initiates the instruction.

Output Devices

Output devices may be adapted to assist individuals with developmental disabilities. These hardware modifications are also designed to provide an individual with increased control over his or her environment. The most commonly used output device for the general population is the printer. A printer may be utilized by many individuals with disabilities, but a variety of additional output devices, including screen magnification, braille, and synthetic speech, are available.

Output devices include printers, screen magnification, braille, and synthetic speech.

Screen Magnification This device enables the individual to enlarge the print on the monitor so that it is easier to see. Screen magnification typically requires an accompanying software program in order to enlarge the print. Software programs vary, but many can enlarge single words, lines on the monitor, and even sections of a document.

Braille Output devices exist that produce documents in braille, which consists of a series of raised dots representing letters of the alphabet. Blind individuals and those with vision difficulties read the text by moving their fingers across the raised dots. Braille keyboards and input devices are also available.

Synthetic Speech Output devices may take the form of synthetic speech. Simply stated, this term refers to speech that is electronically produced. Synthetic speech has been available for several years. Many individuals with developmental disabilities have benefited from augmentative communication systems. These small systems typically communicate by reproducing "canned" phrases or words upon command. However, the quality of speech synthesizers has been poor until recently. Today's speech synthesizers are better able to replicate the human voice. Through the advancement of microcomputer technology, speech synthesizes are also able to reproduce complex communication patterns. The computer can "read" what is written on the screen and turn it into speech.

Software

During the next several years, many new input and output devices, developed specifically for individuals with developmental disabilities, will appear on the market. In considering these devices, it is important to understand that the computer is only a tool. It can do only what it is told to do. Today's technology does not enable the computer to think. It is mindless. Input and output devices enable many individuals with developmental disabilities to have access to computers, but these devices are only part of the equation. Software programs must tell computers what to do. Most of the input and output devices described above would not work without appropriate software programs to direct their activities. For example, a software program establishes the quadrants and interprets a person's touch on the touch-sensitive screen. Software is required for the speech synthesizer to translate from computer language to the human spoken word.

SOFTWARE DIRECTS THE COMPUTER'S ACTIVITIES TO PRODUCE THE DESIRED OUTCOMES.

Literally thousands of software programs are available today. Software is the key to making microcomputers do what is desired. In addition to its traditional use in computer programming, software can assist in performing a variety of diverse tasks. For individuals with disabilities, tasks that previously required motor responses on the part of the individuals may be performed with the aid of computers and appropriate software programs (Casali & Williges, 1990). For example, manipulating paper, filing, and sorting of information now can be performed with the aid of computer software. Software programs can dial the telephone, draw, turn on lights and TVs, activate home security systems, turn pages in a book, and even pay your bills. Specific to the various disability groups (Hagen, 1984), computer software can speak for individuals with hearing impairments or who are nonvocal, produce braille documents or speak for individuals with visual impairments, and even control immediate environments for individuals with physical disabilities. Computer software programs can be used by individuals with learning disabilities as a means of removing the barriers that often exist in pencil-and-paper tasks.

An explosion of available software has occurred during the past decade. The proliferation of new software programs is projected to continue throughout the next decade. Opportunities to engage individuals with developmental disabilities in technology will flourish and create expanded roles for professionals and interdisciplinary teams as they plan services with these individuals.

> ADVANCES IN TECHNOLOGY WILL REQUIRE EXPANDED ROLES FOR INTERDISCIPLINARY TEAMS IN THE PLANNING OF SERVICES.

Table 1 lists information companies specializing in adaptive technology and software programs for individuals with developmental disabilities.

THE PLANNING PROCESS FOR ADAPTIVE TECHNOLOGY

The planning process begins with assessment. This is followed by interdisciplinary team meetings, establishment of goals and objectives,

Table 1. Special needs catalogs

Accent Buyer's Guide
Accent Special Publications
P.O. Box 700
Bloomington, IL 61702

Access to Recreation
2509 E. Thousand Oaks Blvd., Suite 430
Thousand Oaks, CA 91360
(800) 634-4351 or (805) 498-7535
  Catalog of adaptive recreation equipment.

Adaptive Communication Systems, Inc.
P.O. Box 12440
Pittsburgh, PA 15231
(412) 264-2288
  Computer communication equipment.

AT&T Special Needs Center
2001 Route 46, Suite 310
Parsippany, NJ 07054
(800) 233-1222

Bristol-Myers Co.
Guide to Consumer Product Information
P.O. Box 14177
Baltimore, MD 21268
  Personal care, household, medical, and pain treatment resources.

(continued)

Table 1. *(continued)*

Consumer Care Products, Inc.
Sheboygan Falls, WI 53085
  Ergonomically designed equipment.

Consumer's Guide to Toll-Free Hotlines
P.O. Box 19405
Washington, DC 20036
  Ralph Nader booklet; cost is $1.

Dorothy O'Callaghan
P.O. Box 19083
Washington, DC 20036
  Directory of more than 200 mail-order catalogs specializing in the particular
  needs of people with disabilities.

Equipment Shop
P.O. Box 33
Bedford, MA 01730

Heidico Inc.
P.O. Box 3170
Blaine, WA 98230

Hydra-Fitness
P.O. Box 599
Belton, TX 76513-0599
(800) 433-3111
  Fitness machines for people with physical disabilities.

IBM National Support Center for Persons with Disabilities
2500 Windy Ridge Parkway
Marietta, GA 30067
(800) 426-2133

Kemp & George
2515 E. 43rd St.
Chattanooga, TN 37422
(800) 343-4012
  Products for the home.

MARC Mercantile, Ltd.
Div., HAC Box 3055
Kalamazoo, MI 49003
(800) 445-9968 (Voice) or (616) 381-2219 (TDD)
  Special needs catalog for people with hearing impairments.

J.L. Pachner, Ltd.
33012 Lighthouse Court
San Juan Capistrano, CA 92675
  Products to assist sportsmen with disabilities.

Radio Shack Catalog for People with Special Needs
At local Radio Shack stores or from:
300 One Tandy Center
Fort Worth, TX 76102

(continued)

Table 1. (*continued*)

Sears Home Health Care Products Specialog
Sears, Roebuck and Co.
3333 W. Arthington St.
Chicago, IL 60607
  Order by phoning nearest Sears catalog store.

Sonic Alert
209 Voorheis
Pontiac, MI 48053
(313) 858-8957 (Voice/TDD)
  Products for people with hearing impairments.

Special Toys 4 Special Kids
11834 Wyandot Circle
Westminster, CO 80234
  Toys to educate and aid development.

Stuart's Sport Specialties
7081 Chad St.
Anchorage, AK 99502
(907) 349-8377
  Outdoors catalog.

Swedish Rehab
100 Spence St.
Bay Shore, NY 11706
(800) 645-5272
  Utensils and objects for people with limited hand use.

TherAdapt Products, Inc.
17W163 Oak Lane
Bensenville, IL 60106
  Pediatric equipment.

Ways and Means
The Capability Collection
28001 Citrin Drive
Romulus, MI 48174
(800) 654-2345
  General catalog.

Woodworker's Catalog
The Woodworker's Store
21801 Industrial Blvd.
Rogers, MN 55374
(612) 428-2199

COMPUTERS, SOFTWARE, AND GADGETS

Adaptive Communication Systems, Inc.
P.O. Box 12440
Pittsburgh, PA 15231
(412) 264-2288
    Long Range Optical Pointer (LROP), used as a head pointer for persons who
    cannot operate a standard computer keyboard.

(*continued*)

Table 1. *(continued)*

Aesir Software Engineering
P.O. Box 3583
Pinedale, CA 93650
 Single switch computer software.

Aids and Appliances Review
Carroll Centre for the Blind
770 Centre St.
Newton, MA 02158
(617) 969-6200
 Comprehensive overview of aids for the blind. Issue 9 and 10 (a combined
 issue) deals with voice-oriented computer aids. Issue 11 deals with braille-
 oriented computer aids.

American West Engineering
2144 S. 1100 East, Suite 150
Salt Lake City, UT 84106
 Multimouse, single-handed data entry device for IBM computers, ideal for
 persons with use of only one hand. By pressing two or more buttons on the
 palm-shaped chord keyboard, all the keys on a standard IBM keyboard can
 be emulated. Available for right or left hand.

Apollo Electronic Visual Aids
P.O. Box 2755
2932 Lassen St.
Chatsworth, CA 91311
(213) 700-2666
 Large-print computer terminal and typing system.

Arts Computer Products
145 Tremont St., Suite 407
Boston, MA 02111
(617) 482-8248
 Large-print terminal, talking terminal.

Assistive Device Database System (ADDS)
American Information Data Search, Inc.
2326 Fair Oaks Blvd., Suite C
Sacramento, CA 95825
(916) 925-4554 (modem)
 Write for information before calling.

Arnold Balliet
Cascade Graphics Development
1000 South Grand Ave.
Santa Ana, CA 92705
(714) 474-6200
 Cash III Voice Controlled System enables people with limited or no use of
 their hands to operate programs by voice, including using the telephone,
 turning pages, turning on a light, and opening a door.

(continued)

Table 1. (*continued*)

BAUD (Blind Apple Users' Discussion)
Audio-tech Laboratories, Joe Giovanelli
1158 Stewart Ave.
Bethpage, NY 11714
(516) 433-0171
   Bimonthly, cassette-only newsletter discussing microcomputer applications;
   emphasis on Apple software and Computer Aids, Inc. products.

The Catalyst
Western Center for Microcomputers in Special Education
1259 El Camino Real, Suite 275
Menlo Park, CA 94025
(415) 326-6997
   Information on recent research, hardware, software, and applications to
   special education.

Clark Technologies
Lee Brown
16205 Fantasia Drive
Tampa, FL 33623
(813) 962-4105 or 223-8155
   Braillink paperless brailler and a talking terminal.

Closing the Gap
5139 Wentworth Ave. S.
Minneapolis, MN 55419
(612) 665-6573
   Bimonthly newsletter.

ComputAbility Corp.
101 Route 46
Pine Brook, NJ 07058
   Complete Apple or IBM computer systems for people with disabilities.

Computer Shopper
P.O. Box 1419
Titusville, FL 32781

Cyberon Corp.
Eliot Friedman
1175 Wendy Road
Ann Arbor, MI 48103
(313) 994-0326
   Cybertalker speech terminal, Apple Cyber Card.

Designing Aids for Disabled Adults (DADA)
1024 Dupont St., Unit 5
Toronto, Ontario M6H 2A2
CANADA
(416) 533-4494
   PC A.I.D. makes IBM computers more accessible to persons with physical
   disabilities. With PC A.I.D. the computer can be operated with a single
   switch.

(*continued*)

Table 1. *(continued)*

Electronic Specialties
5230 Girard Ave. North
Minneapolis, MN 55430
(612) 521-0008
   AVOS System: Hardware is Osborne 1 or Zorba Computer with speech
   output; software includes word processing, database, and communications
   programs.

Enable Software
Robert Artusy
2340 Martin Luther King Jr. Way, Suite B
Berkeley, CA 94704
(415) 540-0389
   Talking software for Radio Shack Models 3 and 4 and for the Kaypro; for
   screen review and for word processing.

Hadley School for the Blind
700 Elm Street
Winnetka, IL 60093
(800) 323-4238; in Illinois, (312) 446-8111
   Home-study computer literacy course.

Hy-Tek Manufacturing Inc.
412 Bucktail Lane
Sugar Grove, IL 60554
(312) 466-7664
   Voice Interactive Computer System (V.I.C.). IBM-compatible, also features
   voice output and is available in three basic CPU configurations.

IBM Voice Communication Option
IBM Corp.
National Support Center for Persons with Disabilities
2500 Windy Ridge Parkway
Marietta, GA 30067
(800) 426-2133

Intelligent Modem
Phone-TTY, Inc.
202 Lexington Ave.
Hackensack, NJ 07601
(201) 489-7889 (Voice or TTY)

National Braille Press
88 Stephen Street
Boston, MA 02115
(617) 266-6160
   Various publications, including those dealing with computers and people with
visual impairments.

National Easter Seal Society
Attention: Jane Minton
70 Eastlake St.
Chicago, IL 60601
(312) 726-6200
   Computer Disability News newsletter.

(continued)

Table 1. *(continued)*

National Technology Center, American Foundation for the Blind
Elliot M. Schreier, Director
15 West 16th St.
New York, NY 10011
(212) 620-2080
  Information about large print for PC.

Playback
Edward L. Potter
1308 Evergreen Ave.
Goldsboro, NC 27530
(919) 736-0939
  Cassette newsletter, information about audio equipment and computer aids.

Psycho-linguistic Research Associates
2055 Sterling Ave.
Menlo Park, CA 94025
(415) 854-1771
  Hardware and software for talking Zenith Heathkit Computer and software for speech in Radio Shack computers.

Raised Dot Computing
Attn: David Holladay
408 South Baldwin St.
Madison, WI 55703
(608) 257-9595
  Personal computer applications for people with visual impairments. Both braille and audio subscriptions available.

Softwarehouse
3080 Olcott Dr., Suite 125A
Santa Clara, CA 95054
(408) 748-0461
  SLIC works, an IBM-compatible PC program. Shareware product, which means a user can purchase it on disk and try the program before registering.
  For more information and free catalog of other products, contact Softwarehouse.

Special Times
Cambridge Development Lab
86 West St.
Waltham, MA 02154
(800) 637-0047
  Primarily for parents and teachers of children with learning disabilities or problem-solving difficulties.

Street Electronics Corporation
6420 Villa Real
Carpinteria, CA 93013
(805) 684-4593
  Speech synthesizers for computers.

Technical Innovations Bulletin
IRTI 26699 Snell Lane
Los Altos Hills, CA 94022
(415) 948-8588
  Interviews about and demonstrations of computer and other technology.

(continued)

Table 1. *(continued)*

Trace Center
The Waisman Center
University of Wisconsin-Madison
1500 Highland Ave.
Madison, WI 53705
(608) 262-6966
 Registry of software for people with disabilities, workshops on computer
 access.

Vtek (formerly Visualtek)
1735 W. Rosecrans Ave.
Gardena, CA 90249
(213) 329-3463
 Large-print computer access devices for Apple and IBM PC.

SPECIALIZED COMPUTER SOFTWARE

AARON
AESIR Software Engineering
P.O. Box 5383
Pinedale, CA 93650
 Word processor anticipates words.

Electronic 31-Day Calendar
Computer Users of America
5028 Merit Drive
Flint, MI 48506
 With voice.

Hartley Courseware, Inc.
133 Bridge St.
Dimondale, MI 48821
(517) 646-6458
 Instructional programs.

IBM Augmented Phone Services
IBM Corp.
National Support Center for Persons with Disabilities
2500 Windy Ridge Parkway
Marietta, GA 30067
(800) 426-2133

Lambert Software Co.
P.O. Box 1257
Ramona, CA 92065
(619) 789-1438
 Instructional/retraining software.

Listen to Learn
IBM Corp.
IBM Direct, PC Software Dept.
One Culver Road
Dayton, NJ 08810
 Word processor with voice.

(continued)

Table 1. *(continued)*

Micro-Interpreter I "The Finger-speller"
Edu Tec, Inc. (formerly Microtech Consulting Company, Cedar Falls, Iowa)
7070 Brooklyn Blvd.
Minneapolis, MN 53005
(414) 784-8075

PC-Fingers
Midwest Health Programs, Inc.
408 West Vermont
P.O. Box 3023
Urbana, IL 61801
(217) 367-5293

Prompt-Writer
Syn-Talk Systems & Services
70 Estero Avenue
San Francisco, CA 94127
  Word processor with voice.

Rapsheet
BAUD
337 S. Peterson
Louisville, KY 40206
  Spreadsheet with voice.

Special Education Software Center
3857 North High Street
Columbus, OH 43214
(800) 327-5892

TDD Emulation
Phone-TTY, Inc.
202 Lexington Avenue
Hackensack, NJ 07601
(201) 489-7889 (Voice or TTY/TDD)

Tele-Talk
Computer Users of America
5028 Merit Drive
Flint, MI 48506
  Phone/address list with voice.

ThinkTank
Living Videotext Inc.
2432 Charleston Road
Mountain View, CA 94043
  Outliner.

Word Talk
Computer Aids Corp.
4320 Stevens Creek Blvd., Suite 290
San Jose, CA 95129
  Word Processor with voice.

Source: Adapted from Hoffa and Morgan (1990).

development of instructional strategies, and monitoring and evaluation. At the heart of the process is the agency's mission statement or purpose statement. The remaining steps in the process evolve around this statement. The introduction and advancement of adaptive technology require agency staff members to rethink their roles and the purpose of each step in the process.

Mission Statement

The agency's mission statement is at the center of the planning process. It defines the purpose of the agency for the staff, the consumers, and the community. With the direction it provides, agency staff members can identify the goals and objectives needed to accomplish the mission statement. Both the mission statement and the subsequent goals and objectives should include the agency's commitment to adaptive technology.

EXERCISE 2

Review of Agency Mission

Review your agency's mission statement and goals and objectives. Do they contain information about adaptive technology? Are staff members free to explore the use of adaptive technology?

Assessment

Traditional assessment strategies include using either a norm-referenced or criterion-referenced test to assess an individual's strengths, interests, and needs, but these assessments do not include the individual's need for adaptive technology and his or her ability levels in that area.

Because traditional assessments assist team members in understanding an individual's current abilities, they are critical to the team's determination of how the individual might benefit from adaptive technology. Interdisciplinary team members must consider additional assessment strategies to determine the need for adaptive technology of each individual with a developmental disability. For example, the individual's interest in using adaptive technology, appropriate input/output devices, correct positioning of equipment, and how the equipment is to be used should be included as assessment strategies. Careful attention should be given to the individual's need for communication and increased control and autonomy over his or her environment.

DURING THE ASSESSMENT PROCESS, STAFF MEMBERS SHOULD BEGIN TO CONSIDER HOW ADAPTIVE TECHNOLOGY MAY BE USED BY THE INDIVIDUAL WITH A DEVELOPMENTAL DISABILITY. SPECIAL ATTENTION SHOULD BE GIVEN TO THE INDIVIDUAL'S NEED TO COMMUNICATE AND WAYS IN WHICH HE OR SHE CAN EXERCISE MORE CONTROL OVER THE ENVIRONMENT.

Interdisciplinary Team Decisions

The utilization of adaptive technology can offer many challenges to the interdisciplinary team. As noted in the previous section, numerous input and output devices are currently available and new ones are constantly appearing on the market. Software is also rapidly changing. To use this advanced technology appropriately, the interdisciplinary team must obtain current information about the technology and understand the applications and potential benefits of input and output devices and software programs. Because these factors may not be readily apparent to the team, it must decide on methods of learning how adaptive technology might be used within the agency and/or community by individuals with developmental disabilities.

In directing their efforts, team members should not overlook the information that can be provided by the individuals with developmental disabilities regarding their interests and desires to utilize adaptive technology. This information may not always be direct. An individual may not say specifically that he or she is interested in using a computer, but indirect information from the individual or another team member may indicate a need for increased control over the individual's environment, such as maintaining the temperature, turning lights on and off, and answering the telephone. In exploring options for obtaining such goals, the team should consider the use of adaptive technology.

Once the team decides to use adaptive technology, appropriate input and output devices and software programs that will enable the individual to achieve his or her goals must be identified and discussed.

THE INTERDISCIPLINARY TEAM MUST DEVELOP METHODS OF OBTAINING CURRENT INFORMATION ABOUT ADVANCES IN TECHNOLOGY AND UNDERSTAND THE APPLICATIONS AND POTENTIAL BENEFITS OF NEW INPUT AND OUTPUT DEVICES AND SOFTWARE PROGRAMS.

Goals, Objectives, and Instructional Strategies

Goals and objectives are components of effective instructional strategies. Instructional strategies are the written plan of how to teach a skill. They may include goals and objectives written specifically for an individual to learn how to use a computer or a piece of adaptive technology.

It is important, however, to remember that adaptive technology is merely a tool. In this sense, adaptive technology is only a part of the instructional strategy and is used to achieve a higher-level goal or objective. In other words, the words *computer* and *adaptive technology* may not appear in either the goal or objective. Yet, they would be identified as a part of the instructional strategy, which is the vehicle for teaching a goal or objective.

> COMPUTERS AND ADAPTIVE TECHNOLOGY ARE ONLY TOOLS THAT CAN ASSIST INDIVIDUALS WITH DEVELOPMENTAL DISABILITIES TO ACHIEVE GOALS AND OBJECTIVES.

Monitoring and Evaluation

The monitoring and evaluation process completes the cycle. The role of staff members in monitoring and evaluation is threefold: 1) ensure that the team has addressed the critical areas of assessment; 2) successfully identify the strengths, interests, and needs of the individual with a developmental disability, and 3) ensure that the stated goals and objectives and resulting instructional strategies are producing the desired results.

Adaptive technology places additional demands on staff roles related to the monitoring and evaluation functions. Specifically, staff members must ensure that the chosen adaptive technology is producing the desired results. An agency may be tempted to "stick" with one approach to adaptive technology. The result may be reliance on a single approach, rather than a pursuit of better adaptive technology options for individuals with developmental disabilities.

> STAFF MEMBERS INVOLVED IN MONITORING AND EVALUATION PLAY A CRITICAL ROLE IN ENSURING THAT CHOSEN STRATEGIES, INCLUDING ADAPTIVE TECHNOLOGY, ARE PRODUCING THE DESIRED OUTCOMES.

CHOOSING APPROPRIATE ADAPTIVE TECHNOLOGY

Selecting appropriate adaptive technology, both hardware and software, requires careful consideration on the part of agency staff members. They may wonder whether to purchase the computer or the software first and be undecided about what input/output devices to buy. The answer in each case is fairly simple and direct—the agency should purchase nothing at this stage.

Adaptive technology is a consumer-driven process based on assessment of an individual's abilities, interests, and needs. The design and implementation of an adaptive technology program must follow this critical step of assessment. Staff members must identify the intent of the adaptive technology and the outcomes they hope to achieve before making decisions about hardware and software.

Adaptive technology can be very expensive. The selected vendors should be asked to demonstrate the hardware and available input/output devices prior to any decision to purchase. The same applies to software. Although software is not as expensive as hardware, its costs can add up. Staff members should request a full demonstration and expect vendors to identify clearly how individuals with developmental disabilities can benefit from using their software.

Finally, no hardware or software should be purchased without considering the ethics of technology and its use. The design and implementation of adaptive technology must be guided by philosophical principles established by each agency. Otherwise, computers may be used to take the place of human contact. Technology can lead staff members in an unwanted direction, or the agency can use technology to move in a desirable direction. It is imperative for the agency to establish clear guidelines that staff members can follow during this process.

REGARDLESS OF THE ADAPTIVE TECHNOLOGY USED, ITS APPLICATION MUST BE DETERMINED BY THE NEEDS OF THE INDIVIDUALS FOR WHOM ITS USE IS INTENDED. THE AGENCY SHOULD REQUEST DEMONSTRATIONS OF BOTH HARDWARE AND SOFTWARE PRIOR TO PURCHASE.

SUMMARY

As the field of computer technology advances, more hardware and software will be available to meet the needs of individuals with developmental disabilities. New input and output devices will provide greater access to the computer. Software programs will offer opportunities for increased independence and autonomy. As a result, individuals with developmental disabilities will have more control over daily decisions and ultimately over their own lives.

The use of adaptive technology will affect the way in which agency staff members conduct assessments and interdisciplinary team meetings, establish goals and objectives, design implementation strategies, and perform monitoring and evaluation. Adaptive technology is a tool, only one of many tools available to the team in helping an individual to achieve his or her stated goals and objectives.

Adaptive technology is a consumer-driven process. No hardware or software should be purchased without a clear understanding of the strengths, interests, and needs of the individual with a developmental disability. Staff members should then request hardware and software vendors to demonstrate the potential benefits of their products.

Finally, staff members need guidelines for the use of technology within the agency. Guidelines help them to make decisions about the nature and direction of programs. No technology should be considered if it is intended to replace human contact.

BIBLIOGRAPHY

Casali, S.P., & Williges, R.C. (1990). Data bases of accommodative aids for computer use with disabilities. *Human Factors, 32*(4), 407–422.

Cawley, J.F., & Murdock, J.Y. (1987). Technology and students with handicaps. *Contemporary Educational Psychology, 12,* 200–211.

Evans, C. (1981). *The making of the micro: A history of computers.* New York: Van Nostrand Reinhold.

Hagen, D. (1984). *Microcomputer resource book for special education.* Reston, VA: Reston Publishing Company, Inc.

Hoffa, H., & Morgan, G. (1990). *Yes you can: A helpbook for the physically disabled.* New York: Pharos Books.

Lander, R.E. (1989). Computer accessibility for federal workers with disabilities: It's the law. *Communications, 32,* 952–956.

Mahaffey, R.B. (1985). An overview of computer applications. *Topics in Language Disorders, 6*(1), 1–10.

Vanderheiden, G.C. (1981, January). Practical application of microcomputers to aid the handicapped. *Computer.*

ADDITIONAL RESOURCES

J. Bear and D.M. Pozerycki (1992), in *Computer wimp no more: The intelligent beginner's guide to computers* (Berkeley: Ten Speed Press), provide an excellent overview of computers, their purpose, and how to use them. This is a good general reference book about personal computers.

G. Church and S. Glennen (1992), in *The handbook of assistive technology* (San Diego: Singular Publishing Group, Inc.), cover assistive technology in detail and recommend many hardware and software programs for use by individuals with developmental disabilities.

W.E. Wang and J. Kraynak (1990), in *The first book of personal computing* (Carmel: SAMS), offer an excellent source of information about personal computers.

SELF-APPRAISAL

INSTRUCTIONS

The following questions will help you evaluate your knowledge about adaptive technology. For true-false questions, check the correct answer. For multiple choice questions, circle the correct answer(s).

Note: There may be more than one correct answer for some questions.

1. Adaptive technology refers to the application of sophisticated electronic principles and/or devices to the solution of problems faced by individuals with disabilities in day-to-day living.
   ___ True   ___ False
2. Adaptive technology and assistive technology refer to the same process.
   ___ True   ___ False
3. Which of the following are input devices:
   a. Keyboard
   b. Light pen
   c. Mouth stick
   d. Mouse
   e. All of the above
   f. None of the above
4. Which of the following are output devices?
   a. Color monitor
   b. Braille print
   c. Printer
   d. Synthetic speech
5. One goal of adaptive technology is to give individuals with developmental disabilities greater control over their environments.
   ___ True   ___ False
6. Computer software tells the computer what to do.
   ___ True   ___ False
7. Which of the following will be affected by adaptive technology:
   a. The agency's assessment process
   b. The agency's interdisciplinary team process
   c. Goals, objectives, and instructional strategies
   d. Program monitoring and evaluation
8. In making decisions about adaptive technology, the hardware should be purchased first.
   ___ True   ___ False

9. Adaptive technology is a consumer-driven process.
   ___ True   ___ False
10. Adaptive technology should not be used if its goal is to replace human contact.
   ___ True   ___ False

CASE STUDY

Eric Roberts is a young adult with cerebral palsy. He has limited range of motion and his mobility is enhanced through the use of an electric wheelchair. He is able to communicate with an augmentative communication system.

Mr. Roberts graduated from the local community college 6 months ago. He earned an associate in arts degree with a major in computer-assisted design. Mr. Roberts has applied to numerous local businesses for employment. He is particularly interested in architectural firms and engineering companies.

Mr. Roberts needs a personal care attendant to assist him in getting up and preparing for work. He has arranged for transportation to a number of possible employment situations.

He has a support network of friends from school and family and participates in community life. He is generally optimistic that the new Americans with Disabilities Act will increase opportunities for him in the near future.

Situation

Mr. Roberts has secured a job with AVCO Engineering, Inc. He will work with a computer to design pollution-free automobile engines. During the job interview, Mr. Roberts and the employer discussed a number of adaptive technology applications that might enhance Mr. Roberts's performance. The employer is willing to accommodate his technology needs.

1. Discuss alternative input devices that Mr. Roberts might use.
2. What guidelines would you recommend in the selection of hardware and software for Mr. Roberts?
3. Are there any ethical considerations that AVCO should address in thinking about adaptive technology and the future employment of individuals with developmental disabilities?

ANSWER KEY TO
SELF-APPRAISAL AND CASE STUDY

SELF-APPRAISAL

1. True
2. True
3. e
4. a, b, c, d
5. True
6. True
7. a, b, c, d
8. False
9. True
10. True

CASE STUDY ANSWER GUIDELINES

1. Mr. Roberts should explore many different input devices, including a light pen, mouth stick, touch-sensitive screen, touch tablet, joy stick, mouse, and even the human voice. In making the decision, Mr. Roberts should consider what he wishes to accomplish. Clearly defining the desired outcomes will aid Mr. Roberts in making the best choice.

2. Agency staff members should consider multiple guidelines that would apply to the selection of hardware and software. The most critical guideline relates to not purchasing any hardware or software before clearly defining the desired outcomes. Such questions as the following need to be addressed before any hardware or software is purchased: What do we wish to accomplish? What is our goal? What have we already tried? Is there anything else available that will achieve the same results? Another guideline to implement is one that recognizes the selection of adaptive technology as a consumer-driven process. The individual with a developmental disability must choose the best option for himself or herself after considering available options.

3. Every company should discuss ethical considerations when using adaptive technology. For example, the selection of an input device does not mean that it would apply to all individuals with developmental disabilities in all situations. Ethically, the company should consider adaptive technology on an individual basis. In addition, adaptive technology should not be used if it is intended as a replacement for human contact.

chapter 13 — Supported Employment

<p>

chapter 13 Supported Employment

LEARNING OBJECTIVES

Upon completing this chapter, the reader will be able to:

1. Define supported employment.
2. Identify the recipients of supported employment services.
3. Identify three different models of supported employment.
4. State the differences among the three supported employment models.
5. State two new roles for the human services agency staff in the provision of supported employment services.
6. State the differences between a job developer and an employment specialist.
7. Identify the future direction of the supported employment program.

INTRODUCTION

Since 1980, there has been a significant shift in service models of day programs for individuals with developmental disabilities. Rather than forcing individuals to work their way through a series of day programs, ranging from sheltered workshops to work activity centers to actual employment, human services agencies have recognized the value of participation in meaningful, productive work and have developed an array of work options for individuals with developmental disabilities.

This chapter explores the shift to supported employment. It begins by defining supported employment and providing a brief history of its development. Various supported employment models are discussed, as well as the implications for direct service workers participating in the different models. The chapter concludes with a discussion of potential future directions of individuals with developmental disabilities in supported employment programs.

DEFINITION

PL 102-569, the Rehabilitation Act Amendments of 1992 define supported employment as:

> competitive work in an integrated work setting with on-going support services for individuals with severe handicaps who traditionally have been unable to perform competitive work or who have performed competitive work only intermittently. It includes transitional employment for individuals with chronic mental illness. (*Federal Register*, 57[122])

This definition has three noteworthy components. First, supported employment is paid employment. It is not a program to get people ready for work. Getting people ready for work, or prevocational training, has been the focus of sheltered workshops and work activity centers. Supported employment places individuals in real jobs that pay money for the completion of work tasks.

SUPPORTED EMPLOYMENT IS PAID EMPLOYMENT.

Second, as implied in the definition, supported employment is intended for individuals with severe disabilities. These individuals will need ongoing staff support in order to remain employed. Identified supports are provided to individuals in work settings in order to ensure successful work experiences.

SUPPORTED EMPLOYMENT IS INTENDED FOR INDIVIDUALS WITH SEVERE DISABILITIES.

Third, the definition indicates that work is to take place in integrated settings. A major goal of the supported employment program is the integration of individuals with developmental disabilities into work environments with nondisabled peers. By working in integrated settings, individuals with developmental disabilities have increased opportunities for establishing relationships with individuals other than human services employees.

SUPPORTED EMPLOYMENT TAKES PLACE IN INTEGRATED SETTINGS.

Changes in Supported Employment

The new supported employment regulations contain numerous changes over previous regulations. The two key changes include the number of hours an individual must work and the provision of support services.

The old regulations required the individual to work at least 20 hours per week. Many people felt this regulation should be more individually determined and oriented toward outcomes. An individual may benefit from supported employment but be unable to work 20 hours. The new regulation recognizes the differences that exist among various individuals with developmental disabilities and has dropped the minimum-hour requirement. Supported employment could range from 1 hour per week for one individual to 39 hours per week for another.

The old regulations required that support services be provided at the work setting. The new regulations permit support services outside the workplace. Again, use of this option would be individually determined. Some individuals with developmental disabilities may not want the job coach in the workplace and prefer receiving services in other settings. The new regulation permits the delivery of services in settings negotiated between the individual with developmental disabilities and his or her job coach.

MODELS OF SUPPORTED EMPLOYMENT

Many different models of supported employment exist. During the past several years, new models have emerged as human services workers refined their abilities to provide services to individuals with severe disabilities. Additional models may be designed as more experience is gained in providing support services.

The most common supported employment models are enclaves, mobile crews, and individual placements.

Through the implementation of these three models, more and more individuals with developmental disabilities are participating in paid work. As the service system changes to recognize the contributions of these individuals to business and industry, the sooner the goals of normalization and the civil rights of individuals with developmental disabilities can be realized.

Enclaves

In the enclave model, individuals with developmental disabilities, typically in groups of three to eight, are placed in work settings with nondisabled peers. The members of an enclave may work in a variety of groupings. Some may work as a group in the same work area and complete similar tasks, while others may work in scattered work sites within the same company. Still others may work in pairs throughout the company. The enclave model offers the advantages of integration, training, supervision, and wages for individuals with developmental disabilities.

> In the enclave model of supported employment, three
> to eight individuals work with nondisabled peers in
> the work setting.

The enclave model meets the requirements of community integration as detailed in the federal definition of supported employment. Integration is achieved during normal work breaks that occur throughout the day, such as lunch breaks and morning and afternoon coffee breaks.

Because workers are in close proximity to each other, the enclave model is economical in the training and supervision of workers. Training and supervision are provided to the group. This is an important feature of the enclave model because it offers individuals with developmental disabilities who are in need of ongoing, continuous supervision the opportunity to participate in work settings while receiving the supports they need. The link between training and supervision helps to ensure successful work placement of individuals.

Finally, enclaves allow individuals with developmental disabilities to receive fair compensation for completed work. The individuals have the same access to work as nondisabled workers. They receive pay for their work. Benefits may be included at some work sites, depending on what is negotiated in the initial contract.

> An enclave offers the advantages of work integra-
> tion with nondisabled peers and ease in supervision
> and training by human services agency staff.

The enclave model still exists in many supported employment work sites, but its popularity has diminished in favor of the individual placement model.

Mobile Crews

The second most popular model of supported employment is the mobile crew. There are typically three to eight individuals assigned to a mobile crew. As implied by its title, the crew does not work at one site but moves from site to site. It is based out of a truck, a van, or even several cars. Members of mobile crews can provide a variety of services throughout the community, such as janitorial, landscaping, and groundskeeping services.

> In the mobile crew model of supported employment,
> three to eight individuals move from one work site to
> another.

The advantages of integration, training, supervision, and wages described under the enclave model also apply to the mobile crew model of supported employment. The mobile crew model offers an additional advantage. It is particularly suited for rural areas where large businesses or business opportunities are not readily available.

THE MOBILE CREW MODEL OF SUPPORTED EMPLOYMENT IS PARTICULARLY SUITED FOR RURAL AREAS.

One noteworthy disadvantage of this model is the seasonal nature of work for some crews. For example, in the northern areas of the country, landscaping and groundskeeping may be seasonal employment. Human services agencies should investigate alternative work options for members of mobile crews during the off months.

Individual Placement Model

The individual placement model, sometimes called the *supported jobs model*, is the most common type of supported employment. In the individual placement model, individuals with developmental disabilities are matched with available jobs in the community. An individual's strengths and interests are considered in locating suitable work options. Supports are provided within the workplace as needed in order to ensure continued work success.

THE INDIVIDUAL PLACEMENT MODEL MATCHES THE INDIVIDUAL'S STRENGTHS AND INTERESTS TO AVAILABLE JOBS.

The individual placement model differs from the enclave and mobile crew models in that it is best suited for individuals with developmental disabilities who require minimal ongoing supervision. When an individual is placed in an appropriate work environment, training and supervision by the agency staff are intensive at first to ensure that the individual understands the work requirements. These supports are then gradually reduced until the individual is performing with minimal supervision.

The individual placement model offers many advantages. The opportunities for community integration are much greater than with either the enclave or mobile crew model. A single worker with a developmental disability in the workplace, versus a group of six to eight individuals, is much more approachable. Nondisabled workers may view the individual as a part of the work team. They are often more likely to include the individual with developmental disabilities in parties and other social events hosted by coworkers.

THE INDIVIDUAL PLACEMENT MODEL OFFERS THE GREATEST
OPPORTUNITY FOR INTEGRATION WITH NONDISABLED PEERS.

Another advantage of the individual placement model is the opportunity to match the individual's strengths and interests to the work placement. Greater overall success in supported employment may be observed in situations where the individual's goals and desires determine the nature and location of work. This process may increase the likelihood of job satisfaction and, consequently, job performance and longevity.

With individual placement, the person with a developmental disability has more opportunity to become a permanent employee of the company and receive company benefits.

THE INDIVIDUAL PLACEMENT MODEL INCREASES THE LIKELI-
HOOD THAT THE INDIVIDUAL WITH DEVELOPMENTAL DISABIL-
ITIES WILL BECOME A PERMANENT EMPLOYEE OF THE COMPA-
NY.

SHIFT IN STAFF ROLES

Supported employment requires the human services agency to shift from a focus on the person's disability and what he or she cannot do to a focus on work and the requirements of getting the job done. By definition, supported employment assumes that individuals with developmental disabilities are workers. This means that *all* individuals with developmental disabilities, regardless of the level of their involvement, can participate in work. The failure of an individual to succeed in a work setting is a failure of professionals to recognize the assistance or technology required for that person's success. Assisting individuals with developmental disabilities to participate in work settings requires a shift in staff roles.

SUPPORTED EMPLOYMENT, BY DEFINITION, ASSUMES THAT
INDIVIDUALS WITH DEVELOPMENTAL DISABILITIES ARE
WORKERS.

In order for individuals with developmental disabilities to participate in supported employment, the staff of the human services agency must assume roles and responsibilities that differ from those in traditional programs. This shift in roles and responsibilities requires the staff to perform tasks in a different manner. For example, rather than teachers or counselors, staff members will become job developers or employment specialists. Both of these roles are critical to the success of supported employment and the placement of individuals with developmental disabilities in work settings.

SUPPORTED EMPLOYMENT MAY REQUIRE SOME HUMAN SERVICES WORKERS TO ASSUME DIFFERENT ROLES AND RESPONSIBILITIES IN PROVIDING SUPPORTED EMPLOYMENT SERVICES.

Job Developer

The work of the job developer takes place primarily before the individual with developmental disabilities is placed in a work setting. The job developer performs several functions, including market analysis, worker placement, and follow-up assessments.

The job developer must clearly understand what work is available for a given geographic area. This involves the implementation of a market analysis. To accomplish this task, the job developer must know the area in which work placements for individuals with developmental disabilities are desired. A market analysis is tedious work and often takes several months to complete. It also requires ongoing review to ensure that the human services provider understands the changes in job demographics and work requirements over time.

A JOB DEVELOPER CONDUCTS A MARKET ANALYSIS TO UNDERSTAND WHAT WORK IS AVAILABLE FOR A GIVEN GEOGRAPHIC AREA.

The process of completing a market analysis is critical to the success of supported employment. Only through a thorough market analysis can a range of work possibilities be offered to an individual with developmental disabilities. He or she can then make a choice among many types of employment opportunities.

Information needed for the market analysis comes from many sources. The help wanted ads in the local newspaper and in trade journals, and even bulletin boards in community centers, offer a starting place in understanding the local job market. Other strategies may include joining local civic organizations, hosting a breakfast meeting of local business leaders to discuss the job market, or conducting one-to-one meetings with the chief executive officers of local businesses. Local church groups also may be sources of information about the job market and work availability.

A JOB DEVELOPER GATHERS WORK INFORMATION FROM A VARIETY OF SOURCES, RANGING FROM NEWSPAPERS TO LOCAL CIVIC GROUPS TO SPECIAL EVENTS HOSTED FOR BUSINESS LEADERS.

In addition to conducting a market analysis and obtaining a clear picture of the job market and work availability, the job developer must understand the individuals with developmental disabilities who will be placed in jobs. The job developer must know their strengths and interests and ask them where they would like to work and what types of jobs they would like to have. Through an understanding of each individual, the job developer is better able to match that person with a potential employer. This process also helps to ensure greater personal employment satisfaction for individuals with developmental disabilities.

A JOB DEVELOPER RECOMMENDS POTENTIAL WORK BASED ON KNOWING AN INDIVIDUAL'S STRENGTHS AND INTERESTS.

Finally, the job developer continually monitors the employment match between the employer and the individual with a developmental disability. Ongoing follow-up assessments build positive working relationships. They also help to ensure that the employer is satisfied with the work of the individual. In a situation where the employer has concerns about the individual's performance, the job developer, assisted by other appropriate agency personnel, can intervene and prevent continued dissatisfaction.

Many jobs are obtained as the result of personal contacts and referrals from those contacts. To this end, the job developer must be able to develop and maintain an effective network of personal contacts in the business arena. This type of network increases the likelihood of supported employment becoming an integral part of the human services agency, as well as the lives of individuals with developmental disabilities.

A JOB DEVELOPER BUILDS A NETWORK OF PERSONAL CONTACTS IN BUSINESS.

Employment Specialist

The work of the employment specialist picks up where the work of the job developer ends. Whereas the job developer must learn about the types of work available in a given geographic area, the employment specialist must understand the nature of the work required for a particular job. The employment specialist is typically an employee of the human services agency. Some agencies use such titles as job coach, employment coordinator, job trainer, job advocate, or placement coordinator. These terms describe the same job functions and are interchangeable with the term employment specialist. The critical role of the employment specialist is to provide the necessary support required by the individual with a developmental disability to be successful in performing a given work task. This support usually includes training, fading, and follow-up monitoring services.

AN EMPLOYMENT SPECIALIST UNDERSTANDS THE WORK REQUIRED FOR THE COMPLETION OF A PARTICULAR JOB.

The role of the employment specialist as trainer is important if the individual with a developmental disability is to become independent in performing the work task. Once a job has been identified by the job developer and the individual placed at the work site, the employment specialist works alongside the individual as he or she performs the work. As a trainer/teacher, the employment specialist completes a task analysis of the work to be done and employs error-free teaching methods to teach the individual how to complete the task independently as described in Chapter 7. The employer is assured that the work will be completed as scheduled during the training process. In other words, the employment specialist may, for a period of time, assume responsibility for the actual work completed.

THE EMPLOYMENT SPECIALIST WORKS WITH THE INDIVIDUAL WITH A DEVELOPMENTAL DISABILITY AND TEACHES THE SKILLS REQUIRED FOR COMPLETION OF THE WORK.

As the individual with a developmental disability is able to do more and more of the actual work, the employment specialist does less. This process of eliminating or reducing the assistance provided by the employment specialist as the individual learns a new skill is called *fading*. Fading is a very important role of the employment specialist. The goal of fading is to create independence in the performance of a task. The task may be an activity of daily living, such as hand washing, or it may be a work task, such as mopping a floor. Successful fading eliminates assistance in a timely manner and does not create a dependency on the employment specialist for completion of a task.

FADING STRATEGIES ARE EMPLOYED UNTIL THE ASSISTANCE OF THE EMPLOYMENT SPECIALIST IS NO LONGER NEEDED.

Fading is a difficult skill for some human services personnel to learn. Many view their jobs as taking care of or doing for individuals with developmental disabilities. This attitude, if taken by an employment specialist, results in these individuals becoming dependent on the employment specialist. A more appropriate attitude is one that fosters the independence of individuals with developmental disabilities. In the workplace, these individuals must be seen as capable of acquiring work skills. The employment specialist must consider what he or she does as a temporary arrangement until the work skills are learned.

Employment specialists collect data throughout the training and fading process. Data are used to guide decisions regarding the fading process and the continued need for assistance from the employment specialist. Initially, the employment specialist may be present at the work site daily. As the data indicate that the individual with a developmental disability is ready for fading procedures, the employment specialist may reduce the frequency and intensity of his or her visits to the work site until they are no longer needed. For some individuals, the level of support may be reduced to an occasional phone call. For others, a daily check may be required. At this point, the employment specialist shifts from the fading process and responsibility for completion of the work task to ongoing follow-up and monitoring services.

FOR SOME INDIVIDUALS WITH DEVELOPMENTAL DISABILITIES, THE LEVEL OF SUPPORT MAY BE REDUCED TO AN OCCASIONAL PHONE CALL; FOR OTHERS, A DAILY CHECK MAY BE REQUIRED.

The employment specialist monitors the work of the individual with a developmental disability to ensure that he or she continues to perform at an acceptable level. The individual's work productivity should remain constant. The employment specialist plays an important role in monitoring quality assurance. Should the individual's performance fall below an acceptable level, the employment specialist can shift roles back to that of a trainer and increase his or her support until the individual's productivity is again acceptable. In this manner, the employment specialist monitors the individual's performance and ensures a positive working relationship with the employer.

THE EMPLOYMENT SPECIALIST CAN SHIFT ROLES BACK TO THAT OF A TRAINER AND INCREASE THE LEVEL OF SUPPORT PROVIDED IF REQUIRED BY THE INDIVIDUAL WITH A DEVELOPMENTAL DISABILITY.

FUTURE DIRECTION OF SUPPORTED EMPLOYMENT

Predicting the future of any service is risky. At best, all that one can do is try to understand what may occur if current trends continue. The emphasis on integration of workers with severe disabilities into the workplace remains a primary motivation for supported employment.

THE EMPHASIS ON INTEGRATION OF WORKERS WITH SEVERE DISABILITIES INTO THE WORKPLACE REMAINS A PRIMARY MOTIVATION FOR SUPPORTED EMPLOYMENT.

As the concept of supported employment matures and as more employers realize the advantages of supported employment, the roles of both the human services employee and the nondisabled worker in the workplace will continue to change. The current trend indicates that supported employment will become more the responsibility of the employer and less the responsibility of the human services agency. Agency staff roles and responsibilities will need to continue toward building positive relationships within natural settings.

As these significant changes occur, both job developers and employment specialists may need to view their relationships with employers and employees differently. This concept builds on what takes place naturally within most work environments, which are primarily informal support networks for all employees. Most employees give and receive help for many of life's problems through the informal support network system. Future supported employment programs will emphasize and build on these informal, natural support systems.

FUTURE SUPPORTED EMPLOYMENT PROGRAMS WILL EMPHASIZE AND BUILD ON THE INFORMAL, NATURAL SUPPORT SYSTEMS THAT OCCUR WITHIN THE WORKPLACE.

The possible relationships and role changes are highlighted in Table 1. The various options in the table suggest different roles for both the human services staff and the employer. The table also suggests that the future of supported employment lies in the creation of an array of service options available to meet the needs of individuals with developmental disabilities, as well as those of potential employers.

SUMMARY

Supported employment is paid work for individuals with severe disabilities. Currently, federal government regulations require that individuals work in integrated settings at least 20 hours per week. It has been recommended that this requirement be relaxed in favor of individually determined hours of work. Supported employment focuses on the abilities of individuals and assumes that all individuals, regardless of the severity of disability, can become employed. Currently, human services agencies coordinate work opportunities through enclaves in business, mobile work crews, or individual placement models. The enclave model has become less popular in recent years as more individuals choose the individual placement model.

The supported employment goal of integration in the workplace is achieved in all three models. The individual placement model, however, offers the greatest potential for integration. Often, integration is achieved when individuals with developmental disabilities become

Table 1. Community employment support options

| Option | Support person/role | | Responsible to | Agency role |
	Initial	Ongoing		
Job coach	Job coach trains	Coach fades; worker is presumed independent	Agency	Direct: training and follow-up
Mentor	Job coach trains: supervision is transferred to mentor	Mentor remains on site, providing support and supervision	Company	Indirect: matching and support for mentor
Training consultant	Job coach trains with the coworkers/supervisor	Coworkers/supervisor provide support, supervision, and additional training	Company	Indirect: consultation and stipend
Job sharing	Job coach identifies job sharer, then trains and assists	Job sharer remains on site	Agency and company	Indirect: matching; support for job-sharer, stipend
Attendant	Attendant trains and assists (may need some assistance from job coach)	Attendant remains on site at worker's discretion	Worker	Possibly initial training; afterward little or no intervention

Source: Nisbet, J., & Hagner, D. (1988). Natural supports in the workplace: A reexamination of supported employment. *Journal of The Association for Persons with Severe Handicaps, 13*(4), 260.

employees of a company and enjoy the same benefits as their non-disabled peers.

Job developers and employment specialists are critical to the success of supported employment. The job developer, a specialist in job demographics for a given geographic area, conducts a market analysis to learn what work is available. Based on the job developer's knowledge of an individual with a developmental disability and his or her strengths and interests, the individual is offered a choice among the available job options.

The employment specialist understands the nature of work required for the completion of a given job. The employment specialist employs effective teaching strategies, including task analysis and error-free teaching methods, to teach work independence to individuals with developmental disabilities. Fading procedures are then employed to foster independence. Ongoing support services are defined by the individuals' and their need for support. This requires the employment specialist to be flexible in defining job duties and responsibilities and the provision of services.

Both the job developer and employment specialist have job duties and responsibilities for monitoring an individual's work placement and ensuring continued success in the work site. These duties may involve troubleshooting with the employer or the individual and often require great flexibility in providing support services.

The future of supported employment is difficult to predict. Given current trends, however, it is likely that integration in the work site will remain a major focus. It is also likely that another major shift in the roles of human services employees will occur. Future supported employment programs will build on the natural support systems that exist in the workplace for most workers. Human services employees may find their roles changing to teachers, coaches, and mentors, not only for individuals with developmental disabilities but for nondisabled workers as well.

BIBLIOGRAPHY

Gardner, J.F., Chapman, M.S., Donaldson, G., & Jacobson, S.G. (1988). *Toward supported employment: A process guide for planned change.* Baltimore: Paul H. Brookes Publishing Co.

Kiernan, W.E., & Stark J.A. (Eds.). (1986). *Pathways to employment for adults with developmental disabilities.* Baltimore: Paul H. Brookes Publishing Co.

Nisbet, J., & Hagner, D. (1988). Natural supports in the workplace: A reexamination of supported employment. *Journal of The Association for Persons with Handicaps, 13*(4), 260–267.

Rehabilitation Act Amendments of 1992, PL 102-569. (October 29, 1992) as reported in *Federal Register, 57*(122).

Sowers, J.A., & Powers, L. (1991). *Vocational preparation and employment of students with physical and multiple disabilities.* Baltimore: Paul H. Brookes Publishing Co.

Wehman, P., & Moon, M.S. (Eds.). (1988). *Vocational rehabilitation and supported employment.* Baltimore: Paul H. Brookes Publishing Co.

ADDITIONAL RESOURCES

J. Kregel, P. Wehman, and M.S. Shafer (Eds.). (1990). *Supported employment for persons with severe disabilities: From research to practice* (Richmond: Rehabilitation Research and Training Center on Supported Employment, School of Education, Virginia Commonwealth University).

P. Wehman, J. Kregel, & M.S. Shafer (Eds.). (1990). *Emerging trends in the national supported employment initiative: A preliminary analysis of twenty-seven states* (Richmond: Rehabilitation Research and Training Center on Supported Employment, School of Education, Virginia Commonwealth University).

SELF-APPRAISAL

INSTRUCTIONS

The following questions will help you evaluate your knowledge about supported employment. For true-false questions, check the correct answer. For multiple choice questions, circle the correct answer(s).

Note: There may be more than one correct answer for some questions.

1. Supported employment is the current fad in human services and is likely not to be here in the next 10 years.
   ___ True   ___ False
2. Supported employment is paid employment.
   ___ True   ___ False
3. Among the guidelines published for supported employment are:
   a. 20 hours of work per week
   b. Integration with nondisabled workers
   c. Provision of ongoing support services
   d. All the above
   e. None of the above
4. Which of the following are current models of supported employment?
   a. Enclaves
   b. Mobile crews
   c. Emerson's services
   d. Individual placement
   e. Murray's
5. The individual placement model offers the greatest opportunities for integration at the work site.
   ___ True   ___ False
6. Supported employment focuses on an individual's abilities and assumes that all individuals with developmental disabilities are workers.
   ___ True   ___ False
7. Which of the following is a false statement?
   a. Job developers understand what jobs are available for a given geographic area.
   b. Job developers are not critical to implementing supported employment.
   c. A job developer and an employment specialist may be different employees.
   d. A market analysis is critical to the job developer.

8. Employment specialist, job coach, employment coordinator, job trainer, job advocate, and placement coordinator are job titles used to describe the same individual.
   ___ True   ___ False

9. Which of the following is a false statement?
   a. An employment specialist understands the work required for the completion of a particular job.
   b. An employment specialist works with individuals with developmental disabilities.
   c. An employment specialist does not need to know teaching strategies.
   d. Fading is important to the employment specialist.

10. Which of the following describe the future of supported employment services?
    a. Predicting the future is risky.
    b. Integration will remain a primary thrust.
    c. Programs will build on the informal, natural support system of the workplace.
    d. None of the above.

CASE STUDY

Eric Roberts is a young adult with cerebral palsy. He has limited range of motion, and his mobility is enhanced through the use of an electric wheelchair. He is able to communicate with an augmentative communication system.

Mr. Roberts graduated from the local community college 6 months ago. He earned an associate in arts degree with a major in computer-assisted design. Mr. Roberts has applied to numerous local businesses for employment. He is particularly interested in architectural firms and engineering companies.

Mr. Roberts needs a personal care attendant to assist him in getting up and preparing for work. He has arranged for transportation to a number of possible employment situations.

He has a support network of friends from school and family and participates in community life. He is generally optimistic that the new Americans with Disabilities Act will increase opportunities for him in the near future.

Situation

Mr. Roberts needs supports in the work environment. Currently, the state provides supports through the statewide supported employment program. Mr. Roberts wants to work 40 hours per week. His job coach states that he is not able to unbundle support services and provide the individual supports needed by Mr. Roberts.

1. What advice would you give the job coach?
2. Which of the supported employment models would best suit Mr. Roberts's needs?

ANSWER KEY TO SELF-APPRAISAL

1. False
2. True
3. d
4. a, b, d
5. True
6. True
7. b
8. True
9. c
10. a, b, c

CASE STUDY ANSWER GUIDELINES

1. The federal regulations governing supported employment do not limit the number of hours an individual may work. Mr. Roberts may work 40 hours per week and continue to receive needed supports to ensure his successful employment.
2. Mr. Roberts has typical intelligence and is educated. Therefore, an individual placement model would best suit him. Mr. Roberts is capable of negotiating his employment contract and the support services that he needs.

section IV

MAINTAINING PERSPECTIVES: GUIDELINES FOR INDIVIDUAL EMPLOYEES

chapter 14	Coping with Stress and Burnout

LEARNING OBJECTIVES

After reading this chapter, the reader will be able to:

1. Define the differences between stress and burnout.
2. List five symptoms of job stress and burnout.
3. List five causes of job stress and burnout.
4. List five methods for decreasing job stress and preventing burnout.
5. Identify three causes of stress in his or her life and three methods for decreasing stress.

INTRODUCTION

As an employee in a human services agency, you may be aware of a high rate of staff turnover. Some agencies experience 50%-100% turnover in a year. Often, the staff members complain about stress. Sometimes they skip work to take a "mental health day." High turnover may be a symptom of stress and burnout.

Stress and burnout are major problems in the modern workplace and receive strong attention in the media and elsewhere. Magazine articles and books appear regularly on coping with stress and eliminating burnout. Consultants offer seminars on stress and burnout. But stress and burnout are not just trendy. Illness and accidents tied to stress are involved in more than 75% (Hanson, 1986, p. 11) of the time lost from work. Controlling stress is an important factor in disease prevention. Job-related stress decreases the ability of the immune system to fight infection and disease. It can harm your mental and physical health and even kill you. Burnout costs human services agencies billions of dollars each year.

Job-related stress and burnout in human services differ from the stress and tedium that often afflict workers in manufacturing plants and service repair occupations. The differences are due to the people and work involved in human services. This chapter describes stress and burnout. You will learn to recognize the symptoms and causes of stress. More importantly, you will learn to recognize and control stress. You can prevent burnout.

DEFINITIONS

The terms *stress* and *burnout* are sometimes used to describe the same situation, but they refer to two different phenomena. Most employees in human services agencies experience stress. Stress can be controlled. Uncontrolled stress can result in burnout.

Stress

Stress is defined as a response of the human body to demands placed upon it. Stress can be positive or negative. A job promotion, for instance, would generally be considered a positive stress. An automobile accident would be a negative stress. You are constantly faced with stress. The positive stresses are the challenges you face to improve yourself. As a result, you often deliberately place yourself in stressful situations. For example, you may decide to take an evening course at the university. The course will be demanding. The key to coping with stress is knowing how much positive or negative stress you can tolerate. For instance, you probably would not take four courses during the same semester while working full time.

People often give their best performances in times of stress. Olympic records are not set on lonely training fields but in the stress of competition, before large crowds and television cameras. The same is true with actors, poker players, and politicians. Their best performances take place under stress.

Too much stress, however, can push people over the line. Family problems, stalled traffic, and a missed meal can lower the efficiency of any performer. Too many demands, too many details, and no free time can cause moments of mental confusion. Too little stress, however hard, can lower performance. Retirees find that simple tasks that once took little time under normal stress now stretch on for days. A lack of stress dulls physical and mental awareness.

STRESS IS A RESPONSE OF THE HUMAN BODY TO DEMANDS PLACED UPON IT.

Stress can have many causes. Jobs, personal finances, family relationships, rush-hour traffic, crowds, and loud noise can cause stress.

These are discussed in more detail in a later section on Causes of Stress and Burnout. The impact of stress is determined by how each individual reacts to it and interprets it. Stressors are very similar to reinforcers. All individuals have their own menu of stressors. Loud noise and traffic may be a stressor to one person but not to another person.

Most people generally react poorly to negative or unpleasant stressors. A death in the family, personal illness, or financial loss generally result in a negative response. Some people who cannot cope with negative stress also do not react well to positive stressors. For them, a vacation, a visit by close friends, or professional recognition can be as difficult as negative stressors.

Stress, then, is present throughout life. People constantly adjust and readjust to situations. They learn to cope with positive and negative stressors. Some stress is normal. All jobs, for instance, involve some amount of stress. Work in a human services agency is sometimes frustrating. It is hard work. The key is to learn how to cope with stress.

Burnout

Burnout occurs when, as a result of continuing intense and negative pressures, a person finds no meaning or attraction in his or her job. For example, it can result from the constant emotional pressure and stress of working intensely with people for long periods of time. Burnout is typically associated with the "I just don't care anymore" or "There is no point to what I do" mentality. Unrelieved stress can lead to burnout.

Generally, burnout results in three outcomes. First, people who have reached burnout report low energy levels; they feel constantly fatigued. Second, they also experience emotional exhaustion. They feel sorry for themselves and provide little or no support to others. Third, burnout results in mental exhaustion. This occurs when people develop negative attitudes toward themselves, their jobs, and perhaps their careers.

BURNOUT IS A CONDITION OF PHYSICAL AND MENTAL EXHAUSTION THAT CAN RESULT FROM CONTINUOUS EMOTIONAL PRESSURE OF WORKING INTENSELY WITH PEOPLE FOR PROLONGED PERIODS OF TIME.

SYMPTOMS OF STRESS

A common set of physical reactions generally occurs in stressful situations. When faced with stress, the human body goes on an action-alert status. Normal operating systems are bypassed. The blood sugar level rises. Oxygen flow increases and more blood is directed to the heart. Blood pressure rises. The secretion of stomach acid increases. In extreme cases, adrenaline is released into the blood. The body remains on alert until the stress is removed. Body functions then return to normal.

EXERCISE 1

Social Readjustment Rating Scale

Thomas H. Holmes and colleagues at the University of Washington identified 43 life events that require adaptive or coping behaviors. Note the impact of positive stressors. A person who experienced more than 150 points in one year was defined as having a life crisis. Circle those events that have happened to you in the last year.

Life event	Mean value
1. Death of spouse	100
2. Divorce	73
3. Marital separation	65
4. Jail term	63
5. Death of close family member	63
6. Personal injury or illness	53
7. Marriage	50
8. Fired at work	47
9. Marital reconciliation	45
10. Retirement	45
11. Change in health of family member	44
12. Pregnancy	40
13. Sexual difficulties	39
14. Gain of new family member	39
15. Business adjustment	39
16. Change in financial state	38
17. Death of close friend	37
18. Change to different line of work	36
19. Change in number of arguments with spouse	35
20. Mortgage over $10,000	31
21. Foreclosure of mortgage or loan	30
22. Change in responsibilities at work	29
23. Son or daughter leaving home	29
24. Trouble with in-laws	29
25. Outstanding personal achievement	28
26. Spouse begins or stops work	26
27. Beginning or end of school	26
28. Change in living conditions	25
29. Revision of personal habits	24
30. Trouble with boss	23
31. Change in work hours or conditions	20

(continued)

EXERCISE 1

(*continued*)

32.	Change in residence	20
33.	Change in schools	20
34.	Change in recreation	19
35.	Change in church activities	19
36.	Change in social activities	18
37.	Mortgage or loan less than $10,000	17
38.	Change in sleeping habits	16
39.	Change in number of family get-togethers	15
40.	Change in eating habits	15
41.	Vacation	13
42.	Christmas	12
43.	Minor violations of the law	11

Source: Holmes and Rake (1967).

When people are exposed to constant stress, the body may not return all the way to normal. Physical symptoms of chronic stress begin to occur. This stress frequently results in headaches, backaches, and high blood pressure. Chronic stress lowers resistance to cold and flu viruses. Although research is not conclusive, stress has been linked with heart disease and ulcers. A variety of illnesses, including those listed in Table 1, may be brought on by continued exposure to stress. These illnesses can also serve as escape routes for coping with long-term stress.

In addition to illnesses, many other symptoms of stress serve as warning signs. They let you know that too much stress is building. Symptoms differ among people. Some people have difficulty sleeping; others experience constant emotional tension. Typical physical and mental signs of stress are listed in Tables 2 and 3.

Table 1. Some illnesses induced by exposure to stress

Acne	Fatigue
Alcoholism	Frigidity
Allergies	Headache
Asthma	Heart conditions
Colitis	Impotence
Constipation	Insomnia
Dermatitis and eczema	Obesity
Diabetes	Peptic ulcers
Diarrhea	Rheumatoid arthritis

Adapted from Greenberg and Valletutti (1980).

Table 2. Typical physical signs of stress

Alcohol dependency	Indigestion
Diarrhea	Muscle spasms
Drug addiction	Nausea
Dry throat and mouth	Nightmares
Excessive weight change	Pain in back, neck, and chest
Excessive nervous energy	Psychoses
Fatigue	Shortness of breath
Fainting	Sleeplessness
Frigidity	Stuttering
Headaches	Sweating
Heartburn	Tooth grinding
High blood pressure	Trembling
Impotence	Vomiting
Impulsive eating	

Adapted from Greenberg and Valletutti (1980).

SYMPTOMS OF BURNOUT

The symptoms of burnout are more difficult to analyze. Most people enter the human services field to help others. In burnout, the initial attitude of compassion turns to not caring. The desire to help and to make a contribution and the urge to be creative turn into a "nobody really cares" mentality.

EXERCISE 2

Burnout Self-Diagnosis

Following is a list of 21 experiences. Using the frequency scale of 1 (never) to 7 (always), answer the question: How often do you have any of the following experiences?

1 = never; 2 = once or twice; 3 = rarely; 4 = sometimes; 5 = often; 6 = usually; 7 = always.

1. Being tired _____
2. Feeling depressed _____
3. Having a good day _____
4. Being physically exhausted _____
5. Being emotionally exhausted _____
6. Being happy _____
7. Being "wiped out" _____
8. Feeling "burned out" _____

(continued)

EXERCISE 2
(*continued*)

9. Being unhappy _____
10. Feeling rundown _____
11. Feeling trapped _____
12. Feeling worthless _____
13. Being weary _____
14. Being troubled _____
15. Feeling disillusioned and resentful about people _____
16. Feeling weak and helpless _____
17. Feeling hopeless _____
18. Feeling rejected _____
19. Feeling optimistic _____
20. Feeling energetic _____
21. Feeling anxious _____

Scoring the self-diagnosis:

Add up the values you gave items 1, 2, 4, 5, 7, 8, 9, 10, 11, 12, 13, 14, 15, 16, 17, 18, 21. This is sum A. _____
Add up the values you gave items 3, 6, 19, 20. This is sum B. _____
Subtract the sum B from 32. This is sum C. _____
Add sum A and C. This is sum D. _____
Divide sum D by 21. This is your burnout score _____.

What the score means:

A score between 2 and 3 means you are okay.
A score between 3 and 4 means you are at risk of burnout.
A score between 4 and 5 means you are experiencing burnout.
A score higher than 5 is a probable indication that the burnout is severe.

Adapted from Pines, Aronson, and Kafry (1981).

Table 3. Typical mental signs of stress

Anxiety	General irritability
Apprehension about approaching weekends and vacations	Impulsive behavior
	Inability to concentrate
Constant uneasiness	Inability to laugh
Depression	Irrational fears
Feeling of rejection by family	Lack of concentration
Feeling of parental failure	Reoccurring sense of hopelessness
General boredom	Suppressed anger

Adapted from Greenberg and Valletutti (1980).

Physical burnout is usually easy to detect. It results in general fatigue and carries over into off-the-job behavior. Usually, physical burnout can be corrected by a few days away from the job or a vacation.

Psychological or emotional burnout is a more complicated problem. Some people become burned out in environments that do not provide emotional support to employees. As a result, many of the initial symptoms and behaviors of burnout are not sufficiently appreciated because they are present in many of the staff and the process seems rather normal until the final phases.

A common symptom of burnout is undirected anger. Unjustified by special circumstances, this anger boils and ferments near the surface. Unfulfilled expectations fuel the anger. The anger is then directed against supervisors, colleagues, or the people participating in the program.

Another common symptom of burnout is simply withdrawal. In this type of burnout, staff members have no energy. They cannot be challenged. They hang on, put in the time, and hope that no one will expect too much from them.

UNDIRECTED ANGER AND WITHDRAWAL ARE SYMPTOMS OF BURNOUT.

CAUSES OF STRESS AND BURNOUT

The many causes of stress and burnout interact in various ways and affect people differently.

Everyday Hassles and Headaches

The reasons for stress and burnout are present in the normal day. Bad news on the radio, commuting, car trouble, family feuds, and staying on your diet can cause stress and burnout. Natural transitions in life cause stress. Marriage, divorce, moving, retirement, leaving home, and changing jobs can cause stress. Finally, some people make their own stress. Guilt, perfectionism, worry, frustration, and procrastination all lead to stressful situations.

Frustrated Role Expectations

Job-related stress can develop as soon as an employee begins work. At that time, the new employee develops a series of expectations about the job. These expectations come from many sources, including the employee's imagination, the job interview, wish fulfillment, or the physical environment. If this series of expectations is close to reality, there is little stress. However, there can be a large gap between expectation and reality. If so, the employee begins work in a high-stress situation.

The issue of expectations is related to the problem of role ambiguity, or uncertainty. This is best illustrated by the frustrated worker who exclaims "I just don't know what I am supposed to do." Every person in an organization plays several roles. There are different expectations about how employees will behave, depending on their roles.

Role ambiguity can cause confusion for new staff members when they interact with people with developmental disabilities. This is particularly true for those in small residential programs. A staff member may not be certain if he or she is a counselor, house parent, residential adviser, teacher, or trainer. Each of these titles implies a slightly different role. Anyone who works with people with developmental disabilities needs a very clear role definition. Without such a definition, stress is inevitable.

Another source of stress is role conflict. This is illustrated by the worker who exclaims, "I can't play both roles at the same time." Some roles are mutually exclusive and simply cannot be played at the same time. For example, a staff member in an apartment program cannot be both a peer and a residential counselor.

Role conflict becomes a problem when the staff attempt to sustain formal and informal roles simultaneously. For example, a formal role might be that of supervisor of a landscape crew of five workers and the informal role that of peer and coworker. Stress builds when the two roles cannot be sustained at the same time.

Work Overload

Stress also results from work overload. There are two kinds of work overload. The first is a consequence of working excessive hours or squeezing too much work into regular work hours. It also includes situations in which the staff are forced to work and make decisions without reasonable planning and preparation. This type of overload causes physical and emotional stress and leads to burnout.

Another dangerous outcome can result from this kind of work overload. Overly pressured staff find it difficult to provide an individualized program for each person. As a result, they are forced to provide group activities and perform maintenance work. Lack of staffing and overload thus cause programs to shift emphasis from a developmental growth orientation to a make-do model. The staff are frustrated, and the goals of the agency are threatened.

The second type of overload is periodic. It results in an irregular work load. Sudden and excessive demands for service disrupt schedules. The mere absence of a coworker due to illness can double the number of people that another staff person must work with that day.

Demands of Human Services Work

Most human services agencies provide programs to people who have a need. This poses a reactive situation in which staff members must continually confront people's needs and problems and attempt to respond to them. The irony is that when you are successful and meet those needs, the people no longer need your agency. They leave and are replaced by others with needs. Very few people approach a human services agency to announce they are doing fine. This continual giving to meet the needs of others is a major source of stress and burnout in human services.

In addition, many staff members have difficulty leaving work issues at work. (This is almost impossible for live-in residential staff.) They think about other people's needs long after they leave work. This inability to "leave work at work" leads to two complications: First, staff members cannot find relief from the needs and demands of others, and, second, they inject work stress into their home situations.

TO AVOID EXTRA STRESS: "LEAVE WORK AT WORK."

Job stress may be personal, but it is not private. Overreaction to stress—reflected in anger, anxiety, boredom, high blood pressure, depression—is not confined to work. It can shape your interactions with friends, families, and coworkers. In fact, the symptoms of job stress often appear in nonwork settings. You cannot "blow up" in front of a supervisor without fear of consequences, but you can explode at home. Unfortunately, those at home may not understand the reason for your behavior. In fact, they may wrongly relate it to something they did.

Human services agency employees also feel stress when they are given very limited authority. They are asked to assist people in developing new skills and making decisions but sometimes play no role in the agency's planning process. Frustration and stress result from asking staff members to implement policy and procedures developed without their input.

Workers in human services agencies are not typically provided high job status, salaries, or other rewards. Some find initial job satisfaction from aspects of work other than salary. In the long run, however, they will not continue to be creative and energetic without adequate compensation.

Finally, working with people with developmental disabilities can be frustrating and stressful. Teaching new skills and behaviors can be repetitive and time-consuming. This can lead to tedium and burnout. Some people may have strange and difficult behaviors that are stressful to deal with. In addition, people with developmental disabilities do not learn as quickly as other people. In some instances, they do not achieve what you expect. You may feel disappointed or frustrated because you work so hard but feel you achieve little.

Inadequate Workplace Environment

The workplace itself can also produce stress. Although not uncommon in business and industry, this issue is especially important in human services. Many human services agencies operate in less than adequate work settings. Overcrowding and lack of private space are not unusual in large residential programs. Buildings designed as schools or offices frequently house vocational and work programs. Because they were not intended for such use, their lighting, traffic patterns, and noise levels may be stressful. Noise, in particular, has a direct relationship to stress. The eye has an automatic control regulating the amount of light that enters it. The ear, however, has no control. It is open all the time. When the ear detects unexpected sound, the body goes on alert. In severe cases, heartbeat, blood pressure, and muscle tension increase.

EXERCISE 3

Stages of Mental Burnout

If you suspect you are suffering from burnout, complete the following exercise. Check each if it is true for you.

1. I am not at risk of burnout.
2. The public doesn't know anything about my job.
3. The system cannot change.
4. My family really doesn't understand how hard I work.
5. There is no satisfaction in my work; I do it for the money.
6. People with developmental disabilities are the only ones who really understand my good work.
7. This job is impossible.
8. Burnout strikes people who are not determined to succeed.
9. People in human services don't know how good they've got it.
10. No matter how much I put into the job, there is very little change.
11. The administration prevents us from doing an effective job.
12. My knowledge about the causes of burnout should prevent it from happening to me.
13. I should do more to let my coworkers know how much I do accomplish.
14. My main concern is a comfortable retirement.
15. I can move up in the agency by taking on the jobs nobody else will do.
16. The problems of the people I work with are due to their own weakness.
17. Burnout is not an important issue in my job.
18. If the agency provided better supervision, I could do a better job.
19. The agency doesn't really care about people.
20. Most of my coworkers are indifferent about the true quality of service.

(continued)

EXERCISE 3

(continued)

21. Just getting up and going to work in the morning makes me tired.
22. I have not experienced any symptoms of burnout.
23. My supervisors know more about how to do my job tasks than I do.
24. If I would take a few more courses, I could accomplish much more on my job.
25. Nobody in the agency takes my suggestions seriously.

Scoring the stages of mental burnout:

Circle the numbers below that correspond to the items you checked. Count the number of circled items in each column. The column with the most circled items best describes your stage of burnout. Now total the number of circled items in each column. If there are no real differences between columns and your score is under 12, you are not at immediate risk of burnout. If there are no real differences between columns and your score is above 16, you could be experiencing the burnout process.

	Denial	Blaming resentment	Over-compensation	Repression	Resignation
	1	4	6	2	3
	9	11	13	7	5
	12	16	15	10	8
	17	19	18	21	14
	22	20	24	25	23
Number of circled items in each column:	___	___	___	___	___
Total score	_____				

Categories of Mental Burnout

1. Denial—This stage of burnout is characterized by a sense of immunity from burnout. The lack of awareness is often found among new employees and graduate students.
2. Resentment—At this stage, anger begins. Employees do not blame themselves; rather, they place the origin of the problem in or blame on others.
3. Overcompensation—In this stage, employees begin to feel a little incompetent and devote extra hours to eliminating the shortcoming.
4. Depression—This stage is typified by feelings of hopelessness and tiredness.
5. Resignation—At this point, other feelings have subsided. The employee has lost the caring and creative energy.

Adapted from Welch, Medeiros, and Tate (1982).

MANAGEMENT OF STRESS AND BURNOUT

Stress and burnout can be limited and controlled. Burnout is not inevitable. Working with people with developmental disabilities is not a dead-end process. Far from it—creativity and commitment can be fostered in human services agencies

Controlling Stress

One key to managing stress is control. Peter Hanson (1985, p. 16) writes about two groups of workers. Both groups experienced very distracting noises of people yelling, horns honking, and machinery clanging. One group had a button on top of the desk that would turn off the noise. The other group did not.

The productivity of the group with the button was constantly higher than that of the group without the button, even though no one ever pushed the button. Our lives are much the same. We tend to perform better when we have a sense of control over the sources of stress. Hanson (1985, p. 16) counsels, "Learn to ignore what you can't control, and learn to control what you can."

"LEARN TO IGNORE WHAT YOU CAN'T CONTROL, AND LEARN TO CONTROL WHAT YOU CAN."

Understanding Stress and Burnout

The first step in controlling stress and burnout is to understand them. One approach is to use the ABC chart described in Chapter 9. Under B, for behavior, list a behavior that you are concerned about. The behavior, such as being late, skipping work, shouting at other employees, or making careless teaching mistakes, could indicate fatigue, boredom, anger, or other symptoms of stress. Now, under A, for antecedents, list the possible reasons for the symptomatic behavior, such as excessive work load, lack of recognition, and lack of role definition. If the behavior is a symptom of stress and if you can identify some possible reasons for the stress, you can then try some alternative solutions.

One of the first questions to ask is: Who is responsible for the stress? Is the stress work-induced? Are you creating the stress? For example, does your supervisor tell you to work extra hours or to think about work issues over the weekend? Or, do you work extra hours to do a good job? Many people enter human services with a strong impulse to help. They equate extra work with extra help. The need to succeed, to accomplish, can also lead to stress. The need to overachieve, or "workaholism," can lead to stress.

Some people also work extra hard when they sense they are failing. Other staff members become stressed because they are disorganized. In short, you need to determine who is creating the stress. If the agency is causing the stress, you will have to talk with your supervisor. If you are overworking and stressing yourself, you need to make some changes.

In some instances, it is your perceptions of your work, and not the work itself, that cause the stress. Most people make "mountains out of molehills." Most events are not "disastrous," "horrible," or "awful," no matter what you say. It is human nature to attach too much meaning to most events. Then you end up worrying about the meaning you created.

Most people attach too much meaning to events. Then they worry about the meaning they created.

Reducing Stress and Burnout

The most crucial element in reducing stress and avoiding burnout is the development of a social support system. A social support network is a group of people who share your ideas and values. These people can provide help when you need it. There are six basic functions of the social support system:

1. *Listening.* You need someone who will listen to your concerns, who will listen without giving advice or telling you how he or she had the same problem, but even worse.
2. *Technical support.* You need someone who will provide honest feedback on the work you do.
3. *Technical challenge.* You need someone who will constructively challenge your thinking. This will encourage you toward greater creativity and productivity.
4. *Emotional support.* You need people to stand beside you in hard times. They need to stand with you even if they are not in total agreement with your position.
5. *Emotional challenge.* You need trusted friends who may not understand the technical aspects of your job. However, they can say, "Are you really trying your best on this project?"
6. *Reality testing.* You need associates who can help you test your perception of reality. "Are things as they appear?" "Am I correct in looking at the problem this way?" These are reality-testing questions others can help you with.

You must not expect any one person to fulfill all of these functions. You should learn which members of your support system provide which function(s). Ideally, within a work group, each of the functions is provided by some combination of people.

Can you identify your social support system?

Each person must develop an individual approach to coping with stress. The techniques of personal coping and stress reduction are many and varied. You can learn specific details in college courses, workshops, and seminars. You can also obtain information at the public library and from a local health clinic or your physician.

Use your common sense in evaluating stress reduction programs. Beware of programs that promise to reduce stress through special diets or other means. For instance, hanging upside down from inversion boots will probably not decrease stress.

Any reasonable stress reduction program should contain some elements of the following 10 strategies:

1. Exercise. Numerous studies indicate that physical exercise helps a person to cope with stress. Exercise strengthens the cardiovascular system. It decreases boredom. Most people feel relaxed after they exercise. Exercise also results in enhanced self-image and greater personal confidence. You need to choose your own form of exercise. Pick one that you enjoy, is convenient, and conforms to your lifestyle. Aerobic exercises, such as jogging, bicycle riding, swimming, walking, and dancing, are valuable because they build the cardiovascular system. Take normal precautions when you begin to exercise. See Table 4 for general guidelines for beginning an exercise program.

2. Maintain good diet and nutrition. Advice on diet and nutrition has become an American pastime. Again, keep a commonsense approach. Correct eating habits are necessary. Skipping breakfast and eating fast-food lunches and late dinners may eventually con-

Table 4. Guidelines for beginning an exercise program

1. Begin your exercise program gradually.
2. Begin and conclude your exercise program with warm-up, stretching, and cool-down exercises.
3. Exercise on a regular schedule, three to four times each week.
4. Drink plenty of fluids.
5. Wait $1\frac{1}{2}$–$2\frac{1}{2}$ hours after a major meal before exercising.
6. Do not exercise if ill or injured.
7. Use the proper equipment. Various activities require special shoes. Use eye protectors for racket sports.
8. Monitor your physical exertion by taking your pulse.
9. Be alert to distress signals from your body. Dizziness, nausea, loss of breath, pain, faintness, and disorientation are signs of physical stress.
10. In many instances you should consult your physician prior to beginning an exercise program. This is especially true for anyone over 40 years old or under a physician's care.

tribute to stress. Poor diet and eating habits can lead to anxiety, fatigue, depression, and excessive weight gain. Americans consume too much salt, sugar, caffeine, fat, and cholesterol, ingredients all found in quick-order convenience foods. A proper diet that is nutritionally balanced should include small amounts of cholesterol, sugar, and salt.

3. *Create opportunities for learning.* People have a need to learn and explore. Be curious. Enrich your life during and after work. Search for new ways to interact with the people with whom you work. A willingness to learn and explore also contributes to a sense of importance and self. Without these outlets, some employees quickly lapse into tedium and burnout.

4. *Set reasonable standards for yourself.* Avoid the self-destructive urge to compete with others for power, money, or fame. Preoccupation with the quest for achievement can cause a double stress. The first is the continual need for higher achievement; the second results from the absence of other rewards and pleasures.

5. *Emphasize variety.* Variety is the key factor in preventing boredom and stress. This is true for both work and nonwork situations. Introducing variety requires two conditions. First, add challenge by trying new tasks rather than repeating tasks you have already mastered; second, allow yourself to make mistakes in attempting new tasks.

6. *Participate in your own self-improvement.* In Chapters 8 and 9, you learned how to alter behaviors. You can change your own behavior, but first you must be aware of the causes of your stress. Then you must decide to take the responsibility for change. Finally, you must recognize what things you can change and what things are beyond your control.

7. *Know your energy limits.* There is a limit to your energy, so you must pace yourself. If you are going to move in high gear, do two things: first, determine how far you can go at top speed, and, second, slow down when you reach that point. Identify your flameout point—the point at which you work harder and harder but accomplish less and less. Plan ahead how far you are going to push yourself. Do not allow yourself to run into stress.

8. *Provide for your own relaxation.* Home should not be an extension of the workplace. You must have a life that is distinct from work. Try not to work at home, and be careful about bringing work problems home. This can pose particular problems for live-in residential staff. They may need to incorporate special relaxation techniques into their daily routines. Although discussing problems with a friend, relative, or spouse can sometimes provide an important outlet, it can also re-create the stressful experience.

Such discussions do not always help you to cope with the situation.

9. *Reward yourself.* Make a list of rewards within your budget that you most enjoy. Limit the list to those that you can provide yourself. This may include such items as taking a walk, taking a nap, playing tennis, listening to music, attending the theater or the movies, or going to a baseball game. Use this list to reward yourself.

10. Continuous sacrifice over prolonged periods of time increases the likelihood of stress and burnout. Worry only about issues over which you have some power. There is no sense in worrying about events and circumstances that you cannot control. Pay attention, and spend your time on events you can influence and control.

SUMMARY

Stress is a reality of employment. Some work environments are more stressful than others. Human services workers are prone to stress. Prolonged stress leads to burnout.

Stress and burnout can be controlled. Using a behavioral approach, you can analyze stressful situations and find out which events are stressful. You can also alter events so that you avoid or decrease the stress and possible burnout.

Staff members often create stress by misinterpreting situations or other people's motives. People's behavior should be interpreted in a situational context, rather than in terms of personality.

The development of social support systems is crucial for each staff member. The system should provide listening, technical and emotional support, challenge, and reality-testing functions.

Finally, each human services worker needs a personal approach to coping with stress. This should include exercise, diet and nutrition, and good mental health components.

BIBLIOGRAPHY

Greenberg, S.F., & Valletutti, P.J. (1980). *Stress and the helping professions.* Baltimore: Paul H. Brooks Publishing Co.

Hanson, P.G. (1986). *The joy of stress.* Kansas City, MO: Andrews, McMeel, & Parker.

Holmes, T.H., & Rake, R.H. (1967). The social readjustment rating scale. *Journal of Psychosomatic Research, 11,* 213–218.

Makower, J. (1982). *Office hazards: How your job can make you sick.* New York: Caroline House.

Pines, A.M., Aronson, E., & Kafry, D. (1981). *Burnout: From tedium to personal growth.* New York: Free Press.

Welch, I.D., Medeiros, D.C., & Tate, G.A. (1982).Burnout—*How to enjoy your job again when you've just about had enough.* Englewood Cliffs, NJ: Prentice Hall.

ADDITIONAL RESOURCES

C.H. Browner, K.A. Ellis, T. Ford, J. Silsby, J. Tampoya, and C. Yee (1987), in Stress, social support and health of psychiatric technicians in a state facility, *Mental Retardation,* 25(1), 31–38, explore the impact of social support on stress among staff in a state psychiatric facility.

P. Edwards and R. Miltenberger (1991), in Burnout among staff members at community residential facilities for persons with mental retardation, *Mental Retardation,* 29(3), 125–128, explore the impact of burnout on both supervisory and direct service staffs

S. Faelten (1988), in *Take control of your life: A complete guide to stress relief* (Emmaus, PA: Rodale Press), explores the causes of stress from bad news to on-the-job stress; from self-made stresses, such as guilt and perfectionism, to natural life-cycle transitions, such as divorce, retirement, or graduation. Coping techniques and methods of prevention are presented in 89 chapters, with about six or seven pages per topic.

H. Selye has written extensively on the topic of stress. See, for example, Selye (1969), *Stress without distress* (New York: McGraw-Hill); Selye (1976), *The stress of life* (New York: McGraw-Hill); and Selye (Ed.) (1983), *Selye's guide to stress research* (Vol. 3) (New York: Van Nostrand Reinhold).

SELF-APPRAISAL

INSTRUCTIONS

The following questions will help you evaluate your knowledge about stress and coping with burnout. For true-false questions, check the correct answer. For multiple choice questions, circle the correct answer(s).

Note: There may be more than one correct answer for some questions.

1. Stress and burnout are major problems in the workplace.
   ___ True   ___ False
2. You can prevent burnout
   ___ True   ___ False
3. Causes for stress include
   a. Job
   b. Personal finances
   c. Loud noise
   d. Family relationships
4. Burnout results in the following outcomes:
   a. Low energy levels
   b. Emotional exhaustion
   c. Mental fatigue
   d. Hyperactivity
5. Stress can cause the following changes in the human body:
   a. Increased sugar in the blood
   b. Increased oxygen flow
   c. Increased blood pressure
   d. Increased stomach acid
6. Illnesses induced by stress include:
   a. Alcoholism
   b. Headaches
   c. Heart conditions
   d. Insomnia
7. The following are major causes of stress and burnout in the work setting:
   a. Role ambiguity
   b. Role conflict
   c. Work overload
   d. Too many close personal relationships
8. The first step in controlling stress and burnout is to understand them.
   ___ True   ___ False

9. Basic functions of the social support system include:
   a. Listening
   b. Technical support
   c. Emotional support
   d. Reality testing
10. Any reasonable stress reduction program should include:
   a. Exercise
   b. Diet and nutrition
   c. New learning opportunities
   d. Setting reasonable standards for personal expectations

CASE STUDY

Kathy Bennis is a new employee of Monroe Enterprises, a private non-profit agency providing employment evaluations and placement services for adults with mental retardation. Ms. Bennis completed a 2-year program in psychology at the nearby community college. At age 21, she decided to begin work at Monroe Enterprises and to pursue her bachelor of arts degree at the state university's evening college.

The agency accepts people with developmental disabilities for a 6- to 8-week employment evaluation process. During this time, the person is evaluated in a variety of job skills that range from operating power tools to performing general office support services. The agency also determines the person's preference for employment options. Finally, the agency places people with developmental disabilities in supervised employment situations in private business.

The agency's orientation program consists of 2 half-day orientation sessions for all employees who have joined the agency during each 2-month period. All supervising personnel are expected to provide follow-up consultation on a monthly basis throughout the 6-month probationary period.

Ms. Bennis's job requires that she monitor the individual progress of workers in the supervised employment setting. She is out in the field an average of 6 hours a day. The remaining 2 hours are devoted to paperwork in an office she shares with two other staff members who perform evaluations at Monroe Enterprises.

Situation

Until recently, Ms. Bennis shared a house with a close friend. Two months ago, the friend moved out of the state. This has created both personal and financial hardships for Ms. Bennis. She feels stressed and depressed. Her unclear job description has recently resulted in unexpected job responsibilities. She has called in sick on several occasions during the past couple of weeks.

1. What are the major issues that Ms. Bennis should examine?
2. How would you suggest that Ms. Bennis systematically analyze her stress?
3. What steps or actions could the agency take to provide a more supportive work environment?

ANSWER KEY TO
SELF-APPRAISAL AND CASE STUDY

SELF-APPRAISAL

1. True
2. True
3. a, b, c, d
4. a, b, c, d
5. a, b, c, d
6. a, b, c, d
7. a, b, c
8. True
9. a, b, c, d
10. a, b, c, d

CASE STUDY ANSWER GUIDELINES

1. Major issues include developing new relationships, resolving the financial difficulties, and identifying Ms. Bennis's responsibilities at work.
2. First, construct an ABC chart as described in Chapter 9. This will help Ms. Bennis to understand the possible reasons for her stressful behaviors. Understanding is the first step toward resolving difficulties. Second, Ms. Bennis can decide who or what is responsible for the stress. Third, she can choose the best coping strategies for dealing with the stressful situations.
3. The agency should more clearly define Ms. Bennis's job description and provide consultation on a monthly basis. Ms. Bennis's office location could be changed so that she shares work space with people who perform similar duties and responsibilities. The agency could also provide opportunities for the development and growth of informal support networks. These could include regular staff meetings, special lunches, and social events after work.

chapter	Working
15	with
	Families

LEARNING OBJECTIVES

Upon completing this chapter, the reader will be able to:

1. Identify four stages in parents' lives when the need for information and support with regard to raising a child with developmental disabilities is critical.
2. Identify 10 different parental roles.
3. Identify four expectations of parent behaviors.
4. State three approaches to the delivery of parent-training services.

INTRODUCTION

During the past decade, professionals in the field of human services have directed increased attention to the needs of parents of children with developmental disabilities. As a result, programs designed to support parents have grown. Professionals recognize that parents play a critical role in assisting children reach their fullest potential.

This chapter deals with working with the families of children with developmental disabilities. Parents undergo various stages of personal growth and development as their child grows to adulthood. This chapter defines and explores these stages. The parents' changing needs for information and supportive services during these stages are discussed. In addition, guidelines for the delivery of family-centered services are presented. Specific guidelines are also provided for working with parents of both school-age children and individuals older than 21 years.

LIFE-CYCLE REACTIONS

All parents require information and support as they raise their children. Numerous books are available to assist parents when a child is sick, learning to walk, or experiencing sibling rivalry. In addition, friends, neighbors, and other family members are readily available to provide advice and suggestions about raising children. However, when a child with a developmental disability is born, the necessary information and support are often not available. Models of parenting and information about disabilities are sometimes difficult to identify. Without appropriate resources, parents may become isolated from family, friends, and professionals, who often seem unable to identify with the emotional issues experienced by the parents.

The need for information and support among parents of children with developmental disabilities varies from family to family. The need will also change as parents pass through several defined stages in their lives. The most significant stages include when the child is born, when the child enters a school program, when the child leaves a school program to begin employment, and when the child moves away from home.

Birth of a Child with a Developmental Disability

Parents prepare for months for a child's arrival. This time is often characterized as a time of dreaming of the perfect child—whom the child will look like and how he or she will succeed in life. However, these dreams can be quickly shattered by the realization that the "perfect" child has been born with a disability. At such times, a typically joyous event often becomes a time of emotional disorganization. Parents feel disbelief, sadness, and grief at the loss of their dreams. Anxiety, anger, denial, guilt, and a sense of failure are among other emotions parents may experience during this period. Some parents blame themselves or others for their situation. Other parents search for a cure for the disability. Some parents experience a period of depression and withdraw from friends and family. Whereas some parents may experience these emotions for a few days or weeks, other parents feel these emotions, to varying degrees, for a lifetime and are never able to understand and accept their child's disability.

Services to parents at the time of birth of a child with a developmental disability should be designed to provide family support and information. Learning effective communication skills helps the staff to provide emotional support. As a staff member, you should empathize with the parents' feelings. You should encourage them to ask questions that will increase their understanding of the child's disability. Opportunities to talk to other parents of children with disabilities may provide additional support to a family. These strategies can help parents to better come to terms with their feelings. Intense emotional changes can be expected during this period as the family seeks to understand and accept the child.

The informational needs of parents generally center on available community services. When the child requires additional evaluations, parents need to know what agencies or professionals specialize in evaluations. Parents may also require assistance to understand the technical terms used to describe their child's disability. In addition, parents may need information about counseling services to help them cope with their feelings. The parents' possible need for counseling should be viewed as a positive step. Providing counseling services represents an important part of helping the family. The availability of these resources improves your effectiveness in working with families during this stage.

EXERCISE 1

Evaluations and Supports

List on a separate sheet of paper the agencies and/or professionals in your community who specialize in evaluating infants. Also, identify counseling or other support programs available to parents.

The Child's Entrance into Educational Programs

The second critical time for sharing information with parents is when the child enters an educational program. At that time, parents begin a relationship with the schools that can last as long as 21 years. The time when a child starts school is particularly difficult for most parents. For some, it is when the child's disability is first discovered. For others, the differences between their child and other children become more apparent.

The Education for All Handicapped Children Act of 1975 (PL 94-142), known since its 1990 reauthorization as the Individuals with Disabilities Education Act (1990), guarantees parents specific rights in the development of their child's educational program. These rights are important in building successful relationships between educational programs and the home. Parents of young children may be less familiar with their rights than parents of older school-age children. IDEA defines specific due process rights that safeguard a child's placement in a free and appropriate public education. Table 1 lists parental due process rights as guaranteed under IDEA.

IDEA also mandates parental involvement in the educational process. The law views parents as equal partners in planning the child's

Table 1. Parental rights under PL 94-142

The right to examine all school records concerning their child

The right to obtain an independent evaluation

The right to an interpreter or translator

The right to determine whether the hearing will be closed or open to the public

The right to advice of counsel and representation by counsel at the hearing

The right to bring their child to the hearing

The right to keep their child in his or her current educational placement until all due process hearing appeals have been completed

The right to written notification about the hearing in the primary language or mode of communication of the parent

The right to present evidence and testimony

The right to prohibit the introduction of any evidence that has not been disclosed to parents at least 5 days prior to the hearing

The right to cross-examine and to challenge all testimony presented during the hearing

The right to receive a verbatim transcript of the hearing, at reasonable cost

The right to appeal the decision of the hearing officer or hearing panel

---

educational program. This involvement of parents in the educational placement of the child is detailed in Table 2.

The cooperative relationship developed between the school and family is mutually beneficial. Parents may need support and training in order to participate fully in the educational process. With such assistance, they can provide carryover of educational activities into the

Table 2. Parental involvement in the educational process

Written parental permission is secured before assessment.

Parents or guardians are informed in writing of the assessment results.

Parents are informed of their right to participate in the functions of the Admissions, Review, and Dismissal Committee.

Parents are invited to participate in the development of the individualized education program (IEP). The IEP includes:

A statement of present level of functioning

A statement of annual, short- and long-term goals

A statement of specific special education and related services to be provided and the extent to which the child will participate in general education

Projected date for initiation of each service and expected duration

Objective criteria for evaluation of effectiveness of the IEP

A statement concerning any special transportation needs

Parents approve the IEP.

Parents review the appropriateness of the IEP within 60 school days of its initiation. Parents must be informed of the results of the review.

Parents receive a written summary of the IEP on an annual basis.

---

home. Parents can also act as important community advocates for a local educational agency.

The needs of parents are primarily informational when their child enters an educational program. Educational, health, and human services staffs should be prepared to provide information on IDEA, as well as on additional state laws that may affect educational programs. Parents may also need information on such issues as normal developmental sequences, behavior management techniques, and instructional activities and materials for use at home. Information related to specialized services, such as occupational, physical, and speech-language therapy, should be available to parents. Most parents need support from agency staff in learning to build and maintain relationships with teachers and other school officials.

Parents may continue to need emotional support during the school years. Some needs may relate to the family's acceptance of the child's disability. Other concerns may relate to lack of school achievement, feelings of competition with other parents, and family conflicts that are related to or intensified by the child with a developmental disability. Staff members should encourage families to express these emotions. When appropriate, they should encourage the family to participate in parent support groups, parent education programs, and family counseling sessions.

EXERCISE 2

Defining Forms and Identifying Agencies

Define the most commonly used terms in the educational process. List these on a separate sheet of paper.

Identify agencies or professionals in your community who can support parents in meeting their emotional needs. List these on a separate sheet of paper.

In addition to the reauthorization of PL 94-142 in 1990 (PL 101-476) alluded to above, other enactments by Congress (e.g., PL 99-457, PL 102-119) have expanded the original legislation and significantly strengthened the roles of parents and families in the decision-making process. Some highlights of these federal laws are discussed below.

PL 99-457, the Education of the Handicapped Act Amendments of 1986, recognizes that the family is the constant force in the child's life, while professionals come and go. The major thrust of this legislation calls for services that are family centered. Services are to be reflected in the individualized family service plan (IFSP). The law establishes no new services but focuses on the coordination of existing services. It offers incentives to the states to provide services for individuals with disabilities from birth through age 2 (Part H of the legislation) and from age 3 through age 5 (Section 619).

PL 101-476, the Education of the Handicapped Act Amendments of 1990, changes the name of the legislation to the Individuals with Disabilities Education Act (IDEA). The legislation also changes the terminology used throughout the original law, in which the focus is on the condition. In PL 101-476, the preference is for "people-first" language, with the focus on the person. The term *disability* replaces the former term *handicap*; for example, *handicapped children* become *children with disabilities*. Finally, the legislation calls for each eligible individual by age 16 years to have "transition services" identified in the individualized education program (IEP). Transition services promote the individual's movement from school to adult services.

PL 102-119, the Individuals with Disabilities Education Act Amendments of 1991, more clearly defines many of the requirements originally identified in PL 99-457. The legislation encourages states to consider strategies for serving children *at risk* for having a developmental delay and underserved populations, including low-income, minority, and rural children and their families. The legislation introduces the term *service coordination*, which replaces the former term *case management*. It also introduces the concept of strengths; the term *need statements* for family assessments on the IFSP is replaced with the phrase *resources, priorities, and concerns*.

The Child's Transition from School

Transition refers to the period of 3–5 years before the end of educational services when the family and school officials begin to plan the child's future. The transitional process has been largely ignored in the past. If no transition is planned, parents may suddenly discover that there are no available vocational or residential programs upon the child's completion of school or that there are long waiting lists to enter these programs. Planning during the transitional period is critical if the person with developmental disabilities is to continue receiving services in an uninterrupted manner. This can be a very stressful time for parents, for they will be working within the educational system while attempting to learn about services for young adults.

Parents are often reluctant to think about the time when their child will be leaving the educational program. They may feel discouraged by a long waiting list for new services. They may also be apprehensive about involvement with a new agency that requires different roles and expectations for the family.

During the transition, the staff must prepare parents in planning for the future while assisting them to remain involved in the present educational process. Parents will need information about community services for adults. The staff should assist parents in obtaining information about employment, residential, and other community support services and help them to investigate potential financial obligations. In addition, the staff should identify procedures for applying for supplemental security income (SSI) and other state or federal support benefits to which the person with developmental disabilities is entitled.

EXERCISE 3

Transitioning

Identify community-based supported living and employment programs. How do parents explore these services during transition?

What are the local procedures for applying for SSI benefits when the person with developmental disabilities becomes an adult?

When the Child Leaves Home

Finally, parents need support and information as their adult child prepares to leave home. In most instances, parents have had the responsibility of making decisions for their child for more than 2 decades. They have been their child's providers and advocates. These roles change when the child reaches the age of majority and is legally considered an adult. An adult assumes responsibility for making decisions about his or her home, work, and life. Parents need support in defining and understanding this new role for their son or daughter. Information about their child's home and work environments may help the parents to feel more secure about the child's independence.

During this time, parents sometimes become increasingly concerned about their child in the event of their own deaths. The staff should be aware of community resources that can provide information to parents regarding wills, trusts, custody issues, and other concerns related to their child's well-being. Parents of a child with severe disabilities need support if the child continues to remain in the home after reaching adulthood.

During this stage, parental need for emotional support may be even greater than the need for information. Parents find it hard to "give up" their child. It is emotionally difficult for them to accept the fact that their young adult son or daughter is now expected to make decisions that were formerly made by them. Parents may be concerned also for the safety and well-being of their child who now lives outside the home.

The informational and supportive needs of parents during all of these stages provide opportunities for parents to grow and to understand better their child and themselves. Agency staff can assist parents to discover their own strengths, potentials, and talents, as well as those of their child. Staff members should recognize the many different mental, physical, emotional, and social needs of parents and utilize available resources to assist them whenever possible.

EXERCISE 4

Future Planning

Identify the agencies or professionals available to assist parents in planning for their child's future. List these on a separate sheet of paper.

GUIDELINES FOR STAFF

A number of guidelines can assist you in developing working relationships with parents. Certain guidelines apply to all parents. However, staff members working with parents of school-age children should use different approaches than those working with families in which the children are adults.

Parental values and expectations with regard to the child with developmental disabilities have changed during the past decade. The following currently accepted statements regarding the role of parents in caring for and educating their child with developmental disabilities reflect some of these changes:

Parents focus on the care and needs of the child within the context of the entire family.

Parent-training programs are family-focused systems.

Parents play a major role in their child's growth and development.

Parents benefit most from professional input when needs are defined by the parents.

Models for working with parents are consistent with the families' needs.

Parents are most likely to participate in a program of services when they have actively participated in planning programs.

Effective communications between parents and agency staff depend on the staff's understanding of the basic structure and needs of the family. Family concerns for health, income, housing, and personal

Table 3. Roles parents assume

1. Accountant	19. Housekeeper
2. Breadwinner	20. Housewife, househusband
3. Caregiver	21. Judge
4. Chauffeur	22. Learner
5. Child-care worker	23. Listener
6. Community worker	24. Lover
7. Companion	25. Mother
8. Consoler	26. Nurse
9. Cook	27. Nutritionist
10. Counselor	28. Peacemaker
11. Disciplinarian	29. Playmate
12. Doctor	30. Psychologist
13. Electrician	31. Referee
14. Entertainer	32. Seamstress
15. Father	33. Security guard
16. Friend	34. Teacher
17. Gardener	35. Umpire
18. Guardian	

relationships may at times take priority over the child with a disability. Realizing that parents often have priorities other than those related to their child increases the staff's ability to work more effectively with the family. Table 3 lists a few of the many life roles assumed by the average parent.

Sometimes you will not know which role is of primary importance to the parents. For instance, when you ask the parents to assume the role of teacher, they may be more concerned about their lack of money to pay the bills. The demands of day-to-day living decrease the time, energy, and resources available for issues related to a child with developmental disabilities. When parents demonstrate little interest in program issues, you should explore the family's priorities at that time. This orientation helps you to develop realistic expectations of families.

Staff Expectations of Parent Behaviors

Intervention programs should recognize that all parents are not alike. They have different interests, likes, and dislikes. They have diverse outlooks on life, depending on their individual attitudes, values, and beliefs. Specific agency services are not useful or appropriate for all families. It would be difficult to develop one program that would meet the needs of all parents. Agencies should appreciate the differences among families and identify alternative resources from which parents may choose. Referring parents to resources that closely match their needs is an important responsibility for staff members.

EXPECT EACH FAMILY TO BE DIFFERENT.

When working with parents in their homes, keep in mind, too, that individual family homes vary. Parents' taste in furniture, interior decor, and their sense of orderliness may differ from yours. You cannot expect parents to live as you do. It bears reemphasizing: Staff members must respect the family's interests and tastes and not try to change them.

EXPECT EACH HOME ENVIRONMENT TO BE DIFFERENT.

Families have different views about raising children. For this reason, you should offer parents several alternatives in any given situation. People in general, and parents in particular, want to control their own lives. When they ask for information or advice, they want to know what alternatives exist. Providing a range of solutions enables parents to make decisions that best meet their individual needs and family situation. Parents may choose an approach that is different from the one you would recommend. The responsibility for making decisions about their own lives rests with parents.

EXPECT PARENTS TO HAVE DIFFERENT VIEWS TOWARD CHILD REARING.

Finally, parents want and need specific information at specific times in their lives. Professionals sometimes provide information without asking parents what they need. However, giving parents information when they do not want it or need it wastes staff time. For example, providing information about alternative living arrangements to the parents of an infant with a disability may confuse the parents as well as the staff. The agency staff have a responsibility to understand families and to be sensitive and responsive to their needs for information.

EXPECT PARENTS TO WANT AND NEED INFORMATION AT DIFFERENT TIMES IN THEIR LIVES.

Guidelines for Working with Parents of School-Age Children

Parents continue to become more involved in planning intervention programs for children with developmental disabilities. State and federal laws mandate that parents be involved in the design of their child's individualized education program (IEP). Parents are crucial members of the interdisciplinary team and provide other team members with important information related to aspects of the child's strengths and needs. Information shared between the home and the agency helps the individual to grow in both settings. Agency staff and parents need to increase their abilities to establish and maintain effective working relationships with each other.

Programs for parents provided by educational agencies should focus on the priorities of the entire family. Programs should stress techniques that assist parents and that support and enhance the development of the child. Professionals should remember that parental priorities may differ from educational priorities. Programs that focus only on the child with developmental disabilities are rarely successful, because they do not take into account the strengths and needs of the family unit and parental priorities. Educators must consider not only child-related issues but also those related to the entire family. Parents must be viewed not as part of the problem but as part of the solution.

Strategies of Parent-Oriented Programs

Programs for parents can take many different directions and serve various functions. Programs can be structured and formal; for example, parents and professionals can enter into a contract that lists the desired services in detail. However, programs for parents can also be informal, with professionals, for example, simply providing verbal responses to parents' requests. Regardless of the process, parent-oriented programs give parents social and emotional support, information, and opportunities for parental participation. These parent-training services can be provided through a home-based program, a center-based program, or a combination of home- and center-based programs.

Home-Based Programs

Home-based services, provided exclusively in the parents' home, have both advantages and disadvantages. The parents may feel more psychologically secure meeting in their own home than in the professional's office. As an invited guest, however, the professional must abide by the informal rules established by the parents within their home. Services provided in home-based programs are often initiated and directed by parents.

Working in the home environment promotes a trusting relationship among the parents, agency staff, and the person with a developmental disability. Parents may be cautious at first because they are asked to share their world with strangers. They are asked to invite people into their homes who will see and feel how they live. As trust develops and relationships mature, however, a solid foundation is provided for future work. Professionals, in turn, must adjust their expectations to the immediate needs and circumstances of the family and learn to appreciate the problems and anxieties of the parents.

Home-based programs also allow professionals direct observations of parent–child interactions in the natural environment. This helps them to make recommendations that can be readily implemented and evaluated. Programs for parents are generally more effective when they are provided in the environment where the skills will be used. By providing parent training in the home, rather than solely within the confines of a clinic or school, the professional can gain insights into the family situation and provide suggestions and training that have more direct relevance for the family. In addition, parents have the opportunity to give immediate feedback on new techniques. Thus, the professional is able to identify factors in the home environment that might interfere with or enhance the possibility of successfully implementing a program. The home-based program allows the parents and professionals to concentrate on issues and techniques that are directed specifically to the parents and child.

As a disadvantage, the home environment may offer too many distractions for effective parent–professional interactions. Such distractions may prevent worthwhile use of the professional's time. Scheduling home visits at varying times can help to identify the least distracting times of day.

Center-Based Programs

Center-based services are provided in a classroom, clinic, or private office. In a center-based program, the focus of control generally rests more with the professionals, who usually determine what is discussed. Professionals, nevertheless, should be responsive to the concerns of parents participating in the program.

The information shared in a center-based program can address either individual or group needs. Providing presentations to large groups of parents in a center-based program allows agency staff to share general information more easily and less expensively. Group experiences also permit parents to learn from and exchange information with each other. They can share their experiences and observe how other families interact. Finally, center-based programs provide opportunities for the development of social support networks independent of the professional or service agency.

There are limitations to providing services in center-based programs. Some parents, for instance, may not be ready for a group experience. In these cases, families may need individualized and specialized assistance that cannot be provided through a group process. In addition, center-based programs do not permit the professional to view normal interactions between the parents and child in the home. This limitation often prevents the professional from gaining a full understanding of the parents' and family's needs.

Home- and Center-Based Programs

A combination of home- and center-based approaches can offer the advantages of both programs. The dual approach provides general information in group settings, allows development of informal supports for parents, and provides opportunities for parents to observe other parents. Specific information and training also take place during the home visit. This approach to parent training is comprehensive because it provides two strategies for working with families.

In summary, no specific type of program guarantees that all families will participate. Responsiveness to family needs is more important than the location or format of the program. Accountable programs are parent/family oriented and parent directed. No single approach can meet the needs of all parents. Nonparticipating families are not necessarily irresponsible. Rather, agency staff should consider whether their services meet the needs of these parents. In some cases, the staff can direct parents to other agencies providing parent training that more closely approaches their needs.

The Appendix lists agencies and organizations that serve individuals with developmental disabilities and their families.

Also listed in the Appendix are the parent-training and information centers located across the country. These centers, funded through the Office of Special Education Programs, are designed to provide information that will improve the relationship between parents and professionals and increase the ability of the parents to participate in the decision-making process as it relates to their child's education. The Appendix also lists professional organizations that are active in issues related to developmental disabilities.

Guidelines for Working with Parents of Adult Children

Guidelines are not well defined for staff relationships with parents of adults. However, as community-based services for adults with developmental disabilities increase, the need to establish guidelines becomes increasingly important. The staff needs guidelines to assist parents in developing new roles for interacting with agency personnel. Parents no longer will be responsible for making decisions for their children.

Sometimes parents feel that the staff are taking over their responsibilities. They may feel jealous and resentful, until they begin to understand and accept their new roles as parents of an adult. The staff should support the parents as they adjust to this new role, while continuing to assist people with developmental disabilities in making their own decisions and participating more fully in community life.

Age differences may influence your effectiveness with parents. Parents, for example, may consider your goals for their children idealistic or unrealistic. Then, too, older parents may view younger staff members as inexperienced and immature. Despite difficulties that may arise, the staff must be responsive to parents' interests and priorities.

Each family exhibits a unique set of circumstances and needs. Professional expectations and goals must be consistent with those of the family. Professionals cannot structure the life of the family. They must be aware of the possibility of creating additional stress in families by trying to force parents to adopt their own values and beliefs. All families need confidence and motivation. Parents need the technical ability to cope, to develop parenting skills, and to increase their own potential so that they feel more adequate and competent in meeting their child's needs.

Guidelines for Working with Families

Programs for parents have been available for many years. Yet, the emphasis of these services or the primary recipients of the services have been parents and their children. Human services agencies must address the needs of all family members, including mothers, fathers, siblings, grandparents, and other significant individuals. The staff should ensure that an array of services is available to all members of the family. For example, educational programs, counseling, and discussion groups can be offered to siblings, fathers, and/or grandparents. The needs of these individuals should be considered as an integral part of the agency's services.

AGENCIES MUST ADDRESS THE NEEDS OF ALL FAMILY MEMBERS, INCLUDING MOTHER, FATHER, SIBLINGS, GRANDPARENTS, AND OTHER SIGNIFICANT INDIVIDUALS.

PARENTS AS PEOPLE

Parents are always people first. Having a child does not magically prepare a person for the duties and responsibilities of parenting. A caring and thoughtful person is generally a caring and thoughtful parent. A loving person is usually a loving parent. A confused and neurotic person, however, may have some difficulties with the role of parent.

New parents experience many different emotions as they struggle to learn their new roles. These emotions include joy, frustration, confusion, and wonder. There are few courses that prepare a person for parenting. Most people rely on their own experience and that of their parents, friends, or neighbors to develop needed parenting skills. When a child is born with a disability, however, the parents face a situation where there are even fewer guidelines or models of behavior.

The situation of parents of a person with a developmental disability is no different from that of other individuals who experience a variety of difficult personal and emotional issues in their lives. Attitudes and decisions made by individuals reflect their own experiences. There are no right or wrong attitudes or decisions. There are only individual ones.

Most people typically experience changes in feelings and emotions in response to major events in their lives. Parents of children with developmental disabilities experience these same changes. Changes in attitude and behavior also should be expected when parents learn their child has a disability. The change is a natural response to a difficult situation.

An agency's parent-training and counseling program must help parents to see themselves as people first. They are people with mental and physical strengths and limitations like all other people.

SUMMARY

Agencies that provide ancillary services for parents need to determine if they are creating or eliminating stress in the family. Programs providing services for parents rather than with parents should not be encouraged. An agency that does not view the parent as a partner tends to diminish the parental role.

Parents need social and emotional support, information, and opportunities to participate in their child's program of care and education. The amount of services needed will vary from family to family. For most parents, times of crisis generate a need for information and support. These times include the birth of a child with a developmental disability, the child's entry into educational programs, the child's transition into adulthood, and the child's leaving home to live independently. Agency staff must be responsive to parents' needs. The staff should be aware of services provided to parents by other agencies. This enables the staff to present parents with a variety of service options, so that parents can choose the option that best meets their unique needs.

Agencies have several options in the development of services. They may choose to provide parent-training programs that are home based, center based, or a combination of the two. Regardless of the service option available, the agency should view parents as people first. Programs should challenge parents to grow as people.

BIBLIOGRAPHY

Dunst, C.J., Trivette, C., & Deal, A. (1988). *Enabling and empowering families: Principles and guidelines for practice*. Cambridge, MA: Brookline.

Hanft, B.E. (Ed.). (1989). *Family-centered care: An early intervention resource manual*. Rockville, MD: American Occupational Therapy Association.

Salisbury, C.L., & Intagliata, J. (Eds.). (1986). *Respite care: Support for persons with developmental disabilities and their families*. Baltimore: Paul H. Brookes Publishing Co.

Turnbull, A.P., & Turnbull, H.R. (1978). *Parents speak out*. Columbus, OH: Charles E. Merrill.

ADDITIONAL RESOURCES

L. Edelman (Ed.) (1991), in *Getting on board: Training activities to promote the practice of family-centered care* (Bethesda, MD: Association for the Care of Children's Health), provides an excellent resource training guide for teaching others about family-centered care.

H. Featherstone (1980), *A difference in the family* (New York: Basic Books), is an account of the author's experiences as a parent of a child with developmental disabilities.

J.E. May (1991), in *Fathers of children with special needs: New horizons* (Bethesda, MD: Association for the Care of Children's Health), provides information about fathers of children with developmental disabilities and their needs.

R. Perske and M. Perske (1981), in *Hope for the families: New directions for parents of persons with retardation or other developmental disability* (Nashville: Abingdon Press), provide new perspectives on family life for children with disabilities and their parents.

T.L. Shelton, E.S. Jeppson, and B.H. Johnson (1989), in *Family-centered care for children with special health care needs* (Washington, DC: Association for the Care of Children's Health), provide an excellent overview of family-centered care and several checklists to be used in implementing family-centered care.

SELF-APPRAISAL

INSTRUCTIONS

The following questions will help you evaluate your knowledge about working with families. For true-false questions, check the correct answer. For multiple choice questions, circle the correct answer(s).

Note: There may be more than one correct answer for some questions.

1. Attitudes toward parents do not affect the quality of parent-training services.
   ___ True   ___ False
2. Which of the following statements should guide parent support programs?
   a. Parents should focus all their energy on the care and treatment of the child.
   b. Parent-training programs are child-focused, child-driven systems.
   c. Parents are part of their child's problem.
   d. None of the above.
3. Parents should be forced to participate in agency-sponsored parent-training activities.
   ___ True   ___ False
4. Parent training and parent support services are effective when they are:
   a. Provided in an environmentally specific manner
   b. Provided within the confines of a clinic
   c. Provided within the confines of the home
   d. All the above
5. Which of the following are realistic expectations of parent behaviors?
   a. All parental needs for information and support are the same.
   b. All home environments are different.
   c. All parents have the same outlook on life.
   d. All parents have similar views about raising children.
6. Information is important to parents only when they are ready for or need the information.
   ___ True   ___ False
7. Which of the following is the best method for determining information and support needs of parents?
   a. Using norm-referenced tests to obtain assessment data
   b. Asking experienced professional staff

    c. Asking the parents

    d. Asking friends and neighbors of the parents

8. Parents pass through several difficult stages in their lives. These include which of the following:

    a. A child is born with a developmental disability

    b. The child enters a school program

    c. The child leaves the school program

    d. The child leaves home

9. Which of the following represent realistic approaches to the design of agency-sponsored parent-training programs:

    a. Home-based

    b. Center-based

    c. Home/center-based

    d. None of the above

10. Parents should be viewed as people first.

    ____ True   ____ False

CASE STUDY

Susan Williams is a 34-year-old woman who lives with her parents in Washington County, Maryland. She has Down syndrome and severe mental retardation. She is 43 pounds overweight. Her hearing and eyesight are normal.

At age 28, she entered a job-training program at the county vocational center, operated by Tri-County Employment, Inc. She remained in that program for 6 years. For the past 6 months, she has worked in a job station at the nearby Holloway Inn.

Situation

The Washington County Council for Human Services recently opened a new alternative living unit (ALU). The house counselors suggested that Ms. Williams move into the ALU. Ms. Williams agreed to the move. Mr. and Mrs. Williams are opposed to the move, which took place several weeks ago. They have repeatedly called the director of the council to protest the house counselor's lack of regard for their feelings about Susan's move.

1. Should the council transfer Ms. Williams from the ALU because of her parents' objections?
2. Mr. and Mrs. Williams recently met the 22-year-old house counselor. What attitudes or feelings may interfere with the relationship between the parents and the house counselor?
3. What concerns do you think Mr. and Mrs. Williams may have regarding their daughter's move to the ALU?

ANSWER KEY TO
SELF-APPRAISAL AND CASE STUDY

SELF-APPRAISAL

1. False
2. d
3. False
4. a
5. b
6. True
7. c
8. a, b, c, d
9. a, b, c
10. True

CASE STUDY ANSWER GUIDELINES

1. No. The council staff should continue to make Ms. Williams's needs and wishes its primary consideration. Staff members should work closely with the family to help them understand the importance of their daughter living away from home.
2. The age difference may influence the relationship between parents and staff. Mr. and Mrs. Williams may view the counselor as inexperienced and immature. They may think the staff is too young and therefore be hesitant about their daughter living in the ALU.
3. Mr. and Mrs. Williams may feel they are being replaced by the house counselors. They may resent the loss of control in decision making related to their daughter. Mr. and Mrs. Williams may experience confusion regarding their new roles as parents of an independent adult.

Resources

Agencies and organizations serving individuals with developmental disabilities and their families are listed below.

SELECTED NATIONAL INFORMATION AND ADVOCACY GROUPS

These are some of the many organizations that offer information and advocacy to professionals and parents of children and adolescents with disabilities. The groups included here are arranged as follows: those providing general information, those offering help with specific topics, and useful hotlines and clearinghouses.

GENERAL INFORMATION

Association for the Care of Children's Health (ACCH)
7910 Woodmont Ave., Suite 300
Bethesda, MD 20814
(301) 654-6549

Canadian Association for Community Living
Kinsmen Building
York University
4700 Keele St.
North York, ON
CANADA M3J 1P3
(416) 551-9611

Children's Defense Fund
25 E Street NW
Washington, DC 20001
(202) 628-8787

Christian Council on Persons with Disabilities
1324 Yosemite Blvd.
Modesto, CA 95354
(209) 524-7993

Coalition on Sexuality and Disability
122 East 23rd St.
New York, NY 10010
(212) 242-3900

Congress of Organizations of the Physically Handicapped
16630 Beverly Ave.
Tinley Park, IL 60477-1904
(708) 532-3566

The Council for Exceptional Children (CEC)
1920 Association Dr.
Reston, VA 22091
(703) 620-3660

Federation for Children with Special Needs
95 Berkeley St.
Suite 104
Boston, MA 02116
(800) 331-0688 (in MA)
(617) 482-2915

Mothers United for Moral Support (MUMS)
150 Custer Court
Green Bay, WI 54301
(414) 336-5333

National Association of Protection and Advocacy Systems
900 Second St. NE, Suite 211
Washington, DC 20002
(202) 408-9514

(continued)

SELECTED NATIONAL INFORMATION AND ADVOCACY GROUPS
(continued)

**National Center for Youth with
  Disabilities**
Adolescent Health Program
University of Minnesota
Box 721
UMHC
Harvard Street at East River Road
Minneapolis, MN 55455
(800) 333-6293
(612) 626-2825

National Easter Seal Society
70 E. Lake St.
Chicago, IL 60601
(312) 726-6200 (4258-TDD)

**National Information Center for Children
  and Youth with Disabilities (NICHCY)**
P.O. Box 1492
Washington, DC 20013
(800) 999-5599
(703) 893-6061
(703) 893-8614 (TDD)

**National Information System for Health-
  Related Services**
Center for Developmental Disabilities
University of South Carolina
Benson Bldg., 1st Fl.
Columbia, SC 29201-9980
(800) 922-9234
(800) 922-1107 (in SC)

National Organization on Disability
910 16th St. NW, Suite 600
Washington, DC 20006
(800) 248-ABLE
(202) 293-5960
(202) 229-1187 (in MD)

**National Parent Network on Disabilities
  (NPND)**
1600 Prince St., Suite 115
Alexandria, VA 22314
(703) 684-NPND
(703) 684-6763 (Voice/TDD)

ACCESSIBLE HOUSING

**Accessible Housing Research and
  Training Ctr.**
North Carolina State
University School of Design
Box 8613
Raleigh, NC 27695-8613
(919) 515-3082

**Office of Fair Housing and Equal
  Opportunity**
(800) 424-8590
(202) 708-4252 (in DC)

ADOPTION

Adoptive Families of America
3333 Hwy. 100 N
Minneapolis, MN 55422
(612) 535-4829

Adopt a Special Kid (AASK)
3530 Grand Ave.
Oakland, CA 94610
(510) 451-1748

**Children's Adoption Resource
  Exchange (CARE)**
1039 Evarts St. NE
Washington, DC 20017
(202) 526-5200

National Adoption Center
1218 Chestnut St.
Philadelphia, PA 19107
(800) TO-ADOPT

National Adoption Information
11426 Rockville Pike
Suite 410
Rockville, MD 20852
(301) 231-6512

CAREER COUNSELING

**ERIC Clearinghouse on Handicapped
  and Gifted Children**
1920 Association Dr.
Reston, VA 22091-1589
(703) 264-9474

Job Accommodation Network (JAN)
West Virginia University
809 Allen Hall
P.O. Box 6123
Morgantown, WV 26506
(800) 526-7234
(800) 526-4698 (in WV)
(800) 526-2262 (in Canada)
(800) DIAL JAN (Bulletin board phone
  lines; Voice/TDD)

Job Opportunities for the Blind (JOB)
National Federation of the Blind
1800 Johnson St.
Baltimore, MD 21230
(800) 638-7518
(301) 659-9314

(continued)

SELECTED NATIONAL INFORMATION AND ADVOCACY GROUPS
(continued)

National Clearinghouse on Postsecondary Education for Individuals with Disabilities
HEATH Resource Center
American Council on Ed.
1 Dupont Circle, Suite 800
Washington, DC 20036-1193
(800) 54-HEATH
(202) 939-9320

National Job Training Partnership, Inc.
1620 I Street NW
Washington, DC 20006
(202) 887-6120

Technical Assistance for Special Populations Program (TASPP)
National Center for Research in Vocational Education (NCRVE)
University of Illinois Site
345 Education Bldg.
1310 S. Sixth St.
Champaign, IL 61820
(217) 333-0807

EDUCATION

Association on Higher Education and Disability (AHEAD)
P.O. Box 21192
Columbus, OH 43221
(614) 488-4972 (Voice/TDD)

National Committee for Citizens in Education
900 Second St. NE, Suite 8
Washington, DC 20002
(800) NETWORK
(301) 997-9300
(202) 544-9495 (in DC)

National Information Center for Educational Media
4314 Mesa Grande SE
Albuquerque, NM 87108
(505) 265-3591

LEGAL ASSISTANCE

American Bar Association Center on Children and the Law
1800 M Street NW, Suite 300
Washington, DC 20036
(202) 331-2250

Disability Rights Education and Defense Fund, Inc. (DREDF)
2212 Sixth St.
Berkeley, CA 94710
(415) 644-2555

Mental Health Law Project
1101 15th St. NW, Suite 1212
Washington, DC 20036-5002
(202) 467-5730

National Center for Law and the Deaf
Gallaudet University
800 Florida Ave. NE
Washington, DC 20002
(Mailing address only)

Pike Institute
Harry Beyer, Director
Boston University
School of Law
765 Commonwealth Ave.
Boston, MA 02215
(617) 353-2904

RARE DISORDERS

Lethbridge Society for Rare Disorders
#100B 515-7 Seventh St. S
Lethbridge, AB
CANADA T1J 2G8
(403) 329-0665

National Information Center for Orphan Drugs and Rare Diseases
P.O. Box 1133
Washington, DC 20013-1133
(800) 456-3505

National Organization for Rare Disorders (NORD)
100 Rt. 37, P.O. Box 8923
New Fairfield, CT 06812-1783
(800) 999-NORD
(203) 746-6518

REHABILITATION

Canadian Rehabilitation Council for the Disabled
45 Sheppard Ave. E, Suite 801
Willowdale, ON
CANADA, M2N 5W9
(416) 250-7490

(continued)

SELECTED NATIONAL INFORMATION AND ADVOCACY GROUPS
(continued)

**Kinsmen Rehabilitation Foundation of
British Columbia**
2256 West 12th Ave.
Vancouver, BC
CANADA V6K 2N5
(604) 736-8841
(604) 738-0603 (TDD)

**National Rehabilitation Information
Center**
8455 Colesville Rd., Suite 935
Silver Spring, MD 20910
(800) 346-2742 (Voice/TDD)
(301) 588-9284

World Rehabilitation Fund
386 Park Ave., Suite 500
New York, NY 10016-4901
(212) 725-7875

SIBLING SUPPORT

Siblings for Significant Change
United Charities Building
105 East 22nd St., Room 710
New York, NY 10010
(212) 420-0776

Sibling Information Network
The A.J. Pappanikou Center on Special
Education and Rehabilitation: A
University-Affiliated Program
991 Main St.
East Hartford, CT 06108
(203) 282-7050

TRAVEL AND EXCHANGE

Mobility International
P.O. Box 3551
Eugene, OR 97403
(503) 343-1284 (Voice/TDD)

Travelin' Talk
P.O. Box 3534
Clarksville, TN 37043-3534
(615) 552-6670

HOTLINES

Direct Link for the disABLED, Inc.
P.O. Box 1036
Solvang, CA 93464
(805) 688-1603

**National Digestive Diseases Information
Clearinghouse**
9000 Rockville Pike
Box NDDIC
Bethesda, MD 20892
(301) 468-6344

**National Jewish Center for Immunology
and Respiratory Medicine**
1400 Jackson St.
Denver, CO 80206-2762
(800) 222-LUNG

National Spinal Cord Injury Hotline
Montebello Hospital
2201 Argonne Dr.
Baltimore, MD 21218
(800) 526-3456

Social Security Administration Hotline
(800) 772-1213
(800) 325-0778 (TDD)

**U.S. Architectural Transportation
Barriers Compliance Board**
For information related to the Americans
with Disabilities Act.
(800) USA-ABLE

SELECTED NATIONAL ORGANIZATIONS
FOR SPECIFIC DISABILITIES OR CONDITIONS

These national groups offer needed services, resources, and support to parents and professionals. Services provided may include rehabilitation, housing, advocacy, information, networking, and more.

Amputation
National Amputation Foundation
12-45 150th St.
Whitestone, NY 11357
(718) 767-0596

**Amyotrophic Lateral Sclerosis (Lou
Gehrig Disease)**
Amyotrophic Lateral Sclerosis Association
21021 Ventura Blvd., Suite 321
Woodland Hills, CA 91364
(800) 782-4747
(818) 990-2151

(continued)

SELECTED NATIONAL ORGANIZATIONS
FOR SPECIFIC DISABILITIES OR CONDITIONS
(continued)

Arthritis
American Juvenile Arthritis Organization
Arthritis Foundation
1314 Spring St. NW
Atlanta, GA 30309
(404) 872-7100

Arthrogryposis
Avenues, National Support Group for
   Arthrogryposis Multiplex Congenita
P.O. Box 5192
Sonora, CA 95370
(209) 928-3688

Asthma and Allergy
Asthma and Allergy Foundation of America
1125 15th St. NW, Ste. 502
Washington, DC 20005
(800) 7-ASTHMA

Ataxia
National Ataxia Foundation
750 Twelve Oaks Center
15500 Wayzata Blvd.
Wayzata, MN 55391
(612) 473-7666

Attention Deficit Disorder
C.H.A.D.D. (Children with Attention Deficit
   Disorders)
499 NW 70th Ave., Suite 308
Plantation, FL 33317
(305) 587-3700

National Attention Deficit Disorder
   Association (ADDA)
(800) 487-2282

Autism
Autism Society of America
8601 Georgia Ave., Suite 503
Silver Spring, MD 20910
(301) 565-0433

Families of More Able Autistic People
MAAP Newsletter
P.O. Box 524
Crown Point, IN 46307
(Mailing address only)

National Autism Hotline/Autism Services
   Center
Pritchard Building
605 Ninth St., P.O. Box 507
Huntington, WV 25701-0507
(304) 525-8014

Birth Defects
Association of Birth Defect Children
Orlando Executive Park
5400 Diplomat Circle, Suite 270
Orlando, FL 32810
(407) 629-1466

March of Dimes Birth Defects Foundation
1275 Mamaroneck Ave.
White Plains, NY 10605
(914) 428-7100

National Birth Defects Center
Franciscan Children's Hospital
30 Warren St.
Boston, MA 02135
(617) 787-5958

National Network to Prevent Birth Defects
701 East St. SE
Washington, DC 20003
(202) 543-5450

Brain Diseases
Children's Brain Diseases Foundation
350 Parnassus Ave.
Suite 900
San Francisco, CA 94117
(415) 565-6259

Brain Tumor
American Brain Tumor Association
3725 N. Talman Ave.
Chicago, IL 60618
(312) 286-5571

Cancer
AMC Cancer Information Center
1600 Pierce St.
Lakewood, CO 80214
(800) 525-3777

American Cancer Society
46 Fifth St. NE
Atlanta, GA 30308
(800) ACS-2345
(404) 320-3333

Candlelighters Childhood Cancer
   Foundation
7910 Woodmont Ave., Suite 460
Bethesda, MD 20814
(800) 366-2223

Corporate Angel Network
Westchester County Airport
Building 1
White Plains, NY 10604
(914) 328-1313

(continued)

**SELECTED NATIONAL ORGANIZATIONS
FOR SPECIFIC DISABILITIES OR CONDITIONS**
(continued)

Familial Polyposis Registry
Mt. Sinai Hospital
500 University Ave., Suite 1157
Toronto, ON
CANADA M5G 1X5
(416) 586-8334

National Cancer Institute Information
　　Resource Branch
9000 Rockville Pike
Building 31, Room 10A30
Bethesda, MD 20892
(800) 4-CANCER

Cerebral Palsy
American Academy for Cerebral Palsy and
　　Developmental Medicine (AACPDM)
P.O. Box 11086
Richmond, VA 23230-1086
(804) 282-0036

United Cerebral Palsy Associations
　　(UCPA)
1522 K Street NW
Suite 1112
Washington, DC 20005
(800) 872-5827
(202) 842-1266

CHARGE Association
CHARGE Accounts
c/o Quota Club
2004 Parkade Blvd.
Columbia, MO 65202
(314) 442-7604

Chronic Illness
Families of Children Under Stress
　　(FOCUS)
P.O. Box 1058
Conyers, GA 30207
(404) 483-9845

Parents of Chronically Ill Children
1527 Maryland St.
Springfield, IL 62702
(217) 522-6810

Cleft Palate
Cleft Palate Foundation
1218 Grandview Ave.
Pittsburgh, PA 15211
(800) 24-CLEFT
(412) 481-1376

Prescription Parents
c/o Laura Cohen
P.O. Box 161
W. Roxbury, MA 02132
(617) 527-0878

Congenital Hypoventilation Syndrome
Congenital Hypoventilation Syndrome
　　Parent Support Network
71 Maple St.
Oneonta, NY 13820
(Mailing address only)

Cornelia de Lange Syndrome
Cornelia de Lange Syndrome Foundation
60 Dyer Ave.
Collinsville, CT 06022-1201
(800) 753-CDLS
(800) 223-8355
(203) 693-0159

Craniofacial Disorders
AboutFace
Betty Bednar
199 Crowns Ln., 3rd Fl.
Toronto, ON
CANADA M5R 3P4
(416) 944-3223

AboutFace U.S.A.
Pam Onyx
1002 Liberty Lane
Warrington, PA 18976
(800) 225-FACE

FACE of Sarasota
P.O. Box 1424
Sarasota, FL 34230
(813) 955-9250

FACES—National Association for the
　　Craniofacially Handicapped
P.O. Box 11082
Chattanooga, TN 37401
(615) 266-1632

Hemifacial Microsomia/Goldenhar
　　Syndrome Family Support Network
Cynthia Fishman, R.N.,
and Richard Fishman
84 Gleniffer Hill Rd.
Richboro, PA 18954
(215) 364-3199

International Craniofacial Foundation
10210 N. Central Expressway, Suite 230,
　　LB37
Dallas, TX 75231
(800) 535-3643
(214) 368-3590

Let's Face It
P.O. Box 711
Concord, MA 01742
(508) 371-3186

(continued)

SELECTED NATIONAL ORGANIZATIONS
FOR SPECIFIC DISABILITIES OR CONDITIONS
(continued)

National Foundation for Facial
Reconstruction
317 East 34th St., 9th Floor
New York, NY 10016
(800) 422-FACE
(212) 263-6656

Cri Du Chat (5p-)
The 5p- Society
11609 Oakmont
Overland Park, KS 66210
(913) 469-8900
(215) 233-3503

Crohn Disease and Ulcerative Colitis
Crohn's & Colitis Foundation of America
444 Park Ave. S., 11th Floor
New York, NY 10016-7374
(800) 343-3637

Cystic Fibrosis
Cystic Fibrosis Foundation
6931 Arlington Rd.
Bethesda, MD 20814
(800) FIGHT CF
(301) 951-4422

Diabetes
American Diabetes Association
National Service Center
1660 Duke St.
Alexandria, VA 22314
(800) 232-3472
(703) 549-1500

Canadian Diabetes Association
78 Bond St.
Toronto, ON
CANADA M5B 2J8
(416) 362-4440

Juvenile Diabetes Foundation International
432 Park Ave. S
New York, NY 10016
(800) 223-1138
(212) 889-7575

Down Syndrome
Association for Children with Down
Syndrome
2616 Martin Ave.
Bellmore, NY 11710
(516) 221-4700

Canadian Down Syndrome Society
Box 52027, Edmonton Trail RPO
Calgary, AB
CANADA T2E 8K9
(403) 253-5835

Caring, Inc.
P.O. Box 400
Milton, WA 98354
(206) 922-8607

National Down Syndrome Congress
(NDSC)
1800 Dempster St.
Park Ridge, IL 60068-1146
(800) 232-6372
(708) 823-7550

National Down Syndrome Society
666 Broadway, Suite 810
New York, NY 10012
(800) 221-4602
(212) 460-9330

Dyslexia
Dyslexia Research Institute
4745 Centerville Rd.
Tallahasse, FL 32308
(904) 893-2216

Orton Dyslexia Society
Chester Building, Suite 382
8600 LaSalle Rd.
Baltimore, MD 21204-6020
(800) 222-3123
(410) 296-0232

Dystonia
Dystonia Medical Research Foundation
First City Building
777 Hornby St., Suite 1800
Vancouver, BC
CANADA V6Z 2K3
(604) 661-4886

Dystonia Medical Research Foundation
8383 Wilshire Blvd., Suite 800
Beverly Hills, CA 90211
(213) 852-1630

Epilepsy
The Epilepsy Foundation of America (EFA)
4351 Garden City Dr.
Landover, MD 20785
(800) EFA-1000
(301) 459-3700

Fragile X Syndrome
National Fragile X Foundation
1441 York St., Suite 215
Denver, CO 80206
(800) 688-8765
(303) 333-6155

(continued)

SELECTED NATIONAL ORGANIZATIONS
FOR SPECIFIC DISABILITIES OR CONDITIONS
(continued)

Galactosemia
Parents of Galactosemic Children
c/o Linda Manis
20981 Solano Way
Boca Raton, FL 33433
(407) 852-0266

Gaucher Disease
National Gaucher Foundation
19241 Montgomery Village Ave., E-21
Gaithersburg, MD 20879
(800) 925-8885
(202) 393-2777

Genetic Conditions
Alliance of Genetic Support Groups
35 Wisconsin Circle, #440
Bethesda, MD 20815-7015
(800) 336-GENE
(301) 652-5553

National Foundation for Jewish Genetic
  Diseases
250 Park Ave.
Suite 1000
New York, NY 10177
(212) 371-1030

Growth Disorders
Human Growth Foundation
P.O. Box 3090
Falls Church, VA 22043
(800) 451-6434
(703) 883-1773

Guillain Barré Syndrome
Guillain Barré Syndrome Foundation
  International
P.O. Box 262
Wynnewood, PA 19096
(215) 667-0131

Head Injuries
National Head Injury Foundation
1776 Massachusetts Ave., NW, Suite 100
Washington, DC 20036-1904
(800) 444-6443 (Family Helpline)
(202) 294-6443

Hearing Impairments
Alexander Graham Bell Association
  for the Deaf
3417 Volta Place NW
Washington, DC 20007
(202) 337-5220
(Voice/TDD)

American Deafness and Rehabilitation
  Association
P.O. Box 251554
Little Rock, AR 72225
(501)663-7074 (Voice/TDD)

American Society for Deaf Children
  (ASDC)
814 Thayer Ave.
Silver Spring, MD 20910
(800) 942-ASDC

American Speech-Language-Hearing
  Association (ASHA)
10801 Rockville Pike
Rockville, MD 20852
(800) 638-8255 (Voice/TDD)
(301) 897-5700

Auditory-Verbal International, Inc.
6 S. Third St., Suite 305
Easton, PA 18042
(215) 253-6616

Better Hearing Institute
P.O. Box 1840
Washington, DC 20013
(800) EAR-WELL (Voice/TDD)

Canadian Hearing Society
Information Services
271 Spadina Rd.
Toronto, ON
CANADA M5R 2V3
(416) 964-9595
(416) 964-0023 (TDD)

Captioned Films & Videos for the
  Deaf/Modern Talking Picture Services
5000 Park St. N
St. Petersburg, FL 33709
(800) 237-6213
(813) 541-7571

Deafpride, Inc.
1350 Potomac Ave. SE
Washington, DC 20003
(202) 675-6700 (Voice/TTY)

Deaf-REACH
3521 12th Street NE
Washington, DC 20017
(202) 832-6681

HEAR Now
4001 S. Magnolia Way, Suite 100
Denver, CO 80237
(800) 648-HEAR (Voice/TDD)

(continued)

SELECTED NATIONAL ORGANIZATIONS
FOR SPECIFIC DISABILITIES OR CONDITIONS
(continued)

International Hearing Society
20361 Middlebelt Rd.
Livonia, MI 48152
(800) 521-5247
(313) 478-2610

International Organization for the Education
of the Hearing-Impaired
3417 Volta Place NW
Washington, DC 20007
(202) 337-5220
(Voice/TDD)

John Tracy Clinic
806 W. Adams Blvd.
Los Angeles, CA 90007
(800) 522-4582 (Voice/TDD)
(213) 748-5481
(213) 747-2924 (TTY)

LISTEN, Inc.
P.O. Box 27213
Tempe, AZ 85285
(602) 921-3886

National Association for the Deaf (NAD)
814 Thayer Ave.
Silver Spring, MD 20910-4500
(301) 587-1788
(301) 587-1789 (TDD)

National Captioning Institute
5203 Leesburg Pike
Falls Church, VA 22041
(800) 533-WORD
(800) 321-TDDS (TTY)
(703) 998-2400 (Voice/TTY)

National Cued Speech Association
P.O. Box 31345
Raleigh, NC 27622
(919) 828-1218 (Voice/TDD)

National Information Center on Deafness
Gallaudet University
800 Florida Ave. NE
Washington, DC 20002-3695
(202) 651-5051
(202) 651-5052 (TDD)

National Technical Institute for the Deaf
Rochester Institute of Technology
Lyndon Baines Johnson Bldg.
P.O. Box 9887
Rochester, NY 14623-0887
(716) 475-6400

Self Help for Hard of Hearing People
(SHHH)
7800 Wisconsin Ave.
Bethesda, MD 20814
(301) 657-2248
(301) 657-2249 (TDD)

Signing Exact English (SEE) Center for the
Advancement of Deaf Children
P.O. Box 1181
Los Alamitos, CA 90720
(213) 430-1467

Tripod-Service for the Hearing-Impaired
2901 N. Keystone St.
Burbank, CA 91504
(800) 352-8888 (Voice/TDD)
(800) 2-TRIPOD
(Voice/TDD in CA)

VOICE for Hearing-Impaired Children
124 Eglington Ave. W, Suite 420
Toronto, ON
CANADA M4R 268
(416) 487-7719

Heart Disorders
American Heart Association
7272 Greenville Ave.
Dallas, TX 75231-4596
(214) 373-6300

Heart, Lung, and Blood Disorders
National Heart, Lung and Blood Institute
P.O. Box 30105
Bethesda, MD 20824
(301) 951-3260

Hemophilia
Canadian Hemophilia Society
1450 City Councillors, Suite 840
Montreal, PQ
CANADA H3A 2E6
(514) 848-0503

National Hemophilia Foundation (NHF)
110 Green St., Room 303
New York, NY 10012
(212) 219-8180

Hereditary Diseases
Hereditary Disease Foundation
606 Wilshire Blvd., Ste. 504
Santa Monica, CA 90401
(213) 458-4183

(continued)

SELECTED NATIONAL ORGANIZATIONS
FOR SPECIFIC DISABILITIES OR CONDITIONS
(continued)

**Hereditary Hemorrhagic Telangiectasia
(Osler-Weber-Rendu Syndrome)**
Hereditary Hemorrhagic Telangiectasia
(HHT) Foundation (Osler-Weber-Rendu
Syndrome)
P.O. Box 8087
New Haven, CT 06530
(203) 785-7056

Huntington Disease
Huntington Disease Society of America
140 West 22nd St., 6th Floor
New York, NY 10011-2420
(212) 242-1968

Hydrocephalus
Guardians of Hydrocephalus Research
  Foundation
2618 Ave. Z
Brooklyn, NY 11235
(718) 743-4473
(800) 458-8655

Hydrocephalus Association
870 Market St., Suite 955
San Francisco, CA 94102
(415) 776-4713

National Hydrocephalus Foundation
400 N. Michigan Ave., Suite 1102
Chicago, IL 60611-4102
(815) 467-6548

Immune Deficiency
Immune Deficiency Foundation (IDF)
P.O. Box 586
Columbia, MD 21045
(301) 730-8837

Incontinence
Help for Incontinent People (HIP)
P.O. Box 544
Union, SC 29379
(800) BLADDER
(803) 579-7900

Simon Foundation for Continence
P.O. Box 835
Wilmette, IL 60091
(800) 23-SIMON

Intraventricular Hemorrhage
I.V.H. Parents
P.O. Box 56-1111
Miami, FL 33256-1111
(305) 232-0381

Kidney Disorders
American Kidney Fund
6110 Executive Blvd. #1010
Rockville, MD 20852
(800) 638-8299
(301) 881-3052

National Kidney Foundation
30 East 33rd St., 11th FL.
Cynthia Wolkovich
New York, NY 10016
(800) 622-9010
(212) 889-2210

Polycystic Kidney Research (PKR)
  Foundation
922 Walnut St., Suite 411
Kansas City, MO 64106
(800) PKD-CURE
(800) 444-8197
(816) 421-1869

Lactic Acidosis
Lactic Acidosis Support Group
1620 Marble Ave.
Denver, CO 80229
(303) 837-2117
(303) 287-4953

Landau-Kleffner Syndrome
C.A.N.D.L.E. Support Group
(Childhood Aphasia, Neurological
  Disorders, Laundau-Kleffner Syndrome,
  and Epilepsy)
4414 McCampbell Dr.
Montgomery, AL 36106
(205) 271-3947

Laurence Moon Bardet Biedl Syndrome
Laurence Moon Bardet Biedl Syndrome
  Network
124 Lincoln Ave.
Purchase, NY 10577

Laurence Moon Bardet Biedl Syndrome
  Network
18 Strawberry Hill
Windsor, CT 06095
(203) 688-7880

Learning Disabilities
Learning Disabilities Association of
  America
c/o Jean Petersen
4156 Library Rd.
Pittsburgh, PA 15234
(412) 341-1515
(412) 341-8077

(continued)

SELECTED NATIONAL ORGANIZATIONS
FOR SPECIFIC DISABILITIES OR CONDITIONS
(continued)

Learning Disabilities Association of Canada
323 Chapel St., Suite 200
Ottawa, ON
CANADA K1N 7Z2
(613) 238-5721

National Center for Learning Disabilities
99 Park Ave.
New York, NY 10016
(212) 687-7211

Leukemia
Leukemia Society of America
600 Third Ave., 4th Floor
New York, NY 10016
(212) 573-8484

Leukodystrophy
United Leukodystrophy Foundation
2304 Highland Dr.
Sycamore, IL 60178
(800) 728-5483
(815) 895-3211

Liver Disorders
American Liver Foundation
Ari Mararel
1425 Pompton Ave.
Cedar Grove, NJ 07009
(800) 223-0179
(201) 256-2550

Lung Diseases
American Lung Association
1740 Broadway
New York, NY 10019
(212) 315-8700

Lupus Erythematosis
American Lupus Society
3914 Del Amo Blvd., Suite 922
Torrance, CA 90503
(800) 331-1802 (Information Line)
(213) 542-8891

Lupus Foundation of America, Inc.
4 Research Place, Suite 180
Rockville, MD 20850-3226
(800) 558-0121
(301) 670-9292

Lyme Disease
Lyme Disease Foundation
P.O. Box 462
Tolland, CT 06084
(203) 871-2900

Macular Diseases
Association for Macular Diseases, Inc.
210 East 64th St.
New York, NY 10021
(212) 605-3719

Maple Syrup Urine Disease
Maple Syrup Urine Disease Family Support Group
c/o Bonnie Koons
8017 Jonestown
Harrisburg, PA 17112-9715
(717) 652-1386

Marfan Syndrome
National Marfan Foundation
382 Main St.
Port Washington, NY 11050
(800) 8-MARFAN
(516) 883-8712

Mental Illness
Academy of Clinical Mental Health Counselors
5999 Stevenson Ave.
Alexandria, VA 22304
(703) 823-9800, ext. 384

Federation of Families for Children's Mental Health
1021 Prince St.
Alexandria, VA 22314-2971
(703) 684-7710

National Mental Health Association
1021 Prince St.
Alexandria, VA 22314-2971
(800) 969-6642
(703) 684-7722

Mental Retardation
The ARC, a national organization on mental retardation
500 E. border St., Suite 300
P.O. Box 300649
Arlington, TX 76010
(800) 855-1155
(817) 261-6003

Canadian Association for Community Living
Kinsmen Bldg.
York University
4700 Keele St.
North York, ON
CANADA M3J 1P3
(416) 661-9611

(continued)

SELECTED NATIONAL ORGANIZATIONS
FOR SPECIFIC DISABILITIES OR CONDITIONS
(continued)

Multiple Sclerosis
National Multiple Sclerosis Society
733 Third Ave.
New York, NY 10017
(800) 227-3166
(212) 986-3240

Muscular Dystrophy
Muscular Dystrophy Association (MDA)
3330 E. Sunrise Dr.
Tucson, AZ 85718-3208
(602) 529-2000

Myasthenia Gravis
Myasthenia Gravis Foundation (MGF)
53 W. Jackson Blvd., Suite 660
Chicago, IL 60604
(800) 541-5454
(312) 427-6252

Neurofibromatosis
National Neurofibromatosis Foundation
Sherland Peterson
141 Fifth Ave., Suite 7-S
New York, NY 10010-7105
(800) 323-7938
(212) 460-8980

Neurological Disorders
National Institute of Neurological Disorders
  and Stroke
9000 Rockville Pike
Building 31
Room 8A-16
Bethesda, MD 20892
(301) 496-5751

Newborns with Illness
Parent Care, Inc.
9041 Colgate St.
Indianapolis, IN 46268-1210
(317) 872-9913

Niemann-Pick Disease
Niemann-Pick Type C Foundation, Inc.
22201 Riverpoint Trail
Carrollton, VA 23314
(804) 357-6774

Noonan Syndrome
Noonan Syndrome Society
c/o Susan Espinoza
1278 Pine Ave.
San Jose, CA 95125
(408) 723-5188

Orthopedic Problems and Burns
International Shriners Headquarters
Maribel Matias
2900 Rocky Point Dr.
Tampa, FL 33607
(800) 237-5055
(813) 281-0300 (in FL)

Osteogenesis Imperfecta
Osteogenesis Imperfecta Foundation, Inc.
5005 W. Laurel St., Suite 210
Tampa, FL 33607
(813) 855-1161

Ostomy
United Ostomy Association
Michelle Dev Brock
36 Executive Park, Suite 120
Irvine, CA 92714-6744
(800) 826-0826
(714) 660-8624

Paralysis
American Paralysis Association
500 Morris Ave.
Springfield, NJ 07081
(800) 225-0292
(201) 379-2690 (in NJ)

Parents of Children Who Have Died
A.M.E.N.D.
(Aiding Mothers and Fathers Experiencing
  Neonatal Death)
c/o Maureen Connelly
4324 Berrywick Terrace
St. Louis, MO 63128
(314) 487-7582

Compassionate Friends
P.O. Box 3696
Oak Brook, IL 60522-3696
(708) 990-0010

Parkinson Disease
National Parkinson Foundation
1501 Ninth Ave. NW
Miami, FL 33136
(800) 327-4545
(800) 433-7022 (in FL)

Prader-Willi Syndrome
Prader-Willi Syndrome Association
6490 Excelsior Blvd., E-102
St. Louis Park, MN 55426
(800) 926-4797
(612) 926-1947

(continued)

SELECTED NATIONAL ORGANIZATIONS
FOR SPECIFIC DISABILITIES OR CONDITIONS
(continued)

Psoriasis
National Psoriasis Foundation
6443 SW Beaverton Hwy., Suite 210
Portland, OR 97221
(503) 297-1545

Rett Syndrome
International Rett Syndrome Association
8511 Rose Marie Dr.
Ft. Washington, MD 20744
(301) 248-7031

Reye Syndrome
National Reye's Syndrome Foundation
P.O. Box 829
Bryan, OH 43506
(800) 233-7393
(419) 636-2679

Rubinstein-Taybi Syndrome
Rubinstein-Taybi Parent Group
414 E. Kansas
Smith Center, KS 66967
(913) 282-6237

Scoliosis
National Scoliosis Foundation
72 Mt. Auburn St.
Watertown, MA 02172
(617) 926-0397

Seizure Disorder
THRESHOLD—Intractable Seizure
   Disorder Support Group
c/o Barbara Schwan
29 Melrose Terrace
Middletown, NJ 07748
(908) 957-0714

Short Stature
Little People of America
P.O. Box 9897
Washington, DC 20016
(800) 24-DWARF

Parents of Dwarfed Children
c/o Margaret B. Badner
11524 Colt Terrace
Silver Spring, MD 20902
(301) 649-3275

Sickle Cell Disease
National Association for Sickle Cell
   Disease (NASCD)
3345 Wilshire Blvd., #1106
Los Angeles, CA 90010-1880
(800) 421-8453
(213) 736-5455

Spina Bifida
Spina Bifida Association of America
   (SBAA)
4590 MacArthur Blvd. NW
Suite 205
Washington, DC 20007-4226
(800) 621-3141
(202) 944-3285

Spina Bifida Association of Canada
33 Wellington Crescent
Winnipeg, MB
CANADA R3M 0A8
(204) 452-7580

Spinal Cord Injuries
National Spinal Cord Injury Association
   (NCCSCI)
6721 Pine Creek Court
McLean, VA 22101-5519
(703) 533-8518

National Spinal Cord Injury Association
600 W. Cummings Park
Suite 2000
Woburn, MA 01801
(800) 962-9629
(617) 935-2722

Stuttering
National Center for Stuttering
200 East 33rd St.
New York, NY 10016
(800) 221-2483
(212) 532-1460 (in NY)

National Stuttering Project
2151 Irving St., Suite 208
San Francisco, CA 94122-1609
(415) 566-5324

Stuttering Foundation of America
P.O. Box 11749
Memphis, TN 38111-0749
(800) 992-9392
(202) 363-3199

Sudden Infant Death Syndrome
National Sudden Infant Death Syndrome
   (SIDS) Alliance
10500 Little Patuxent Pky., Suite 420
Columbia, MD 21044-3505
(800) 221-SIDS
(301) 964-8000

(continued)

SELECTED NATIONAL ORGANIZATIONS
FOR SPECIFIC DISABILITIES OR CONDITIONS
(continued)

Tay-Sachs Disease
National Tay-Sachs and Allied Diseases
  Association
2001 Beacon St., Suite 304
Brookline, MA 02146
(617) 277-4463

Terminal Illness
Children's Hospice International
901 N. Washington St., Suite 700
Alexandria, VA 22314
(800) 242-4453
(703) 684-0330

Tourette Syndrome
Tourette Syndrome Association
42-40 Bell Blvd.
Bayside, NY 11361-2861
(800) 237-0717
(718) 224-2999

Treacher Collins Disease
Treacher Collins Foundation
c/o Hope Charkins-Drazin and David
  Drazin
P.O. Box 683
Norwich, VT 05055
(802) 649-3020

Trisomy 18, 13
Support Organization for Trisomy 18, 13 &
  Related Disorders
c/o Barb Van Herreweghe
2982 S. Union St.
Rochester, NY 14624
(716) 594-4621

Tuberous Sclerosis
National Tuberous Sclerosis Association
8000 Corporate Dr., Suite 120
Landover, MD 20785
(800) 225-NTSA
(301) 459-9888

Turner Syndrome
Turner Syndrome Society
Sandi Hofbauer
Executive Director
7777 Keele St., 2nd Floor
Concord, ON
CANADA L4K 1Y7
(416) 660-7766

Urea Cycle Disorders
National Urea Cycle Disorders Foundation
4559 Vauxhall Rd.
Richmond, VA 23234
(804) 275-2285

Visual Impairments
American Council of the Blind
1155 15th St. NW., Suite 720
Washington, DC 20005
(800) 424-8666
(202) 467-5081

American Foundation for the Blind
15 West 16th St.
New York, NY 10011
(800) AFB-LIND (232-5463)
(212) 620-2147 (in NY)

American Printing House for the Blind
1839 Frankfort Ave.
P.O. Box 6085
Louisville, KY 40206-0085
(800) 223-1839
(502) 895-2405

Blind Children's Center
4120 Marathon St.
Los Angeles, CA 90029
(800) 222-3566
(800) 222-3567 (in CA)

Canadian National Institute for the Blind
1929 Bayview Ave.
Toronto, ON
CANADA M4G 3E8
(416) 480-7415
(416) 480-7414

Institute for Families of Blind Children
P.O. Box 54700
Mail Stop #111
Los Angeles, CA 90054
(213) 669-4649

National Association for Parents of the
  Visually Impaired
2180 Linway Dr.
Beloit, WI 53511
(800) 562-6265

National Association for Visually
  Handicapped
22 West 21st St., 6th Fl.
New York, NY 10010
(212) 889-3141

National Federation of the Blind
1800 Johnson St.
Baltimore, MD 21230
(301) 659-9314

(continued)

SELECTED NATIONAL ORGANIZATIONS
FOR SPECIFIC DISABILITIES OR CONDITIONS
(continued)

National Retinoblastoma Parent Group
603 Fourth Range Rd.
Pembroke, NH 03275
(603) 224-4085

National Society to Prevent Blindness
500 E. Remington Rd.
Schaumburg, IL 60173-4557
(800) 331-2020 (National Center for Sight)
(708) 843-2020

Parents and Cataract Kids (PACK)
c/o Geraldine Miller
P.O. Box 28
Collingswood, NJ 08108
(215) 293-1917

Recording for the Blind
20 Roszel Rd.
Princeton, NJ 08540
(609) 452-0606

Retinitis Pigmentosa Foundation Fighting
   Blindness
P.O. Box 900
Woodland Hills, CA 91365
(800) 344-4877
(818) 992-0500

Retinoblastoma Support Group
c/o Susan Laventure
603 Fourth Range Road
Pembroke, NH 03275
(603) 224-4085

Stargardt Disease Self-Help Network
Tom Perski
Edwin and Lois Deicke Ctr.
219 E. Cole Ave.
Wheaton, IL 60187
(708) 690-7115

Vision Foundation
818 Mt. Auburn St.
Watertown, MA 02172
(800) 852-3029 (in MA)
(617) 926-4232

Vitiligo
National Vitiligo Foundation
P.O. Box 6337
Tyler, TX 75711
(214) 534-2925

Williams Syndrome
Williams Syndrome Association
P.O. Box 3297
Baldwin, MO 63022-3279
(314) 227-4411

Wilson Disease
Wilson Disease Association
P.O. Box 75324
Washington, DC 20013
(703) 636-3003
(703) 636-3014

Wolf-Hirschhorn Syndrome (4p-)
4p- Parents Group
c/o Tom & Becky Richardson
3200 Rivanna Court
Woodbridge, VA 22192
(703) 491-0309

Wolf-Hirschhorn Syndrome (4p-) Support
   Group and Newsletter
c/o Brenda Grimmett
5536 Virginia Ct.
Amherst, OH 44001
(216) 282-1460

FEDERAL AGENCIES

These government agencies offer parents and professionals information on services and regulations. The Federal Information Center (FIC) can help you find information about federal government services, programs, and regulations. FIC can also tell you which federal agency to contact for assistance. Contact the national FIC for individual states' toll-free 800 FIC numbers at: P.O. Box 600, Cumberland, MD 21502, (301) 722-9098.

AMERICANS WITH DISABILITIES ACT

**American Federation for the Blind and
   Gallaudet University**
(202) 223-0101 (Voice/TDD)

**The Arc (formerly the Association for
   Retarded Citizens of the U.S.)**
(800) 433-5255

(continued)

FEDERAL AGENCIES
(continued)

Association of Handicapped Student Service Programs in Post Secondary School Education
(800) 247-7752 (Voice/TDD)

Department of Transportation
(202) 366-9305
(202) 202-7687 (TDD)

Disability Rights Education Defense Fund
(800) 466-4232 (Voice/TDD)

Equal Employment Opportunity Commission
(800) USA-EEOC
(800) 800-3302
(202) 663-4494 (TDD)

Federal Communications Commission
(202) 632-7260
(202) 632-6999 (TDD)

Office of Fair Housing and Equal Opportunity
(800) 424-8590
(202) 708-4252 (in DC)

President's Committee on Employment of People with Disabilities
1331 F Street NW, Ste. 300
Washington, DC 20004-1107
(202) 376-6200
(202) 376-6205 (TDD)

Regional Disability Business Accommodation Centers
(6179 349-2639
(617) 354-6618 (TDD)

U.S. Architectural Transportation Barriers Compliance Board
(800) USA-ABLE

DISABILITY

Administration on Developmental Disabilities
200 Independence Ave. SW
349F Humphrey Building
Washington, DC 20201
(202) 690-6590

National Information Center for Children & Youth with Disabilities (NICHCY)
P.O. Box 1492
Washington, DC 20013-1492
(800) 999-5599
(703) 893-6061
(703) 893-8614 (TDD)

National Institute of Neurological Disorders and Stroke (NINDS)
9000 Rockville Pike
Building 31, Room 8A-16
Bethesda, MD 20892
(303) 496-5751

National Library Service for the Blind and Physically Handicapped
Library of Congress
1291 Taylor St. NW
Washington, DC 20542
(202) 707-5100

Senate Subcommittee on Disability Policy
113 Hart Senate Office Bldg.
Washington, DC 20510
(202) 224-6265

EDUCATION

National Head Start Association
201 N. Union St.
Suite 320
Alexandria, VA 22314
(703) 739-0875

Office of Special Education and Rehabilitation Services Clearinghouse on Disability Information
U.S. Department of Education
Switzer Building
330 C Street SW
Room 3132
Washington, DC 20202-2524
(202) 205-8723

GENERAL INFORMATION

Administration for Children, Youth and Families
330 C Street SW
Washington, DC 20201
(202) 205-8347

Very Special Arts
1331 F Street NW
Suite 800
Washington, DC 20004
(202) 628-2800
(202) 737-0645 (TDD)

(continued)

FEDERAL AGENCIES
(continued)

HEALTH

Health Care Financing Administration
Inquiries Staff
Room GF-3
East Lowrise Building
Baltimore, MD 21207
(Mailing address only)

Maternal and Child Health Bureau
Parklawn Building
5600 Fishers Lane
Room 1805
Rockville, MD 20857
(301) 443-2170

**Medicare/Medigap Information and
   Second Surgical Opinion Program**
Department of Health and Human Services
   Health Care Financing Administration
Baltimore, MD 21235
(800) 638-6833
(800) 492-6603 (in MD)

**National Center for Education in
   Maternal and Child Health**
38th and R Streets NW
Washington, DC 20057
(202) 625-8400
(202) 625-8410
(Clearinghouse)

**National Institute of Child Health and
   Human Development**
National Institutes of Health
9000 Rockville Pike
Building 31, Room 2A03
Bethesda, MD 20892
(301) 496-3454

**Office of Disease Prevention and Health
   Promotion**
National Health Info. Center
National Institutes of Health
P.O. Box 1133
Washington, DC 20013-1133
(800) 336-4797

HOTLINES

Consumer Information Ctr.
P.O. Box 100
Pueblo, CO 81002
(Mailing address only)

Consumer Product Safety Commission
(800) 638-2772

District Internal Revenue Services
Tax Information
(800) 829-1040
(800) 829-3676 (forms)

FIRS
(Federal Info. Relay Service)
(800) 877-8339
(202) 708-9300 (in DC)

SSA Hotline
(Social Security Administration)
(800) 772-1213
(800) 325-0778 (TDD)

TDD and TTY Operator Services
(800) 855-1155
(202) 708-9300 (in DC)

MENTAL HEALTH

Mental Health Policy Resource Center
1730 Rhode Island Ave. NW
Suite 308
Washington, DC 20036
(202) 775-8826

**National Association of Psychiatric
   Treatment Center for Children**
200 L Street NW
Washington, DC 20036
(202) 955-3828

**National Consortium for Child Mental
   Health Services**
3615 Wisconsin Ave. NW
Washington, DC 20016
(202) 966-7300

PROFESSIONAL ORGANIZATIONS

These groups offer valuable services to parents and professionals by identifying appropriate qualifications and standards of practice of their members. Some can help locate qualified practitioners. They have been arranged alphabetically by subject matter. (From: Annual directory of national organizations, 1991–92. *Exceptional Parent* [1991, September] *21* (6), pp. D4–D20; reprinted by permission.)

DENTISTRY

Academy of Dentistry for the
   Handicapped
211 E. Chicago Ave., 17th Fl.
Chicago, IL 60611
(800) 621-8099, ext. 2660
(312) 440-2660

DEVELOPMENTAL DISABILITIES

American Association of University
   Affiliated Programs for the
   Developmentally Disabled
8630 Fenton St., Suite 410
Silver Spring, MD 20910
(301) 588-8252

(continued)

PROFESSIONAL ORGANIZATIONS
(continued)

National Association of Developmental
  Disabilities Councils
1234 Massachusetts Ave. NW, Suite 103
Washington, DC 20005
(202) 347-1234

EDUCATION
American Council of Rural Special
  Education (ACRES)
Western Washington Univ.
Miller Hall, Rm. 359
Bellingham, WA 98225-9092
(206) 676-3576

American Federation of Teachers
555 New Jersey Ave. NW
Washington, DC 20001
(800) 238-1133
(202) 879-4400

National Association of Private Schools for
  Exceptional Children
1522 K Street NW, #1032
Washington, DC 20005
(202) 408-3338

National Association of State Directors of
  Special Education
1800 Diagonal Rd., #320
Alexandria, VA 22314
(703) 519-3800

National Education Association/Human &
  Civil Rights Equal Access Program
1201 16th Street NW
Washington, DC 20036
(202) 833-4000

EXCEPTIONAL CHILDREN
Council for Exceptional Children
1920 Association Dr.
Reston, VA 22091-1589
(703) 264-9474

HOME CARE
National Association for Home Care
519 C Street NE
Stanton Park
Washington, DC 20002
(202) 547-7424

MEDICINE
American Academy for Cerebral Palsy and
  Developmental Medicine
P.O. Box 11086
Richmond, VA 23230-1086
(804) 282-0036

American Academy of Pediatrics
141 NW Point Blvd.
P.O. Box 927
Elk Grove Village, IL 60009-0927
(708) 228-5005

American Medical Association
515 N. State
Chicago, IL 60610
(312) 464-5000

Association for the Care of Children's
  Health
7910 Woodmont Ave., #300
Bethesda, MD 20814
(301) 654-6549

MENTAL HEALTH
National Mental Health Association
1021 Prince St.
Alexandria, VA 22314
(800) 969-6642
(703) 684-7722

MENTAL RETARDATION
American Association on Mental
  Retardation
1719 Kalorama Rd. NW
Washington, DC 20009
(800) 424-3688
(202) 387-1968

National Association of State Mental
  Retardation Program Directors
113 Oronoco St.
Alexandria, VA 22314
(703) 683-4202

ORTHOTICS AND PROSTHETICS
American Orthotic and Prosthetic
  Association
1650 King St., Suite 500
Alexandria, VA 22314
(703) 836-7116

Association of Children's Prosthetic-
  Orthotic Clinics
6300 N. River Rd., #727
Rosemont, IL 60018-4238
(708) 698-1694

PSYCHIATRY
American Academy of Child and
  Adolescent Psychiatry
3615 Wisconsin Ave. NW
Washington, DC 20016
(202) 966-7300

(continued)

PROFESSIONAL ORGANIZATIONS
(continued)

American Psychiatric Association
1400 K Street NW
Washington, DC 20036
(2029 682-6000

PSYCHOLOGY
American Psychological Association
The Ethics Office
750 First Street NE
Washington, DC 20002
(202) 336-5930

National Association of School
  Psychologists
8455 Colesville Rd.
Room 1000
Silver Spring, MD 20910
(301) 608-0500

REHABILITATION
Council of State Administrators of
  Vocational Rehab.
P.O. Box 3776
Washington, DC 20007
(202) 638-4634

National Institute for Rehabilitation
  Engineering
P.O. Box T
Hewitt, NJ 07421
(201) 853-6585

National Rehabilitation Association
1910 Association Dr., #205
Reston, VA 22091-1502
(703) 836-0850
(703) 836-0852 (TDD)

Rehabilitation International
25 East 21st Street
New York, NY 10010
(212) 420-1500

RESNA
1101 Connecticut Ave. NW
Suite 700
Washington, DC 20036
(202) 857-1199

RESIDENTIAL PLACEMENT
National Association of Private Residential
  Resources
4200 Evergreen Ln., #315
Annandale, VA 22003
(703) 642-6614

RESPIRATORY CARE
American Association for Respiratory Care
11030 Ables Lane
Dallas, TX 75299
(214) 243-2272

SEVERE DISABILITIES
The Association for Persons with Severe
  Handicaps (TASH)
11201 Greenwood Ave. N
Seattle, WA 98133
(206) 361-8870

SOCIAL WORKERS
National Association of Social Workers
750 First St. NW, Suite 700
Washington, DC 20002
(800) 638-8799
(202) 408-8600

THERAPY
American Alliance for Health, Physical
  Education, Recreation and Dance
1900 Association Dr.
Reston, VA 22091
(703) 476-3400

American Art Therapy Association
3101 Park Center Dr.
Alexandria, VA 22302
(703) 820-4940

American Occupational Therapy
  Association
P.O. Box 1725
Rockville, MD 20849-1725
(301) 948-9626

American Physical Therapy Association
1111 N. Fairfax St.
Alexandria, VA 22314
(703) 684-2782

National Association for Music Therapy
8455 Colesville Rd., #930
Silver Spring, MD 20910
(301) 589-3300

National Therapeutic Recreation Society
2775 S. Quincy St., Suite 300
Arlington, VA 22206
(703) 820-4940

(continued)

Parent Training and Information Centers

The Parent Training and Information (PTI) program views parents as full partners in the educational process and a significant source of support and assistance to each other. The following PTIs are funded by the Division of Personnel Preparation, Office of Special Education Programs (OSEP), U.S. Department of Education, "to provide training and information to parents to enable such individuals to participate more effectively with professionals in meeting the educational needs of handicapped children," as stated in PL 98-199. PTI projects help parents to:

Better understand the nature and needs of their child's condition
Provide follow-up support for the educational programs of their children
Communicate more effectively with special and regular educators, administrators, related services personnel, and other relevant professionals
Participate in educational decision-making processes, including development of the child's IEP
Obtain information about the programs, services, and resources available to their child with a disability

Parent training and information centers are listed below:

ALABAMA
Special Education Action Committee, Inc.
P.O. Box 161274
Mobile, AL 36616-2274
(800) 222-7322 (in AL)
(205) 478-1208

ALASKA
Parents as Resources Engaged in Networking and Training Statewide (PARENTS)
P.O. Box 32198
Juneau, AK 99803
(800) 478-7678 (in AK)
(907) 790-2246

ARIZONA
Pilot Parent Partnerships
2150 E. Highland Ave., Suite 105
Phoenix, AZ 85016
(602) 468-300l

ARKANSAS
Arkansas Disability Coalition
10002 W. Markham St., Suite B17
Little Rock, AR 72205
(501) 221-1330 (Voice/TTY)

CALIFORNIA
Parents Helping Parents
535 Race St., Suite 140
San Jose, CA 95126
(408) 288-5010

Team of Advocates for Special Kids, Inc.
100 W. Cerritos Ave.
Anaheim, CA 92805-6546
(714) 962-6332

COLORADO
PEAK Parent Center
6055 Lehman Dr., #101
Colorado Springs, CO 80918
(800) 284-0251 (TDD)
(719) 531-9400

CONNECTICUT
Connecticut Parent Advocacy Center (CPAC)
5 Church Ln.
P.O. Box 579
East Lyme, CT 06333
(800) 455-2722 (in CT)
(203) 739-3089 (TTY)

DELAWARE
Parent Information Center of Delaware, Inc.
700 Barksdale Rd., Suite 6
Newark, DE 19711
(302) 366-0152
(302) 366-0178 (TDD)

FLORIDA
Family Network on Disabilities
1211 Tech. Blvd., Suite 105
Tampa, FL 33619
(800) 825-5736
(813) 623-4088

GEORGIA
Parents Educating Parents
ARC of Georgia
1851 Ram Runway, Suite 104
College Park, GA 30337
(404) 761-2745 (PEP)
(404) 761-3150 (STOMP)

(continued)

PARENT TRAINING AND INFORMATION CENTERS
(continued)

HAWAII
Learning Disabilities Association of Hawaii
200 N. Vineyard Blvd., #103
Honolulu, HI 96817
(808) 536-2280 (Voice/TDD)

IDAHO
Idaho Parents Unlimited
4696 Overland Rd., Suite 478
Boise, ID 83705
(208) 342-5884
(800) 242-4785 (in ID)

ILLINOIS
Designs for Change
220 S. State St., Rm. 1900
Chicago, IL 60604
(312) 922-0317

Family Resource Center on Disabilities
20 E. Jackson Blvd., Rm. 900
Chicago, IL 60604
(312) 939-3513
(800) 952-4199 (in IL)

INDIANA
IN*SOURCE
833 Northside Blvd., Building 1, Rear
South Bend, IN 46617
(800) 332-4433 (in IN)
(219) 234-7101

IOWA
Iowa Pilot Parents
33 North 12th St.
P.O. Box 1151
Fort Dodge, IA 50501
(800) 383-4777
(515) 576-5870

KANSAS
Families Together, Inc.
1023 S.W. Gage Blvd.
Topeka, KS 66604
(913) 273-6343

KENTUCKY
Kentucky Special Parent Involvement
  Network (KY-SPIN)
318 W. Kentucky St.
Louisville, KY 40203
(800) 525-7746
(502) 589-5717/584-1104

LOUISIANA
Project PROMPT
UCP of Greater New Orleans
1500 Edwards Ave., Suite O
Harahan, LA 70123
(800) 766-7736 (in LA)
(504) 734-7736

MAINE
Maine Parent Federation, Inc. (SPIN)
P.O. Box 2067
Augusta, ME 04338-2067
(800) 325-0220
(207) 582-2504

MARYLAND
Parents' Place of Maryland
7257 Parkway Dr., Suite 210
Hanover, MD 21076
(301) 379-0900

MASSACHUSETTS
Federation for Children with Special Needs
95 Berkeley St., Suite 104
Boston, MA 02116
(800) 331-0688 (in MA)
(617) 482-2915 (Voice/TTY)

MICHIGAN
Citizens Alliance to Uphold Special
  Education (CAUSE)
313 S. Washington Sq. #40
Lansing, MI 48933
(800) 221-9105 (in MI)
(517) 485-4084

Parents Are Experts
UCP of Metro Detroit
17000 W. Eight Mile Rd., Suite 380
Southfield, MI 48075
(313) 557-5070

MINNESOTA
PACER Center
4826 Chicago Ave. S
Minneapolis, MN 55417
(800) 53-PACER (in MN)
(612) 827-2966

MISSISSIPPI
Mississippi Parent Advocacy Center
  (MS-PAC)
332 New Market Dr.
Jackson, MS 39209
(800) 231-3721 (in MS)
(601) 922-3210

(continued)

PARENT TRAINING AND INFORMATION CENTERS
(continued)

MISSOURI
Missouri Parents Act (MPACT)
1722 S South Glenstone, Suite 125
Springfield, MO 65804
(800) 66-MPACT (in MO)
(417) 882-7434 (TDD)
or
625 N. Euclid, Suite 405
St. Louis, MO 63108
(800) 284-6389 (in MO)
(314) 361-1660 (TDD)
or
1115 E. 65th Street
Kansas City, MO 64131
(816) 333-6833

MONTANA
Parents Let's Unite for Kids (PLUK)
EMC/IHS
1500 North 30th St.
Billings, MT 59101-0298
(406) 657-2055

NEBRASKA
Nebraska Parent's Information and
    Training Center
3610 Dodge St.
Omaha, NE 68131
(800) 284-8520 (in NE)
(402) 346-0525

NEVADA
Nevada Technology Center
288 E. Flamingo, Suite A
Las Vegas, NV 89121
(800) 435-2448 (in NV)
(702) 735-2922

NEW HAMPSHIRE
Parent Information Center
P.O. Box 1422
Concord, NH 03302-1442
(603) 224-6299
(603) 224-7005 (Voice/TDD)

NEW JERSEY
Statewide Parent Advocacy Network
    (SPAN)
516 North Ave. E
Westfield, NJ 07090
(201) 654-7726
(201) 654-SPAN (Voice/TDD)

NEW MEXICO
Education for Parents of Indian Children
    with Special Needs (EPICS Project)
P.O. Box 788
Bernalillo, NM 87004
(505) 867-3396

Parents Reaching Out to Help (PRO)
1127 University Blvd. NE
Albuquerque, NM 87102
(800) 524-5176 (in NM)
(505) 842-9045

NEW YORK
Advocates for Children
24-16 Bridge Plaza S
Long Island City, NY 11101
(718) 729-8868 (Voice/TDD)

Parent Network Center (PNC)
1443 Main St.
Buffalo, NY 14209
(800) 724-7408 (in NY)
(716) 885-1004
(716) 885-3527 (TDD)

Resources for Children with Special Needs
Project Staff
200 Park Ave. S.
Suite 816
New York, NY 10003
(212) 677-4650

NORTH CAROLINA
Exceptional Children's Assistance Center
P.O. Box 16
Davidson, NC 28036
(704) 892-1321

Families First Coalition, Inc.
300 Enola Road
Morgantown, NC 28036
(704) 433-2661

NORTH DAKOTA
Pathfinder Parent Center and Information
    Center
1600 Second Ave. SW
Minot, ND 58701
(701) 852-9426

OHIO
Child Advocacy Center
SOC Information Center
106 Wellington Place
Cincinnati, OH 45219
(513) 381-2400 (TTY)

Ohio Coalition for the Education of
    Handicapped Children (OCEHC)
1299 Campbell Road, Suite B
Marion, OH 43302
(614) 431-1307 (Voice/TDD)

(continued)

PARENT TRAINING AND INFORMATION CENTERS
(*continued*)

OKLAHOMA
Parents Reaching Out in Oklahoma (PRO-
Oklahoma)
1917 S. Harvard Ave.
Oklahoma City, OK 73128
(800) PL94-142
(405) 681-9710

OREGON
Oregon COPE Project
999 Locust St. NE, Box B
Salem, OR 97303-5299
(503) 373-7477 (Voice/TDD)

PENNSYLVANIA
Parent Education Network
333 E. Seventh Ave.
York, PA 17404
(717) 845-9722

Parents Union for Public Schools
311 S. Juniper St., Suite 602
Philadelphia, PA 19107
(215) 546-1212

PUERTO RICO
Asociación de Padres por Bienestar de
Niños Impedidos de PR (APNI)
P.O. Box 21303
Rio Piedras, PR 00928
(809) 763-4665
(809) 765-0345

RHODE ISLAND
Rhode Island Parent Information Center
500 Prospect Street
Pawtucket, RI 02860
(401) 831-3150

SOUTH CAROLINA
Parents Reaching Out to Parents of S.C.
2712 Middleburg Dr., Suite 102
Columbia, SC 29240
(803) 734-3547

SOUTH DAKOTA
South Dakota Parent Connection, Inc.
Nancy Nelson
P.O. Box 84118-4813
Sioux Falls, SD 57118
(800) 640-4553 (in SD)
(605) 335-8844

TENNESSEE
Support and Training for Exceptional
Parents (S.T.E.P.)
ARC of Tennessee
1805 Hayes St., Suite 100
Nashville, TN 37203
(615) 327-0294

TEXAS
Fiesta Educativa
P.O. Box 2579
Laredo, TX 78041
(512) 722-5174

Partnerships for Assisting Texans with
Handicaps (PATH)
6465 Calder, Suite 202
Beaumont, TX 77706
(800) 866-4726
(409) 866-4726

UTAH
Utah Parent Center (UPC)
2290 East 4500 S, Suite 110
Salt Lake City, UT 84117
(800) 468-1160 (in UT)
(801) 272-1051

VERMONT
Vermont Information and Training Network
(VITN)
Vermont/ARC
Champlain Mill
Winooski, VT 05404
(802) 655-4016 (Voice/TDD)

VIRGINIA
Parent Educational Advocacy Training
Center (PEATC)
228 S. Pitt St., Suite 300
Alexandria, VA 22314
(800) 869-6782 (VA,WV,MD)
(703) 836-2953
(703) 836-3026 (TDD)

WASHINGTON
Specialized Training of Military Parents
(STOMP)
Washington PAVE
12208 Pacific Hwy. SW
Tacoma, WA 98499
(206) 588-1741

Washington Parents Advocating Vocational
Education (PAVE)
6316 South 12th St.
Tacoma, WA 98465
(800) 5-PARENT (in WA, Voice/TDD)
(206) 565-2266 (Voice/TDD)

WEST VIRGINIA
West Virginia Parent Training and
Information Center
Schroath Bldg., Suite 1
Clarksburg, WV 26301
(800) 281-1436
(304) 624-1436

(*continued*)

PARENT TRAINING AND INFORMATION CENTERS
(continued)

WISCONSIN
Parent Education Project (PEP)
2001 W. Vlitt
Milwaukee, WI 53206
(800) 231-8382
(414) 937-8380

WYOMING
Parent Information Center
270 Fort St.
Buffalo, WY 82384
(307) 684-5461

Reprinted from *Exceptional Parent* magazine's Annual Directory of National Organizations, 1992–93, published as part of Exceptional Parent's September 1993 issue, Volume 22, Number 6. Copyright (c) 1992 by *Exceptional Parent* magazine, Boston, Massachusetts.

Maintaining Safe Environments

chapter 16

LEARNING OBJECTIVES

After completing this chapter, the reader will be able to:

1. Define five attributes of safe behavior.
2. Identify four methods to increase the effectiveness of first aid given to an accident victim.
3. Identify three unsafe practices that lead to fire, electrical shock, poisoning, and falls in the home.
4. Identify 10 common safety concerns in the kitchen, bathroom, and basement.
5. Identify four safety procedures for working with hand and power tools.
6. Define the main requirements of an accident prevention and report system.

INTRODUCTION

People with developmental disabilities must be given the dignity of risk and the chance to learn. Staff members should be prepared to let people learn from small mistakes. However, no person should be knowingly given the chance to learn from a dangerous accident.

Accidents are major social and economic problems. For example, more highway deaths occur each year than the total number of combat deaths during the entire Vietnam War. Between 1900 and 1980, there were 7 million deaths from accidents of all types in the United States. During the same period, there have been 700 million injuries and $750 billion in economic loss from these injuries. About 20% of the injuries caused permanent disability.

Before you finish reading this chapter, four people will die in an accident in this country. In addition, 400 people will be injured in accidents nationwide. In terms of age groups, accidents kill more children than the six major children's diseases. More people between the ages of 15 and 24 die from accidents than from all other causes. Accidents are the major cause of death of persons between the ages of 1 and 44.

More accidents occur at home than in any other place. There are about 27 million injuries in homes each year. About 5 million of these injuries require bed rest. Accidents on the job cost over 200 million person days of lost work each year. These accidents also cost billions of dollars.

Although accident prevention is important for all people, agencies serving people with developmental disabilities must pay particular attention to safety. These agencies have a responsibility to maintain safe environments. They may be liable for some accidents. Injury and death from accidents also can be a major source of public concern and scandal. Some people point to accidents as proof that persons with developmental disabilities cannot live in the community.

ACCIDENTS

An accident is an unplanned act or event resulting in injury or death to people or damage to property. Accidents are not really accidental. Most accidents take place for obvious reasons. About 85% of accidents are caused by unsafe behavior. You can reduce accidents by changing your own behavior and the behaviors of people with developmental disabilities. Table 1 lists individual attributes for safe behavior.

MOST ACCIDENTS ARE CAUSED BY UNSAFE BEHAVIOR.

Unsafe environments cause the remaining 15% of accidents. Machines and equipment in the home and at work require proper maintenance and use. Improper use of equipment and machinery creates an unsafe environment. Protective equipment and procedures can prevent accidents. Such practices as using ungrounded electrical appliances, storing gasoline in an automobile trunk, and squeezing 10 people into a canoe cause unsafe environments.

DISORDER CAUSES ACCIDENTS. KEEP THE HOME AND WORK-PLACE FREE OF CLUTTER. GOOD HOUSEKEEPING REDUCES ACCIDENTS.

Control over the environment reduces accidents. Knowledge, skills, and protective habits prevent unsafe behavior. A clean and orderly living space promotes safety. This is important for staff safety and

Table 1. Individual attributes for safe behavior

1. Know your physical limitations. Work within them. Do not attempt to perform activities unless you know you have the physical capabilities.
2. Know how to perform a task. Be aware of any hazards associated with a task. Knowledge about tasks is necessary before attempting to do them.
3. Practice performing a task. Competent skill levels reduce accidents. People should be trained to perform job duties to the best of their abilities.
4. Develop habits of performing tasks in a safe manner. Skills repeated over and over become habits. Safe habits become automatic safety measures.
5. Develop a concern about safety. A concerned but realistic attitude toward safety will decrease unsafe behavior and reduce the likelihood of accidents.

accident prevention. People with developmental disabilities have the same safety needs as the staff. They need to exercise control over the environment. They also need to develop the right knowledge, skills, and habits. Finally, they need to learn how to maintain clean and orderly environments. Teaching people the right skills and attitudes can prevent behaviors that result in accidents. The staff must set the example and level of expectation.

FIRST AID

Not all accidents can be prevented. You should be prepared to give immediate assistance to an injured person. The following four steps can increase your chances of giving effective first aid:

1. Take a first aid course every 3 years. Even though you know first aid, you may hesitate in an emergency; therefore, it is important to have a ready knowledge of what to do in any type of emergency. Also, take a course in cardiopulmonary resuscitation. These courses are usually given by the Red Cross, local YMCAs, hospitals, and community colleges.
2. Store a first aid kit in an accessible and convenient location.
3. Keep a chart that describes first aid measures for trauma, ranging from poisoning to frostbite.
4. Post a list of emergency telephone numbers next to the telephone. Numbers for the physician, poison control center, fire department, police department, ambulance, and hospital should be listed.

ACCIDENTS IN THE HOME

As stated earlier, the home is a primary site of accidents. An average of 3.5 million disabling injuries take place yearly in the home. Each year, about 27,000 people are killed in home accidents. The cost of home accidents exceeds $7 billion each year.

Fire

Fire is the most dangerous household accident. Injury and death result from smoke inhalation, burns, and heat. Smoke inhalation causes most of the deaths. Modern plastics do not burn quickly, but they produce large amounts of very toxic smoke. Fire and smoke are especially dangerous for people who do not make quick decisions or who move slowly.

Causes of Fire

Electrical malfunctions are a major cause of fires. Wires overheat when too many appliances are operated off extension plugs in one outlet. Frayed and cut electrical cords can cause both electrical shock and fire. Replacing blown fuses with new fuses of higher amperage can cause wires to overheat.

In some instances, the staff can identify potential problems. For example, an unusual odor from an appliance or heating equipment can signal a malfunction. Also, fuses or circuit breakers that blow or trip repeatedly indicate trouble. You should identify problems, but you may not be able to provide a solution. In general, consult a qualified electrician for electrical problems.

Many fires are also caused by defective or misused heating equipment. Fires often occur in cold weather when heating systems are pushed beyond capacity. All gas, oil, and electrical heating systems should be inspected each year. In wood-burning systems, chimney flues and stove pipes should be cleaned on a regular basis. When possible, avoid using kerosene heaters. If they must be used, purchase only those with independent laboratory approval. Follow safety instructions. Never use kerosene heaters when people are sleeping or if no one is in the room.

Cigarette smoking is a threat to health and can also lead to injury by fire. Over 15% of all home fires are caused by cigarettes. Smoking in bed is a bad risk because the blood picks up carbon monoxide from the tobacco smoke quicker than it does oxygen. This can increase drowsiness, cause a person to fall asleep, and lead to potential disaster.

Many flammable liquids are found in the home and workplace. Gasoline, cleaning fluids, paint products, turpentine, kerosene, and spot removers can explode when exposed to an open flame or external heat. Never store volatile liquids in closed areas, such as car trunks, garage cabinets, or basement rooms where there is no air circulation. Do not keep volatile liquids in unmarked containers. Do not store or use volatile liquids near sources of heat or an open flame. Discard any rags, cardboard, or newspapers that have absorbed volatile liquids. Finally, do not substitute one dangerous liquid for another. For example, never use gasoline in a kerosene heater.

Strategies To Minimize Injury by Fire

The threat to personal safety by fire can be reduced through four pre-cautionary strategies. First, develop and practice a fire evacuation plan. In an emergency, follow the escape plan. Stay close to the floor where there is more oxygen but less heat and smoke. Take short breaths. Cover your face and hair with a wet cloth. Open ward doors with extreme caution. Never open hot doors. Close all doors and windows when evacuating a room. Meet at a preselected place outside the building. Determine if all people are present. Do not reenter the building until it is safe.

IN A FIRE:

STAY CLOSE TO THE FLOOR.

TAKE SHORT BREATHS.

NEVER OPEN HOT DOORS.

CLOSE ALL DOORS AND WINDOWS WHEN EVACUATING A ROOM.

A second precaution is to install smoke detectors. They are an inexpensive warning device. Because smoke rises, the detectors should be placed on the ceiling. They can also be placed high on an inside wall just below the ceiling. In general, halls, bedrooms, and the bottoms and tops of stairwells are the best locations for detectors. Your local fire department can provide advice.

Third, have fire extinguishers available. Various types of fire extinguishers are designed for different types of fires. A class A extinguisher fights fires of solid combustible material, such as wood or textiles. Class B extinguishers combat fires of flammable liquids or gases. A class C extinguisher controls electrical fires but can also be used on fires involving liquid, gas, and solid material. Consult your local fire department about the need for number, type, and location of fire extinguishers.

The fourth precaution in preventing a serious disaster is to report a fire promptly. The first minutes after a fire is discovered are the most important. The chances of containing a fire decrease markedly after the first 6 or 8 minutes. The first priority, however, is to get everyone out of the building. After evacuation, call your local emergency telephone number from a nearby telephone. When reporting a fire, be brief, accurate, and speak in a clear voice. Provide your name, address, and the identity of the nearest cross street. Give your location on the block. Describe any special landmarks or street arrangements.

Electrical Shock

Electrical shock is a serious and common danger. Severe shock can damage vital organs, stop heartbeat and respiration, and lead to death.

Additional injuries often result when the person violently jerks away from the source of electricity. Appliances and lighting fixtures in good working order reduce the possibility of electrical shock. Regularly inspect and replace damaged wiring. Do not run temporary wiring across the floor. Also, never use an electrical appliance while you are standing on wet ground or if your hands are damp. Finally, use a three-prong plug or otherwise ground electrical equipment.

MOISTURE AND ELECTRICITY ARE A DANGEROUS COMBINATION.

If someone does receive a serious shock, determine if the person is still in contact with the electrical source. If so, turn off the electrical current or remove the source from the person. Do not touch the person or source of current. Instead, use wood, hard plastic, or rolled-up newspaper to move the source of electricity away from the person. Then, give the victim artificial respiration and summon an ambulance.

EXERCISE 1

Emergency Telephone Numbers

Go to the nearest agency telephone. Is the list of emergency telephone numbers available? What are the numbers for the fire department, ambulance, and poison control center?

Poisons

An increasing number of accidental poisonings occur each year. Approximately 3,300 of 300,000 annual poisonings in this country result in death. About 66% of the deaths are caused by ingesting lethal amounts of medications, such as aspirin, barbiturates, sleeping pills, and tranquilizers. The remaining 34% of poisoning deaths result from taking unspecified solid and liquid substances. Accidents can be reduced by keeping all medicines, including nonprescription drugs, and other poisonous substances away from regular food and drink. Never store poisonous materials in unmarked or easily confused containers. Finally, the telephone number of the nearest poison control center should be readily available. Call the center even if you only suspect someone has consumed a dangerous substance. Table 2 lists common household poisons.

Common symptoms of poisoning are nausea, vomiting, headache, and coughing, but these symptoms occur in only about 10% of all poisoning cases. A variety of other symptoms, including stomach pain,

Table 2. Common household poisons

Cleaning aids	Cosmetics
Ammonia	Astringents
Bleach	Nail polish remover
Detergents	Maintenance items
Drain cleaners	Gasoline
Dyes	Insect sprays
Cleaning fluids	Paint products
Lye	Glues
Medical items	Animal poison
Antiseptics	Miscellaneous items
Aspirin	Benzene
Cough syrup	Aerosol sprays
Cold medications	Kerosene
Iodine	Typewriter cleaner
Prescription and over-the-counter medications	
Rubbing alcohol	

breathing difficulty, weakness, confusion, diarrhea, ringing in the ears, and sweating, may be associated with poisoning because poisons can attack many different parts of the body.

The treatment for most poisoning victims is generally mild (Silverman, 1984). About 60% of all cases require no treatment or application of water or milk to areas affected by the poison, such as skin, mouth, or stomach. The use of ipecac to induce vomiting is needed in about 17% of cases. Only 2% of poison victims require intravenous fluids, and another 2% need their stomachs pumped. Dialysis, oxygen, or heart monitoring procedures are required in less than 1% of cases. In 80% of telephone calls to poison hot lines, assistance is provided over the telephone and there is no need for a visit to a health specialist.

When poisoning has occurred, you will need emergency medical help, but there are six things to do:

1. Make sure the person is breathing. If the person is not breathing, call for immediate medical assistance.
2. Remove any possible obstruction from the mouth or throat. Lay the person on his or her back and move the jaw upward. This will open the airway to the lungs. Provide mouth-to-mouth resuscitation, if necessary.
3. Call for immediate medical assistance if the person is unconscious or having a convulsion. Lay the person on his or her stomach and turn the head to the side. Do not give an unconscious or convulsing person anything to eat or drink.

4. If the person is conscious, give 8 ounces of water to dilute the poison.
5. Induce vomiting with syrup of ipecac if the victim is awake and alert, has not already vomited, and is showing symptoms of poisoning. Do not give ipecac if the poison is a petroleum or caustic agent.
6. Call the nearest poison control center and be prepared to answer the following questions:

What substance was involved?
How much was involved?
What is the person doing now?
What are the age and weight of the person?
Does the person have any illness?
Is the person taking any drugs or medications?

EXERCISE 2

Antidotes for Poisons

Ask the program director or your supervisor where there is a list of antidotes for various poisons. List the available antidotes.

Falls

Falls are the most serious threat to life around the home. Adequate fencing around all outside stairs, porches, and balconies can reduce the likelihood of injury from falls. Do not use the stairs for storage. Also, maintain proper lighting in all stairwells and hallways. Because so many falls result from slipping on wet surfaces, install necessary grab bars and mats in bathing areas. Finally, never carry objects in your arms or on your shoulder in such a way as to hinder your field of vision.

SAFETY AT HOME

In the Kitchen

The kitchen is a central room with many purposes ranging from preparing meals, to washing dishes, to ironing clothing, to feeding the dog, to talking on the telephone. To ensure both safety and health, the kitchen must be kept clean and orderly. Dishes should be washed and food put away after each meal. Spills can result in slips and skids and should be cleaned up immediately.

Pilot lights in gas stoves should be inspected periodically. If you must use a match to ignite a burner, light the match before turning on the burner. Electric stoves also present a potential hazard. A burner that is on but not glowing can still be very hot. Never place your hand on a burner.

The kitchen is a likely place for accidental fires. In case of fire, follow the procedures given in the preceding section on accidents in the home. In addition, if there is a grease fire on the stove, do not pour water on the flames. This will only spread the flames. Instead, cover the flames with a cooking pan lid or extinguish the fire with a class C fire extinguisher.

EXERCISE 3

Safety in the Kitchen

Do you:	Yes	No
Know what class fire extinguisher is in the kitchen?	___	___
Keep handles of cooking pots turned inward?	___	___
Keep curtains secure so they do not blow over the stove?	___	___
Keep electrical cords and appliances away from sinks containing water?	___	___
Store poisonous cleaning materials in clearly identified areas away from food?	___	___
Use a sturdy, balanced step stool for climbing?	___	___
Light the match before turning on a gas burner?	___	___
Dry your hands before using electrical appliances?	___	___
Prevent steam burns by lifting the far side of pot lids?	___	___
Use pot holders (not paper towels, dish towels, or napkins) when handling hot containers?	___	___
Return foods promptly to the refrigerator?	___	___
Make sure that all poisonous and flammable substances are stored in original containers?	___	___
Discard all chipped and cracked foodware?	___	___
Ensure the kitchen is adequately wired?	___	___
Avoid burns from microwave ovens in which the food becomes hot but the oven remains at room temperature?	___	___

Adapted from Olson (1981).

In the Bathroom

The most common accidents in the bathroom result from falls and electrical shocks. Most surfaces in the bathroom—tile walls and floor, porcelain tubs, and showers—become very slippery when wet. The proper combination of rugs, mats, and hand bars will prevent slips and falls.

Electricity and water are a deadly combination. Separate them. Never use an electric razor, radio, hair dryer, or other electrical appliance near water. Never grab an appliance or light fixture with wet hands or while standing in the tub or shower.

EXERCISE 4

Safety in the Bathroom

Do you:	Yes	No
Check the water temperature with your hand before showering or bathing?	——	——
Avoid storing glass bottles near the bathtub or shower?	——	——
Use nonskid mats in the shower?	——	——
Use rubber-backed rugs on bathroom floors?	——	——
Use necessary grab bars and handrails?	——	——
Avoid using electrical appliances in the bathroom?	——	——
Insulate all electric pull chains?	——	——
Dispose of razor blades in closed containers?	——	——
Clearly mark all medicines?	——	——
Read the label before taking medicines?	——	——

Adapted from Olson (1981).

In the Basement

In some homes, the basement serves as a laundry room, workshop, storage area, and recreation center. The water heater, furnace, and electrical service panel are located there. Understand how these major utilities operate. Know when to call for service. Also, know the location of the pilot light for gas heating units.

Review the operation of the circuit breaker panel or fuse box. Some new appliances, such as microwave ovens and hair dryers, draw large amounts of electricity. If fuses keep blowing, the electrical system should be checked. Also, keep extra fuses available for the occasional need.

EXERCISE 5

Safety in the Basement

Do you:	Yes	No
Maintain well-lighted and well-ventilated work areas?	——	——
Know how to change a fuse?	——	——

(continued)

EXERCISE 5

(continued)

Do you:	Yes	No
Know where the main water and gas valves are located?	___	___
Know where the main electric switch is located?	___	___
Know how to light the pilot lights on the gas furnace and hot water heater?	___	___
Use drying racks and not clotheslines in the basement?	___	___
Know whom to call if you suspect a gas, oil, or water leak?	___	___

Adapted from Olson (1981).

SAFETY AT WORK

Safety Programs

The greatest reduction in the frequency of accidents has occurred in the workplace. A major incentive for safety has been the financial cost of accidents to employers. Direct employee supervision has contributed to the reduction, as have state and federal laws regulating conditions of safety.

Aggressive and organized safety programs by business and industry are the primary reason for the decline in accidents. Most employees accept and participate in these safety education programs. The emphasis on safety has become common in the workplace, unlike the residential setting where life is less regimented and more relaxed.

Many of the safety concerns in the residential setting—fires, falls, and hazardous chemicals—extend to the vocational training program and the job site. The same precautions apply to both residential and work settings. For example, the primary causes of accidents in business and industry are falls, improper handling of objects, improper use of equipment, contact with hazardous materials, and outdated physical facilities.

CONCERNED AGENCY STAFF CAN REDUCE ACCIDENTS.

Estimates place the lost time from industrial accidents in 1978 at 245 million employee-days. The financial loss was about $23 billion, or approximately $240 per worker. There are no separate figures on accidents in activity centers and workshops. But in light of the above figures, it should not be surprising that they do occur. As in business and industry, the staffs of activity centers, workshops, and job stations in industry should actively promote worker safety.

Power Tools and Machinery

The increasing emphasis on meaningful work and integrated employment means that more people are being exposed to power tools and machinery. They must be trained in the use of this equipment. The risk of accidents can be reduced by basic safety practices. An important general rule is always to work in clean, well-lighted areas. Dim lights and clutter invite accidents; put tools away immediately after use.

When using hand tools, keep both hands behind the cutting edge. Always cut, grind, and sand in motions away from the body. When necessary, use a vise or clamp to hold work in place. This is particularly important when using knives, chisels, and saws.

When working with power tools, observe safety rules. Use the right equipment for the job. Keep all machine guards in place. Wear safety glasses but no loose clothing or jewelry. Make sure power equipment is properly grounded. Also, do not use electrical equipment in damp areas. Never use a metal ladder or stool when working with electrical tools.

Disconnect hand tools by holding the plug. Do not pull on the cord. If equipment becomes abnormally hot, have it inspected and, if necessary, repaired. Finally, avoid using an extension cord. If you must, make sure it has the same ampere rating as the equipment.

Make sure employees and trainees know how to operate power tools prior to beginning work.

Lawn maintenance and landscaping require the use of gasoline and electrically powered equipment. Sturdy shoes and work gloves are generally required. Pay particular attention to the storage and use of gasoline. Never use it around a flame. Always pour gasoline in well-ventilated outdoor areas. Do not store gasoline in the trunk of the car. Vapors can ignite and explode. Never pour gasoline when the engine is running or still hot. Turn the engine off and let it cool before refueling.

There are basic safety rules for using a power lawn mower. Never cut the grass by pulling the machine toward you. Do not stand downhill of the mower. Always wear heavy shoes or boots. Clear away any debris before mowing the lawn. Finally, turn off the machine during breaks and after finishing the job.

Hand shears should be stored with blades in a closed position. When using electrical shears, sling the extension cord over the shoulder opposite the hand holding the equipment. This will minimize the risk of cutting the electrical cable.

Dangerous Materials and Chemicals

Accidents from dangerous substances result from skin contact, swallowing, or inhalation. Hazardous substances can cause strong skin reactions. Paint thinners, cleaning agents, and solvents can irritate the skin. Some people are sensitive to common cleaning agents.

Trainees and employees can inadvertently swallow harmful substances. This can happen when they eat in work areas where chemicals are stored. For this reason people should avoid eating where they work. In addition, chemicals and cleaning agents should never be stored in food or beverage containers.

Foreign substances also can be inhaled. Dust is a particular problem in older buildings without adequate ventilation. Proper maintenance and housekeeping minimize dust.

Handling of Materials

Most people in training programs handle materials. Common accidents happen because of improper lifting. Many injuries occur, for example, from bending over the object and pulling up from the back; stress on the back muscles causes injury. The proper technique is to lift by bending the legs.

In addition, cuts are caused by materials with sharp edges. The use of work gloves decreases cuts, injuries from wood splinters, and other hand injuries.

Finally, accidents can result from carrying materials that block the field of vision. Impaired vision increases the risk of slips, falls, and collisions with furniture or equipment.

Noise

Noise can adversely affect people in activity centers and work training programs. Noise levels exceeding 90 decibels during the 8-hour work day can result in significant hearing loss over extended periods of time. Findings on the short-term impact of noise on workers have not been conclusive. Preliminary indications are, however, that noise causes fatigue, frustration, and, as a result, accidents. Noise levels may be a special concern in training programs in facilities originally designed as schools, churches, or offices. The staff should pay particular attention to the noise level in buildings not designed as work centers. Table 3 lists the potential physical effects of various noise levels.

ACCIDENT PREVENTION AND REPORTS

Work training and work sites should stress accident prevention. Training in accident prevention and performance incentives can help people with developmental disabilities to develop job-related safety awareness and skills. Training in accident prevention does not mean providing overprotection. The staff should prepare people to function in complex environments. Many routine safety precautions are learning tasks for people with developmental disabilities.

TRAINING IN ACCIDENT PREVENTION IS NOT OVERPROTECTION.

In addition to training and incentive programs, work and residential programs should utilize an accident record system. The system is needed to record facts about each accident so that general trends can be analyzed. An accident report of each injury should contain the following eight items:

1. Person injured
2. Type of physical injury
3. Part of the body affected by the injury
4. Source of injury
5. Accident type (the event that resulted in the injury)
6. Hazardous conditions (circumstances that caused the accident type)
7. Location of the accident
8. Unsafe action (statement of the violation of a commonly accepted safe procedure that directly resulted in the accident)

The agency should have a first aid program that is explained to and understood by all program staff. In addition, each staff member should accept personal responsibility for ensuring an accident-free environment. This should not be done by removing people with development disabilities from risks. Rather, you should assist them to recognize risks and exercise responsible precautions.

SUMMARY

There must be a concern for accidents and safety promotion in home, work, and leisure-time activities. Most accidents can be prevented if you change your behavior and that of others.

Table 3. Physical effects of noise levels

Physical effect	Noise level (dB)	Noise source
Hearing damage	140	(Pain threshold)
	130	Rock band
	110	Motorcycle
Mental stress	100	Food blender
	90	Loud street noise
Task interference	65	Radio
	50	Quiet conversation
	10	Whisper

Adapted from Makower (1982).

People with developmental disabilities should learn about safety and accidents through small, nondangerous learning situations. They should never confront major learning situations with potentially dangerous consequences without prior instructions.

Commonsense behaviors and concerns that can help prevent accidents are similar in both residential and work environments. The right attitude about safety, accident prevention, and general behavior is more important than technical information.

Staff members should take first aid courses and cardiopulmonary resuscitation courses every 3 years. When confronted with an accident situation, they can then move in a thoughtful but timely manner.

BIBLIOGRAPHY

Denton, D.K. (1982). *Safety management: Improving performance*. New York: McGraw-Hill.

Groner, N.E. (1988). Fire safety practices. In M.P. Janicki, M.W. Krauss, & M.M. Seltzer (Eds.), *Community residences for persons with developmental disabilities: Here to stay* (pp. 317–325). Baltimore: Paul H. Brookes Publishing Co.

Makower, J. (1982), *Office hazards: How your job can make you sick* (p. 81). New York: Caroline House.

National Safety Council. (1991). *Accident prevention manual for industrial operations*. Chicago: National Safety Council.

Olson, N.Z. (1981). *Personal and family safety and crime prevention*. New York: Holt, Rinehart & Winston.

Silverman, H. (1984). *The consumers' guide to poison protection*. New York: Avon Books.

Smith, D. (1983). *Dennis Smith's fire safety book: Everything you need to know to save your life*. New York: Bantam Books.

ADDITIONAL RESOURCES

The Bennett Information Group (1990), in *The green pages: Your everyday shopping guide to environmentally safe products* (New York: Random House), identifies simple things that people can do to help the environment without seriously affecting their lifestyles. It identifies common substances found around the home that have an adverse environmental/health effect.

A. Cote and J. Linville (Eds.). (1986), in *Fire protection handbook* (Quincy, MA: National Fire Protection Association), provide a detailed and authoritative examination of fire protection.

R.H. Dreisbach and W.O. Robertson (1987), in *Handbook of poisoning: Prevention, diagnosis & treatment* (Norwalk, CT: Appleton & Lange), provide a detailed introduction to poisons.

The National Fire Protection Association, Batterymarch Park, Quincy, MA 02269, is the national clearinghouse and publisher of standards, procedures, codes, and other materials concerning fire safety, life safety codes, and fire protection.

A.M. Pope and A.R. Tarlov (Eds.). (1991), *Disability in America: Toward a national agenda for prevention* (Washington, DC: National Academy Press), is a comprehensive treatment of disability and prevention. Various chapters cover the introduction to disability, the magnitude of disability, disability prevention, and the prevention of injury-related disability.

D. Rousseau, W.J. Rea, and J. Enwright (1988), in *Your home, your health, and well being* (Berkeley: Ten Speed Press, 1988), cover indoor air quality, health, and safety.

SELF-APPRAISAL

INSTRUCTIONS

The following questions will help you evaluate your knowledge about maintaining safe environments. For true-false questions, check the correct answer. For multiple choice questions, circle the correct answer(s).

Note: There may be more than one correct answer for some questions.

1. The following will decrease accidents:
   a. Changing your behavior
   b. Increasing control over the environment
   c. Maintaining good housekeeping
   d. Using protective equipment and procedures
2. Rendering effective first aid can be increased by:
   a. Taking a course in first aid
   b. Keeping first aid kits in accessible locations
   c. Posting emergency telephone numbers near the telephone
   d. Telephoning families or next of kin prior to rendering assistance
3. Most deaths from fire are caused by:
   a. Flame
   b. Heat
   c. Smoke
   d. Burns
4. Effective strategies for minimizing injury from fire include:
   a. Practicing fire evacuation plans
   b. Installing smoke detectors
   c. Making fire extinguishers available
   d. Reporting fires promptly
5. In cases of poisoning, you should:
   a. Find the container
   b. Identify the substance and administer the antidote
   c. Telephone the poison control center
   d. Induce vomiting
6. When using hand tools:
   a. Report to the shop foreman
   b. Keep both hands behind the cutting edge
   c. Always cut, grind, or sand away from the body
   d. When necessary, use a clamp or vise to hold work in place

7. Noise levels exceeding 70 decibels during an 8-hour work day over an extended period of time can result in a significant hearing loss.

    ___ True   ___ False

8. An accident report system should record the following:
   a. Type of physical injury
   b. Source of injury
   c. Hazardous condition
   d. Unsafe act

9. Extinguish grease fires in the kitchen by:
   a. Pouring water on the flame
   b. Pouring baking soda on the flame
   c. Covering the flame with a cooking pan lid
   d. Using a class C fire extinguisher

10. About 85% of accidents are caused by unsafe behavior.

    ___ True   ___ False

CASE STUDY

Kathy Bennis is a new employee of Monroe Enterprises, a private, non-profit agency providing employment evaluations and placement services for adults with developmental disabilities. Ms. Bennis completed a 2-year program in psychology at the nearby community college. At age 21, she decided to begin work at Monroe Enterprises and to pursue her bachelor of arts degree at the state university's evening college.

The agency accepts people with developmental disabilities for a 6- to 8-week employment evaluation process. During this time, the person is evaluated in a variety of job skills that range from operating power tools to performing general office support services. The agency also determines the person's preference for employment options. Finally, the agency places people with developmental disabilities in supervised employment situations in private businesses.

The agency's orientation program consists of 2 half-day orientation sessions for all employees who have joined the agency during each 2-month period. Follow-up consultation is provided on a monthly basis throughout the 6-month probationary period. Ms. Bennis's job requires that she monitor the individual progress of workers in the supervised employment setting. She is in the field an average of 6 hours a day. The remaining 2 hours are devoted to paperwork in an office she shares with two other staff members who perform evaluations at Monroe Enterprises.

Situation

Ms. Bennis returns from the supervised employment setting. While walking through the agency's employment evaluation program area, she notices that the work area is littered with packaging materials. In addition, water is accumulating on the floor near the carpentry station. This presents a potential work hazard for people who are carrying packing materials to and from the work training stations.

1. Why should Ms. Bennis express her concern regarding the clutter to her supervisor?
2. What specific hazard is presented by the accumulation of water on the floor by the carpentry station?
3. Ms. Bennis is concerned that people placed in the supervised employment settings have not been adequately prepared to deal with on-the-job safety considerations. The employment evaluation process at Monroe Enterprises shelters people from many learning situations. How should Ms. Bennis resolve this dilemma?

ANSWER KEY TO
SELF-APPRAISAL AND CASE STUDY

SELF-APPRAISAL

1. a, b, c, d
2. a, b, c
3. c
4. a, b, c, d
5. a, b, c
6. b, c, d
7. False
8. a, b, c, d
9. c, d
10. True

CASE STUDY ANSWER GUIDELINES

1. The clutter is an obvious invitation to an accident. In addition, it provides a poor training model for the workers. Workers should be trained to maintain accident-free environments.
2. Water and electricity do not mix. Workers in the carpentry station use a variety of electrical tools. The presence of water increases the risk of electrical shock. In addition, water on the floor increases the risk of injury due to slipping. Again, staff responsibility is to maintain a safe environment.
3. First, Ms. Bennis can recommend that the agency increase its emphasis on safety education. Second, she could recommend that more training take place in real work situations. Finally, while supervising individuals in the community, she could provide an appropriate model for concerns over safety.

Drugs and Medications

chapter
17

LEARNING OBJECTIVES

Upon completing this chapter, the reader will be able to:

1. Identify the three categories of medications commonly used by people with developmental disabilities.
2. Identify potential side effects of some medications.
3. Identify staff responsibilities for medical treatment of a person with a developmental disability.
4. Identify five elements contained within a medication plan.

INTRODUCTION

In 1985, approximately 143 million people in the United States had used prescription drugs at some point in their lives. An estimated 75 million Americans are taking one or more drugs on a routine basis. Pharmacists fill about 6 billion prescriptions each year. About 80% of these prescriptions are written for people who are not in hospitals. These drugs are administered and monitored without the direct supervision of medical staff. In addition, most U.S. citizens have occasion to use one or more of the 200,000 available nonprescription (over-the-counter) drugs.

This chapter covers the general use of drugs and describes how these substances work within the body. The common categories of drugs used by individuals with developmental disabilities are pre-

---

The terms *drug* and *medication,* generally used interchangeably, are so used in this chapter. Both refer to any chemical compound that may be used in the diagnosis, treatment, or prevention of disease or other abnormal condition, for the relief of pain or suffering; or to control or improve any physiological or pathological condition.

sented. The side effects frequently associated with these drugs are then described, as well as staff responsibilities for supervising people who take them. Finally, a method for documenting the use of drugs within a program is reviewed.

EXERCISE 1

Medical Records

Study your agency's medical records for each person you are working with in the program. Identify the medications each person is taking.

DEFINITION OF A DRUG

A drug is a chemical substance used in the medical treatment of a person. When taken in prescribed or recommended dosages, the chemical is designed to benefit the person using it by relieving symptoms or curing an illness.

The methods by which drugs are prepared and dispensed today are considerably different from those used a century ago. In the past, a doctor's prescriptions were taken to a pharmacist, who prepared the needed mixtures from various plants and/or minerals. Today, private manufacturers produce the hundreds of thousands of drugs on the market, and the role of the pharmacist is to dispense the medication according to the doctor's prescription. Before each new drug product reaches the consumer market, it must pass standards for safety and effectiveness established and monitored by the U.S. Food and Drug Administration.

DRUGS AND MEDICATIONS REFER TO THE CHEMICAL SUBSTANCES USED IN THE MEDICAL TREATMENT OF AN ILLNESS.

The two major classifications of drugs are prescription and nonprescription. Prescription drugs, which require written doctor's orders, are designed to relieve symptoms or to cure the underlying disease. Because of a relatively narrow safety margin, their use must be carefully monitored.

In contrast, nonprescription drugs do not require written doctor's orders and are available over the counter at local drugstores. They do not cure diseases but are designed to relieve the symptoms associated with an illness. They can alleviate discomfort, but the body's natural defense mechanism provides the cure. Nonprescription drugs have a wider margin of safety than prescription drugs. However, this does not mean they are harmless. They can cause serious problems if they are not used according to the directions. Also, neither prescription nor nonprescription drugs should take the place of a visit to your physician when you have a major discomfort or illness.

PRESCRIPTION DRUGS ARE OBTAINED ONLY BY WRITTEN DOC-
TOR'S PRESCRIPTIONS. NONPRESCRIPTION DRUGS ARE AVAIL-
ABLE OVER THE COUNTER AT THE LOCAL DRUGSTORE.

When taken with a prescribed medication, nonprescription drugs may alter the intended effect of the prescribed medication. For this reason, it is critical that you consult your doctor or pharmacist before using nonprescription drugs if you are already using a prescription drug for the treatment of a condition or illness.

EXERCISE 2

Drug Identification

For every drug listed in Exercise 1, identify those that are prescription drugs and those that are nonprescription drugs.

HOW DRUGS WORK

The human body is a complex chemical organism. Effective body functioning depends on internal chemical processes. Drugs are also chemicals but are foreign to the body's natural chemistry. Drugs are prescribed to assist the body's natural chemical system. Alone, they do not cure what is wrong with a person. They produce chemical actions that modify or change a particular bodily function, thus allowing the body's natural defense system to restore health.

DRUGS AND MEDICATIONS PRODUCE CHEMICAL REACTIONS IN
THE BODY THAT ENABLE THE BODY'S NATURAL DEFENSE SYS-
TEM TO RESTORE HEALTH.

The task for the physician is to determine which drug will produce the desired effect. The success of drug treatment depends on the physician's ability to select the right drug for the individual and the illness. It depends, also, on the correct dosage taken at the recommended time of day. This selection process is important because the drug interacts with or interrupts the delicate chemistry of the body. The physician can never be sure that the prescribed drug will react in the way it is intended. For this reason, careful monitoring of drug treatment is important.

SUCCESSFUL DRUG INTERVENTION DEPENDS ON SELECTING THE RIGHT DRUG, USING THE RIGHT DOSAGE, AND ADMINISTERING THE DRUG AT THE RIGHT TIME OF DAY.

Taking any medication poses some potential hazards. These hazards are referred to as both side effects and precautions to drug use. Side effects are the undesirable reactions to a drug. Usually, they are an expected and predictable result of drug use and are unavoidable. Side effects can range from the mild to the extreme and depend on such factors as allergic reactions to the drug, the dosage, and when the drug is taken.

Precautions are the conditions under which the drugs are administered. Taking a drug before meals or after meals and avoiding use of alcohol while on a drug are examples of common precautions. Special precautions are generally written on the medication container. However, people with developmental disabilities or the staff should ask the physician to identify precautions associated with each drug. Ignoring precautions may result in unwanted or adverse side effects.

SIDE EFFECTS ARE THE UNDESIRABLE, YET USUALLY PREDICTABLE, RESULTS OF DRUG USE. PRECAUTIONS IDENTIFY THE CONDITIONS UNDER WHICH THE DRUG IS USED.

> **EXERCISE 3**
>
> Side Effects and Precautions
>
> Identify the side effects and precautions for each drug listed in Exercise 1.

Because it is not always possible to predict accurately an individual's reaction to a particular drug, the person taking a prescribed medication and the staff should know the possible side effects. Unfortunately, even the physician cannot predict the exact side effects of a prescribed drug.

Knowledgeable users can contribute to the management of their own drug therapy. Each person should know the intended purpose of the medication, precautions, potential side effects, and duration of the prescription. This knowledge can contribute to a safe and proper medical treatment. As a staff member, you should provide this knowledge to assist each person, when possible, to administer his or her own medication.

A WELL-INFORMED INDIVIDUAL CONTRIBUTES SUBSTAN-
TIALLY TO HIS OR HER OWN MEDICAL TREATMENT.

USE OF MEDICATIONS BY PEOPLE WITH DEVELOPMENTAL DISABILITIES

Approximately one-half of all people with developmental disabilities take one or more drugs routinely. The most common types of medications prescribed for people with developmental disabilities include antipsychotic, antianxiety, antidepressant, stimulant, and antiepileptic drugs.

Antipsychotic and Antianxiety Drugs

Antipsychotic and antianxiety drugs are the medications most frequently prescribed for people with developmental disabilities. These drugs are prescribed primarily to chemically alter the person's behavior. They are generally used for aggressive, destructive, and/or self-abusive behaviors. However, there are differences between these two categories of drugs. Antipsychotic drugs generally are strong or major tranquilizers. Antianxiety drugs refer to minor tranquilizers. Antipsychotic drugs are prescribed more often than antianxiety drugs.

Antipsychotic and antianxiety drugs have both short- and long-term side effects. Drowsiness, apathy, and lethargy are the most common short-term side effects. To a lesser degree, some individuals may experience a dry mouth, blurring of vision, urinary retention, abdominal pain, and constipation. Some people may experience motor restlessness; abrupt spasms of the head, neck, and upper back muscles; or body rigidity and a shuffling gait. In some instances, additional medications may be prescribed to alleviate these side effects. Weight gain and constant motor tremors appear to result from long-term use of antipsychotic and antianxiety drugs. The long-term effects of these drugs on learning, performance, and adaptive behaviors are not known at this time. Table 1 describes the antipsychotic and antianxiety drugs commonly prescribed.

Antidepressant Drugs

Antidepressant drugs are frequently prescribed for the treatment of depression in adults. This is especially true when the symptoms include psychomotor disabilities, sleep disorders, loss of appetite, weight loss, and constipation. Antidepressants have also been proved effective in such conditions as bed-wetting, childhood hyperactivity, school phobia, intense fright at night, head banging, and incontinence. They are generally prescribed for people with developmental disabilities to

Table 1. Antipsychotic and antianxiety drugs

Common name (brand name)	Intended effects	Potential side and adverse effects
Chlorpromazine (Thorazine)	Restoration of emotional calm Relief of severe anxiety Relief of agitation	Drowsiness Dryness of mouth Nasal congestion Constipation Skin rash Increased appetite and weight gain
Thioridazine (Mellaril)	Restoration of emotional calm Relief of severe anxiety Relief of psychotic behavior	Drowsiness Lethargy Blurred vision Nasal congestion Dryness of mouth Constipation Skin rash Headaches
Haloperidol (Haldol)	Restoration of emotional calm Relief of severe anxiety Relief of agitation Relief of psychotic behavior	Drowsiness Lethargy Blurred vision Dryness of mouth Constipation Impaired urination Transient drop in blood pressure Skin rash Insomnia Restlessness Anxiety Agitation Headache Dizziness Weakness
Chlordiazepoxide (Librium)	Relief of mild to moderate anxiety and nervous tension	Drowsiness Lethargy Unsteady gait Skin rashes Dizziness Fainting

(continued)

Potential side and adverse effects (*continued*)	Extended use	Special storage instructions
Parkinson's disease–like disorder Muscle spasms Muscle twitching Convulsions Decreased blood pressure Fainting	Tardive dyskinesia Eye changes Cataracts Impaired vision	Lid tightly closed Light-resistant container
Lightheadedness Confusion Agitation Restlessness Nausea Vomiting Loss of appetite Convulsions	Tardive dyskinesia Impaired vision	Lid tightly closed Light-resistant container
Lightheadedness Heart palpitations Rapid heart rate Reduced appetite Nausea Vomiting Diarrhea Parkinson's disease–like disorder Muscle spasms Convulsions Depression Confusion Hallucinations	Tardive dyskinesia	Airtight container Protect from light
Slurred speech Nausea Acute excitement Hallucinations Rage Depression	Psychological and/or physical dependency Impairment of liver functioning	Store in a dry place Airtight container Light-resistant container

(continued)

Table 1. (*continued*)

Common name (brand name)	Intended effects	Potential side and adverse effects
		Blurred vision
		Double vision
Diazepam (Valium)	Relief of mild to moderate anxiety and nervous tension	Drowsiness
		Lethargy
		Unsteady gait
		Skin rashes
		Dizziness
		Fainting
		Blurred vision
		Double vision

treat behavioral disorders, such as hyperactivity and aggressive behaviors.

The most common side effects of antidepressant drugs are dryness of the mouth, drowsiness, lethargy, nausea, and motor tremors. More serious long-term side effects include an adverse effect on the heart and constant motor tremors. Table 2 describes the antidepressant drugs most commonly used.

Stimulant Drugs

Stimulants are generally prescribed to treat minimal brain dysfunction, hyperactivity, and attentional deficit disorders. The intended outcome is to improve the attention span of the individual.

They are commonly administered in the treatment of behavioral deficits. They are often prescribed for individuals who demonstrate short attention spans, aggressive behavior toward others, impulsiveness, and restlessness.

The most common short-term side effects of stimulants are decreased appetite, coupled with weight loss, insomnia, headaches, and rapid or irregular heartbeat. Other possible side effects include dizziness, drowsiness, increased verbal behavior, and drug-induced psychosis. A possible long-term side effect of administering stimulants to children and adolescents may be the suppression of growth. Table 3 describes the stimulants commonly used.

Antiepilepsy Drugs

Antiepilepsy drugs are used in the treatment of seizure disorders. People with developmental disabilities have an increased incidence of epilepsy. The percentage of individuals with developmental disabil-

Potential side and adverse effects (*continued*)	Extended use	Special storage instructions
Parkinson's disease– like disorder		
Slurred speech	Psychological and/or physical depen- dency	Store in a dry place
Nausea		Tightly closed container
Acute excitement		Light-resistant container
Hallucinations	Impairment of liver function	
Rage		
Eye pain		
Glaucoma		
Emotional depression		

ities who also have epilepsy increases with the severity of disability. Approximately 50% of individuals with profound developmental disabilities have seizure disorders.

Antiepilepsy drugs, when effective, are successful in the treatment of epilepsy; however, only 50% of all individuals with epilepsy can achieve seizure control through the use of these medications. The nature and unpredictability of the side effects associated with the drugs also require that they be closely monitored. Side effects vary among individuals. The most common are decreased attention span, decreased motor performance, increased hyperactivity, drowsiness, loss of appetite, unsteady gait, slurred speech, and irritability. Table 4 details the antiepileptic drugs most commonly used.

STAFF RESPONSIBILITIES

Medications should not be the intervention of choice in the treatment of behavioral disorders. The interdisciplinary team should first investigate environmental factors that could be influencing the individual's behaviors. The team should also consider nutritional or behavioral interventions prior to medical treatment. Finally, drugs should not be prescribed for an individual who is annoying agency staff. Medications are never used for the convenience of the staff.

IN GENERAL, ADMINISTRATION OF A DRUG IS NOT THE FIRST RESPONSE TO AN INAPPROPRIATE BEHAVIOR.

The decision to administer a drug as the first intervention strategy may only mask the true problem. The use of drugs in this situation is

Table 2. Antidepressant drugs

Common name (brand name)	Intended effects	Potential side and adverse effects
Imipramine (Tofranil)	Gradual improvement of mood and relief of emotional depression	Drowsiness Blurring of vision Dryness of mouth Constipation Impaired urination Increased appetite for sweets Weight gain Tiredness Skin rash Hives Swelling of face or tongue Drug fever Nausea Headache
Desipramine (Norpramin) Nortriptyline (Aventyl, Pamelor) Phenelzine (Nardil)	Mood elevators General improvement of mood and relief of emotional depression	Drowsiness Blurring of vision Dryness of mouth Constipation Impaired urination Skin rash Hives Swelling of face and tongue Drug fever Nausea Indigestion Weakness
Phenelzine (Nardil)	Relief of certain types of mental depression	Rapid heartbeat Stiff or sore neck Chest pains Nausea Vomiting Constipation Diarrhea Fainting
Tranylcypromine (Parnate)	Gradual relief of emotional depression and improvement of mood	Insomnia Lightheadedness Dizziness Weakness Feeling of faintness Skin rash Headache Vertigo

Potential side and adverse effects (*continued*)	Extended use	Special storage instructions
Dizziness Weakness Unsteady gait Tremors Confusion Hallucinations Agitation Restlessness Nightmares Numbness Tingling Pain Loss of strength in arms and legs	No problem expected	Store in a dry place Tightly closed container
Unsteady gait Tremors Confusion Hallucinations Agitation Restlessness Nightmares Numbness Tingling Pain Loss of strength in arms and legs	No problem expected	Store in a dry place Tightly closed container
Unusually active Excitable Talkative Drowsiness Dryness of mouth Tiredness Weakness Insomnia	May be toxic to liver	Store in a dry place Tightly closed container
Agitation Confusion Impaired memory Tremors Blurred vision Nausea Vomiting Sweating	Conversion of mental depression into a state of hypomania (excessive mental and physical activity—excitement, agitation, loud and rapid talking, delusional thinking)	Store in a dry place Tightly closed container Store at room temperature

Table 3. Stimulant drugs

Common name (brand name)	Intended effects	Potential side and adverse effects
Pemoline (Cylert)	Treatment of behavioral problems in children	Loss of appetite Trouble sleeping Dizziness Drowsiness Headaches Increased irritability Depression
Amphetamine (Benzedrine)	Treatment of narcolepsy (the uncontrolled desire to sleep or sudden attacks of sleep at irregular intervals)	Chest pains Skin rash Unusual and uncontrolled movements of the head, neck, arms, and legs Irritability
Dextroamphetamine sulfate (D-amphetamine) (Dexedrine)	Treatment of narcolepsy Reduction of restlessness, distractibility, and impulsive behaviors characteristic of the abnormally hyperactive child Suppression of appetite in the management of weight reduction, using low-calorie diets	Nervousness Increased heart rate Insomnia Hives Headaches Dizziness Overstimulation
Methylphenidate hydrochloride (Ritalin)	Improved mood, confidence, initiative, and performance in states of fatigue and depression Reduction of restlessness, distractibility, and impulsive behavior in the abnormally hyperactive child	Nervousness Insomnia Skin rash Drug fever Joint pains Decreased appetite

not a permanent solution to the problem. The intervention strategy is effective only so long as the person is on medication; the problem often re-emerges when the medication is discontinued. An additional consideration is whether the intended benefits of the drug outweigh the potential side effects. The interdisciplinary team should determine if it is preferable for a person to have a few seizures or to function under the

Potential side and adverse effects (*continued*)	Extended use	Special storage instructions
Nausea Skin rash Stomachache Seizures Hallucinations Uncontrolled movement of eyes	Dyskinetic movements Rapid heartbeat	Store in a dry place Tightly closed container
Nervousness Restlessness Trouble sleeping Blurred vision Constipation Diarrhea Loss of appetite	Mood or mental changes Habit forming	Store in a dry place Tightly closed container
Increased blood pressure Psychotic episodes Weight loss Skin rashes Insomnia Excitability	Personality changes Severe psychological dependency Habit forming	Store in a dry place Tightly closed container Light-resistant container
Nausea Dizziness Drowsiness Headaches Excessive bruising	Suppression of growth	Store in a dry place Tightly closed container

influence of a drug. The combination of medications with other behavioral and educational interventions is often the more desirable and successful strategy.

Finally, even when a drug is effective in eliminating a behavior, the individual does not learn new and more desirable behavior patterns. The use of a drug does not take the place of a written behavior manage-

Table 4. Antiepilepsy drugs

Common name (brand name)	Intended effects	Potential side and adverse effects
Phenobarbital (Luminal)	Relief of mild to moderate anxiety or tension Sedation sufficient to induce sleep Prevention of epileptic seizures	Skin rashes Localized swelling Drug fever Dizziness Unsteadiness Nausea Vomiting Diarrhea Joint and muscle pain Unusual bleeding or bruising
Phenytoin sodium (Dilantin)	Prevention of epileptic seizures	Sluggishness Drowsiness Pink to red to brown coloration of urine Rash Headache Dizziness Staggering
Primidone (Mysoline)	Prevention of epileptic seizures	Drowsiness Lethargy A sense of mental and physical sluggishness Skin rash Dizziness Vertigo Unsteadiness
Carbamazepine (Tegretol)	Prevention of certain complex types of epileptic seizures	Dryness of mouth and throat Constipation Impaired urination Skin rash Itching Drug fever Headaches Dizziness Drowsiness

Potential side and adverse effects (*continued*)	Extended use	Special storage instructions
Drowsiness Lethargy A sense of mental and physical sluggishness Headaches Impaired vision Slurred speech Depression	Psychological and/or physical dependence	Store in a dry place Tightly closed container
Slurred speech Confusion Muscle twitching Nausea Vomiting Constipation Excessive hair growth	Weakened bones Lymph gland enlargement Possible liver damage Numbness and tingling of hands and feet Continual back-and-forth eye movement Bleeding, swollen, or tender gums	Store in a dry place Tightly closed container
Impaired coordination Reduced appetite Nausea Vomiting Nervousness Irritability Emotional disturbance	Lymph gland enlargement Thyroid gland enlargement Anemia Rickets in children and osteomalacia in adults (insufficient calcium to the bones)	Store in a dry place Tightly closed container
Unsteadiness Fatigue Blurred vision Confusion Water retention Hair loss Mental depression Agitation	Impaired liver functioning Possible liver damage Hair loss Ringing in ears	Store in a dry place Tightly closed container

ment plan, nor does it relieve the interdisciplinary team of its responsibility to develop an effective plan. The use of a drug as a behavior management technique should automatically alert the team to develop a written behavior management plan. The goal of the plan is to eliminate the need for drug intervention. This is true even in instances where the individual requires a drug for an acute psychiatric disorder. The medication should be administered within the context of a habilitation team process and written plan.

DRUGS DO NOT TAKE THE PLACE OF WRITTEN BEHAVIOR MANAGEMENT PLANS, NOR DO THEY RELIEVE THE INTERDISCIPLINARY TEAM OF ITS RESPONSIBILITY TO DEVELOP EFFECTIVE PLANS. THIS IS ALSO TRUE FOR INDIVIDUALS WITH ACUTE PSYCHIATRIC DISORDERS.

EFFECTS OF MEDICATIONS

Physicians generally do not have the opportunity to observe an individual for an extended time period before prescribing a medication. Moreover, individuals rarely have emotional outbursts or seizures during a doctor's appointment. As a result, the physician relies on information provided by the individual or by people familiar with the person. The staff may be asked to provide specific information about an individual that will assist in the diagnosis and treatment of medical problems. When a medication is administered, the dosage is gradually increased or decreased until the desired therapeutic effect is achieved. Information from agency staff is often crucial in changing and monitoring drug dosage. This information pertains to alterations in the person's behavior, noted side effects, and the desired outcome of drug treatment. The staff should be knowledgeable about the effects and uses of medications.

Be familiar with the medications prescribed for each person. Be aware, also, each time a person takes a specific medication. Note any physical, behavioral, or emotional changes that occur. Any changes during the first few days of medication may be the direct result of the new drug. Observed changes should be reported to the interdisciplinary team and to the physician, depending on the degree of changes.

INTERVENTION STRATEGIES AND MEDICATIONS

Drug treatment is considered successful if it produces the effect desired. Penicillin, for instance, may cure a throat infection after a few days. The medication thus produces the desired effects. Similarly, antiepilepsy medication may result in decreased seizure activities.

As mentioned earlier, drugs may also produce a range of undesired reactions in the individual. The severity of each undesired effect depends on the individual. An undesired effect of taking penicillin, for example, can range from an upset stomach to a dangerous allergic reaction. Drug treatment is an individual intervention process.

In some instances, a particular drug treatment may not be effective. For example, an antiepilepsy drug may not change seizure activity. The physician must then either increase the dosage or try other medications.

MEDICATION PLANS

Each person taking a prescription drug should have a medication plan that contains the following information:

Purpose and desired effect of the drug
Response time for accomplishing the desired effect
Undesired effects that may occur
Special consideration when other medications are taken
Special administration or storage instructions
Conditions under which to notify the physician

Each of these facets of a plan is discussed below.

Purpose and Desired Effect of the Drug

Why was the medication prescribed? There must be clear answers to this critical question. Is the drug taken for medical treatment, or is it being given for the convenience of the staff? This is a particularly relevant question when medications are given for the treatment of behavioral disorders.

Response Time

Most medications do not react immediately with the body. Drugs may be taken for several days before the desired effects are noticeable. Therefore, you must know how soon the medication is expected to take effect.

Undesired Effects of the Medication

You should recognize when a drug is causing an undesired side effect. You should also cooperate with the physician to ensure that the medication is compatible with educational and/or habilitation goals. For example, a side effect of a particular medication may be drowsiness. Increased drowsiness may interfere with the individual's performance in learning or work situations. In this case, you should cooperate with the physician in identifying other medications that produce the desired effects without causing drowsiness.

Both the individuals taking drugs and the staff must recognize the physical, behavioral, and emotional side effects of medications. Some medications may cause a person to become irritable, withdrawn, or overactive. Administration of some medications requires consultation with other professionals. For example, certain seizure medications that cause excessive gum growth may require consultation with a dentist. Or, a nutrition consultation may be necessary when a drug causes loss of appetite.

Possible Interactions with Other Drugs

When a person is taking two different medications, be aware of the possible effects one drug may have on the other. One medication may cause the other to have increased side effects, or one drug may cause the other to be less effective in treating the problem. A final consideration is that when taken together, the two medications may produce a reaction that is altogether different from the expected reaction of each individual drug. This reaction may be totally unpredictable and possibly dangerous.

Special Administration or Storage Instructions

Some medications require special administration or storage instructions. Note if medications are to be taken before a meal, after a meal, or with specific beverages. While some medications are being taken, use of other medications or substances, such as alcohol, may need to be avoided.

In addition, certain medications require refrigeration or storage in dark containers. The pharmacist or physician can identify these special considerations.

Conditions for Notifying the Physician

The physician should be notified immediately if any of the noted side effects are present. In addition, other symptoms may appear that are not noted in the drug literature. Notify the physician should any of the following occur:

Difficulty walking or maintaining balance
Slurred speech
Reported vision difficulty
High fever
Seizures (if unusual for the individual)
Confusion or incoherence
Vomiting or diarrhea
The wrong medication and/or dosage mistakenly given

Finally, you should feel free to call the physician if you have any questions or concerns. It is better to be safe and to have all concerns answered.

SUMMARY

Drugs are given for specific reasons. They produce desired biochemical reactions. No drug is curative. Rather, drugs assist the body's natural defense mechanism.

There are predictable side effects with any drug use. The severity of the side effects varies from individual to individual. The physician must select the right drug, in the right dosage, at the right time.

An estimated one-half of all people with developmental disabilities take one or more drugs routinely. As a staff member, you should assist people with developmental disabilities to learn safe and proper administration of drugs.

Finally, each person who takes drugs should have a medication plan. This plan should detail the purpose and desired effects of the drug, response time for accomplishing the desired effects, undesired effects that may occur, special considerations when taken with other medications, special storage instructions, and conditions under which to notify the physician.

BIBLIOGRAPHY

Aman, M.G., & Singh, N.N. (Eds.). (1988). *Psychopharmacology of the developmental disabilities.* New York: Springer-Verlag.

Gadow, K.D. (1988). *Pharmacotherapy and mental retardation.* Boston: Little, Brown.

ADDITIONAL RESOURCES

Consumer Reports Books. (1991), The complete drug reference (Mount Vernon, NY: Consumers Union), is a complete reference book on prescription and over-the-counter drugs.

SELF-APPRAISAL

INSTRUCTIONS

The following questions will help you evaluate your knowledge about drugs and medications. For true-false questions, check the correct answer. For multiple choice questions, circle the correct answer(s).

Note: There may be more than one correct answer for some questions.

1. Drugs and medications are chemical substances used in the medical treatment of a person.
   ___ True   ___ False

2. The term *nonprescription* drugs refers to the drugs and medications no longer needed by the person.
   ___ True   ___ False

3. Prescription drugs:
   a. Are obtained from a pharmacist
   b. Require a doctor's prescription
   c. Have a narrow margin of safety
   d. Have side effects

4. Drugs assist the body's natural defense mechanism in curing an illness.
   ___ True   ___ False

5. The success of drug treatment depends on the physician's ability to select the:
   a. Right drug
   b. Right dosage
   c. Right time of day for the drug to be administered
   d. Right generic form or brand name

6. Common drugs used for people with developmental disabilities include:
   a. Antipsychotic drugs
   b. Antianxiety drugs
   c. Antidepressant drugs
   d. Stimulants

7. The use of drugs and medications is the best approach to dealing with behavior problems in individuals.
   ___ True   ___ False

8. The physician decides what medications are needed based on:
   a. Direct observations of the individual
   b. Reports of the individual from the staff
   c. Reports from the interdisciplinary team
   d. Previous medical records

388

9. The dosage of a prescribed drug is rarely changed.
   ___ True   ___ False
10. For every drug and medication given, the following information should be known:
    a. The purpose and desired effect of the drug
    b. The response time for the drug
    c. Undesired effects of the drug
    d. Special storage instructions

CASE STUDY

Robert Daniels is a 53-year-old male with a diagnosis of severe mental retardation and a seizure disorder. Mr. Daniels has lived in a large state-operated intermediate care facility for persons with mental retardation (ICF/MR) since he was 18 years old. The county service coordination program has been working with Mr. Daniels, the ICF/MR, and a local residential provider to begin Mr. Daniels's transition into a four-person group home.

The institution staff have expressed concern about Mr. Daniels's ability to change his place of residence at age 53, as well as about the possibility of injury resulting from seizures. The community residential staff are concerned about these issues but feel that Mr. Daniels should move to the group home.

The service coordinator has identified a day program for Mr. Daniels. Many of Mr. Daniels's friends from the institution attend the program, which stresses socialization skills and leisure-time skills. The day program supplements the leisure-time program by transporting all 38 participants on community field trips to the local playground, swimming pool, restaurant, and other places.

The group home staff plan to develop more age- and culturally appropriate leisure-time activities for Mr. Daniels. They also plan to collect data over a 2-month period to document the frequency and type of his seizure activity. This information will be used in determining whether or not Mr. Daniels should continue to wear a protective helmet. Mr. Daniels has indicated to the service coordinator that he does not want to wear a helmet.

Situation

At a recent interdisciplinary team meeting, the group home staff expressed concern regarding Mr. Daniels's increased seizure activity. Data kept on seizure activity indicate that the change occurred shortly after his last physical examination. The service coordinator read the physician's report, which indicated a change in Mr. Daniels's medications. Mr. Daniels is now taking phenobarbital and phenytoin sodium (Dilantin). The physician indicated no need to see Mr. Daniels again until his next physical in 1 year.

1. Identify and discuss the information that all staff should have on the drugs Mr. Daniels is taking.
2. Identify and discuss the information that should be shared with the physician.
3. What recommendations would you make to the team regarding Mr. Daniels's use of medications and his work placement?

ANSWER KEY TO
SELF-APPRAISAL AND CASE STUDY

SELF-APPRAISAL

1. True
2. False
3. a, b, c, d
4. True
5. a, b, c
6. a, b, c, d
7. False
8. a, b, c, d
9. False
10. a, b, c, d

CASE STUDY ANSWER GUIDELINES

1. All staff should know the following information on each drug:

   The purpose and desired effects of the drug
   The response time for accomplishing the desired effects
   The undesired side effects that may occur
   Special considerations when more than one drug is being taken
   Conditions under which to notify the physician

   This information is needed to monitor Mr. Daniels's medical treatment.
2. The physician should be notified of any changes observed by the staff. The increased seizure activity and any other changes should be reported immediately. The staff should ask the physician why Mr. Daniels will not be seen for a year when his seizure rate has increased and when the medication has just been changed.
3. All staff should be alerted to the potential side effects associated with the change in medication. Drowsiness and sluggishness are potential side effects of both phenobarbital and Dilantin. Mr. Daniels should be observed for evidence of these side effects. The service coordinator could also ask the physician if other drugs could be administered that would not have these adverse side effects.

| chapter | Management |
| 18 | Responsibilities |

LEARNING OBJECTIVES

Upon completing this chapter, the reader will be able to:

1. Describe the differences between theory X and theory Y management approaches.
2. Identify four different management styles.
3. Define three rules for effective communication.
4. Identify six rules for reducing defensive behaviors.
5. Describe the six steps for effective problem solving.
6. Describe the seven requirements for effective negotiating.

INTRODUCTION

Many human services agency employees think that management issues are the responsibility of directors, administrators, and supervisors. This is generally true. All agency employees, however, whether or not they are directors, administrators, or supervisors, are called on to use management skills. You can develop and practice some of these skills, including those related to communication, problem solving, group process, conflict resolution, time management, and negotiation. Before considering these topics, however, this chapter reviews basic management concepts.

MANAGEMENT THEORY

A large body of information exists about management. There are many different theories about administration, leadership, and motivation, most of them based on contrasting views of human behavior. McGregor (1957) described these differing approaches as theory X and theory Y.

According to McGregor, theory X is a traditional approach to management that rests on three assumptions about people:

1. The average person dislikes work and will avoid it whenever possible.
2. Most people must be directed or threatened with punishment in the work situation.
3. The average person avoids responsibility, has little ambition, and wants security.

Theory X maintains that employees require close supervision. Authority is vested at the top and is delegated down. Employees work because of the threat of punishment or for the reward of a paycheck.

Theory Y, McGregor said, places greater emphasis on individual capabilities. It stresses the positive side of employee behavior. Theory Y rests on a very different set of five assumptions:

1. Physical and mental efforts in work are as natural as play or rest.
2. Punishment is not the only method for making people work toward organizational objectives.
3. The average person will accept responsibility.
4. Most people can exercise imagination and creativity in problem solving.
5. The intellectual capabilities of most employees are not fully utilized.

THEORY X MAINTAINS THAT EMPLOYEES REQUIRE CLOSE SUPERVISION.

THEORY Y PLACES GREATER EMPHASIS ON INDIVIDUAL CAPABILITIES.

Theory X may create a self-fulfilling prophecy that results in a vicious cycle. The blame for poor job performance is placed on the worker. The solution is greater supervision, punishment, or other restrictive measures. This only decreases the worker's sense of worth and self-esteem, thus leading to a further loss of motivation and productivity.

Theory Y, by contrast, lays the problem of poor performance at the feet of management. Problems, such as employee laziness or lack of cooperation, result from the failure of the agency's methods of control and organization. Management is held responsible for motivation and productivity. This does not mean that employees have no responsibility for performance. Certainly, employees who perform poorly can be found in agencies highly committed to theory Y, but probably the percentage of such employees is lower than in other agencies.

Human services agencies seldom adopt a total theory X or theory Y approach. Rather, they blend elements of both. Theory Y, however, is closer to the developmental model in human services. A human services agency should stress the capabilities and motivation of both its employees and consumers. The set of assumptions the agency holds about people applies to staff and consumers. Both supervisors and staff should develop the qualities of successful leaders and managers noted in Table 1.

MANAGEMENT STYLES

The different approaches to employee performance are reflected in various management styles. Likert (1967) developed a sequence of four management styles for organizations:

1. *Exploitative authoritarian*   In this system of management, all decisions are made at the top. Communication flows from the top to the bottom. Employees are told what to do. They are not able to voice their opinions. There is no teamwork.
2. *Benevolent authoritarian*   This model of management allows for some upward communication. Some contact occurs between management and workers, but teamwork is not encouraged.
3. *Consultative*   Communication takes place between management and staff. Workers feel responsible for and committed to organizational goals. Management makes policy decisions. Specific decisions are made at lower levels.

Table 1.   Qualities of successful leaders and managers

Develop qualities that are found in successful leaders and managers. Pay attention to:

Urgency—Make it a standard practice to complete work on time. Be interested in the job. Make suggestions and offer insight.

Caring—Let others know that you care about the dignity, rights, and feelings of people.

Opportunity—There is an adage that success is due to plain dumb luck. Dumb luck is helpful only if you are prepared for the lucky opportunity.

Sufficiency—Know how much energy you can put forth and what the return will be. Always insist upon quality. However, extra effort that results in marginal outputs is wasted.

Common sense—"The problem with common sense," remarked a case manager after an exasperating day, "is that it is just not that common." Common sense is not a substitute for knowledge; it is a requirement for making decisions.

---

4. *Participative* Communication takes place between management and staff. Both groups feel mutual trust and confidence. There is a commitment to organizational goals. Teamwork is encouraged.

Research has shown that, in general, the participative management style and theory Y systems are more productive than the authoritarian theory X systems. Table 2 illustrates the importance that employees place on management's feedback and input on their work performance. Nevertheless, many agencies continue to operate in theory X fashion.

MANAGEMENT PRACTICES IN TRANSITION

Organizations that provide services and supports to people with developmental disabilities display various management practices. You will need to determine if your agency uses a theory X or a theory Y approach. In a similar manner, you will have to figure out which management style your supervisor likes best. In addition to understanding your present situation, you should be aware of how management in human services may change in the future as a result of support service models. Supported living, supported employment, and family support programs are leading to smaller units of service and are placing more responsibility on the staff who provide support and services.

Reduction of Defined Hierarchies

When people with developmental disabilities make more decisions, organizational hierarchy (rank of authority) becomes less important.

Table 2. Elements of job satisfaction, as ranked by employees and managers

	Employees	Managers
Interesting work	1	5
Appreciation of work done	2	8
Feeling of being in on things	3	10
Job security	4	2
Good pay	5	1
Promotion and growth	6	3
Good working conditions	7	4
Loyalty to employees	8	7
Help with personal problems	9	9
Tactful discipline	10	6

From Jeffries, E. (1992). The heart of leadership. *Total Quality Newsletter,* 3(1), 3; reprinted with the permission of Lakewood Publications, 50 South Ninth St., Minneapolis, MN 55402.

Ranking: 1 = most important
10 = least important.

This means that the decision-making system in human services agencies is beginning to change. Vertical reporting systems of supervisor and employees are being replaced by peer networks. These peer networks of staff pass information across horizontal lines and provide each other with support and feedback. The pathways for exercising influence and making changes have increased. Bennis (1989) has noted that, in the new organizations, leaders emerge as they learn to influence and persuade without direct authority.

Changes in Middle Manager Roles

The role of middle managers is changing from that of boss to that of mentor and coach. The focus of attention is switching from "how the new employee is doing" to "how well the coach is teaching." The new employee's performance depends on the capability of the coach. Successful middle managers no longer tell new employees what to do but teach them why and how to do their tasks. This requires on-the-job, day-to-day communication with the staff. A lack of regular feedback to the staff can prevent new staff members from developing skills and insights.

Learning Experiences of Organizations

People with developmental disabilities and the staffs of service and support agencies all learn through experience. This fact becomes even more obvious as services become more individualized and decentralized. Fewer rules and procedures guide decision making by the staff and individuals with developmental disabilities. Both the staff and people with developmental disabilities learn together how to adapt and change. The knowledge gained through experience in problem solving can produce new insights and leadership skills.

Experiential learning (or that derived from experience) is an unrecognized source of leadership for people with developmental disabilities and for new staff members. Leaders emerge through a process of reflecting on experience. Organizations must allow both people with developmental disabilities and staff members the freedom to succeed or fail. What is needed, wrote Bennis (1989, p. 182), is "an organization's commitment to providing its potential leaders with opportunities to learn through experience in an environment that permits growth and change."

FUNDAMENTAL SKILLS

Traditional service organizations stressed policy, procedure, and supervision. New decentralized support programs require some structure, but they also need more staff skills. Communication and problem-solving skills, as well as the ability to deal with differences, negotiation, time management, and feedback, are primary requirements for all staff members.

Communication

Good communication begins with good listening. The first rule of effective communication is to listen to the speaker. In order to listen, you have to stop talking. Also, you have to delay thinking about what you want to say. Individuals sometimes listen to only parts of a discussion. They hear only what they want to hear.

The second rule of effective communication is to be an active listener. An active listener helps to clarify the meaning of messages by paraphrasing statements. State your understanding of the message you received. You do this when you say, "Do you mean . . . ?"

An effective and active listener reaches for more information. Help the speaker to focus on solutions and conclusions. Assist in this process by asking "how" and "what" questions, such as the following:

What do you want?
What is missing?
How would you like to see it change?
What would you like to do?
How could you make that happen?
What additional information do you need?

Avoid asking "why" questions. "Why" questions tend to make people defensive. Also, they focus on the past and on problems; they do not address solutions and the future. Table 3 includes suggestions for effective listening.

Table 3. Suggestions for effective listening

---

1. Stop talking—
   You cannot talk and listen at the same time.
2. Make the talker feel comfortable and relaxed—
   See the other person's point of view; allow open discussion.
3. Demonstrate that you are interested—
   Do not yawn or take telephone calls during the conversation.
4. Allow time for the point to be made—
   Do not interrupt or head for the door.
5. Do not become angry—
   Do not speak in anger. When you speak in anger, you may communicate the wrong message.
6. Do not argue or criticize—
   Bringing up arguments and criticisms only raises defensiveness.
7. Ask questions—
   This is concrete evidence that you are interested.

The third rule of effective communication is to convey the message you intend. Make sure that you send the right message by stating the intention of the communication. Why are you communicating? Are you giving information or trying to influence a decision? You also need to identify your frame of reference. For instance, are you speaking as an employee or as a baseball fan? Are you speaking as an angry employee or as a motivated employee?

Also, state your assumptions; the receiver may not be aware of them. For example, you suggest to your supervisor that the workshop should close early. Without explaining that you think it will snow, however, you are not communicating your assumptions. Finally, you can be more specific by giving examples of what you mean.

Communication is also more effective if you speak in the receiver's language. Understand the receiver. Make statements the person will understand. Use examples that are part of the receiver's frame of reference. As an illustration, avoid using examples from the vocational program when talking to the residential staff about mealtime behaviors.

In addition, communication is improved by sending consistent messages. For example, if you change your intentions, assumptions, or frame of reference, you will likely change what the receiver hears. The receiver will then become confused.

AVOID ASKING "WHY" QUESTIONS. "WHY" QUESTIONS CAN MAKE PEOPLE DEFENSIVE.

Finally, you can ensure effective communication by sending repeated messages. It does not hurt to repeat yourself. You can also communicate the same idea in different ways—by using new wording, gesturing with your hands, or varying the tone and volume of your speech.

Nonverbal Communication

The effectiveness of your listening and sending skills is greatly influenced by nonverbal communication. This refers to messages given in nonverbal, and generally nonwritten, communication. Nonverbal communication takes place when body motions convey meaning. Facial expressions, for example, can indicate surprise, sadness, anger, or joy. The eyes also communicate. Avoiding another person's glance is sometimes considered evasive. Staring at another person is not polite. Frequency of eye contact and pupil dilation also conveys meaning. Most importantly, the eyes signal a willingness or reluctance to communicate. For example, frequent withdrawal of eye contact ends a conversation. The hands, arms, and legs are also used in communication. Crossed arms and legs generally indicate defensiveness; rapid movement of the hands and arms shows excitement and intensity.

Your distance from another person sends messages. Personal space zones surround most individuals. People 12 feet or more from you generally go unnoticed. The business or social zone extends from 4 to 12 feet away from the other person. Most business and social interaction takes place in this sphere. A distance of 1–4 feet is a personal zone for very close relationships. The space within 1 foot is usually reserved for intimate relationships.

There are many other types of nonverbal communication. One's manner of dress, the arrangement of office space and furniture, and the time that events take place convey meaning. Touch and smell carry messages. Decoration, posture, and type of automobile are additional forms of nonverbal communication.

Defensive Communication

Effectiveness of communication is increased when the verbal and nonverbal messages are consistent. Nonverbal communication should reinforce verbal messages. For example, if you calmly ask your supervisor for instructions while standing 12 feet away with your arms crossed, you are sending a mixed message. Similarly, you are confusing the communication if your facial expression and eyes indicate anger but your verbal message is calm in content, tone, and volume. Mixed and confusing communication can be perceived by the listener as a threat. The fear of threat causes defensive behavior, which then results in defensive listening. This prevents the listener from sensing the motives, values, and emotions of the sender. Six aspects of "defensiveness—supportiveness" that influence the perceptions of the receiver are:

1. *Evaluation–description*　Speech that appears to evaluate can increase listener defensiveness. Try to describe situations. Attempt to avoid judging or evaluating others.
2. *Control–creativity*　Verbal and nonverbal communication that attempts to control people causes defensiveness. Trying to persuade the listener to accept a predetermined outcome causes defensive behavior. Instead, the sender should indicate a desire to work with the listener to identify and solve problems in a creative manner, rather than forcing a solution.
3. *Strategy–spontaneity*　If the sender is perceived as working through an elaborate strategy, the listener may become suspicious. Spontaneity in a discussion conveys to the listener that he or she is not a victim of hidden manipulation. This does not mean that planning should not take place prior to meetings. It does mean that the listener is allowed to participate in the direction of the discussion.
4. *Neutrality–empathy*　Sometimes the listener feels that the sender's neutrality in speech indicates a lack of concern for the listener's welfare. Communication that conveys empathy, or concern, reduces defensiveness.

5. *Superiority–equality*   When the sender communicates superiority in power, wealth, or intelligence, for example, the listener may become defensive. Downplaying differences in status, ability, and power reduces defensive behavior.
6. *Certainty–open-minded*   Attitudes of certainty and arrogance lead to defensiveness. The sender who appears willing to accept different positions may cause less defensiveness. Problem solving, rather than debating, increases the supportive climate.

EXERCISE 1

Behaviors and Messages

Assume you are participating in a team meeting. The behaviors listed in the left column are exhibited by other team members. In the right column, write out the message the behavior would send you, as shown in behavior No. 1.

Behavior	Message
1. Team members dispute your information and ask where you received it.	The team members do not place a high regard on my abilities to gather information.
2. A team member arrives late and leaves early, citing the pressure of other meetings.	
3. Team members tell you that your presence helped the meeting along. Your clarifying and summarizing statements were very helpful.	
4. Two team members avoid eye contact and do not talk to each other.	
5. Team members provide concise and well-documented reports.	

Feedback

Providing feedback is a vital aspect of communication. In giving feedback, remember the six rules listed above for reducing defensive behaviors. In addition, keep feedback specific, rather than general. Telling your peers that they made mistakes may not be particularly helpful. Instead, you can be specific and say, "You used the admission form instead of the following form."

FEEDBACK SHOULD BE SPECIFIC, RATHER THAN GENERAL.

Also, focus on the behavior, not the person. Telling a person that he has "talked 10 minutes longer than anyone else" is more acceptable than calling him a "loudmouth." In addition, the feedback should focus on a behavior under the control of the receiver.

Feedback should address the needs of the receiver. Feedback that makes you feel good may be of little use to the receiver. Feedback should be solicited by the receiver or volunteered by the sender; it should never be imposed by the sender. The amount of feedback depends on the capacity of the receiver, rather than the feelings of the sender. Sometimes you may have a great deal to say but you recognize that the receiver can work with only part of it. Finally, feedback should share information but not provide advice. Feedback should be descriptive, not judgmental. Table 4 summarizes rules for providing helpful feedback.

Problem Solving

The patterns of problem solving are the same whether you are working with a management team, with people with developmental disabilities, or on your own. You can apply the same method in different situations. Problem solving can be broken down into seven steps:

1. Define the problem. The written definition of the problem should be a specific statement that is neither too general nor too narrow.
2. Identify criteria for evaluating possible solutions. For example, consider a person with a developmental disability who needs a residential placement. The concept of least restrictive alternative and the principle of normalization are two criteria that you could use to evaluate solutions.
3. Identify sources of information. You can talk with others who had the same problem.
4. Generate as many solutions as possible. Identify all possible alternatives. List even those that seem silly. The most serious mistake you can make is to list only the first solution that comes to mind. Always ask, "What are the alternatives?"
5. Make a decision and choose the best alternative. Apply the decision criteria to each of the possible alternatives. Choose the alternative that best meets the criteria. You also must determine if the

Table 4. Rules for helpful feedback

Feedback is:
Descriptive, not evaluative
Specific, not general
Relevant to the needs of the receiver
Desired by the receiver
Timely
Concerned with a behavior over which the receiver has control

resources are available to implement the alternative. If the resources are not available, you will need to pick the next best alternative.

6. Implement the alternative. Define individual duties and responsibilities.

7. Define a method to evaluate the alternative. The evaluation plan should define the data that will be needed. The plan should state who will conduct the evaluation. A time-line should be established.

This decision and problem-solving process can be used in many different solutions. The process is rather straightforward if you are the only decision maker. But what if several people are required to make a decision as a team? In this case, the consensus method is preferred.

The consensus method is an example of the participative management style, mentioned in the earlier section on management styles. In consensus decision making, every member of the group has an equal opportunity to influence the decision. Final decisions must be unanimous. This is not the same as voting or leaving the final decision to the supervisor. Consensus requires that team members display good communication and group process skills.

Differences of opinion will surface during the consensus decision-making process. However, if all team members try to reduce defensiveness and provide effective feedback, consensus can be reached. Other decision-making methods may be quicker. Some may involve less work. The advantage of consensus is that when the decision is made, all team members are committed to the decision and less time is needed to carry it out. Table 5 indicates the time frame for several decision-making models.

Table 5. Time frame for group decisions

Approach	Time required to make a decision	Time required to develop a commitment to the decision	Time needed to implement the decision	Average total time
Leader-imposed decision	Short	Long	Long	Long
Group consensus with leadership	Moderate	Short	Short	Moderate
Group consensus with no leadership	Long	Moderate	Moderate	Long

Source: Adapted from Morris and Sashkin (1976).

SMALL GROUP PROCESS

The success of consensus depends on the effectiveness of the small group process. The purpose of small group meetings is to concentrate on a common objective. One group may be the team that develops the individualized service plan (ISP). Another group may consist of administrators working on a plan for new vocational services. All small groups do both *content* work and *process* work. Content work is the *what* of the meeting. Defining problems, evaluating alternatives, and choosing solutions are examples of content. Issues related to the ISP or the new vocational service are content work.

Process work is the *how* of the meeting. Mediating differences of opinion, helping others contribute ideas, praising others, and adding humor are examples of process. Moving the discussion to a successful conclusion is the process of the meeting.

In order to complete its content and process work, members of the group must complete five activities:

1. Initiating—suggesting new ideas or ways to work
2. Clarifying—clearing up complicated ideas
3. Coordinating—integrating and tying ideas together
4. Summarizing—keeping work focused and offering conclusions
5. Logistical—arranging the meeting and taking notes

In addition to completing tasks, groups need to build unity and confidence. In order to provide a supportive setting for group members, maintenance functions are required:

1. Supporting—team members providing support to each other
2. Harmonizing—mediating differences and relieving tension
3. Gatekeeping—helping or allowing all members to participate in the discussion
4. Providing feedback—team members giving constructive feedback to one another
5. Following—allowing others to take the lead

EXERCISE 2

Group Meeting Report

Arrange to attend a small group meeting. The group should consist of four to seven members. Observe the group interaction and determine how often members of the group do the following:

1. Attempt to define or clarify the problem:
   Often   Sometimes   Never

(continued)

EXERCISE 2

(continued)

2. Listen and try to understand all points of view:
   Often   Sometimes   Never
3. Ask questions to clarify issues:
   Often   Sometimes   Never
4. Encourage and support each other:
   Often   Sometimes   Never
5. Identify alternatives but defer judgment:
   Often   Sometimes   Never
6. Attempt to gather all the facts:
   Often   Sometimes   Never
7. Accept differences of opinion:
   Often   Sometimes   Never
8. Provide constructive feedback to each other:
   Often   Sometimes   Never

Conflict Resolution

Differences between individuals can grow into conflicts. In general, there are three types of conflict. The first results from failure in communication or lack of understanding. Different interpretations can result from miscommunication. Providing the correct information (and undoing any damaged egos) generally solves the problem. For example, two counselors may engage in a heated discussion because the director of residential programs gave them conflicting instructions.

Substantive problems, the second type of conflict, are more difficult to manage. Two department directors wanting the same space and inequalities in a pay scale are two examples. Differences in responsibility and authority or disagreements over the patterns of work allocation can cause substantive problems.

Substantive problems can be solved structurally or behaviorally. Structural solutions take place when you remove the basis for the conflict. For example, inequalities in the pay scale can be corrected and work allocated in a fair manner. Behavioral solutions take place when those in conflict work through their problems and resolve the conflicts.

The third type of conflict occurs when two people have different personal feelings or values. Unless one of the parties is willing to change his or her values (a rare situation), the differences remain. In this case, the best solution is to agree to disagree.

A wide variety of methods or approaches are available to deal with conflict. The use of each depends on the particular circumstances, as described in the following five examples:

1. *Avoiding and smoothing*   These two approaches require no decisions. Avoiding the conflict means that it is never openly dis-

cussed. In smoothing the conflict, the manager recognizes that "the conflict is due to two different personalities." The manager simply asks the people to get along; these are a legitimate responses when two people cannot reach agreement. Using these approaches too frequently, however, may indicate that needed decisions are not being made.

2. *Unilateral mode* A decision is made by one of the two parties. The decision is made without consulting others. It may only increase the conflict. The advantage of the unilateral mode is that a decision is made. This approach is least useful in interpersonal conflicts.

3. *Forcing mode* Issues may be discussed, but one party uses power to influence the outcome. Many decisions in an agency are forced. The manager assesses a situation and makes a decision. In interpersonal conflicts, forcing deals only with the immediate situation; the personal ill feelings remain.

4. *Bargaining* This approach involves an exchange of information. However, it also results in posturing and distortion of information. Bargaining is a less than optimal approach because it reduces openness and trust between the parties.

5. *Problem solving* To use this approach, both parties must face their differences. Each must have a positive reason for negotiating a solution. This approach may take a bit longer, and it requires high interpersonal skills.

Negotiation

Many conflict situations can be avoided if you negotiate differences constructively. Through negotiation, differences are not allowed to escalate into conflicts. More importantly, interpersonal relationships are not damaged, as often happens when conflicts occur.

There are six rules of successful negotiation (Fisher & Ury, 1981). The first rule is to separate the person from the problem. You may have to negotiate with a reasonable person who has a terrible problem. Separate the two so that you do not approach the individual as a terrible person with a problem. Also, try to view the problem as the other person does. Understanding the motives of the other person does not mean that you accept them.

SEPARATE THE PERSON FROM THE PROBLEM.

The second rule is to never deduce another's motives from your own fears. People tend to assume that adversaries will consciously and deliberately do just what they fear. Avoid interpreting in the worst light what an opponent says or does.

DO NOT DEDUCE ANOTHER'S MOTIVES FROM YOUR OWN FEARS.

The third rule of successful negotiation is to be consistent in applying the motivation-outcome rule. This rule states that you will expect others to judge you in the same manner that you judge them. People tend to judge others by what others do, while judging themselves by their intentions. Be consistent. You can judge motives or outcomes. Be sure you apply the same measures to both yourself and your adversaries.

JUDGE OTHERS BY THE SAME MEASURES BY WHICH YOU WANT
TO BE JUDGED.

The fourth rule is to focus on interests and not on position. Multiple positions can satisfy a single interest. You can argue your interest without becoming locked into a particular position. Also, the most powerful interests are generally basic human needs. These include security, economic well-being, sense of belonging, recognition, and autonomy.

FOCUS ON INTERESTS, NOT POSITIONS.

Consider this example of interests and position. Assume that you are a staff member in a supported employment program. You have taken the position that you need a salary increase. There could be multiple interests for wanting an increase in pay. You may feel you deserve more recognition; you may also feel you have increased your productivity, or that you work harder than other employees. If your interest is recognition, a salary increase is only one position. Other positions that could potentially satisfy this interest are more verbal feedback or increased job responsibilities.

A fifth rule of successful negotiation is to give positive support to the other party. The level of support corresponds to the intensity of your attack on the problem. The more you attack the problem, the more you support the other person. This may perhaps result in the person disassociating himself or herself from the problem.

BE HARD ON PROBLEMS BUT EASY ON PEOPLE.

Good negotiating also requires options for mutual gain. The sixth rule, then, is to find solutions that represent a gain for both parties. The other party does not have to lose in order for you to succeed. In some instances, negotiations are successful because each party wants a different outcome or has a different interest.

FIND OPTIONS FOR MUTUAL GAIN.

TIME MANAGEMENT

Many aspects of time management are important to employees who are not in management positions. Human services agencies are very labor intensive. Agencies accomplish objectives by direct staff work. Automation, computers, and robots cannot do direct tasks in human services. As a result, the expenditure of time is an important issue. Staff time is the major capital resource of the human services agency.

Time management is a life-management process. You will never have enough time to do everything that you enjoy or that is important. Most people would like more time for travel, sports, hobbies, or relaxation. Many people would like some extra time to think about what is really important in relation to the limited time they have.

The reality of limited time requires certain resolutions about how you deal with time. For example, you should:

Recognize the importance of assigning priorities to events and tasks. Identify the most important personal and work goals. Decide how you will accomplish those.

Be aware that the decision to take on a task means that you will be unable to do another task. What is the other task? How important is it?

Time management at work begins with your job description, which should provide the duties and responsibilities of your position. After reading it, you should know why you were hired, what you are expected to do, how you should do it, and what resources are required. The job description provides the first information about managing your time. Agency policy and procedure can provide additional information about work hours, breaks, and other time issues.

The mission statement of the agency should also help you to set priorities. If the agency lacks a mission statement or does not have a job description, be concerned. You cannot manage your time if the agency cannot identify its goals or has not defined your duties.

TIME MANAGEMENT IS A LIFE-MANAGEMENT PROCESS.

In addition, conscious and unconscious agreements use up your time. You may make various agreements about time distribution. For example, you agree to complete the achievement reports by Friday and you attend staff meetings every Monday morning. Other agreements are more unconscious. For example, your past behavior has indicated that you will listen to coworkers whenever they stop by.

EXERCISE 3

Unconscious Agreements

List five unconscious agreements you may have made that result in wasted time. How can you renegotiate those agreements?

Agreement	Method for renegotiation
1.	
2.	
3.	
4.	
5.	

As you develop priorities for your time, make two lists. First list the tasks you must do to complete the job. Then list the tasks you want to do. This second list is a statement of personal work goals. You will need a good balance between the many tasks required by the agency and the personal work goals that are important to you.

In generating your list, consider aspects of priority and output. Priority means those tasks that must be completed as soon as possible. Activities can be either low or high priority. Output refers to the importance of the task to you. Tasks also have a high or low output. The irony is that many high-output tasks are not high priority. The routine tasks of organizational maintenance have high priority. In arranging your time, pay attention to low-priority, high-output tasks. They may become complicated, risky, or challenging. But until you give those tasks time, there cannot be any major achievements.

Many tasks are low-priority, low-output activities. These include writing progress reports on ISPs, ordering teaching materials, or completing agency reports. Sometimes you may see these as time wasters.

However, these are really responsibilities that are required as part of the job. Perhaps you can suggest ways to do those tasks more efficiently.

Real time wasters can be separated into two groups. Group A consists of wasters that are caused by people or circumstances outside the agency. Group B consists of wasters under the control of agency staff. Table 6 lists examples of both types of time wasters.

EXERCISE 4

Time Wasters

Review your own situation. Generate your own list of group A and group B time wasters.

Group A	Group B

After examining your own time-management situation, you may conclude that you have too much work. If you are feeling overwhelmed and frustrated, determine if any of the following may be true:

You are attempting to do too much.
You need to say, "no," more often.
You have a need to feel busy.

Table 6. Time wasters

Group A	Group B
Meetings	Boredom
Telephone calls	Procrastination
Supervisors	Forgetfulness
Forms	Too much work
Reports	Inability to say, "no"
Confused agency goals	Poor attitude
Conflicting priorities	No organization
Drop-ins	

You have not clearly defined your goals.

You are too disorganized.

You like to feel busy. Being busy lets you avoid high-output, low-priority goals.

If you decide that any of these may be true, draw up a plan to better manage your time. Increasing your time-management skills provides a natural reinforcer—you will have more time to do what you want.

EXERCISE 5

Time Management Self-Survey

Determine your time management skills and eliminate your time wasters.

Fill out a daily time log and identify those events that occupied most of your time. How could you decrease the time spent on those events?

Time of day	What took place?	How long did it take?	Comments

SUMMARY

The human services agency staff are provided many opportunities to exercise good management skills. These skills can improve your ability to communicate and participate in team meetings. They should help you to deal with conflict and to increase your negotiation capabilities. Good skills increase your personal satisfaction while on the job and allow more time to do those activities you enjoy.

Improving your management skills helps you to be more effective and efficient in providing services to people with developmental disabilities. Good communication, problem-solving, and time-management skills give you more time for direct service. Moreover, the quality of service is enhanced.

Finally, developing basic management skills is a primary requirement for being a good manager. You can begin to produce and refine those skills. Pay particular attention to management skills that provide the biggest output for people with developmental disabilities, the agency, and yourself.

BIBLIOGRAPHY

Bennis, W. (1989). On becoming a leader. Reading, MA: Addison-Wesley.

Fisher, R., & Ury, W. (1981). Getting to yes: Negotiating agreement without giving in. Boston: Houghton Mifflin.

French, W.L., & Bell, C.H. (1984). Organization development: Behavioral science interventions for organization development. Englewood Cliffs, NJ: Prentice Hall.

Jeffries, E. (1992, January). The heart of leadership. Total Quality Newsletter, 3(1) 3.

Likert, R. (1967). The human organization. New York: McGraw-Hill.

McGregor, D. (1957). The human side of enterprise. Management Review, 46, 22–28; 88–92.

Morris, W.C., & Sashkin, M. (1976). Organization behavior in action: Skill building experiences. New York: West Publishing Co.

Schon, D.A. (1983). The reflective practitioner: How professionals think in action. New York: Basic Books.

ADDITIONAL RESOURCES

W. Bennis and B. Nanus (1985), in Leaders (New York: Harper & Row), and W. Bennis (1989), in On becoming a leader (Reading, MA: Addison-Wesley), point to the differences between leaders and managers. J. Kouzes and B. Posner (1987), in The leadership challenge: How to get extraordinary things done in organizations (San Francisco: Jossey-Bass), provide a practical manual on leadership.

G.S. Bernstein and J.A. Halaszyn (1989), in "Human services? . . . That must be so rewarding.": A practical guide for professional development (Baltimore: Paul H. Brookes Publishing Co.), provide a practical approach to key issues in career development for staff in human services. Chapters include time management, stress management, communication, professional relationships, professional development, and how to work with other people's issues.

W.E. Deming (1982), in Quality, productivity, and competitive position (Cambridge, MA: MIT Center of Advanced Engineering Study), provides an overview of Deming's Fourteen Points of quality management that pertain to quality in production and service settings. K. Albrecht and R. Zemke (1985), in Service America; Doing business in the new economy (New York: Warner Books), and V. Ziethaml, A. Parasuraman, and L. Berry (1990), in Delivering quality services: Balancing customer perceptions and expectations (New York: Free Press), narrow the focus to quality management in service settings. Zeithaml et al., in particular, have much to offer the human services industry.

C. Green and D. Reid (1991), in Reinforcing staff performance in residential facilities: A survey of common managerial practices, Mental Retardation,

29(4), 195–200, discuss alternative methods for providing feedback to staff to reinforce performance.

R. Horner, L. Thompsen, and K. Story (1990), in Effects of case manager feedback on the quality of individual habilitation plan objectives, *Mental Retardation*, 28(4), 227–231, describe the relationship between providing staff feedback and the quality of service plans.

R.M. Kanter (1989), in The new managerial work, *Harvard Business Review*, November–December, 85–92; A. Cohen and D. Bradford (1990), in *Influence without authority* (New York: John Wiley & Sons), discuss the emerging trend of managing and leading through the use of influence rather than hierarchical authority.

H. Koontz and H. Weihrich (1990), *Essentials of management* (5th ed.) (New York: McGraw-Hill), is a basic text on management.

L. Leritz (1987), in *No fault negotiating: A simple and innovative approach for solving problems, reaching agreements and resolving conflicts* (New York: Warner Books), supplements Fisher and Ury (1981) on negotiating skills.

T. Peters and R. Waterman (1982), in *In search of excellence* (New York: Harper & Row); T. Peters and N. Austin (1985), in *A Passion for excellence* (New York: Random House); and T. Peters (1987), in *Thriving on chaos: Handbook for management revolution* (New York: Alfred A. Knopf), address the theme of management for excellence.

SELF-APPRAISAL

INSTRUCTIONS

The following questions will help you evaluate your knowledge about management skills. For true-false questions, check the correct answer. For multiple choice questions, circle the correct answer(s).

Note: There may be more than one correct answer for some questions.

1. The theory X management model makes these assumptions about people:
   a. The average person dislikes work
   b. The average person will accept responsibility
   c. Most people must be directed in the work setting
   d. The intellectual capabilities of most employees are not fully utilized
2. The theory Y management model makes these assumptions about people:
   a. Physical and mental efforts in work are natural.
   b. Punishment is not the only method for making people work.
   c. The average person avoids responsibility.
   d. Personal goals are incompatible with work goals.
3. The four different management styles include:
   a. Exploitative—authoritarian
   b. Benevolent—authoritarian
   c. Participative
   d. Consultative
4. The following are rules for effective communication:
   a. Type all messages
   b. Speak very loudly
   c. Speak very slowly
   d. Listen closely
5. Feedback is:
   a. Evaluative
   b. General
   c. Descriptive
   d. Judgmental
6. The steps in problem solving after defining the problem, identifying criteria for evaluating solutions, and identifying sources of information include:
   a. Generating alternatives
   b. Choosing the best alternative

    c. Making changes in policy and procedure

    d. Evaluating the alternative

7. The following are maintenance functions required for the small group process:

    a. Supporting

    b. Harmonizing

    c. Clarifying

    d. Coordinating

8. Which of the following are methods for dealing with conflict:

    a. Avoiding and smoothing

    b. Unilateral mode

    c. Forcing mode

    d. Bargaining

9. Effective time management indicates that you should concentrate on low-priority, high-outcome tasks.

    _____ True   _____ False

10. Successful negotiation requires that you:

    a. Separate the person from the problems

    b. Focus on interests, not positions

    c. Remain truthful and share all information

    d. Find options for mutual gain

CASE STUDY

Kathy Bennis is a new employee of Monroe Enterprises, a private non-profit agency providing employment evaluations and placement services for adults with developmental disabilities. Ms. Bennis completed a 2-year program in psychology at the nearby community college. At age 21, she decided to begin work at Monroe Enterprises and to pursue her bachelor of arts degree at the state university's evening college.

The agency accepts people with developmental disabilities for a 6- to 8-week employment evaluation process. During this time, the person is evaluated in a variety of job skills that range from operating power tools to performing general office support services. The agency also determines the person's preference for employment options. Finally, the agency places people with developmental disabilities in supervised employment situations in private business.

The agency's orientation program consists of two half-day orientation sessions for all employees who have joined the agency during each 2-month period. All supervising personnel are expected to provide follow-up consultation on a monthly basis throughout the 6-month probationary period.

Ms. Bennis's job requires that she monitor the individual progress of workers in the supervised employment setting. She is out in the field an average of 6 hours a day. The remaining 2 hours are devoted to paperwork in an office she shares with two other staff members who perform evaluations at Monroe Enterprises.

Situation

Ms. Bennis began work 1 week after the last orientation session. Therefore, she has had to wait 2 months for the next session. During this time, she has noticed that her actual job responsibilities are different from those in her job description. In addition, she does not feel that she is part of a work group because she spends so much time out of the office. This situation is aggravated because the monthly supervision has not been provided on a regular basis.

1. What difficulties could arise from delaying the orientation for 2 months?
2. What difficulties arise when employment duties are different from those detailed in the job description?
3. Ms. Bennis feels that decisions regarding agency policy and procedures should be made more quickly. Her concern is that too much time is spent in reaching a consensus. What advice would you provide Ms. Bennis?

ANSWER KEY TO
SELF-APPRAISAL AND CASE STUDY

SELF-APPRAISAL

1. a, c
2. a, b
3. a, b, c, d
4. d
5. c
6. a, b, d
7. a, b
8. a, b, c, d
9. True
10. a, b, d

CASE STUDY ANSWER GUIDELINES

1. New employees may not know what to do when uncertainties and issues arise. More importantly, employees begin without understanding the basic mission and values of the organization. Finally, the agency employee has a responsibility to consistently follow established policy and procedures. The employee orientation should provide new workers with an overview of the agency's policies and procedures.

2. In this situation, employees are sometimes asked to execute duties they were not trained to perform. Differences between actual duties and the job description also create confusion about what duties and responsibilities new staff members are expected to assume. Finally, these differences increase the possibility of interpersonal conflict among staff members because roles and responsibilities are not well defined.

3. Consensus decision making does take more time than decisions imposed by a single individual. However, the time needed to develop agreement on the decision and then to implement the decision is shorter in consensus decision making.

Maintaining and Enhancing Quality of Services

LEARNING OBJECTIVES

Upon completing this chapter, the reader will be able to:

1. Identify six traditional methods of quality enhancement.
2. Define quality of life measures.
3. Define quality as satisfaction with services.
4. Identify aspects of quality as defined by people with disabilities.
5. Identify the three dimensions of choice.
6. State six questions the staff can ask to determine quality.

INTRODUCTION

The growth of services for people with developmental disabilities has resulted in concern about the quality of services. In the late 1960s and 1970s, exposés revealed terrible conditions in certain public institutions. Attempts during the 1970s to decrease the number of persons living in public psychiatric institutions resulted in some mismanaged community placement. Without adequate community supports and resources, some people were literally "dumped" in the community.

The present concern is that high-quality services may not be provided at the scattered sites of an increasingly decentralized community support system. As residential facilities for large groups give way to integrated living arrangements, people with developmental disabilities are less visible to agency managers. Maintaining the quality of services for people who reside at various sites throughout the neighborhood is an important responsibility of the agency staff.

QUALITY IN HUMAN SERVICES AGENCIES

In the human services agency, quality is determined at the point of interaction between a staff member and an individual with a developmental disability. Marketing strategies, fund raising, and attractive buildings do not result in quality. Regardless of agency planning, managing, and financing, there can be no positive impact at the point of interaction if the staff do not provide services of high quality for the individual with a developmental disability.

QUALITY IS DETERMINED AT THE POINT OF INTERACTION BETWEEN THE STAFF MEMBER AND THE INDIVIDUAL WITH A DEVELOPMENTAL DISABILITY.

The executive director and senior management may talk about quality, but talk means little unless the staff at the service delivery level put the talk into practice. Quality originates at the bottom of the organization. Daily interactions between the individuals with developmental disabilities and specific staff members determine the level of quality. Senior and mid-level managers may engage in important activities, but the service and support staffs actually deliver the quality.

Methods of Quality Assurance

Quality assurance efforts have generally consisted of surveys or site visits to examine compliance with established standards of care. Four major forms of quality assurance are:

1. *Certification* The state survey agency certifies that the program meets federal standards. Certification enables the state to recover federal funds for the operation of Medicaid community waiver programs and intermediate care facility for persons with mental retardation (ICF/MR) programs.
2. *Licensure* The state awards the agency a license to operate on the condition that a program meets the applicable state regulations. Most states have developed regulations for residential and work/vocational programs.
3. *Accreditation* Independent, third-party accreditation agencies determine compliance with their irrespective standards. The Accreditation Council on Services for People with Disabilities and the Commission on Accreditation of Rehabilitation Facilities are the two prominent accreditation organizations in human services.
4. *Citizen monitoring* Citizens, parents, family members, and people with developmental disabilities are trained and authorized to monitor quality of services according to established guidelines.

From Quality Assurance to Quality Enhancement

During the past decade, there has been a shift from quality assurance to quality enhancement. Some advocates contend that quality assurance programs cannot really assure quality. Instead of guaranteeing or assuring quality, advocates have noted the possibility of increasing, or enhancing, quality. Efforts to increase quality must focus on values and the design of habilitation programs. Quality enhancement stresses the planning and design of programs, rather than the inspection of programs to measure compliance.

QUALITY ENHANCEMENT STRESSES THE PLANNING AND DESIGN OF PROGRAMS, RATHER THAN THE INSPECTION OF PROGRAMS TO MEASURE COMPLIANCE.

A National View of Quality

A 1985 Gallup poll (Rosander, 1989, pp. 48–49) on the quality of American products and services stressed the responsibility of the employee providing the service. The multiple responses of 1,005 persons indicated that quality was associated with:

1.	EMPLOYEE BEHAVIOR, ATTITUDES, AND COMPETENCE	67%
2.	SATISFYING NEEDS	18%
3.	PROMPTNESS OF SERVICE	12%
4.	PRICE	11%
5.	EXPERIENCE	13%
6.	ALL OTHER	58%

Responses to a second question relating to the reasons for poor quality of service were even more dramatic. The multiple responses of 593 persons indicated the following reasons for poor quality of service:

1.	EMPLOYEE BEHAVIOR, ATTITUDES, AND COMPETENCE	81%
2.	TIME (TOO SLOW)	30%
3.	PRICE (TOO EXPENSIVE)	20%
4.	ALL OTHER	35%

A Quality of Life Perspective

A quality of life perspective focuses attention on the viewpoints and desires of the person with a developmental disability. Quality of life is based on the whole person and not on the disability. With this approach, people with developmental disabilities are acknowledged to be similar to other people in society. Good (1988) found that people with developmental disabilities want to:

Have expectations and dreams
Control decisions about their lives
Develop friendships
Feel valued
Make economic and social contributions
Take reasonable risks to accomplish important goals

The quality of life perspective stresses that the important factors related to quality of life apply to all people. There are not two separate sets of measures for the quality of life—one for people with developmental disabilities and one for everyone else.

Approaches to Quality

Two approaches to quality can be found in the field of human services. In the first, more traditional approach, quality is demonstrated by conformity to standards. This definition of quality rests on the assumption that there can be agreement on a set of standards; for example, educators can agree on standards for higher education and the health care industry can agree on a set of standards for hospitals.

Such agreements are also the bases for state licensing and certification programs. The state and federal governments attempt to fashion commonly accepted performance standards as requirements for state licensure and certification for participation in federal programs.

The second approach defines quality in terms of outcomes for the individual. The outcomes can be objective, such as independence, integration, and productivity. Objective outcomes can be measured.

Outcomes also can be more subjective, such as satisfaction with services rendered. In this case, the focus shifts from an objective determination of outcome (e.g., an increase in salary) to the question of satisfaction with the job. The individual may indicate dissatisfaction with the salary but like the job because of its accessibility and the challenge of the work.

Determining quality in service industries is complicated by the following three factors (Zeithaml et al., 1990):

1. Service quality is more difficult to evaluate than product quality. Assessing the quality of a lawn mower or a toaster is easier than determining the quality of a human services program.
2. People do not evaluate services on outcome alone. For example, if the hairstylist is friendly and shows an interest in you as a person, you may overlook the fact that the session took too long or that she left too much curl on the sides.

3. The only considerations that matter in determining service quality are set by the user of the service.

The focus on satisfaction increases control by the individual with a developmental disability and decreases the influence of the human services agency staff. The traditional focus of active treatment and habilitation was intended to further independence, integration, and productivity through training and habilitation by staff. The shift toward satisfaction as a primary outcome means that skill acquisition and support services to promote independence, productivity, and integration are important only if the individual identifies them as important.

Individual satisfaction means that the individual with a developmental disability feels that his or her own personal goals and needs are met by the service system. This is the purpose of habilitation planning, futures planning, and other types of individual planning.

THE FOCUS ON SATISFACTION INCREASES CONTROL BY THE INDIVIDUAL WITH A DEVELOPMENTAL DISABILITY AND DECREASES THE INFLUENCE OF THE HUMAN SERVICES AGENCY STAFF.

INDIVIDUAL COMMENTS ON SATISFACTION AND QUALITY

The following excerpts from presentations and writings of people with disabilities provide individualized and personalized views of satisfaction and quality.

> Everyone has to be up at the same time; in one institution where I lived it was 5:00 A.M., like it or not. At the staff's discretion half of the group was taken to get showers in the morning, half at night. All residents were thinly dressed with inappropriate clothing; an institutional breakfast was then served to the group. Our toothbrushes were lined up in a row, and our teeth were brushed. . . .
>
> I have moved into a house that I rent with two friends who do not have disabilities. For recreation I attend parties with my coworkers and other friends of my choice. I also see my family when it is convenient. I go to the neighborhood bars, movies, and sporting events. For the first time I am experiencing the quality of life that is standard for a person without disabilities. I have been given the opportunity to live my life as I choose. (Kennedy, 1990, pp. 36–37)

> Apart from being unlucky enough to get ALS, or motor neuron disease, I have been fortunate in almost every other respect. . . . I was again fortunate in that I chose theoretical physics, because that is all in the mind. So my disability has never been a serious handicap . . . . (Hawkins, 1988, p. vii)

Independent living is sometimes frightening, dangerous, lonely, frustrating. . . . The "what ifs" could drive one nuts:

What if my electric wheelchair breaks down on Saturday night and I can't get it fixed until Monday?
What if I fall out of my chair while emptying the urinal and no one is there to pick me up for hours?
What if my van breaks down on some back country road in zero-degree weather?
What if I get diarrhea at my job and everyone knows it?
What if my PCA is in a bad mood or gets sick and doesn't want to or can't help me do something for me? . . .

But regardless of how well I plan, living my life will always involve taking chances, even at times, risking my life. That's okay with me! Especially when I consider the alternative: safety. I could live in the sheltered environment of a nursing home or a state institution where everything is taken care of for me, where I don't have to take any responsibility or make any decisions except which soap opera to watch, and even that might not always be my choice . . . No thanks! I'll accept the vulnerability, even when it hurts. (Zimmerman, 1985, pp. 40–41)

I wish I had control of my life instead of people running your own, the staff running your own, my own life, telling me what to do. . . . And not only that, I wish I had more control to have personal friends. And not only me, but Lou and Kendall too. Maybe have a housewarming party. But the staff where me and Kendall live don't understand us. (Matthew, as quoted in Williams, 1990, p. 52)

REASONS FOR LACK OF QUALITY

Four general reasons for poor quality in service industries (Zeithaml et al., 1990) are lack of knowledge, lack of performance goals, lack of ability, and extravagant promises. These reasons apply to human services organizations for people with developmental disabilities.

Lack of Knowledge

Agency staff may not know what individuals with developmental disabilities expect from a service or support. In some instances, the individuals do not have the opportunity to express or explain their goals, aspirations, and needs. Instead, they are assigned to a program because there is an opening. They are matched with available "slots" and expected to live with other individuals and perform tasks in a day habilitation program because they occupy a slot.

Quality demands that services and supports be designed around an individual's goals, aspirations, and needs. This requires staff members to listen to the individual. Mid-level managers and senior agency staff also should be aware of individual expectations because the organization must be managed to meet those expectations.

EXERCISE 1

How do people enter the program? Do they first visit, meet possible peers, and then make a decision? Do they have real options? Or, are they assigned to a slot?

Lack of Performance Goals

Many service organizations prefer to deliver services rather than satisfaction. They are unable or unwilling to establish expectations, or goals, for performance. Instead of quality, their real concern is financial and personnel stability. Sometimes a human services agency defines quality in terms of internal management standards, rather than in terms of services that are important to people with developmental disabilities. For example, the agency may stress subcontract revenue, the number of persons in training, or the number of job placements for the month. Such figures may be important to the agency but not at all important to the people with developmental disabilities receiving services or support. Internal process measures, such as productivity and efficiency, may not cause satisfaction for the individuals with developmental disabilities.

Human services agencies may fail to set performance expectations because of the belief that some aspects of individual satisfaction exceed the capability of the organization. Individual goals and aspirations may not be considered practical when an agency lacks the skills, knowledge, or financial resources to provide satisfaction. The agency may admit that certain outcomes are important but point to a lack of resources as a reason for not achieving those outcomes.

In some instances, the term *infeasible* (incapable of being done) is used when the staff lack the creativity required to help individuals with developmental disabilities achieve their goals and aspirations. Staff members must be open to innovation and practice changing the way they think about challenges. They should not dismiss as infeasible the goals and aspirations of these individuals because of their own lack of creativity or because the agency stresses uniformity and regulation more than creativity and innovation.

MANY GOALS AND ASPIRATIONS OF PEOPLE WITH DEVELOPMENTAL DISABILITIES ARE DISMISSED AS INFEASIBLE BECAUSE THE STAFF LACK CREATIVITY OR THE AGENCY STRESSES UNIFORMITY AND REGULATION MORE THAN CREATIVITY AND INNOVATION.

Lack of Ability

A service provider may simply lack the ability to perform at a level high enough to provide satisfaction. In some instances, staff members are not given the necessary information or training to do their jobs adequately. They may lack the ability, skill, or values to provide a support or a service that satisfies the person with a developmental disability. Staff members also may be unaware of performance standards and evaluation methods.

Lack of ability may be related to a poor fit between employee and job. Some individuals lack the value base or the necessary interpersonal skills, or have language barriers that hinder satisfactory work performance. The staff's inability to perform at high levels also may result from inadequate management feedback and reward systems. Management must provide clear feedback on employee performance and show a direct link between individual performance and employee rewards and recognition.

Finally, human services agencies may fail to perform at high levels because of poor teamwork. When agencies design individual support and service programs for people with developmental disabilities, personnel from several agencies usually provide the supports and services that were once offered by a few employees in a centralized location. This newer type of program requires teamwork and coordination.

EXERCISE 2

Feedback for You

How does the organization provide feedback to you on your performance? Do you get feedback on your performance as an individual or as a member of a team?

Extravagant Promises

Promises about services sometimes do not match the services that an agency delivers. In such cases, the agency may be unable to satisfy an individual with a developmental disability because it promised too much and the heightened expectation makes satisfaction more difficult.

Inadequate communication among the planners of services, the providers of services, and the people responsible for program eligibility can result in mixed messages. Different messages about services or supports can cause a person with a developmental disability to have unclear expectations and uncertainty about what is needed for his or her satisfaction.

In addition, some service providers promise individualized supports and services but do not provide them. Often, the package of supports and services that is "the closest available" to individual preference is not adequate.

RELATION BETWEEN QUALITY AND CHOICE

The issues of choice, autonomy, and control over one's life are vital aspects of the quality of life for all people with developmental disabilities. These issues are particularly important for people with cognitive dysfunction. For them, choice has three significant dimensions. The first dimension is experiential. People with mental retardation learn best in specific, concrete situations. They often have difficulty with concepts and abstractions. Significant choices, then, are relevant when the individual has experienced the options from which to choose. For example, a choice between a recreational event in which the individual has participated and a proposed activity that has not been experienced may not be meaningful.

Like other people, individuals with developmental disabilities deserve the opportunity to make choices in a graduated fashion. They should be exposed to and assisted in making small choices with limited risk before they are required to make big choices with significant risk. An agency should examine the training an individual has had in making smaller choices prior to giving that person the opportunity to make significant, but risky, choices.

Many individuals with developmental disabilities have lived in environments where their options for making choices were limited and where they had little exposure to an assortment of experiences that could serve as a basis for decision making. Service providers must recognize patterns of previous opportunity deprivation and assist these individuals to make progressively more involved decisions through exposure to multiple experiences.

The second dimension of choice is collective. Most people make difficult decisions after talking with friends and relatives. Successful coping requires a network that provides a variety of formal and informal supports and feedback. Persons with developmental disabilities need access to the same support network.

SUCCESSFUL COPING REQUIRES A NETWORK THAT PROVIDES A VARIETY OF FORMAL AND INFORMAL SUPPORTS AND FEEDBACK.

A primary responsibility of the program planning team is to ensure that the individual is connected to other significant people who can assist in decision making. The planning team helps the individual to make decisions apart from the formal team meeting. Individual should be connected to peers who can offer advice on their decisions not to bathe, to eat with their fingers, or to refuse to visit the dentist.

The third dimension is creative. Choice is seldom an either-or situation. Yet, team members often discuss the rights and responsibilities of individuals with developmental disabilities as a "Can they?" or "Can't they?" choice. Creativity and multiple options increase the range of choices. The teddy bear is a good example. The question is raised, "Does the individual have the right to choose the teddy bear, even if it violates the normalization principle?" This is the wrong question. Refocus and ask:

- "Why does the person want the teddy bear?"
- "What additional objects, activities, and experiences could we offer the individual that would produce the same or even better outcome?"
- "If we have offered these in the past, have we really reinforced the individual for appropriate choices?"

Another typical choice situation focuses attention on an outcome that might be harmful to the individual. The question is phrased, "Does the person have the right to make a dangerous choice?" Again, this is the wrong focus. Rather, consider the severity of the harm and the extent to which others may be hurt. No one has a right to harm oneself or others, either directly or indirectly. This includes physical harm. The principle also covers instances where individual behavior would cause significant shame or embarrassment for others in a group situation. The rights of the individual to strange behavior must be weighed against the negative impact on the group.

There are no simple solutions to some problems of choice. The issues should not be considered as abstract arguments in a college philosophy seminar. The questions of whether an individual can refuse ear surgery, eat mayonnaise sandwiches, or wear dirty T-shirts can be answered only in concrete situations. For example, does an individual who is representing a group in an important legal hearing have a right to dress in a sloppy manner? Would you order a thick mayonnaise sandwich (that would drip down your arm) during lunch while discussing a job opening? No, probably not, but you might snack on one at home. The focus on yes or no answers, perhaps, should be shifted to assist people with developmental disabilities to make different choices in different circumstances.

Instead of trying to figure out how to answer abstract questions, the staff could use a brainstorming session to test their ability to come up with other outcomes and choices. The group can ask:

- "Does our relationship with the individual allow us to assist her in making the choice?"

- "If our relationship does not offer possibilities, does she need someone else to help her in the situation, such as a friend, an advocate, or a guardian?"
- "Maybe the situation is that the individual does not care about us and we no longer can care about the individual. As a responsible agency, what should we do?"
- "What alternatives could we offer and reinforce that would provide the same outcome for the individual?"
- "What assistance in making choices have we provided in the past? What could we provide at the present time?"

COMPLICATIONS IN QUALITY DETERMINATION

Determining quality and setting up quality improvement programs are not simple tasks. Making the determination can be complicated by differing viewpoints on various issues:

Who is the customer? The response to this question would seem to be the person with a developmental disability, but the question can have multiple answers. The focus of a human services agency sometimes shifts from the individual to funding, regulatory, and administering organizations. At times, the agency is trying to satisfy the state funding agency; at others, it is busy with the concerns of families, advocates, and community groups. The state licensing authority or the ICF/MR survey team often appear to be the primary customer.

EXERCISE 2

Who Do I Work For?

Your first response to the question is that you work for people with developmental disabilities. But, do you ever feel like you really work to meet the demands of:

The board of directors	_____
The executive director	_____
The state funding agency	_____
The state licensing agency	_____
Parents and families	_____
Advocacy groups	_____
The court	_____

What do we want? The preliminary answer is that services and supports should be *responsive* to individual choices, goals, and needs. However, quality assurance systems also hold a human services agency *accountable* for doing what it promised to do. Quality assurance must ensure that the agency makes responsible use of the taxpayers' money. In addition, a quality assurance system is often designed to enforce *compliance* with state licensing requirements and/or federal certification requirements.

What do we measure? A strong argument can be made that quality of services is directly related to the *satisfaction* of the individuals with developmental disabilities who receive the services. Other advocates and researchers argue that quality is directly related to *objective out-comes* in the areas of independence, productivity, and integration. Finally, there is significant opinion that quality is best understood as *conformity with a consensus* about quality.

QUESTIONS ABOUT SUPPORTS AND SERVICES

The services provided by an agency should be of the same quality for all people. The quality should not differ because a person has a disability, is a member of a minority culture, or is color blind. Less quality in services, supports, and settings is sometimes accepted because the human service organization feels that people with developmental disabilities are different and devalued (see Chapter 3, "The Principle of Normalization"). The human services agency should review any practices or procedure that lessen quality because services are provided to people with developmental disabilities. The following questions can help in analyzing assumptions that result in an individual's acceptance of a lower level of quality:

Does the individual work in a real community job setting?
Does the individual use community resources in the same way that his or her neighbors use them?
Does the individual have a network of friends who can help him or her to make decisions?
Does the individual have the opportunity to make significant decisions independently?
Does the individual receive assistance in learning how to make choices?
Is the individual allowed to take risks?
Do the staff have positive expectations for the individual's future?
Is the individual learning skills to accomplish goals that are important to him or her?
Does the individual earn wages that are similar to wages earned by nondisabled workers with similar jobs?
How does the individual's family feel about the places where the individual lives and works?

SUMMARY

Quality of services is determined at the moment the service is rendered. The staff providing a support or service in a particular place and at a specific time control the quality. The role of management is to facilitate and advise the agency staff. The quality of service is determined by interactions at the bottom level of the agency.

Quality is measured by compliance with standards or by the impact of the service on an individual. Impact is determined by measuring outcomes, such as productivity, integration, and independence, or by measuring the individual's satisfaction with the service.

Four general reasons for lack of quality in service settings are:

1. Lack of knowledge of what the individual expects from services and supports
2. Inability to set performance expectations
3. Inability to perform at the level that provides satisfaction
4. Promises that do not match the delivery of services

The key to quality is individual choice. Real choice for people with developmental disabilities requires some experience with a range of alternatives. Choice also requires a formal and informal network of friends and associates who can provide advice. Finally, choice is enhanced by the staff's creativity and ability to envision multiple options.

Determining quality of services is complicated because organizations often do not know who they are trying to satisfy—the person with a developmental disability, the person's family, the funding provider, or the regulator. In addition, human services agencies are often unsure of what they are expected to do. They do not know whether quality will be measured as satisfaction with services, as objective outcomes, or as conformity with a consensus.

BIBLIOGRAPHY

Bradley, V.J., & Bersani, H.A. (Eds.). (1990). *Quality assurance for individuals with developmental disabilities: It's everybody's business.* Baltimore: Paul H. Brookes Publishing Co.

Goode, D.A. (1988). *Quality of life: A review and synthesis of the literature.* Valhalla, NY: The Mental Retardation Institute.

Hawkins, S. (1988). *A brief history of time: From the big bang to black holes.* New York: Bantam Books.

Kennedy, M. (1990). What quality assurance means to me: Expectations of consumers. In V.J. Bradley & H.A. Bersani (Eds.), *Quality assurance for individuals with developmental disabilities: It's everybody's business* (pp. 35–45). Baltimore: Paul H. Brookes Publishing Co.

Rosander, A.C. (1989). *The quest for quality in services.* Milwaukee: American Society for Quality Control.

Schalock, R.L. (1990). *Quality of life: Perspectives and issues.* Washington, DC: American Association on Mental Retardation.

Williams, K. (1990). Unarmed truth: A record of discussion. In V.J. Bradley & H.A. Bersani (Eds.), *Quality assurance for individuals with developmental disabilities: It's everybody's business* (pp. 47–60). Baltimore: Paul H. Brookes Publishing Co.

Zeithaml, V.A., Parasuraman, A., & Berry, L.L. (1990). *Delivering quality service: Balancing customer perceptions and expectations.* New York: Free Press.

Zimmerman, D. (1985). "Let me introduce myself." In A.J. Brightman (Ed.), *Ordinary moments* (pp. 40–41). Syracuse: Human Policy Press.

ADDITIONAL RESOURCES

K. Albrecht and R. Zemke (1985), in *Service America: Doing business in the new economy* (New York: Warner Books), provide a practical guide to quality in service industries.

W. Bennis and B. Nanus (1985), in *Leaders* (New York: Harper & Row), and W. Bennis (1989), *On becoming a leader* (Reading, MA: Addison-Wesley), cover the relationship between quality and leadership.

P.B. Crosby (1979), in *Quality is free* (New York: McGraw-Hill,), provides a guide for the introduction of a quality management program into an organization.

W.E. Deming (1982), in *Quality, productivity, and competitive position* (Cambridge, MA: MIT Center for Advanced Engineering Study), provides an overview of Deming's Fourteen Points of quality management that have direct applications to the provision of services for people with disabilities.

T. Peters and R.H. Waterman (1982), in *In search of excellence* (New York: Harper & Row); Tom Peters and Nancy Austin (1985), *In search of excellence* (New York: Random House); and Tom Peters (1987), in *Thriving on chaos: Handbook for management revolution* (New York: Alfred A. Knopf), address the theme of management for excellence.

SELF-APPRAISAL

INSTRUCTIONS

The following questions will help you evaluate your knowledge about quality enhancement. For true-false questions, check the correct answer. For multiple choice questions, circle the correct answer(s).

Note: There may be more than one correct answer for some questions.

1. Quality is determined at the time and place that service is delivered.
   ___ True   ___ False
2. Quality enhancement stresses planning and implementation of services, rather than inspection of services, to determine compliance.
   ___ True   ___ False
3. The same measures for quality of life apply to people with significant disabilities, those with mild or temporary disabilities, and those with no disabilities.
   ___ True   ___ False
4. Major forms of quality assurance include:
   a. Certification
   b. Licensure
   c. Accreditation
   d. Citizen monitoring
5. The focus on satisfaction as an outcome in human services is complicated by the following:
   a. Service quality is more difficult to evaluate than product quality.
   b. Satisfaction is too subjective.
   c. People do not evaluate service on satisfaction alone.
   d. Service quality is determined by the user.
6. The four reasons for the lack of quality in services are:
   a. No knowledge of what an individual expects from services
   b. An inability to set performance standards
   c. An inability to perform at a level high enough to provide satisfaction
   d. Promises set too high to match the actual delivery of services
7. The important dimensions of choice are:
   a. Experiential
   b. Collective
   c. Holistic
   d. Creative

8. Difficult decisions about choice can best be answered by:
   a. Abstract thinking in hypothetical situations
   b. Examination of the details in concrete situations
   c. Interdisciplinary teams
   d. The individual with the developmental disability
9. People with cognitive disabilities should learn to make small decisions before they are expected to make major decisions.
   ___ True   ___ False
10. Different viewpoints on the following questions complicate determinations of quality:
    a. Who is the customer?
    b. What do we want?
    c. What do we measure?
    d. Why do we ask?

CASE STUDY

Billy Hughes is 20 years old, has a moderate degree of cognitive impairment, and is graduating from the Oak Hills Special Education School next year. Billy currently lives at home and enjoys going to fast-food restaurants, watching sporting events, and helping with chores around the house.

Oaks Hills School, Billy, and his family have been discussing the range of residential, vocational, and leisure options available during the next 3–4 years. Billy has indicated that he would like to continue to live at home. He has also expressed a desire to work in the produce department at the local Lucas Supermarket. There is general agreement that Billy is capable of supported employment and may even be able to secure independent employment.

Situation

During the next year, Billy's individualized education program stresses the development of social competencies needed for the workplace. Billy will also work 3 hours every Saturday in the produce department with a volunteer job coach to determine whether he actually enjoys the work.

1. What issues would you advise Billy, the family, and the school to consider in planning for transition from school to work?
2. What factors would you consider in determining the quality of the educational program provided to Billy during his last year of school.

ANSWER KEY TO
SELF-APPRAISAL AND CASE STUDY

SELF-APPRAISAL

1. True
2. True
3. True
4. a, b, c, d
5. a, c, d
6. a, b, c, d
7. a, b, d
8. b
9. True
10. a, b, c

CASE STUDY ANSWER GUIDELINES

1. The key issue is that of informed choice. The school personnel and the family should assist Billy to make an informed choice about his job and, perhaps, his career. The part-time employment on Saturdays will give Billy work experience in the produce department. He will be able to make decisions based on his actual experience. There are two questions that Billy, the school, and the family should consider. The first is whether there are other jobs and careers that Billy should be aware of and perhaps even try. Has Billy made a choice from several options? Have the school and family helped Billy to explore his options? The second issue is coordinating Billy's last year of school with transition to the world of work. The school should plan to coordinate Billy's instruction from the job coach at the job site and his last year of instruction at school.

2. The quality of the education program depends on two key factors. The first measure of quality is how well the educational program incorporated Billy's goals. Was the program of educational instruction and work preparation built around Billy's goal of working in the produce department? Second, was the education program successful in teaching Billy new skills and abilities?

Glossary

Absence Seizures   Once referred to as *petit mal seizures*, in which the individual does not lose consciousness but experiences momentary loss of mental functioning. The individual may appear to stare blankly into space; his or her eyelids may flutter; the eyes may roll slightly; or the individual may drop whatever he or she is holding at the time.

Accident   An unplanned act or event resulting in injury or death to people or damage to property.

Accreditation   An independent, third-party evaluation of the level of quality in service/support programs as determined by the extent to which the organization incorporates performance measures into practice.

Acquired Immunodeficiency Syndrome (AIDS)   The most severe form of human immunodeficiency virus (HIV) infection. The median incubation time from infection with HIV to a diagnosis of AIDS is about 8–10 years, but considerably shorter duration in the case of infants and children. Clinical symptoms vary and the disease is fatal.

Activity Center   A facility that provides activities to people whose work capabilities are considered limited and perhaps inconsequential.

Adaptive Behavior   Behavior that reflects the extent to which a person meets the standards of independence and social responsibility expected of his or her age and cultural group.

Adaptive Technology   The application of sophisticated electronic principles and/or devices for the solution of problems individuals with disabilities face in daily living. Often, the terms *adaptive technology* and *assistive technology* are used interchangeably.

Advocate   A person who supports and represents the rights and interests of another individual in order to ensure the individual's full legal rights and access to services.

Antianxiety Drugs   Drugs that prevent or relieve the feeling of apprehension, uncertainty, and fear.

Antidepressant Drugs   Drugs that prevent or relieve depression by elevating the mood of the person.

Antiepileptic Drugs   Drugs that combat seizure disorders by controlling or minimizing seizure activity.

Arranging the Environment   An instructional strategy whereby a person's environment is altered to aid in the successful completion of a task.

Assessment An empirical process used to determine whether, and to what degree, an individual has developmental deficits. An assessment identifies the individual's strengths, abilities, needs, and developmental level.

Athetoid Cerebral Palsy Involuntary or purposeless movements. An individual with athetoid cerebral palsy may display abrupt movement of the arms or legs.

Autism A disorder characterized by a pervasive lack of responsiveness to other people, gross deficits in language and communication, nonrational responses to the environment, and absence of delusions and hallucinations, with onset before 30 months of age.

Aversive Behavior Intervention Refers to the application, contingent upon the exhibition of a maladaptive behavior, of extremely unpleasant, startling, or painful stimuli that have a potentially noxious effect. This type of intervention is very controversial.

Baby-Boomers Children born in the years after World War II, between 1945 and 1960.

Barbiturates A group of drugs frequently used as sedatives to soothe, calm, or tranquilize an individual.

Behavior Anything a person does that can be observed and measured.

Behavior Management Techniques designed to influence existing behavior in some predetermined manner, replacing maladaptive or problem behaviors with behaviors that are adaptive and appropriate.

Burnout A physical and mental state of exhaustion and apathy that is the result of continuous emotional pressure from intense work with people for prolonged periods of time.

Cerebral Palsy A disorder of movement and posture due to a nonprogressive defect of the immature brain.

Certification A state agency certifies that a program operated by a provider agency meets standards established by the Health Care Financing Administration for purposes of federal financial participation.

Chaining The process of combining simple behaviors to form a new complex behavior. For example, washing hands is really a series of simple behaviors that, when performed in sequence, result in hand washing.

Community Living Arrangement (CLA) Program that resulted from attempts to reform the Medicaid program during the 1980s. CLA was enacted in 1990 as a new Medicaid state plan option. Funding was originally restricted to eight states.

Complex Partial Seizures Seizure disorder that usually results in the loss of consciousness. The individual may experience an unusual smell, sight, noise, sense of déjà-vu, distorted time, or intense feelings of fear, anger, or anxiety. Complex partial seizures may also be referred to as *psychomotor seizures*.

Comprehensive Term describing the full array of services in a geographical area that are required to meet the needs of persons with mental retardation living in the area.

Consensus A process for group decision making in which the group reaches a unanimous decision without a vote.

Criterion-Referenced Assessments A developmental assessment process whereby an individual is evaluated based upon specific, objective behavioral outcomes. The criterion-referenced assessment process compares the test scores against the individual.

Data Information that is collected and organized for analysis or study. Data are used as the basis for making a decision.

Developmental Disability The Developmental Disabilities Assistance and Bill of Rights Act of 1990 (PL 101-496) defines developmental disability as a severe, chronic disability of a person who is 5 years of age or older that: 1) is attributable to a mental or physical impairment or combination of mental and physical impairments; 2) is manifested before the person attains the age of 22; 3) is likely to continue indefinitely; 4) results in substantial functional limitations in three or more of the areas of major life activity (self-help, receptive and expressive language, learning, mobility, self-direction, capacity for independent living, and economic self-sufficiency); and 5) reflects the person's need for a combination and sequence of special interdisciplinary or generic care, treatment, or other services that are of lifelong or extended duration and are individually planned and coordinated; except that such term, when applied to infants and young children means individuals from birth to age 5, inclusive, who have substantial developmental delay or specific congenital or acquired conditions with a high probability of resulting in developmental disabilities if services are not provided.

Developmental Disabilities Councils (DDCs) DDCs are authorized and funded through the Developmental Disabilities Assistance and Bill of Rights Act of 1975 (PL 94-103) and consist of state agency representatives, people with disabilities and their families, and the general public. Councils assess state needs, plan, and coordinate services. Councils also promote change by providing start-up funding for demonstration programs and dissemination projects.

Developmental Level The level of skill performance in various developmental areas or domains. For example, learning to crawl, to stand, and to walk are various levels of development in the gross motor domain.

Deviant A person whose characteristics and/or behaviors differ from the social norm and the differences are negatively valued.

Diagnosis A statement or opinion of a person's condition that is made on the basis of assessment and evaluation.

Diplegia Cerebral palsy that involves both legs.

Down Syndrome A condition causing mental retardation, resulting from genetic abnormality.

Drug Any chemical compound that may be used in the diagnosis, treatment, or prevention of disease or other abnormal condition; for the relief of pain or suffering; or to control or improve any physiological or pathological condition.

Due Process The process that protects the rights of all people when the government attempts to limit those rights. The government cannot limit or take away rights without giving that person notice and a fair chance to present his or her case.

Dyslexia Term used inconsistently; generally indicates serious reading difficulty; condition characterized by an inability to read more than a few words with understanding.

Enclaves Supported employment option whereby a group of three to eight individuals with developmental disabilities is placed in work settings with nondisabled peers in business or industry.

Epilepsy Condition that describes abnormal brain activity that results in seizures.

Equal Protection A legal requirement that the government treat all people equally despite the fact that people differ by religion, sex, age, and physical and mental ability. The government cannot treat any group differently because of a singular characteristic.

Extinction A behavior management principle whereby a behavior is gradually weakened by withholding reinforcement.

Fading An instructional strategy involving the gradual elimination of special assistance (e.g., physical assistance or modeling) until the person is able to respond independently.

Family Individuals who perform the roles and functions of natural relatives in the lives of individuals, including: parents, brothers, sisters, foster parents, guardians, or surrogates.

Form of Behavior The specific actions performed by an individual in order to accomplish a behavioral function. For examples, nourishment can be obtained through a gastrostomy tube, by being assisted by another person, by eating with one's fingers, by eating with utensils, or by drinking through a bottle. Each behavior form accomplishes the behavioral function of obtaining nourishment.

Function of Behavior The specific outcomes of any behavior. For example, the function of eating is to obtain nourishment.

Generalized Seizures Generalized seizures involve the entire brain. The most common generalized seizures include absence, myoclonic, and tonic-clonic seizures.

Generic Services Services offered or available to the general public, as distinguished from specialized services that are intended for specific groups of people.

Genetic Defect A cause of mental retardation resulting from abnormalities in an individual's genes. Abnormalities in genetic composition that cause mental retardation occur at conception.

Gesturing An instructional strategy in which movement is used to aid in the successful teaching of a skill or concept. Pointing toward the on/off switch while teaching machine use is an example of gesturing.

Goal A general statement of purpose that defines the end result of a program's impact upon an individual.

Graph The visual representation of data.

Guardian An individual who has full or partial legal control and management of a person, or of his or her property or estate, or of both the person and property.

Hemiplegia Cerebral palsy that involves half the body (e.g., the arm and leg on the same side of the body).

Hierarchy The hierarchy of authority describes who reports to whom in an organization. The hierarchy is depicted by the vertical lines on an organizational chart.

Human Immunodeficiency Virus (HIV) A retrovirus that attacks white blood cells, the brain, bowel, skin, and other tissue. HIV is transmitted primarily through sexual contact and the use of shared needles in drug usage.

Human Rights Committee A standing committee of a human services agency that reviews on a regular basis the care, treatment, and human and legal rights of people with mental retardation. The committee usually consists of representatives from the medical, legal, religious, and lay communities.

Human Services Agency An organization that primarily provides health, welfare, social, rehabilitation, medical, and educational services to promote and increase individual health, social development, and functional independence.

Independence The extent to which a person with a disability exerts control and choice over his or her life.

Individual Placement Model Supported employment option in which the individual with a developmental disability is matched with an available job in the community based upon his or her strengths and interests.

Individualized Service Plan (ISP) A written statement of the services an agency provides to the person based on an interdisciplinary assessment. The ISP should include:

A list of goals arranged by priority
Behavioral objectives that must be attained before the goal is achieved
Teaching strategies that detail what the staff will to do assist the person in accomplishing new skills and/or behaviors
Evaluation procedures to determine whether the teaching strategies are assisting the person to accomplish objectives.

Informed Consent The voluntary acceptance of any procedure, program, or practice that is performed by another individual. This requires knowledge of possible outcomes, including adverse reactions and other alternative procedures to accomplish the same outcome.

Instructional Strategy The planned, systematic process used to assist an individual to accomplish an objective.

Integration The use of the same community resources that are used by and available to other citizens and participation in the same community activities in which nondisabled citizens participate, together with regular contact with nondisabled citizens, and residence in homes that are in proximity to community resources.

Intelligence Test A testing procedure that produces an intelligence quotient (IQ). The average or norm score is 100. A score of 68 or below is one criterion for a determination of mental retardation.

Interdisciplinary Team A group of persons representing those professional or service areas responsible for evaluating an individual's needs and designing the individualized service plan (ISP). In addition, the team periodically reviews the individual's response to the ISP and revises the plan as needed.

Intermediate Care Facility for Persons with Mental Retardation (ICF/MR) A residential setting serving four or more individuals and meeting federal ICF/MR requirements. The state receives federal reimbursement for state expenditures for an ICF/MR.

Joy Stick A control stick for access to computer software. A joy stick is attached to a base that moves from side to side, or from top to bottom.

Label A descriptive term used to link the individual with other individuals, characteristics, or attributes. Labels are often used to identify the person as a member of a valued or devalued group.

Least Restrictive Alternative The intervention into a person's life that is the least intrusive and disruptive and that represents the least departure possible from normal patterns of living.

Leisure Time Time that is available after personal care time, sleep, and house and family care time is subtracted from nonwork time.

Licensure A provider agency meets applicable state requirements as a condition for providing services.

Light Pen/Light Pointer A beam of light used to activate computer software.

Measurable One of two conditions of a behavior whereby the behavior is recorded in some quantifiable way. This may include the number or duration of responses.

Medicaid Waiver Medicaid Waiver enables states to "waive" certain Medicaid requirements and provide services to persons with disabilities in community settings rather than in institutional settings.

Medication The administration of remedies or treatments aimed at improving the vital powers of the person.

Mental Illness An acute or chronic illness affecting the brain and mental process.

Mental Retardation Mental retardation refers to substantial limitations in present functioning. It is characterized by significantly subaverage intellectual functioning, existing concurrently with related limitations in two or more of the following applicable adaptive skill areas: communication, self-care, home living, social skills, community use, self-direction, health and safety, functional academics, leisure, and work. Mental retardation manifests before age 18.

Metabolism Physical and chemical processes and reactions in the human body that maintain life.

Mobile Crews Supported employment option whereby three to eight individuals with developmental disabilities move from worksite to worksite. The mobile crew is based out of a truck, van, or even several cars.

Modeling An instructional strategy whereby a skill or behavior is taught by showing or demonstrating the desired behavior.

Monoplegia Cerebral palsy that involves one arm or leg.

Mouse A small rectangular box with a tail connected to a computer that enables an individual to gain access to the computer by moving the mouse across a mat located next to the computer.

Mouth Stick A stick held between the teeth that enables an individual to access the computer.

Myoclonic Seizures Sudden, brief jerking of the affected muscle group. These seizures may involve one or several muscle groups. They may be referred to as *jackknife seizures*.

Negotiation A process by which two or more persons or groups interact with each other to reach an agreement.

Nonprescription Refers to those medications available without a physician's written prescription.

Nonverbal Communication Signals and messages given from one person to one or more other people through facial expressions, body movement, verbal tone, or posture.

Normalization The utilization of culturally valued means in order to establish and/or maintain personal behaviors, experiences, and characteristics that are equally culturally normative or valued.

Norm-Referenced Assessment An assessment process whereby one person's score is compared with those of many other individuals. The purpose of the test is to determine a person's standing relative to the test norm.

Objective A statement of an expected behavior that is related to the achievement of a goal. An objective is always written in behavioral terms.

Observable One of the two requirements in the definition of a behavior. It refers to behaviors that can be seen or heard rather than emotions or feelings that are inferred to exist.

Parents' Movement Beginning in the 1930s and 1940s, the Parents' Movement expanded after World War II and resulted in the formation of the Association for Retarded Citizens (now known as The Arc) in 1950. Early efforts of the Parents' Movement were directed toward the provision of school programs and improving dehumanizing conditions in institutions.

Partial Seizures Seizure disorder in which the individual does not lose consciousness. Rather, the leg or arm on one side of the body may jerk. Also referred to as *focal-motor seizures*.

Personal Care Time Time devoted to personal care involving such activities as dressing, eating, and hygiene.

Physical Assistance An instructional strategy whereby a person is physically led through a behavior by another person. For example, to teach a person to wash his hands, the instructor puts his or her hands over the person's hands and completes the behavior.

Policy A plan or course of action set forth by an agency to influence and determine how decisions are made in particular situations.

Positive Reinforcement The delivery of a reinforcer following a behavior that increases the frequency or strength of the behavior.

Prescription A doctor's written direction for the preparation and administration of a drug.

Procedures A set of established guidelines or methods for conducting the ongoing activity of an agency.

Productivity Engagement in income-producing work that is measured through improvements in income level, employment status, job advancement, or engagement in work that contributes to a household or community.

Protection and Advocacy (P & A) Program Established by the Developmental Disabilities Assistance and Bill of Rights Act in 1975 as a required state program, the Protection and Advocacy programs provide legal and advocacy services on behalf of people with disabilities.

Public Law 94-142 (PL 94-142) Federal legislation also known as the Education for All Handicapped Children Act of 1975. It ensures that all children with disabilities have available to them a free, appropriate public education (FAPE), and it guarantees that the rights of children with disabilities are protected.

Public Law 101-336 (PL 101-336) Also known as the Americans with Disabilities Act (ADA), PL 101-336 is an omnibus civil rights bill that prohibits discrimination against people with disabilities in private sector employment, public services, public accommodations, transportation, and telecommunications.

Public Law 101-476 (PL 101-476) PL 101-476, the Education of the Handicapped Act Amendments of 1990, reauthorized and expanded PL 94-142 and changed the name of the legislation to the Individuals with Disabilities Education Act (IDEA). Part H of IDEA provides assistance to states for statewide early intervention services to infants and toddlers with disabilities and their families. Part H was phased in over the 5 years from 1986 to 1992.

Punishment The delivery of an unpleasant event following a behavior that decreases the frequency or strength of the behavior.

Quality Assurance A procedure that involves reviews and inspections to determine that organizational performance complies with established standards.

Quality Enhancement Organizational activities to improve the outcomes of service and supports for people with disabilities. The focus of quality enhancement is on the outcomes of organizational performance from the individual perspective (i.e., what did the service or support do for the individual?).

Quality of Life The factors that contribute to the fullness of life, as defined by the individual for whom the factors are analyzed.

Quadriplegia Cerebral palsy that involves the entire body, including both arms and both legs.

Reinforcement A basic principle of behavior that refers to procedures used to make behaviors stronger and more likely to occur.

Restraint Any physical or mechanical process used to restrict the movement of an individual or the movement or normal function of a portion of the individual's body, excluding only those devices used to provide support for the achievement of functional body position or proper balance (e.g., positioning chairs) and devices used for special medical and surgical (as distinguished from behavioral) treatment.

Restrictive Program/Procedures A program or instructional strategy that has the potential to abridge the person's legal rights.

Role The characteristic and expected social behavior of an individual that results from the individual's position in an organization or group.

Seclusion Placement of an individual in a locked room.

Service Coordinator Refers to a person who is assigned the responsibility for ensuring, documenting, and evaluating continuity of care for persons receiving health and/or human services.

Side Effects A consequence other than the beneficial effects of a drug; often referred to as the adverse effects produced by a drug.

Social Role Valorization The impact of supports and services in increasing the range and quality of the social roles played by people with disabilities. Social roles might include the roles of student, athlete, neighbor, advisor, worker, friend, or shopper.

Spasticity   A specific type of cerebral palsy that results in high muscle tone; the muscles in the affected area are tight or stiff. Body movements are difficult to control.

Specialized Services   Services that are provided to, or restricted to, certain groups of people who have particular characteristics and/or needs.

Standardized   A characteristic of test design whereby the norms of the test are based on the average score of individuals tested during test construction.

Stigma   An attribute that is deeply discrediting to an individual.

Stimulant   An agent that produces stimulation, and excites functional activity.

Stress   A response of the human body to demands placed upon it.

Support   In contrast to service programs that people enter, supports are designed to meet individual needs in a variety of situations and environments. For example, attendants, special equipment, and therapies can be provided in natural living and employment settings.

Synthetic Speech   Speech that is electronically produced.

Task Analysis   The process of breaking down the content of a complex behavior into smaller and more basic components in order to facilitate learning.

Time-out   A behavior management procedure whereby an individual is removed from a reinforcing situation for a period of time when the person engages in a specified, inappropriate behavior.

Tonic-Clonic Seizures   Once referred to as *grand mal seizures*. It is the most common seizure disorder. It occurs in two phases. During the tonic phase, the body becomes very rigid. If the individual is standing or sitting, the tonic phase will often result in the individual falling to the ground unconscious. The clonic phase that follows also affects the entire body. During this phase, the body jerks in a rhythmic pattern. As time passes, the jerking becomes less intense. The individual will often awaken very tired and confused.

Touch-Sensitive Screens   A screen that fits over the front of a computer monitor and enables an individual to access the computer through touch.

Touch Tablets   A tablet that lies flat on a table and activates computer software through touch.

Transitioning   Refers to the 3–5 years before the end of educational services when the family and school officials begin to plan for the child's future after school.

Two-step Commands   Instructions given to an individual that require the person to follow two sequenced behaviors. For example, asking a person to "Pick up the box and put it in the warehouse" is a two-step command.

University-Affiliated Programs (UAPs)   In 1975, the Developmental Disabilities Assistance and Bill of Rights Act (PL 94-103) authorized and provided funding for university affiliated programs to provide exemplary services, interdisciplinary advanced degree training, dissemination, and technical assistance. As units within colleges and universities, UAPs serve as facilitators of change in both academic and community settings.

Index

Page numbers followed by *t*, *f*, or *n* indicate tables, figures, or footnotes, respectively.